CENTRAL ISSUES IN CRIMINAL THEORY

Central Issues
in Criminal Theory

WILLIAM WILSON
Reader in Criminal Law
Queen Mary
University of London

·HART·
PUBLISHING

OXFORD – PORTLAND OREGON
2002

Hart Publishing
Oxford and Portland, Oregon

Published in North America (US and Canada) by
Hart Publishing c/o
International Specialized Book Services
5804 NE Hassalo Street
Portland, Oregon
97213-3644
USA

Hart Publishing is a specialist legal publisher based in Oxford, England.

To order further copies of this book or to request a list of other
publications please write to:

Hart Publishing, Salter's Boatyard, Folly Bridge,
Abingdon Road, Oxford OX1 4LB
Telephone: +44 (0) 1865 245533 or Fax: +44 (0) 1865 794882
e-mail: mail@hartpub.co.uk
WEBSITE: http//www.hartpub.co.uk

British Library Cataloguing in Publication Data
Data Available
ISBN 1–84113–062–1 (paperback)

Typeset by Hope Services (Abingdon) Ltd.
Printed and bound in Great Britain on acid-free paper by
Bell and Bain, Glasgow

Preface

As George Fletcher has remarked recently these are good times for the theory of criminal law. Not only has there been an enormous upsurge of interest in the philosophical foundations of criminal law but the quality of much of the work is of a very high order and is filtering through into the doctrinal expositions of textbook writers. Even judges are taking note of it. This unparalleled co-operation between judges, commentators and theorists of criminal law present an indication, frustrating at times, that traditional walls between the law presented in textbooks and the social practice of law can be broken down.

I have set myself the task of contributing to this process of communication by highlighting some of the key issues upon which criminal theory seeks to cast its light. The desire to advance communication has important ramifications both for the content of the book and for the way it is written. Criminal theory, in so far as it attempts to chart the philosophical foundations of criminal law, is not an easy subject to grasp or indeed to communicate. True understanding of any phenomenon demands that ideas concerning it are tempered in the fire of argument and counter-argument. Paradoxically, therefore, the very process whereby understanding is achieved is a process capable of interfering with the communication of ideas. It is easy to lose the thread of an argument and its significance when it is forever being tested for weaknesses. Much of what is good in contemporary criminal theory runs this communicative gauntlet. It takes it as read that the reader possesses both the doctrinal knowledge and philosophical sophistication to hit the ground running as it were. As a result, the potential audience for important new ideas and insights is unavoidably squeezed. I have tried, therefore, to ensure that as many channels of communication as possible are kept open by keeping this book relatively short, and by assuming no prior knowledge or significant degree of philosophical sophistication. I have also kept supporting arguments to a minimum, trusting in the intelligent reader to fill in the argumentative gaps where necessary. I do so in the hope that any resulting deficit in depth of analysis is compensated for in the coherence and clarity of the views presented. So as to keep criminal lawyers on board who, I make no apology, are my primary target I make substantial use of hypotheticals and, perhaps a touch more than is usual in works of this kind, of material commonly found in criminal law textbooks.

The general organisational dynamic of the book largely takes care of the choice of issues. The obvious starting point for any attempt to make sense of criminal law is punishment. It is this phenomenon, after all, which generates much of the impetus to rationalise, evaluate, and also attack the premises giving rise to criminal liability. I consider early on the justification for punishment, which is centred, unremarkably, in desert. This notion of desert and the many contradictions it gives rise to inevitably raises issues concerning the structure of criminal liability which in turn uncovers other issues. What makes punishment deserved? Rule-breaking? Culpable wrongdoing? What makes for wrongdoing? What makes wrongdoing culpable such as to warrant punishment? And so on.

Certain stylistic features of the book are worth commenting upon. I have consciously constructed the book in terms of layers of increasing complexity. Each chapter begins with an accessible introduction to the area under consideration so as to afford a firm foundation for considering the issues or challenges identified for discussion. The book itself is structured so as to allow later chapters to build upon the knowledge and insights gleaned earlier. The practical effect is a progressive ratcheting up of the level of complexity on the assumption that once basic premises and other recurrent themes are understood the reader will need less guidance finding her way around the specifics of the individual chapter. Beginners will probably find it beneficial, therefore, to read the book sequentially; chapters 10 and 11 are an altogether different kind of read than chapters 1, 2 and 3, which are of a more introductory character. By constructing the book in this way I have sought to deliver a book which on one level is capable of working as a primer while on another offers something of interest to those already familiar with the terrain.

Chapter 4 appears under the title 'Impaired Voluntariness: A Variable Standard?' in the fall/winter volume of the *Buffalo Criminal Law Review*, 2002, with minor modifications. Permission to publish is gratefully acknowledged.

Thanks are due to Stephen Shute, Jeremy Horder and participants at Birmingham University's seminar series in Criminal Theory. Also participants in legal theory seminar at Queen Mary, University of London.

This book is dedicated to Melanie, Fred and Henry whose patience during the writing of this book has not been inexhaustible.

Contents

Introduction   1

1 Criminalising Wrongdoing   16

Criminalising Wrongdoing   17
    The Harm Principle   19
    Ratcheting Up State Coercion   25
    Moral Wrongdoing   31
Structuring Morality and Autonomy   37

2 Punishing Wrongdoing   43

What is Punishment?   43
Justifying Punishment   45
Punishment as Social Engineering   47
Punishment as Desert   54
Punishment as Communication   61
Reconciling Means and Ends   66
Anchoring Punishments and Penalties: Restoration and Vengeance   71

3 Criminal Wrongdoing: Acts and Omissions   77

The Act Requirement   78
Acts and Actions   79
Moral Responsibility Without Action   82
Autonomy-Based Objections to Criminalising Omissions   91
Legality-Based Objections to Criminalising Omissions   95
Communicating Wrongdoing   99

4 Criminalising Wrongdoing: Voluntariness   103

Characterising Voluntary Behaviour   105
Voluntariness, Defences and the Courts   113
Authorship, Policy and Moral Evaluation   116
Authorship and Control   118
Involuntry Omissions   121
    Voluntariness: A Variable Standard   123
Conclusion   125

5 Intention, Motives and Desert   129

Introduction: Mens Rea and Desert   129
Intention and Responsibility   135
Intention as a Means of Structuring Liability   138
Intention as a Means of Structuring Wrongs   142
  Structuring Homicide   144
The Meaning of Intention   149
Intention, Motive and Doctrinal Rationality   156

6 Causing Harm   161

Introduction   161
Understanding Causation   163
For Which Crimes is there a Causal Requirement?   166
How do we Arrive at a Principled Approach to Causation?   167
Assigning Causal Responsibility   170
  Limiting the Range of Responsible Agents   173
  Omissions   186

7 Attributing Liability to Secondary Parties   195

Accessories as Agents   198
Accessories as Causes or Prime Movers   200
Derivative Liability: Tensions and Instability   203
Withdrawal from Participation   212
Complicity and Causation: A Rational Approach to Criminal
  Attribution?   218

8 Criminal Attempts   225

Conceiving Attempts   226
Criminal Attempts: The Mental Element   232
Incomplete Attempts   235
Voluntary Abandonment   243
Punishing Attempts: The Significance of Resulting Harm   249
Impossible Attempts   252

9 Packaging Criminal Liability   259

Packaging Wrongdoing   259
  Wrongdoing and Harm   259

Packaging Crime 263
Mens Rea and *Actus Reus* 263
Offences and Defences 268
Wrongdoing and Attribution 278
Separating Excuses and Justifications 282
Duress and the Citizen's Code 289

10 Criminal Defences: Setting Limits to Justifications 293

Duress, Necessity and Self-Defence: The Basic Template 293
The Necessity to React 294
Immediacy 295
Proportionality 299
Differentiating Duress, Necessity and Self-Defence 303
Necessity and Self-Defence 306
Setting the Limits 308
The Limits of Self-Defence 310
The Limits of Necessity 315
Justifying Self-Preservation: Necessity and Duress 319

11 Excusing Wrongdoing: Capacity and Virtue 325

Introduction 325
Thresholds of Responsibility 327
Embodying Criminal Defences 329
The Capacity Approach 333
Free Will 336
Drawing the Line 338
The Character Approach 342
Acting out of character 343
Another Look at Character: Deploying Reasons 352
A Unity to Excuses? 356

Bibliography 363
Index 377

Introduction

IN A LOOSE sense criminal theory is the enterprise of subjecting criminal doctrine and its procedures to critical scrutiny. It seeks to tell the story of criminal law in a way which offers more than a merely descriptive account of the rules and procedures governing criminal liability. But there are a number of different stories which can be told about criminal law.[1] The doctrinal writer seeks to explain the content of the rules and procedures in terms of underlying doctrines and principles.[2] Others evaluate those rules and procedures by reference to the purposes, political, ethical and social, criminal law seeks to discharge. Still others analyse the cogency of the different concepts from which criminal liability is fashioned. What is it to act, to cause harm, to intend a consequence, and so on? Then there is the story of the historian who seeks to describe changes in the form and content of criminal law in a way which elucidates historical processes and, in more ambitious accounts, something about law itself.[3] In similar fashion the sociologist pinpoints society and its institutions and processes as the engine room of legal development.[4] The political theorist tells a story which relates the form and content of criminal law to enduring issues of power, authority, and legitimacy.[5] There are other stories which can be told,

---

[1] See generally AR White *Grounds of Liability*, (Clarendon Press, Oxford, 1985) chapter 1and discussion in N Lacey 'Contingency, Coherence, Conceptualism' in RA Duff (ed.) *Philosophy and the Criminal Law* (CUP, Cambridge, 1998) 12–21; 'Philosophy, History and Criminal Law Theory' (1998) 1 *Buffalo Crim LR* 295, 296.

[2] NE Simmonds *The Decline of Juridical Reason*, (Manchester University Press, Manchester, 1984).

[3] See for example E Pashukanis *Law and Marxism* (London, 1978); K Renner *The Institutions of Private Law and Their Social Functions* (London, 1949); EP Thompson *Whigs and Hunters: The Origins of the Black Acts*, (Allen Lane, London, 1975); D Hay 'Property, Authority and the Criminal law' in D Hay *et al.* (eds.) *Albion's Fatal Tree*, (Allen Lane, London, 1975), p 63.

[4] M Weber *On Law in Economy and Society*, (Cambridge, Harvard University Press, 1954); E Durkheim *The Division of Labour in Society*, (Macmillan, London, 1984).

[5] Joel Feinberg's *Harm to Others: The Moral Limits of the Criminal Law*, (OUP, New York 1984); R Dworkin *Taking Rights Seriously*, (Duckworth, London, 1977); M Weber *On Law in Economy and Society*, (Harvard University Press, Cambridge, Mass. 1954).

not only from within the disciplines but stories from the individuals, victims, defendants, officials and so on who are affected by criminal laws and its procedures.

Nicola Lacey has argued that a good story of the criminal law must combine these different perspectives because true understanding of any social practice demands that the story we produce concerning it embraces both the point of view of the participants and the context, social, economic, historical, political, and psychological in which it takes place.[6] The pertinence of this argument is easily understood when we consider the kind of story necessary to illuminate cultural forms, such as art, with less immediate and direct political impact than the practice of criminal law. Where attempts are made to tell the story of art divorced from the social practices of art located within different social, economic and historical contexts these inevitably reduce to ahistorical generalisations. In the archetypal account the 'artistic spirit' is portrayed as the restless inspiration behind art's evolutionary development, ever striving to express itself by challenging and transcending existing forms and contents. Ultimately, however plausible they may first appear, such stories fail to satisfy since they tell us nothing which a fanciful imagination cannot invent for itself. We obtain a more meaningful grasp of the object of analysis from the insights of the cultural historian which quickly explode the myth of any evolutionary strain intrinsic to artistic endeavour. We discover, for example, that the primitivism of medieval painting and its endlessly repetitive iconographic subject matter is not attributable to technical incompetence or limited artistic vision but to the narrow needs of the early churches and the master-governed workshops which arose to satisfy those needs. Likewise we discover that changes in the form and content of art reflect underlying social, economic and political changes rather than the yearnings of a decontextualised artistic spirit. These include the diversification of the churches and the arrival of new sources of patronage, both institutional and personal, following the emergence of an acquisitive merchant class, each with its own new and differentiated formal and substantive demands—landscape, portraiture, myth, eroticism, and so on.[7] Understanding of the contemporary practices of art must rely upon a similar pattern of analysis.[8] It must be rooted in the

[6] See n 1.

[7] A classic example is Ernst Gombrich *The Story of Art*, (Phaidon, London, 1957).

[8] Even populist accounts of the theory and the history of art tend to embrace these contextual dimensions. See for example Robert Hughes' excellent *The Shock of the New* (BBC, London, 1980).

specifics of the art form, say painting, its cultural location, say the West, its political and economic context—globalisation. The global art market emerges as a formal parody of the erstwhile systems which requires no unified, authentic conception of art to sustain it. Hence the endless contemporary debates about what is art/good art. Art as a commodity, rather than as a distinctive self-referential cultural form, owes its value largely to its transferability rather than what it is or represents. Is it sellable? Is there a market for it? What is the nature of that market—private or museum collections, private or corporate investment, corporate interior decoration? And so on.

The classical tradition of theorising about the criminal law eschews this form of contextual analysis, telling rather the insider's story. It attempts to explicate doctrinal rules in terms of underlying moral values. Thus commentators such as Hale, Hawkins, Foster, and Blackstone sought, by rationalisation and systematisation, to present the posited rules 'as applications of an underlying conception of justice.'[9] This process was important because, by contrast with those in other areas of substantive law (and equity), the nature of the functions secured through criminal law tended to impede the development of secure theoretical foundations.[10] To appreciate why, it is necessary only to reflect upon the kind of reasoning necessary to decide whether A owes B money, and that necessary to decide whether A is responsible for B's death. While it is relatively easy to formulate coherent and internally consistent rules governing the creation and discharge of a debt, it is less easy to formulate coherent and consistent rules governing the imputation of criminal liability. We may know a murderer when we see one but how do we capture the elements of murder in the form of a rule capable of providing a consistent blueprint for the disposal of offenders?

Disappointingly, the theoretical foundations of contemporary anglo-american criminal law appear little more secure today than in the time of these classical commentators despite the efforts of theorists of criminal law to improve its stock.[11] The works of Glanville Williams, Jerome Hall, HLA Hart and George Fletcher, in recent decades, have done much to create the impression that there is a theoretical structure out there ready and able to support a rational criminal law. Since William's ground-breaking work *Criminal Law: The General Part*

---

[9] NE Simmonds *The Decline of Juridical Reason*, (MUP, Manchester, 1984) ch 1.

[10] Cf SF Milsom *The Historical Foundations of the Common Law* (Butterworths, London, 1968), ch 14.

[11] G Fletcher 'Fall and Rise of Criminal Theory' in (1998) 1 *Buffalo Crim LR* 275, 277.

theoretical work has, however, tended to centre around issues supposedly common to all crimes, the so-called 'general part' of *actus reus, mens rea*, justification and excuse, rather than exposing and articulating the premises informing individual crimes as once was common. The two former elements are represented as the basic building blocks of criminal offences, the establishment of which (wrongful conduct/ guilty mind) is the irreducible minimum necessary for conviction and punishment. The latter represent the defence elements which operate to ensure that those who are justified in what they do or are otherwise blameless are not subject to conviction although they may fall full square within an offence definition. In line with the ambitions of the codification project this model of liability promises to realise a form of doctrinal rationality dependent only upon the intercession of an informed and disciplined judiciary. Indeed, part of this project seems to be complete since many of the ideas are in common legal parlance through their adoption by textbook writers and others whose own stock has never been higher.

And yet scepticism persists. There are few theorists of any consequence who are not troubled by the sometimes massive disjunctions still existing between the theoretical assumptions underpinning criminal law and the social practice of criminal law. The theoretical gaps resulting from separating doctrine into general and special parts has presented critical commentators with an unstable edifice to attack. Contradictions and incoherence are bound to emerge if the only story offered of criminal law is that which is reducible to broad generalisations. There is little argument about the basic nature of the problem. Where collective goals in order and security are pursued in a context in which individual rights to fair treatment are offered a more than notional guarantee something has to give. More often than not that 'something' is doctrinal rationality. Where argument tends to arise is around the question of whether these sometimes-contradictory demands are reconcilable or whether collective needs will in a generally unprincipled way 'trump' individual rights.

At the broadest level questions can be raised as to the possibility of defining criminal wrongdoing in terms which do not rely upon some partisan moral or political agenda. Alan Norrie has argued that the very form taken by criminal law ensures that what counts as criminal justice is filtered through a context-specific lens which subjugates the individual to collective needs.[12] By concentrating upon individuals and

---

[12] A Norrie *Crime Reason and History* (London, Weidenfeld and Nicholson, 1993) ch 3; *Law Ideology and Punishment*, (Kluwer, 1991) ch IX; *Punishment Responsibility and Justice* (Clarendon Press, Oxford, 2000), ch 3.

their actions, divorced from the context within which actions take place, the broader 'rights and wrongs' which may afford moral legitimacy to theft as a response to hunger or the use of violence to escape political tyranny, gives way to a decontextualised notion of right and wrong within which collective interests in property, personal security and public order override justice to the individual. The result is to deflect attention from the social and other injustices which 'impartial' criminal justice compounds rather than redresses. The inadequacies of the official version are exposed by the resulting contradictions, ambiguities and inconsistencies arising between criminal law as it is practised and the story told of it. A stark and topical example concerns the trial of Mr Milosevic for war crimes. Many observers, by no means all partisan, accept Mr Milosevic's contention that he is a politician who has lost a war. Others insist he is a criminal and should be treated as such. That such disagreement is possible at all suggests we are in need of another, more subtle, story which can be told of Mr Milosevic and his deeds, one capable of reconciling the paradoxical claims that although (world) events are ultimately attributable to social/historical/political/economic forces they are also definable as individual wrongs and so personally attributable to the decisions of the individuals through which those forces are channelled.

It is not difficult to particularise other mismatches between the criminal law's own theory of itself as represented in the general part and the practice of criminal law. The former's traditional focus upon individuals and their works shows itself at odds with the very basis for corporate liability. And yet it seems undeniable that companies are quite capable of causing harm for which they, distinct from any individuals which comprise them, are the proper focus for a finding of accountability. Indicative of the kind of contradictions issuing from this state of affairs is the mismatch between doctrines emerging in support of corporate liability for homicide and the general juridical context in which punishment invariably takes the form of imprisonment and its justification emphasises a rehabilitative or else spiritual and moral dimension to which companies, by their nature, are insensible. This tension hints, once again, at the need for a deeper, richer focus for the institutions of state coercion than the actions of individual 'straws in the wind', one based in institutional dynamics and processes irreducible to the decisions and motivations of individuals.[13]

[13] C Wells *Corporations and Criminal Responsibility* (Clarendon Press, Oxford 1993).

Again, a constant doctrinal irritant have been the attempts to theorise a generally applicable notion of intention or recklessness in the face of the differentiated notions implemented in the practice of criminal law. As shall be explained in chapter 5 it has been all too easy to present this disjunction as indicative of the inability of the system to live up to its organising premises; of its unavoidable susceptibility to political highjack.[14] Another less remarked upon example of mismatch is explored in chapter 4. Here the interaction between the general principles governing defences and liability for omissions on the one hand, and the doctrinal specifics of the crime of murder, on the other, is examined. The doctrinal specifics seem to tell us, by contrast with the premises derived from the general part, that moral involuntariness is a defence to murder, at least where it is committed by omission. The resulting contradiction is that duress is no defence to murder by affirmative action but may be a defence to murder by omission. The social practice of law busies itself with smoothing over these contradictions but textbooks show little inclination to expose or account for them.[15]

Such instances demonstrate, if this were necessary, that to comprehend a social practice as complex as the criminal law it is necessary to go deeper than the account offered by the system itself to present itself as coherent, systematic and principled. Coherent and principled it may be but the coherence and principles it displays may be otherwise than can be captured by any broad generalisations which ignore the substance of criminal law as it is practised.[16] It is hard to resist the conclusion that a major part of the project of theorising about criminal law generally, and the production and systematisation of doctrines governing criminal liability specifically, is less the attempt to expose the inner workings of criminal law, more the attempt to generate the intellectual impetus to organise or attack the criminal law in a manner deemed appropriate by the individual theorist.

Latterly theorists of all persuasions have sought to take more seriously the social practice of criminal law, giving cause for optimism that the contributions of criminal theorists may make a practical contribution to understanding the forms of our social life, if not to the

---

[14] See A Norrie (1993) above n12, chapter 3; (2000), and Norrie above n 12, ch 8.

[15] Cf W Wilson: *Criminal Law: Doctrine and Theory* (Longmans, London, 1998) 86–9.

[16] See J Gardner 'On the General Part of the Criminal Law' In RA Duff (ed.) *Philosophy and the Criminal Law* (CUP, Cambridge, 1998) 205, 244–9.

forms themselves. While critical theory has been hard at work exposing the contradictions and inconsistencies apparent in criminal doctrine other accounts have sought to align more successfully theorising about criminal law from the insider's point of view with the object of theorisation.[17] The concern to produce an account of the moral structure of the criminal law which is true to its subject matter has, for example, stimulated much contemporary interest in character-based theories of responsibility. Theorists, it seems, are increasingly attracted to the idea, doctrinal support for which has usually been overlooked by commentators, that responsibility for the harms suffered by our neighbours and community is not limited to those occasions when individuals act in conscious denial of their rights and interests.[18] Again, doubts have been canvassed, contrary to the premises informing the general part, as to whether it is, has ever been and ever should be necessary to show a full correspondence between the wrong for which the actor is punished and the (subjective) mental attitude which accompanies it. Even for core crimes such as murder it seems to make moral as well as practical sense to hold responsible not merely those who act with death 'in mind' but also those who cause death in the course of committing a violent attack, whether or not death was intended or contemplated.[19] More broadly it has been argued that variation rather than uniformity may be the key to rational criminal doctrine.[20] Given the way our thought processes affect the moral quality of our actions it may be quite apt, for example, for there to be more rather than less variation in the fault elements attached to different offences and for *mens rea* words to have variable meanings according to the context in which the word is used. What, other than the aesthetics of meaning, compels us to conclude that driving recklessly should have the same referent as injuring recklessly or damaging property recklessly? Why do we assume that the

[17] See for example J Gardner 'The Gist of Excuses' (1998) *Buffalo Criminal Law Review* 575; J Horder 'Two Histories and Four Hidden Principles of Mens Rea' (1997) 113 *LQR* 95; S Shute, J Gardner, J Horder (eds.) *Action and Value in Criminal Law* (Clarendon Press, Oxford, 1993) ch 1.

[18] G Fletcher *Rethinking the Criminal Law* (Little Brown Barton, 1978) ch 10; M Bayles 'Character, Purpose and Criminal responsibility' (1982) 1 *Law and Philosophy* 5; RA Duff 'Choice, Character and Criminal Liability' (1993) 12 *Law and Philosophy* 345; K Huigens 'Virtue and Criminal Negligence' in (1998) *Buffalo Criminal Law Review* 431, at 434–9; J Horder 'Gross Negligence and Criminal Culpability' (1997) 47 *U Toronto LJ* 495.

[19] J Horder 'Two Histories and Four Hidden Principles of Mens Rea' (1997) 113 *LQR* 95.

[20] See for example J Gardner 'On the General Part of the Criminal Law' In RA Duff (ed.) *Philosophy and the Criminal Law* above n 16 205.

mental state described as intending grievous bodily harm should be the same mental state referred to in causing grievous bodily harm with intent contrary to section 18 Offences Against the Person Act 1861, and in attempting that same offence?

Although there is clearly an urgent need for theorising criminal law in the manner suggested by Nicola Lacey there remains room, therefore, also for accounts which tell the story of the criminal law from the internal point of view. Given the crucial and potentially injurious social functions criminal law offers to discharge, it is of signal importance for an account to be given which discloses its underlying premises and subjects these and the way they are implemented to critical evaluation. It is this kind of 'middle level' account which is emphasised here.[21] The primary aim is to make sense of the social practice of criminal law and to identify how far it measures up to the goals it sets itself. Typical of this emphasis is the coverage of defences in the final chapter in which the foundational framework of criminal excuses is examined with a view to considering, for example, how far the criminal law does/should excuse those lacking the normal mental/moral furniture to conform their behaviour consistently to rules.

The first two chapters provide a brief overview of theories of criminalisation and punishment. Although these do not form part of the package of 'central issues' which constitutes the bulk of the text they perform a basic scene setting role. It is useful to have some idea about the ideas deployed to justify criminalisation and punishment in the first place if we are to make headway in deciding, for example, what makes or does not make a person an appropriate object of criminal liability. At the outset the range of considerations which potentially underpin a decision to subject others to coercive rules are surveyed and the question posed and considered whether it is ever legitimate to punish those whose conduct is not wrongful by any measure other than that set by the rule itself. This leads into a broader inquiry into whether state punishment is under any circumstances justifiable and, if so, what that justification may be. Two issues in particular are broached. The first is whether the struggle to produce theories of punishment which dissociate retributive and consequentialist concerns is capable of doing true justice to the phenomenon of punishment. The second, implicit in contemporary arguments in favour of restorative approaches to punishment, is whether the state's punitive response should embrace more

---

[21] The phrase is Jules Coleman's. The approach is discussed by N Lacey in 'Philosophy, History and Criminal Law Theory' (1998) 1 *Buffalo Crim LR* 303–7.

radically the idea that punishment offers something of value both to the victim and the wider society, by taking explicit account of the presently covert role played by vengeance in the constitution of desert.

In the remaining chapters the organisational framework of the criminal law itself is surveyed. In chapters 3 and 4 I examine how criminal wrongdoing is conceived, most notably through theorisations of the act requirement, the idea that criminal liability requires someone to have done something wrong rather than, say, simply thinking bad thoughts. Two main themes take up the bulk of chapters 3 and 4. The first theme is the notion that criminal wrongdoing implies a 'doing', act, action or activity.[22] This notion is criticised and the view advanced that there is no particular quality intrinsic to the conduct element in criminal offences other than that it should be capable of forming the subject matter of an effective coercive norm. There is nothing untoward in situational crimes, crimes of possession, or crimes of omission so long as the relevant rule can act as a standard capable of enabling subjects to remain on the right side of the law. On the other hand, I argue that the constitution of criminal wrongdoing requires particular attention to be paid to the criminal law's communicative function. Although the conduct element need take no particular form ideally it should be morally informative, communicating precisely what it is about certain ways of behaving which attracts moral condemnation and punishment. This function, along with law's well understood concern to honour autonomy and the principle of legality, is a major reason for circumspection in the criminalisation of omissions.

The second related theme is the notion that 'doing wrong' presupposes voluntariness, whether of action or omission. The theory behind this is that criminal liability must have some objectively arrived at limits, some basic element upon which responsibility is founded. What is this element? Is it, for example, action *tout court*. Is it volition? Is it the unacted upon capacity to have behaved otherwise? It is widely assumed that a requirement of voluntariness is a liability element distinct from other exculpatory claims. The cogency of this assumption is challenged and the contention advanced that there is no easy distinction to be made between the claim 'I did no wrong/my conduct was involuntary' and the claim 'I was not at fault/my conduct was not blameworthy'. This is most apparent in connection with the structure of liability for omissions where excuses are available which seem to have no direct counterpart for crimes of commission.

[22] See generally M Moore *Act and Crime* (Clarendon Press, Oxford, 1993).

Much of the theoretical interest in criminal attempts, the subject matter of chapter 8, also stems from the linkage which must be shown between a given substantive offence and the kind of activities which will incriminate those who take (unsuccessful) steps towards bringing it about. This interest derives, in the main, from certain unresolved questions informing criminal theory at large which, in the context of liability for attempts, take on a particularly acute character. Foremost amongst these is whether the basis for liability as an attempter is arrived at subjectively or objectively, whether a successful accommodation can be made between a notion of attempt based in harm prevention and one based in wrongdoing, and how far luck should be a factor pertinent to criminal liability.[23] In this chapter I canvass the view that the notion of an attempt is too indeterminate a notion of criminal wrongdoing to ground a rational mechanism for countering or otherwise responding to those who act with harm in mind. Law's preventive function can be more systematically advanced by precisely tailored situational offences and crimes of possession on the one hand, and its punitive function by more extensive use of crimes of ulterior intent, considered in chapter 5, on the other. This latter theme is pursued in chapter 9 where, sharing the view of Antony Duff, I suggest that the criminal law's core function is to set norms rather than simply declaring what shall and shall not be done. If, as is argued in chapter 2, punishment is society's mechanism for expressing condemnation of an agent's anti-social conduct then offence and defence definitions form society's central resource for the dissemination of standards of socially acceptable behaviour. A precondition of communicative efficacy is that crimes are packaged in morally significant ways, hence the greater usefulness of crimes of ulterior intent.[24]

Chapter 5 broaches the way a person's reasons for acting bear on liability. This is a theme developed in chapters 9, 10, and 11. Concentrating upon crime's paradigm mental element, intention, I consider why the criminal law accords the actor's intention rather his/her reasons for acting the primary defining role in the constitution of the offence. Although this focus has the potential for injustice, since deliberate rule breaking rather than moral fault is the primary basis upon which punishment and censure is allocated, it secures the viability of an

---

[23] *Ibid*, ch 8.

[24] An argument put with much force by J Horder 'Crimes of Ulterior Intent' in A Simester and ATH Smith (eds) *Harm and Culpability* (Clarendon Press, Oxford) 1996) 153.

effective normative system. By relegating motives to the 'realm of supervening defences' the clarity of the moral principles enshrined in criminal prohibitions—in relation to crimes of violence, say, the principle that harming people is wrong—can be sustained.[25] Two related issues are broached in chapter 5. The first concerns the theoretical inclination to assume a unified meaning and function for intention. As to intention's functions, it is not used simply to filter, in conjunction with recklessness, those deserving of punishment for their wrongdoing from those who do not, or, alternatively, to grade wrongdoing in terms of seriousness. If it were there would be strong grounds for it carrying the same meaning wherever it was found in the criminal catalogue. More significantly, it is also used as a defining element in criminal wrongdoing. Contrary to traditional assumptions doctrinal rationality rather than challenged may in fact be advanced by the use of variable meanings of intention, depending upon which of these functions is being discharged. The second issue concerns how doctrinal instability may result from the failure to take seriously the way an actor's intentions affect the nature and constitution of his wrongdoing. The upshot is an opportunistic tendency to push types of moral wrongdoing into legal pigeonholes they were not made for, thus compromising doctrinal rationality generally.

In chapters 6 and 7 I address the question of harm and how it is attributed to an actor. To be accountable normally requires some wrongful deed on the part of an actor capable of eliciting the reasoned judgement that it was by this deed that the harm came about. Without such a clear causal nexus judgements of accountability typically will have nothing upon which to bite. Causation doctrine is faced with a problem, however. Not all causal contributions necessarily entail a finding of accountability. Some contributions are too 'remote' to count. Robust policing practices were thought to have ignited an already explosive situation at the time of the Brixton riots in the early eighties. But it was the rioters rather than the police who were held criminally accountable, significant though the latter's causal contribution was. Critics hold that this state of affairs indicates that decisions on causation owe more to political concerns such as the desirability of finding a politically suitable person to bear responsibility than the legal/moral concern to ensure that such person is fairly selected.[26] A way of accommodating this objection must

[25] J Horder 'The Irrelevance of Motive in Criminal Law' in J Horder (ed.) *Oxford Essays in Jurisprudence*, (Clarendon Press, Oxford, 2000) 174.
[26] See for example A Norrie (1993) above n 12 ch 7.

be fashioned if resulting harm is to be allowed to play so great a part in the construction of criminal identities.

Nowhere is this problem of attributing harm to a human agent more apparent than where it is sought to hold an agent accountable for his failure to prevent a harm whose occurrence issues from active causal processes. While all omissions to prevent harm can be understood in a loose sense as 'causes' of that harm we tend to look for the things which make a difference in ascribing causal responsibility and we can rarely be sure that prompt intervention would make such a difference. Nevertheless, particularly where such failure is four square in terms of culpability with harmful action, the absence of such a clear cut causal nexus does not register as a knock-down reason not to hold the omitter to account. Criminal liability for omissions seems to bespeak a different form of attribution in which complex but subtle judgements are made at a pre-theoretical level about the fairness of holding someone accountable for the consequences of passive acquiescence, which judgement is then rationalised, casuistically, in terms of the offence's definitional elements.[27]

Accessoryship, like omissions, also permits liability on the basis of a person's loose association with a primary causal agent rather than his direct instrumentality. The accessory's liability **derives** from the culpable wrongdoing of another, the perpetrator, rather than from his own wrongdoing. This derivative basis to accessorial liability poses acute organisational problems since by abandoning orthodox notions of personal responsibility and loosening the connection with theories of punishment and blame, doctrinal tensions are created. Derivative liability seems to stretch the net of accountability too wide in some respects and too narrow in others. On the one hand those who get caught up in the criminal activities of others stand at risk of being held accountable for criminal actions although they may neither approve nor assent to such actions. On the other, those who procure the commission of wrongdoing by others should, in theory at least, escape liability if, say, the latter avoids conviction by reason of lack of *mens rea* or the existence of a defence. It is not hard to see why there appears to be an intrinsic strain in the evolution of doctrine to replace the derivative nature of liability with a personal inchoate form. Doctrine here appears to instantiate most obviously the dual standards and resulting contradictions proposed in critical accounts. Seemingly it must if it is to convict

[27] A Smart 'Criminal Responsibility for Failing to do the Impossible' [1987] 103 *LQR* 532, 535; G Hughes, 'Criminal Omissions ' (1958) 67 *Yale LJ* 590.

Mr Big for the drug trafficking activities of his 'mules' but not routinely convict the vast raft of others who perhaps satisfying, in formal terms, the liability component of a criminal offence are not a proper subject of condemnation and punishment. This can be achieved effortlessly via the rules of complicity. Principles of causation qualified by the rules governing attribution for complicity circumscribe fairly precisely, while leaving ample room for manoeuvre, the range of people who are properly subject to criminal liability. They restrict liability in the case of those who do not themselves perpetrate in a direct and immediate fashion a criminal harm to those who act **with the intention**[28] **of assisting or encouraging** a blameworthy perpetrator in his. The rules of accessorial liability in conjunction with doctrine governing liability for omissions, are intrinsically suited to make matters of attribution more sensitive to historically and politically rooted moral judgements concerning who is fairly held accountable for harmful events.

In chapter 9 I consider the theoretical inclination to consider offences and defences as separate elements in the construction of criminal liability, as is the separation of defences into excuses and justifications.[29] The impetus to package liability in this way is explained in terms of the position marked out earlier that a rational system of criminal law should ideally be in the business of communicating behavioural norms rather than simply issuing prohibitions. The point of the separation is to ensure that norms of behaviour are articulated with maximum moral clarity. By one set of norms (offence definitions) citizens are offered guidance as to their primary obligations. By another (justificatory defences such as self-defence) citizens are offered guidance as to the circumstances under which they are permitted to infringe the former norms. In this way the moral landscape of crime can best be communicated and appreciated the better to guide citizens' behaviour. In theory, both offence elements and justificatory defences would stand to be included in a 'citizens code'—the civilised state's mechanism for ensuring that all citizens understand how best to conform their conduct to society's standards[30]. Excuses would remain

[28] Nothing less than an intention to assist will do and so questions of definition are here too of central constitutive importance. See for example *J.F. Alford Transport Limited* [1997] *Crim LR* 745.

[29] See J Gardner 'Justification and Reasons' in A Simester and ATH Smith (eds) *Harm and Culpability* (Clarendon Press, Oxford, 1996) 103; cf A Norrie *Punishment Responsibility and Justice* (Clarendon Press, Oxford, 2000), ch 7.

[30] Paul H Robinson 'Rules of Conduct and Principles of Adjudication' (1990) 57 *Univ of Chicago LR* 729; RA Duff (1999).

outside the code. These are claims to avoid punishment, such as provocation, which provide reasons for **officials** to exempt an actor from
(full) punishment and condemnation but do not provide reasons for the
actor to act otherwise than in accordance with his primary obligation.
Two objections to this analysis are posted. The first questions the
cogency of making an analytically secure distinction between excuses
and justifications. The second questions whether it is in any event
implicit in the notion of an excuse that it may not operate to give people
guiding reasons for acting otherwise than the relevant primary norm
would recommend. The defence of duress instantiates both these objections, raising questions as to whether the excuses/justification separation is of any real assistance in determining the proper limits of a
citizens' code.

In chapters 10 and 11 I examine more closely the constitution of
criminal defences. Whether or not it is possible to separate defences
into those which negate the wrongdoing implicit in a defence definition
(justifications) and those which merely negate responsibility for that
wrongdoing (excuses and exemptions) it is possible to discern three
basic claims to avoid criminal liability implicit in the organisational
'templates' of different defences. These templates largely, but not
entirely, map this analytical separation. The templates comprise status-based denials of capacity, defences of impaired voluntariness, and
defences of reasonable reaction. In chapter 10 I examine defences of
reasonable reaction, which largely, but not entirely, map the field of
justificatory defences. Concentrating on duress, self defence and necessity the aim is to explain how a common template sustains their individual internal moral ordering but also creates a framework by which
other cases of excused or justified action may become recognised. I
argue that there are cases, falling outside the traditional defence
boundaries which are yet capable of recognition as involving valid
justificatory claims and consider what the nature of that justification
is.[31] As *Re A*, the case of the conjoined twins, illustrates action is easier to justify where its object (preserving life) is a good one and any
harm wrought is incidental to the actor's purpose rather than the
means by which such purpose is realised. It is for this reason that where
the basis of a person's moral responsibility is located in what he foresees the corresponding fault element is constructed as recklessness
rather than intention. In both cases it is not that we foresee the harm

---

[31] See S Uniacke *Permissible Killing: The Self-Defense Justification of Homicide*
(Clarendon Press, Oxford, 1994) 143–55.

issuing from our actions which constitutes our actions as morally wrong. It is that the reason we have for acting is not good enough to offset the harm which is threatened.

Finally, in chapter 11 I examine those defences which ordinarily fall under the rubric of excuses and exemptions. Having made some preliminary observations as to how excuses are constituted at the moral level I examine the way such excuses are filtered through into criminal doctrine. I suggest that if a person's action is morally defensible this is a strong but not conclusive reason for holding it also to be legally defensible. Correspondingly, if a person's action is morally indefensible this is a strong but not conclusive reason for holding it to be legally indefensible. With this basic focus in mind I examine the leading contemporary theories of excuses with a view to questioning whether a unified theory of excuses is either possible or desirable.

1

Criminalising Wrongdoing

Adam finds Cain bouncing a tennis ball in the living room. He confiscates the ball reminding Cain that since Cain broke a window there has been a rule that balls are not to be played with in the house. Cain objects that he did not think tennis balls counted as they are not apt to do damage. Adam rejects Cain's explanation and the ball remains confiscated. Cain appeals to Eve for support. Eve privately suggests that Cain has not really been naughty and that Cain's explanation is reasonable. Tennis balls do not break windows and the point of the rule was to prevent window damage. Adam replies that a rule is a rule. Although the original point of the rule was to prevent damage to the window, the point of house rules is to make it easy for house members to know what they can and cannot do. Allowing such members to determine the scope of the rule threatens the effectiveness of the rule. So it is proper to couch the rule in terms which prohibit conduct which falls outside the mischief of the rule. Confiscation is not unfair because, although Cain did not deliberately provoke a risk of window damage justifying sending Cain to his room, he did infringe a rule governing the use of balls.

In this private scenario many of the key issues facing the criminal justice system are reflected. What kinds of considerations should underpin a decision to subject others to coercive rules? What is the relationship, if any, between the content of a rule, and standards of good conduct? Is it legitimate to punish those whose conduct is not wrongful by any measure other than that set by the rule itself? Under what circumstances, if any, is it legitimate to punish infringement of a rule? What, if anything, distinguishes punishment from other methods of controlling or responding to unacceptable behaviour? In the next two chapters these issues will be subjected to critical scrutiny beginning, in this chapter, with a consideration of the ideas surrounding the propriety of criminalisation.

CRIMINALISING WRONGDOING

In the family environment the subjects of coercive rules are generally, poor blighters, children. In informal environments such as families adults do not tend to subject themselves to rules. Rules of behaviour are not needed if an agent has a consistent ability and disposition to act reasonably. Few adults would admit to lacking such ability and fewer still would cede the personal autonomy which would thereby transpire. Moreover, rule creation and enforcement requires power and authority of a nature which sits uneasily with the premise of equality between partners but is implicit in the unequal relations enjoyed by parents and children. Where formal rules of behaviour do govern the behaviour of adults outside the framework of law they typically arise as a precondition of membership of social organisations. By such means institutions can minimise the scope for conflict and disagreement which inevitably arise when agents with their own personal interests and standards need to co-operate with others whose personal interests and standards will not always be synchronised. By joining or signing up, a member cedes a degree of freedom to the authority of the institution the better to enjoy the fruits of membership .

Coercive rules in the family domain are typically justified on grounds of paternalism, that is, that the rules are necessary in the interests of the moral and physical interests of the children themselves.[1] Rules designed to ensure a child's moral and social development may include rules against lying, deceit and bad language and, at a broader level, against rowdy, untidy or disruptive behaviour. Rules designed to ensure the child's physical interests may include curfews, boundaries, rules against use of knives and weapons and use of violence. These latter rules express more clearly perhaps, as does the ball prohibition, the essential character of the rules which, generally speaking, operate and are experienced as methods of behavioural control.

No one explanation is capable of accounting for the large number of different criminal offences. We cannot say, for example, as once was fashionable, that the coercive norms of the criminal law necessarily embody collectively acknowledged moral standards. No doubt many of the rules of criminal law do embody such standards. Killing,

---

[1] See SI Benn, ' "Interests" in Politics' (1960) *Proceedings of the Aristotelian Society* 60 130 *et seq.*

stealing, hurting are obvious instantiations of moral prohibitions. They are actions which are criminalised because they are wrong in themselves, that is because they are immoral or, in the language of another age, *mala in se*. But the vast majority of criminal offences embody norms which are not direct reflections of underlying moral norms. Speeding offences and health and safety regulations are not juridical representations of the Ten Commandments updated for a modern world. There is no 'Thou shalt wear a hard hat on a building site or shalt not drive quicker than 70mph on a motorway' norm of behaviour. Such offences we might say are wrong by virtue of being declared wrong rather than by any immorality intrinsic to them. They are *mala prohibita* rather than *mala in se*. Clearly, however, most if not all criminal prohibitions do have some moral reference point in the sense of being instantiations of socially appropriate ways of behaving. Speeding offences and health and safety regulations for example embody the moral principle that we do not unreasonably subject each other to the risk of harm. Putting the matter this way suggests that the criminal law's role in advancing society's moral concerns is simply the flip side of a proposition to which all can subscribe, namely that it functions to advance and secure the interests of its members collective and individual, by punishing deviations from collectively agreed standards of behaviour.[2]

The more interesting object of inquiry for those concerned to understand the present and potential scope of the criminal law concerns therefore not so much uncovering any special characteristic of criminal offences, as specifiying the norms governing the creation of criminal proscriptions. Are there any principles governing what activities may and may not be criminalised? If so it may be possible to construct some form of measure by which to assess the moral propriety of types of criminal prohibition, the constituent elements of individual offences, and perhaps also a framework for interpretation where the rules of substantive law are dogged by ambiguity or inconsistency.

At the political level coercive rules in liberal societies are, in theory at least, subject to ethical constraints. These derive from the premise that the liberal state exists to support individual autonomy and freedom rather than to restrict it.[3] Coercive rules avoid this apparent para-

---

[2] See N Lacey, 'Contingency and Criminalisation' in I Loveland (ed), *The Frontiers of Criminality* (Kluwer, London, 1995).

[3] See generally HJ Paton, *The Moral Law: Kant's Groundwork of the Metaphysic of Morals* (Hutchinson , London, 1948).

dox by criminalising activities and conduct which are hostile to the autonomy of others and by ensuring that individuals are give fair warning of the occasions when their conduct may fall foul of a criminal proscription. Individuals are thus protected by the rules and are also able to use the rules as standards by which to calculate how to conduct themselves with the minimum of state interference. Core criminal activities such as theft and violence express these preoccupations at their simplest. To be an autonomous person in the sense of being the effective author of our own lives requires our ownership and possession of property to be protected from interference and our personal security to be guaranteed. Freedom is thus restricted in order to guarantee autonomy—the more valuable social commodity. Such crimes are then of symbolic importance since they record directly what society is up to in using coercion against citizens.[4] They are criminalised not simply as instances of moral wrongdoing but because the thief or aggressor, in seeking to augment his own life choices, thereby diminishes those same choices of the victim.

The Harm Principle

The apparently paradoxical emphasis on autonomy as guarantor of the legitimacy of state coercion is reflected in the harm principle which takes as the basic limiting principle of state coercion the prevention of harm to others. Given the relative lack of consensus about the values worthy of state enforcement other than those expressed in focal crimes, and the risk of values being introduced into the criminal law for the purpose of meeting partisan rather than community aims, the harm principle is widely recognised as a key ethic in maintaining moral neutrality and ensuring the state serves the interests of the citizenry rather than its own interests.[5] It was first canvassed by JS Mill in his essay 'On Liberty':

> The only purpose for which power can be rightfully exercised over any member of a civilised community against his will is to prevent harm to others. His own good, either physical or moral, is not a sufficient warrant. He cannot rightfully be compelled to do or forebear . . . because in the opinion of others to do so would be wise or even right.[6]

---

[4] What this is may be the subject of contestation. See I Dennis, 'The Critical Condition of Criminal Law' (1997) *Current Legal Problems* 213.

[5] See generally J Raz, *The Morality of Freedom* (Clarendon Press, Oxford, 1986).

[6] JS Mill, 'On Liberty' in J Gray (ed), *On Liberty and Other Essays* (OUP, Oxford, 1991).

At the heart of the principle are two sentiments with which few liberals could possibly disagree. First, the state has the authority to criminalise the causing of harm to other people and activities which conduce thereto. Secondly, the state should keep interference to the minimum necessary to guarantee the maximisation of individual autonomy. The individual should be allowed to do, say, think what he/she likes provided that this does not interfere with the similar rights of others.[7] What more can we ask of a tolerant, rights-respecting society than this? But it is an ambiguous principle. On the one hand, the principle provides a useful check against the potentially overweening power of the state to restrict our liberty. And yet, on the other, the state would provide little more than minimal protection to the interests of its citizens if it allowed any activity save those which caused direct harms to others. More people are killed and injured by thoughtlessness on the roads than ever they are by acts of calculated violence. Similarly the divisive influence of certain antisocial economic practices is more inimical to human flourishing than isolated cases of theft from individuals. A plausible account of the proper scope of the criminal law must, therefore, be able to explain how a proper balance between freedom and welfare and between private and public interests should be struck.[8]

The major modern reformulation of the harm principle is that of Joel Feinberg. He proposes that the criminal law may legitimately criminalise conduct only where it causes harm or serious offence. It may not, however, criminalise conduct simply to satisfy the moral preferences of the majority. It may not criminalise 'non-harmful wrongs'.[9] Harm for the purposes of the harm principle refers to the way a subject's interests may be 'set-back' as a 'consequence of wrongful acts or omissions by others'. So 'minor physical and mental "hurts" and a miscellany of disliked states of mind including various forms of offendedness, anxiety and boredom', since they involve no (quantifiable) set-back of interest, do not count as harms for the purpose of criminalisation.[10]

The idea of set-back allows us to refine the idea of harm somewhat. Most obviously included in this notion of set-back is the kind of direct harm which the victim of attack or theft suffers. But the harm principle can be preyed in aid of criminalising conduct which sets back our

---

[7] See generally J Feinberg, *Harm to Self* (OUP, Oxford, 1986) chs 18–19.
[8] See J Raz, *The Morality of Freedom*, ch 15.
[9] Feinberg, *Harm to Others* (OUP, Oxford, 1984), 36.
[10] *Ibid* 215–16.

interests in less direct and material ways. So it can be used to support the state regulation of dangerous activities such as driving motor vehicles, the possession of potentially dangerous things, and those other social enterprises which create risks of harm when prosecuted without reference to the welfare of citizens who may be affected. Straightforward examples include regulations concerning health and safety, pollution, food safety and so on.

The important feature uniting both types of offence is that their criminalisation is dependent upon a notion of the public interest which has no partisan moral agenda. An efficient, ordered society must necessarily underwrite the interests of individuals in the security of their person and property. Legislating to prohibit violence or to reduce the risks attending everyday activities does not commit the state to a morally controversial view of how citizens should behave. Society is not a suicide club and so the state is properly involved in restricting activities which might contradict this common sense idea.

Harm, thus conceived, is a somewhat richer concept than that subscribed to by, for example, the tort of negligence with its emphasis on material harm to person or property. Consider again the notion of consented to physical harms.[11] Are these 'harms' for the purpose of the harm principle? The answer depends upon an assessment of the interests, if any, which may be set back by the relevant act.[12] A person who undergoes a serious life-saving operation is not 'harmed', for the purpose of the criminal law, by the surgeon's scalpel although he suffers physical injury since no interest of his or any other is thereby setback. On the other hand, individuals may suffer harm even where not the direct victim of a physical attack, say because they are members of the victim's family, and society's collective interests may be harmed where no individual has suffered a set-back to his individual interests. So, while a person who consents to a private bout of fisticuffs may not suffer a set-back to his own interests by dint of such consent, others' interests, including collective interests in security, may be.[13]

The ability of the harm principle to justify the criminalisation of conduct which conduce to indirect or as they are more commonly termed 'remote harms' serves notice of a more general problem which the legitimating power of the harm principle on state coercion tends to conceal, namely that it has no inbuilt mechanism for clarifying how serious and

[11] Feinberg, *Harm to Others* (OUP, Oxford, 1984), 215–16.
[12] *Ibid*; cf H Gross, *A Theory of Criminal Justice* (OUP, New York, 1979), 118.
[13] Feinberg, *Harm to Others*, 221–5.

direct the harm has to be before the state receives its warrant to sanction it through punishment. The harm principle, though its political clout derives from its promise to restrict the occasions when the state may interfere with our liberty, supports in practice interference in potentially every area of our lives save possibly our self-regarding recreational activities. It is ironically, therefore, a principle capable of justifying extremes of state interference.

Feinberg's solution to this problem is to prescribe thresholds of 'seriousness' limiting the applicability of the criminal sanction.[14] The standard mechanism for determining an appropriate threshold for state intervention in cases involving activities which do not involve a direct attack upon the interests of the victim takes the form of a practical equation weighing the gravity of the harm and the likelihood of its occurrence on the one hand, against the social value of the relevant conduct and the degree of interference with personal liberty that criminalisation would involve on the other. This latter is an important qualification. Sexual immorality, say adultery, conduces to harmful consequences and the likelihood of such consequences occurring are relatively high. It may cause distress, and deep psychological harm to family members, particularly children. It may cause financial harm not only to the participants, but also to their families and the wider society. It probably causes more pain, trauma and mental illness to its victims than most serious crimes. Yet most people would concede that it would not be a proper subject for the criminal sanction. The obvious reason for this is that our membership of a society which respects individual autonomy and protects individual freedom necessitates placing outside the realm of the criminal law those features and practices which constitute us as free human beings. At the forefront of these is our sexuality and personal relationships.

Assessing appropriate thresholds of harm whether for purposes of basic criminalisation or for purposes of grading offences is obviously not amenable to strict empirical verification. It is easier to produce examples of wrongs which are obviously fit for criminalisation—say homicide, theft, arson, and rape—than to produce a cogent basis for excluding wrongs too trivial to justify such state sponsored coercion. This might challenge the cogency of the overall project of requiring new crimes to measure up to predetermined thresholds of gravity. But clearly the principles governing criminalisation cannot be a counsel of

---

[14] Feinberg, *Harm to Others*, 221–5.

perfection.[15] After all the gap between substantial and insubstantial wrongs can be closed by reference to the same criteria which informs our assessment of the clear cases.[16] All that is necessary is that we use a consistent approach in weighing the various factors relevant to seriousness.

Grading is a different matter. At the level of basic wrongs entailing direct attacks on personal and property interests grading offences, say crimes of violence, is achieved by marking out crimes of lesser seriousness by both gravity of harm and fault terms. The fault element for crimes of lesser seriousness are typically negligence and recklessness and of greater seriousness knowledge, purpose and intention. The not uncontroversial assumption is that intention and subjective recklessness is a more culpable state of mind than negligence.[17] It is possible to create quite plausible theories to account for the fact that in both law and morality arson is treated more seriously than theft, and murder more seriously than manslaughter or criminal damage. We are also able to account for the fact that certain types of criminal damage (arson) with accompanying states of mind (intention or recklessness as to the risk of death) are punishable within the limits set by the crimes of homicide rather than those of property offences generally. In these uncontroversial cases Feinberg's notion of set-back of interest does most of the work needed of it in explaining why one wrong is more serious than another. His method for assessing seriousness of harm centres upon the victim's loss of choice or opportunity. Murder is a more serious crime than theft because of the relative impact of the activities upon the victim's choices, and manslaughter because of the more culpable attitude displayed. Again, theft justifies criminalisation, whereas dishonest borrowing does not because, *ceteris paribus*, the latter does not seriously diminish the victim's range of choices. She may not be able to read this book, wear this ring, use this lawnmower today but these activities are left open to her another day.

Beyond the paradigm cases just considered this approach is less compelling, however. What measure of lost options allows us to compare in terms of seriousness rape with, say, serious wounding, drunken driving, polluting the waterways or institutional fraud? Von Hirsch and Jareborg have provided a solution for settling appropriate thresholds

---

[15] AJ Ashworth 'Is The Criminal Law a Lost Cause?' (2000) 116 *LQR* 225, 240 *et seq.*

[16] *Ibid* 242.

[17] See AP Simester, 'Can Negligence be Culpable?' in J Horder (ed), *Oxford Essays in Jurisprudence* (Clarendon Press, Oxford, 2000).

of seriousness appropriate for both determining the level at which criminalisation is first appropriate and, thereafter as a means of grading different offences.[18] The mechanism turns our attention from what the victim loses in terms of choice to what he loses in terms of quality of life. Harms are graded according to the effect they have on a person's standard of living assessed according to material criteria such as financial resources and shelter and wider aspects of a good quality of life such as health, dignity, physical amenity, privacy and so on. This is, after all, how we differentiate, common-sensically, between different crimes. It is why we say that torturing someone or robbing them is worse than stealing from them or smashing their window because the effects upon the victim's quality of life are more profound. The significant feature in the analysis is that it provides a cogent basis for comparing what would otherwise be incommensurable interest violations. Serious property crimes, say, which relegate individuals from a position of adequate wellbeing to the level of subsistence can be graded more seriously than, say, non-serious crimes of violence where the victim's global interests are not irreparably affected.

By concentrating on loss of choice and reductions in the quality of life both approaches rightly attempt to generate some consistency between public intuitions of the relative seriousness of different harms and institutional practices of grading and punishment.[19] It provides also a plausible mechanism for integrating crimes against collective interests such as pollution control and health and safety provisions into the general scheme of criminal offences rather than, as present, being shunted away into the regulatory field. A possible weakness in both approaches is a tendency to suppress the significance of the normative packaging of harm. Criminalisation cannot be conceived simply as a matter of addressing harms committed against individuals—we have the civil law for this very purpose. It is also about defining public interests worthy of enforcement and identifying the factors which convert wrongs against individuals into matters of public concern.[20] Private

---

[18] A von Hirsch and N Jareborg, 'Gauging Criminal Harms: a Living Standard Analysis' (1991) 11 *OJLS* 1.

[19] 30 September 2000. Todays newspaper reports that a nun has not been imprisoned for years of child abuse seriously damaging victim's standard of life while a 39-year-old woman has been imprisoned for 2 years for having sex with two 14-year-old boys, prosecution instigated by boys' parents.

[20] J Horder, 'Rethinking Non-Fatal Offences Against the Person' [1994] 14 *OJLS* 335; cf J Gardner in 'Rationality and the Rule of Law in Offences Against the Person' [1994] *Camb LJ* 502.

interests are offered support through the criminal law but only where the protection of those interests is itself a matter of the public interest. At the forefront of such interests is that of individual autonomy. The crimes of rape, assault and theft are examples of offences where the vindication of individual interests in autonomy are subsumed within the public interest. These are attacks on individuals which, as an attack on core values, are experienced as an attack on everyone both as individuals and collectively.[21] It is because public interests can be set-back with no corresponding set-back to private interests that criminalising informal fisticuffs may be legitimate although no individual interests are set-back. Again, it is sometimes argued that trivial cases of theft, say shoplifting, should be decriminalised while serious cases of dishonest borrowing, say those involving valuable goods for long periods, should be criminalised. Analysed in terms of victims' choices there is clearly much to be said for such a view which would support the replacement of the current set of property crimes by a set of offences constituted in terms of the gravity of the set-back. A cogent account of propriety in criminalisation, however, requires something more than a simple weighing of the gravity of the harm to the victim's choices against the harms associated with criminalisation. In particular, the decision to criminalise also requires due weight to be accorded to the reasons why society considers theft differently from dishonest borrowing. At one level, namely that of public morality, it is because theft is a different wrong from dishonest borrowing. At another level it is because society has a stake in maintaining the **integrity** of property relations rather than protecting property interests per se. It is considerations such as these which perhaps explain why stealing a bottle of milk from a shop deserves public condemnation while borrowing someone's jewels for the weekend, or failing to discharge a debt does not.

Ratcheting Up State Coercion

Nevertheless, as far as standard victimising wrongs are concerned the harm principle has an important ideological role to play in keeping the criminal law 'honest'. If an actor does something wrong which sets

---

[21] Cf S E Marshall and RA Duff, 'Criminalisation and Sharing Wrongs' (1998) *Can J of Law and Jurisprudence* 7.

back the interests of others in a more than trivial way this is a good reason to subject him to state coercion in the absence of countervailing reasons. On the other hand state coercion is inappropriate in the absence of sufficient gravity of harm caused or risked to justify the state taking on the mantle of injured party. As explained earlier, however, if the central organising theme governing criminalisation is harm rather than, say, wrongdoing the harm principle threatens to outgrow its usefulness as a support to rather than check on the value of individual liberty and autonomy. We shall examine two areas which pose a particular challenge for the cogency of the harm principle, namely regulatory offences and offences addressing what has been termed 'remote harms'.

The contemporary experience indicates that much new legislation is of a regulatory nature, addressing minor acts of wrongdoing and wrongful omissions. Parking offences, failures to submit tax returns, or to display a tax disc are archetypal examples. On the face of it criminalising such minor harms is inconsistent with the legitimising role which the harm principle fulfils in liberal society. If harm means 'substantial' harm' then such regulatory offences fall foul of the harm principle, raising questions about whether criminal legislation is designed for the convenience of the state rather than for the maximisation of freedom to individuals. The state's justification for the criminalisation of non-serious harms is unambiguously pragmatic. Regulatory offences are a convenient way of securing both the smooth running of society and protecting people's welfare interests. The criminal law is a clear, smart, efficient way of ensuring people keep up to scratch. The harm principle is side-stepped by the implication that regulatory offences are not true crimes—they do not serve to express social condemnation—and therefore there is no need for them to be subject to the same ethical controls. The generalised absence of a fault requirement for regulatory offences makes the same point. The *mens rea* requirement is an obvious hindrance to efficient and effective social regulation for the benefit of all.[22]

The working assumption is that all such regulatory offences are of this nature. Minor harms can then be addressed by a fast track regulatory mechanism with non-custodial penalties balancing minimal procedural safeguards against unjust conviction. In fact, however,

---

[22] See generally WG Carson, 'White Collar Crime and the Institutionalisation of Ambiguity' in G Geis and E Stotland, *White Collar Crime* (Sage, Beverley Hills, 1990).

the system of regulatory offences is a lot more messy than this.[23] Increasingly, for example, activities causing or generating the risk of causing substantial social harms are enacted as part of a regulatory framework, with prosecutions typically initiated by public authorities rather than the police. The rules governing environmental pollution is an obvious example of a crime at once regulatory and yet comparable in terms of potential to harm to traditional crimes of violence and endangerment. The problems posed by this development concern the blurring of the usual linkages between the degree of seriousness of the wrongdoing, the maximum penalties available and the usual procedural safeguards against unjust convictions. Many of these offences, because of their regulatory features and the absence of an appropriate fault element, misrepresent the gravity of the harms addressed. Sometimes, as in the case of pollution, this gravity is pointed up by the existence of maximum penalties comparable to those of traditional crimes. Other times it is obscured by bearing penalties appropriate to an activity causing minor harm. This is made possible by the absence of any systematic legislative endeavour to produce cogent thresholds of gravity outside the sphere of direct victimising harms. Clearly if the harm principle is to create a just and effective framework for addressing wrongdoing with a public dimension this is a key requirement.

Some activities suffer criminalisation although they neither cause direct harm in themselves nor even pose the risk of harm, whether to public or private interests. Nevertheless, like the broad subject matter of regulatory offences, the criminalisation of such activities may be within the legitimising scope of the harm principle. The case of *Brown* gives a pointed illustration of how easy it is to reconceptualise harm so as to criminalise activities which have no direct harm causing potential. The appellants belonged to a group of sado-masochistic homosexuals who performed consensual acts of violence on each other for purposes of sexual gratification. The House of Lords was divided upon the legality of these activities. The minority took the view that such activity should only be made subject to the criminal sanction if it had a public impact, for example if it resulted in injury requiring public expenditure on medical care, or it took place in public such that members of the public were caused offence, or if the activity was conducive to a breach of the peace. The majority while appearing to be actuated by moral

---

[23] AJ Ashworth, *Principles of Criminal law* (OUP, Oxford, 1999); 'Is The Criminal Law a Lost Cause?' (2000) 116 *LQR* 225, 240 *et seq*.

disapproval of the activities concerned nevertheless grounded their reasoning in a broader notion of harm than that accepted by the minority. Lord Templeman in particular emphasised the potential of cults of violence to spread corruptively beyond the participants into the wider society. It would not be in our collective interests, even if no individual was directly affected, for this to happen. The relevant harm for the purpose of assigning the proper limits of the criminal law is not therefore always obvious.[24] An alternative ground for criminalising conduct is that while relatively innocuous in itself the activity may create a slippery slope leading to harmful activities committed either by the actor himself at a later stage or by others influenced by him to do likewise. Equally, it might be argued, it is disingenuous to treat a private bout of fisticuffs to settle an argument as a quintessentially private affair. Our society is not organised like Dodge City, but if private dispute settlement of such a kind became lawful it soon might be.

Brown instantiates the problem of remote harms, that is a harm at one or more stages removed from a risk creating activity. It is a remote harm since the proscribed activity does not create the harm or risk of harm itself but sets in motion causal processes which may do so.[25] For purposes of elucidation reckless driving involves a non-remote harm— the harm being the increased risk of accident and injury, which is a direct set-back to collective interests in physical security. Driving with excess alcohol, by contrast, involves a remote harm. The harm for which the driver is punished is not driving dangerously (a genuine set-back of interests) but doing something which increases the risk of him driving dangerously (a contingent set-back of interests.) Other examples of offences addressing remote harms include weapon possession, and drug possession and supply offences. These are typically justified upon the basis that criminalising the possession or supply of weapons and drugs reduces their use and in turn the likelihood that they will be used to cause harm to public or private interests. While individual instances of weapon/drug possession may pose no threat to such interests, criminalisation is justified on a cumulative basis. A weapons

---

[24] Gross, a modern harm theorist, has described the harms within the potential purview of the criminal sanction as follows: 1. violations of interest in retaining or maintaining what one is entitled to have. 2. offences to sensibility 3. harms consisting in some impairment of collective welfare 4. harms consisting in violations of some government interest.

[25] A useful classification of remote harms can be found in A von Hirsch, 'Extending the Harm Principle: Remote Harms and Fair Imputation' in A Simester and ATH Smith (eds), *Harm and Culpability* (Clarendon Press, Oxford, 1996) 259, at 263–5.

culture such as that existing in the United States seems to make for greater weapons use in unlawful contexts. If a person has a gun or knife in his pocket he is obviously more likely to shoot or stab someone in anger than if he carries only a pocket handkerchief. Correspondingly, decriminalising the possession and/or supply of drugs threatens to sustain a drugs culture in which people turn to narcotics as a hedonistic pursuit which in turn may diminish the individual's capacity to live a socially responsible and economically productive life thereby increasing the risk of lawlessness with attendant harm to society's social and economic structure.

The criminalisation of remote harms poses a problem not least because, contrary to the organising rationale of the harm principle, it may lead to unreasonable restrictions in liberty and autonomy on difficult to substantiate grounds. As *Brown* illustrates, if our grounds for criminalising conduct is that, while relatively innocuous in itself, the activity may create a slippery slope to directly harmful activities the danger is that there will be created slippery slopes without end though with little evidence of meaningful danger at the bottom. Also problematic, particularly with respect to crimes which have censure as their purpose, is the fact that criminalising remote harms holds individuals accountable and subject to censure not on the basis of an act of culpable wrongdoing but of some future event not necessarily of the actor's own making. This contradicts the normal rules of attribution which require both that the individual is to blame for what transpires and for him to have caused it.[27] The person subjected to criminal liability for possessing a weapon cannot be faulted morally if he keeps it under lock and key in his gun room and there is no causal connection between his possession of that weapon and, say, an armed robbery of the bank in his local town. Causal responsibility for social harms inheres in those whose voluntary acts bring them about, rather than in those who create the context, albeit knowingly, within which the decisions to act are made. It is for this reason that, following urban riots, we punish the rioters and not, say, the documentary film maker who alerted the rioters to the social mischiefs in response to which they took to the streets.[28] Likewise, the person who possesses a weapon, takes drugs or engages in consensual sado-masochism which have the potential to

[27] See A von Hirsch, above, n 25, at 265–8. For another example of how citizens may be subjected to liability on the basis not of their own wrongdoing but on the wrongdoing of somebody else see ch 7.

[28] But see Kennedy.

form the first link in a causal chain which leads to a given harm, but is otherwise a model citizen, may reasonably object: 'So there is a risk that others might follow my example, thus fostering a climate of lawlessness. But as long as I do nothing to encourage them why should I suffer the burden of social censure and punishment for things which 'are not my business?'

So that criminalisation does not threaten basic liberties and autonomy modern formulations have sought to cut the harm principle down to the kind of size appropriate to life in a liberal democracy. Prominent among such criteria is that the conduct is generally viewed as wrong and constituting a social threat, that it is amenable to control by the criminal law, could not reasonably be dealt with by other means, and that criminalising it will not produce any likely harmful side effects.[29] The standard harms analysis as qualified by this minimalist ethic is a useful rule of thumb when assessing the propriety of criminalising conduct which involve remote harms. It accounts for the fact that, for example, it is a criminal offence to drive a motor vehicle with blood-alcohol concentrations above a prescribed limit[30] (statistically related to significant increases in road accidents) but no offence to ride a bicycle with such concentration (little evidence that blood concentration of itself and unconnected with instances of riding while intoxicated is related to increased risk of road accidents). It explains also, however, why being drunk in charge of either type of vehicle is a criminal offence (statistically related to significant increases in road accidents).[31]

It is less helpful however in maintaining a cogent link between criminalisation and respect for individual freedom and autonomy. A strong case can be made that where, as in the claim that drug consumption is a slippery slope towards lawlessness, there is no obvious statistical connection between the activity to be criminalised and the harm towards which the activity is supposed to conduce, the standard harms analysis should not in any event be conclusive. Rather, the presumption should be that activities should not be criminalised where it is not possible to impute a given harmful consequence to some culpable action of the actor. As von Hirsch has suggested, only perhaps where the potential

---

[29] Herbert L Packer, *The Limits of the Criminal Sanction* (Stanford University Press, Stanford, 1968), 296.

[30] Section 5. Road Traffic Act 1988.

[31] Section 4.

harm was of such magnitude as to sustain the social and moral arguments in favour of criminalisation in the face of an absence of an imputational link would this presumption be displaced.[32] A topical example is the proposal to criminalise the failure, upon police request, to decode an email message, a proposal designed to enable law enforcement officers to track down terrorists. To be effective such a provision would arguably need to address both culpable failures—terrorist wishes his message to remain secret—and non culpable failures—Mr Bean has lost his decoding key.

Whether or not such a restriction would be any more effective a restraint upon the over-enthusiastic criminalisation of activities which may conduce to remote harms is another question. The problem posed by remote harms is, as explained earlier, a more general problem governing criminalisation policy, namely that of ensuring that state sponsored coercive techniques effect a proper balance between liberty on the one hand and society's welfare interests on the other. It is because there is no demonstrably sound balance to be struck that legislators have little difficulty ratcheting up the boundaries of social control in the face of liberal opposition. It may be that the harm principle is best understood simply as a rallying call for minimalism in criminalisation rather than a principle capable of generating a liberal consensus concerning the proper boundaries of the criminal law.

Moral Wrongdoing

Since autonomy and freedom both qualifies and justifies the state's coercive authority scant attempt is made these days to justify coercive rules by reference to moral or paternalistic concerns. Even laws which appear to have an underlying moral or paternalistic bent, such as those attending drug-taking or seat belt or crash helmet laws have obvious public interests attached to compliance capable of counteracting the high price in terms of loss of freedom and autonomy which coercion implies, not least the economic costs of ministering to those whose physical interests are damaged. While we may concede, therefore, that some moral rules must always be guaranteed by force of the criminal law, it is less easy to give a coherent account of the proper scope of the criminal law **reducible to morality alone**.

[32] 'Extending the Harm Principle: Remote Harms and Fair Imputation' at 268–71.

And yet a consideration of controversial cases for criminalisation such as drugs possession, field sports, pornography, sexual deviance and so on leads to consideration of whether the harm principle is itself capable of underwriting all the various purposes the criminal justice system might reasonably set for itself. As we have seen, state coercion may sometimes be used to counter remote or speculative risks. Here the harm principle is a blunt guide at best in circumscribing the permissible limits. Moral wrongdoing on the other hand is something we can all recognise, can't we? Another problem for Feinberg's restatement of the harm principle concerns activities which, while harmless in his terms, nevertheless cause serious offence. Where such activities, say fornication or oral sex, take place in public there are clearly strong grounds for criminalisation and punishment. Feinberg's position, on the face of it quite consistent with the moral neutrality implicit in the harm principle, is that while society is not entitled to criminalise activities simply upon the basis that they are disapproved of, it may be appropriate to proscribe activities which cause serious (public) offence. Witnessing seriously offensive practices is properly treated as inimical to individual wellbeing although not describable as a set-back to individual interests and not reducible to state sponsored moral coercion.[33] Indicative of such an approach is the following statement of the Wolfenden Committee which in the late 1950s was charged with the task of making recommendations concerning the continued criminalisation of homosexual activity and prostitution. In the Committee's opinion the function of the criminal law,

> is to preserve public order and decency, to protect the citizens from what is offensive or injurious and to provide sufficient safeguards against exploitation and aggravation of others, particularly those who are specially vulnerable because they are young, weak in body or mind, inexperienced, or in a state of special physical, official or economic dependence. It is not in our view the function of the law to intervene in the private lives of citizens.

The most interesting feature in Feinberg's analysis here is his requirement that the offensive conduct take place in public. It is clear why this must be the case if it is to be reconciled with his overall position which is that legislating on grounds of morality alone is unjustified. If conduct which takes place in private causes huge offence, say orgiastic activities going on in a publicly known brothel, its criminalisation could only be explained on the basis that it offended moral

[33] Feinberg *Offence to Others* ch 7.

sensibilities and this because it violated moral norms. What is less clear is why the same analysis does not also explain the criminalisation of similar conduct in public.[34] Very few things offend simply because they are perceived, nasty organic smells and sights are good examples of things that do. Moreover the things that do offend do not seem to offend any the less for occurring in private. Public nudity or fornication might appear to be good counter examples, Feinberg certainly thinks so. But if we look more closely it seems that what offends us is not what we see—deeply moral people do not blanche at witnessing naked people in public per se. What is offensive is the violation of norms. The same act of undressing is inoffensive, if it takes place in an art class, and deeply offensive if it takes place, gratuitously in a place of worship. The same kiss is inoffensive if it takes place between a man and a woman but may be experienced as deeply offensive where it takes place between two men. By criminalising the latter rather than the former it is hard to see how Feinberg succeeds in entirely insulating the content of the criminal law from the possibly tendentious moral preferences of the society he inhabits. Public and private interests are reconciled of a fashion but at the cost of subjecting individuals to the risk of state coercion even for perhaps objectively moral activities which deeply offend the sensibilities of the moral majority.

Leaving this relatively minor qualification to the harm principle aside, as long as wrongdoing is of a nature which provokes a morally authoritative voice of condemnation it might prove both a more stable and a more coherent basis for criminalisation than the speculative notion of harm or offence. This view is obviously plausible when we consider core crimes, namely those concerned with violence and interference with property. These key moral values (for example, that hurting people is wrong) can be seen as directly implicated in the integrity of a society's social and economic structure. They are values which everyone has a stake in. This is readily acknowledged in the various civil law arenas such as contract and tort where harm is conceived largely as a compensatory feature rather than an indicia of wrongfulness. Hence Atiyah, speaking of the law of contract, says:

> The law reflects to a considerable extent the moral standards of the community in which it operates . . . the persons responsible for the development

[34] See generally L Alexander, 'Harm, Offence, and Morality' (1994) 7 *Can Journal of Law and Jurisprudence* 199.

of the law have, almost without exception, been devout Christians. It is therefore not surprising to find that behind the law of contract lies the simple moral principle that a person should fulfil his promises. . .[35]

Does it extend still further? Is it a sufficient basis for criminalisation that a given activity is morally wrong irrespective of any evidence that the activity conduces to harming public or private interests? The legal moralist tradition which opposes the harm principle argues that it is. Sometimes the question whether individual or collective interests have been 'set back' by a particular activity is besides the point.[36] Wrongdoing is about doing wrong not simply causing harm, as the majority in *Brown* concluded. Society is entitled to pursue its own moral lights through the direction of an accountable legislature and even, in more radical accounts, through the creative engineering of a morality-sensitive judiciary. This viewpoint was famously adopted in the 1960s by Lord Devlin who argued against the decriminalisation of homosexuality and prostitution. In his view sexual freedom should give way to the broader claims of community which require key social institutions such as the family to be protected from the potentially subversive effect of a counter sexual culture. It was endorsed in a case decided in the early 1960s to justify restricting the freedom of prostitutes to advertise their services in a magazine.[37]

The basic liberal argument against this view is that it substitutes the harm principle's starting point to criminalisation, namely the enhancement of individual freedom and autonomy, with its polar opposite, namely the enhancement of state control over individual forms of life. This argument demands our attention of course only if we limit the notion of harm to the more direct forms of material harm, which harm theory itself tends not to do. It is not difficult to reformulate Lord Devlin's legal moralism in terms which are consistent with the conceptual thrust if not the ethical spirit of the harm principle. Given that society may criminalise activities which conduce to harm only in its remote sense is it not then entitled to protect itself against moral as much as material harms?

---

[35] PS Atiyah, *Promises, Morals and Law* (Clarendon Press, Oxford, 1981).

[36] See RA Duff and A von Hirsch, 'Responsibility, Retribution and the Voluntary' [1997] *Camb LJ* 103.

[37] 'In the sphere of criminal law I entertain no doubt that there remains in the courts of law a residual power to enforce the supreme and fundamental purpose of the law, to conserve not only the safety and order but also the moral welfare of the state, and that it is their duty to guard against attacks which may be the more insidious because they are novel and unprepared for.' *Shaw v DPP* [1962] AC 220, per V Simonds at 267.

At their most cogent proponents of this tradition, no less than harm theorists and for similar reasons—undesirable social side effects, loss of privacy, diminution of freedom and autonomy—emphasise that state coercion is a necessary evil which should only be embarked upon for the most compelling of reasons.[38] With this minimalist slant the scope of the criminal law's incursions into the purely moral domain is restricted to the promotion of social cohesion where, alongside the protection of key interests, the values concerned, as with incest and bigamy, are so far a part of society's cultural identity that flouting such values would seriously rupture the common sense understandings that allow the individual to make sense of and thus inhabit and sustain the networks of relationships by which a given society is constituted.[39] Liberal society arguably needs protection from forms of life which pose a threat to its continued survival. Accordingly it should have the right to pursue what it determines as a morally correct path and to ensure that path is adhered to by the use of the criminal sanction, if necessary. Is it not appropriate for the state to provide true moral leadership in a world in which everything appears possible? As long as the state treats all citizens with 'equal concern and respect' by ensuring that the key ingredients in what is generally considered to be a good and worthwhile life are available to all, it arguably still has a role to play in upholding such residual ethical imperatives.[40] This is a viewpoint which has been canvassed by Ronald Dworkin and, more recently and more aggressively, by Michael Moore[41] who would include within the generalised concept of wrongdoing not only activity causing harm or offence in Feinberg's terms but also practices which may be wrong for no other reason than they are thought immoral. Rejecting Devlin's measure of immorality, namely majoritarian opinion,[42] Moore nevertheless advocates a role for the state in providing moral leadership in which those activities which can be defined as objectively immoral, and not like sexual

---

[38] See for example N Lacey, (1988) 100; Michael Moore, *Placing Blame* (OUP, Oxford, 1997), 70.

[39] Indicative of such (functionalist) approaches is that of the French sociologist, Emile Durkheim.

[40] R Dworkin, *Taking Rights Seriously* (Duckworth, London, 1977).

[41] *Placing Blame*, 70.

[42] HLA Hart rightly attacked Lord Devlin's method for determining the proper point at which individual freedom is trumped by the state's protective function (universal moral outrage) as responsive to the kind of moral populism which is inconsistent both with the promotion of individual autonomy and moral neutrality. He did not satisfactorily counter his main proposal, however.

deviance immoral simply because people find certain practices offensive, fall within the purview of state control. Matters such as an activity's propensity to cause harm inevitably remain of key significance because harm causing activity is in any plausible account of morality immoral. Indeed, even self-harming acts may be immoral if they damage a person's capacity for moral agency, the capacity to choose to do the right or wrong thing.

Significantly this does not draw any kind of line between the practical concerns of Moore and harm theory since Moore has his own reasons why, notwithstanding the immorality of such conduct, it may not be the subject of state coercion. Not only are there the inevitable social costs referred to earlier but also, what we might term the individual's political trump card, namely his right to define himself as a human being though his choices.[43] As we are wont to say, if people wish to drink themselves to death/into moral *anomie* it is their choice. This libertarian idea has been challenged by Joseph Raz, who otherwise is broadly supportive of the harm principle. For him the state's coercive interventions are not restricted to fostering and maintaining individual autonomy. Autonomy is not inherently valuable. The only value in fostering autonomy is to enable persons to choose between different conceptions of the **good life**.[44] Since morally repugnant choices do not conduce to the good life they are valueless, and therefore not appropriately exempt from state coercion. There is no value worth protecting in allowing an individual the choice between, say, frittering his life away in front of the TV and being a concert pianist. This is not what being a human being is all about.

Raz's position neatly straddles legal moralism and Feinberg's restatement. He agrees with Feinberg that state punishment at least in the form of imprisonment should be reserved for harmful (autonomy reducing) activities rather than harmless immoralities. However, he sides with legal moralism in ceding a degree of moral leadership to the state. He effects this reconciliation by limiting the forms of moral coercion to techniques such as imprisonment, which would significantly impinge upon individual autonomy. So valuable choices can be encouraged by subsidies and valueless choices can be discouraged by taxes. It is easy to object that Raz is no more than a closet legal moralist, hiding his moral authoritarianism under a cover of enlightened penal minimalism which

---

[43] *Placing Blame*, 763–75.
[44] *The Morality of Freedom* (Clarendon Press, Oxford, 1986) ch 15.

is in fact organisationally incoherent. After all, if he is prepared to sign up to taxing immorality there can be no obvious objection to state punishment per se, say in the form of fines or shaming punishments. As will be seen in the next chapter, however, Raz's analysis is a useful starting point for rethinking the relationship between different forms of punishment and associated penal goals—how for example imprisonment in its propensity to visit shame on the offender is aptly tailored to redress shameful actions; how fines, by contrast, are equally apt to redress the taking of illegitimate social and economic short cuts. Such ideas, implicit in most popular discourse concerning criminalisation and punishment, are only infrequently accorded serious attention at the level of penal theory.

STRUCTURING MORALITY AND AUTONOMY

In a politically organised and culturally differentiated society one cannot expect morality to do all the work society would wish of it, namely to set effective standards of 'obligatory behaviour'. For this to be possible there must, at the very least, be an overwhelming consensus guaranteeing the authority of the norm concerned, which in turn demands a high degree of social unity or homogeneity, a social structure which offers offenders no 'corner' in which to hide and which has mechanisms of censure which come into automatic operation when norms are breached. It goes without saying that most modern societies tend to lack such conditions. Using morality as our yardstick for intervention, it is easy to see why such crimes as murder, rape, and theft, perhaps even incest, bestiality, necrophilia, and bigamy, are crimes. It is also fairly easy to see why other morally dubious activities, such as trading while insolvent, fox hunting, pornography, exporting cigarettes and powdered baby milk to the Third World, and the manufacture and sale of weapons of mass destruction should not be criminalised, even though they may be difficult to differentiate morally from the above focal crimes. Although many consider such practices immoral many others do not, or at least do not feel sufficiently disturbed by it to support a plausible case for punishment. The latter (say business people) might argue, for example, that trading while insolvent is a case of 'justified wrongdoing' essential for maintaining the strength and flexibility of a thriving capitalist economy. The former (say consumers) might argue that it is no different from theft or fraud. The lack of consensus reflects an economically, and therefore morally, differentiated society which supposedly gains strength from such a differentiated outlook and which therefore does not seek to repress its every manifestation.

At a broad level the business of government in a liberal society is the reconciliation of potentially conflicting values of freedom and welfare. Freedom is the whole point of liberal democracy but freedom must be tempered by welfare to ensure that all enjoy it. Neither the pursuit of autonomy nor the prosecution of society's key values provides a conclusive lens for understanding the full complexity of function involved in state coercion. As it stands the harm principle does little more than advocate a minimalist state. This neither reflects its true function, nor fulfils what many would see as the state's fundamental responsibility, namely to enable human beings to flourish rather than merely keeping out of their lives as much as possible.[45]

What is clear is that autonomy sometimes must be subjugated to collective interests and, where it is, the ethics which tie criminalisation to occasions of moral wrongdoing inevitably become loosened. Although curtailing freedom is not necessarily inconsistent with maximising the range of individual choices,[46] over a significant area of social life the state restricts freedom so as to achieve some other social good—particularly individual and collective welfare. To explain such activities of the state in terms of the coercive implementation of key social 'moralities', minimising social 'harms' or facilitating individual autonomy does not, then, do justice to the true complexity of the state function. To understand this function it is perhaps more helpful to understand the content of the criminal law as representing a structured negotiation between autonomy, welfare and moral values with autonomy as the key to the overall structuring process.[47] This explains to a degree why those who interfere with the autonomy of others have their own autonomy interfered with via the criminal sanction (typically imprisonment). The law of criminal omissions provides an instructive example of how the structuring process, at least in relation to core crimes, is achieved. Here welfare values are allowed to intrude into doctrine but only where these do not undermine the centrality of autonomy. The stance taken

---

[45] See RA Duff and A von Hirsch, 'Responsibility, Retribution and the Voluntary' [1997] *Camb LJ* 103.

[46] Raz, *The Morality of Freedom*, 380–1.

[47] For a general exploration of this issue see A Brudner, 'Agency and Welfare in the Penal Law' in Shute *et al* (eds), *Action and Value in Criminal Law* (Clarendon Press, Oxford, 1993), 22–7.

by the common law is relatively uniform. It does not enforce the kind of standards of good citizenship which would prompt the responsible citizen to rescue another in serious peril. People could not be the authors of their own destiny if they were under an enforceable obligation to defer their own interests to those of others. Individual freedom takes priority over welfare as a vindication of the principle of autonomy. The exception to the rule, however, shows that welfare is a proper value to be pursued but only where this does not undermine autonomy. If one voluntarily assumes a responsibility of care over another, one may be punished for not discharging it if harm results. This is not considered a diminution of a person's autonomy because, by assuming the obligation, one is deemed already to have chosen to restrict the range of life choices available. It is thus reasonable to insist that the welfare obligation is discharged. It can be seen, in other words, that the present scope of potential liability for omissions is informed by a cogent, though limited, notion of individual autonomy.[48]

The force of contrary opinions on this matter has done much to muddy the conceptual waters surrounding reasoning about the nature and proper limits of the criminal law. An influential view maintains that if facilitating autonomy is genuinely the key item of political morality which informs government, this cannot be achieved by simply preventing direct interferences with it so as to maximise freedom. Under conditions of (relative) freedom, it is disingenuous to assume that individual citizens have an equal capacity to be the author of their own destiny. At an individual level no agent bears all the hallmarks of true moral agency (rationality and free choice) which makes the theory of maximising personal freedom and minimising state interference so tempting. As Raz makes clear the pursuit of autonomy requires the state both to pursue social policies which enable individuals to have an adequate range of choices and to put in place laws which protect people from the consequences of their own vulnerability and of communal living. A society which allows people to fall through the gaps of the social structure into the gutter and allows them to consume and other people to sell them psychotropic drugs shows contempt for rather than respect for individual autonomy. Its notion of autonomy is the freedom of individuals to be pulled this way and that, like straws in the wind, by social forces beyond his/her control.

---

[48] A comparable analysis can be sustained throughout criminal doctrine. See for example p 284, on consent and p 285 on self-defence.

Theorists within this tradition, therefore, may uphold the propriety of paternalistic legislation where it is designed to counter life conditions and events which may lead an individual to choose to remove the power of effective choice over his future action. As Alan Brudner has argued:

> In order that the goals one chooses be authentically ones own or self-determined, one must have a minimum degree of security of life, physical health, education and economic wherewithal. One must also be nurtured in an environment of habits and attitudes that fosters a rational sense of one's worth and of one's capacity to be author of what one becomes. And one must be protected from those who would enslave others by procuring their addiction to substances the need for which exerts a tyranny over one's life choices.[49]

The promotion of autonomy thus requires law to steer a difficult path between competing interests of freedom and welfare. Too much positive intervention diminishes freedom. Too little diminishes the range of choices needed to sustain a life of real autonomy. Such a choice has to be brokered even in the context of core crimes such as murder. Although one cannot consent to be killed, it is clear, for example, that doctors do not unlawfully kill when they withdraw life sustaining therapy from those incapable of recovery and of giving consent. In such circumstances the value attached to the autonomy of the individual outweighs the state's responsibility to ensure that life is maintained.[50]

Other theorists would go further, and require the state to advance communitarian goals which ensure basic standards of welfare are met, if necessary by the criminal law, in addition to prohibiting autonomy-reducing antisocial activities. In Lacey's view, for example, the criminal law has an active role to play in creating the conditions material and ideological necessary to 'protect the autonomy and welfare of individuals and groups in society with respect to a basic set of goods, both individual and collective.'[51] It does so by responding to 'serious and direct threats to and violations of those fundamental interests through behaviour which expresses a rejection of, hostility or total indifference to the basic framework values which a society acknowledges.'[52] Lacey

---

[49] A Brudner, 'Agency and Welfare in the Penal Law', 21, at 41. See n 47.

[50] *In re Quinlan* 70 N.J. 10, 355 A. 2d 647 (1976)

[51] N Lacey (1988), 104–5.

[52] Basic values encompass those concerned with physical integrity, property, health, sexual autonomy, and the protection of such social and collective interests as the preservation of society itself, protecting the environment, the maintenance of some degree of public order and ultimately the upholding of its framework of shared understandings and common values.' *Ibid* 100.

envisions the enforcement of key values as a central state function, rejecting also the supposition that it is only through the prism of set-backs to interests that these values can profitably be recognised. The criminal law is already used uncontroversially to enforce moral obliga-tions divorced from any realistic ambition to minimise social or eco-nomic costs to promote kindness—for example with reference to the regulation of vivisection or the proscribing of cruelty to animals, or to support moral taboos based in a collectively acknowledged apprecia-tion of the fundaments of a good and worthwhile life. However the enforcement of basic values means demanding positive, good stand-ards of behaviour rather than simply refraining from positive acts of mischief. It can be used, for example, to defend proposals to enforce certain basic responsibilities of community such as ensuring that people co-operate with each other so as to promote non-exploitative social and economic relations and other means of fostering collective well-being such as providing reasonable acts of assistance to those in desperate need.

Although, Lacey asserts a central limiting ethic on intervention, namely that the value asserted through the criminal sanction is recog-nised in a given society as central to its integrity, and acknowledges the importance of defending individual rights against collective needs, criminalisation on the basis of communitarian principles runs the risk of lending legitimating support to an authoritarian system of law.[53] This is of real significance, however well intentioned it may be, given the empirical reality of criminalisation practices. The criminal law inevitably reflects the way in which politically organised society pro-tects and reconciles the interests valued in a given society. This has a good side and a bad side. The good side is that it facilitates the state's role in providing moral leadership. The bad side is that the state's moral leadership may serve to advantage one section of society at the expense of another. Politics and economics have as great a role to play here as morals. It is politics, or more precisely political economy, which dictates the continued criminalisation of drug use rather than the implacable resistance to the practice of a morally unified community. It is politics which determines the neutral state attitude to the manu-facture of weapons of mass destruction rather than the equivocal voice of the moral community. Allowing moral values to determine the lim-its of the criminal sanction offers to legitimate an already over zealous

---

[53] See n 44.

use of the criminal law for purposes of social control. The harm principle, albeit in a diffuse and ambiguous way, at least has as its organising principle the idea that state coercion is an evil to be entered into only exceptionally. We may not wish to go so far as to conclude, with Feinberg, that activities should not be criminalised unless they cause serious offence or conduce to serious harm to defined social or individual interests. His conviction, considered in the next chapter, that punishment is the visible symbol of the moral condemnation which certain forms of (harmful) wrongdoing elicits effectively commits him to this narrow view. However, we may wish to concede, given the state's constitutional propensity to prosecute narrowly defined political objectives at the expense of individual autonomy, that the normal presumption must be against state coercion on grounds of morality alone or paternalism.

If this appears a recipe for conservatism in criminalisation it should be pointed out that the inevitable lens through which our assessment of the propriety of criminalisation is focused is that of punishment or, more particularly, its paradigm form of imprisonment. Because of imprisonment's symbolic significance and its unique autonomy-defeating nature this requires it to be limited to cases where no other form of coercion will do, where the wrongdoing concerned is unambiguously immoral and where (strictly) defined public interests are set back. Inevitably, this must lead us most of the way down the road to embracing the harm principle but it does not commit us, as Raz has explained, to the unnecessary corollary that moral leadership and coercion in areas lying outside the field of influence of the harm principle should not be undertaken. As long as this does not involve an attack on the individual's own autonomy it seems quite reasonable for the state to weight the choices, through all the mechanisms at its disposal, in favour of those which conduce to individual human flourishing on the one hand and collective well-being on the other.

2

Punishing Wrongdoing

CENTRAL TO AN understanding of the criminal justice system is the phenomenon of punishment. It is through an understanding of the rationale of punishment that we can arrive at a cogent basis for evaluating both contemporary penal practices and the content of the criminal law. Theorists of punishment tend to espouse one of two basic approaches. The reductionist approach sees punishment as an instrument of social control designed to reduce antisocial activity, typically through isolation and deterrence, less typically through rehabilitation and education. The retributivist approach sees punishment as a morally appropriate and/or necessary response to wrongdoing by which, just as reward is the just response to good deeds, punishment is the just response to wrongdoing. It will be appreciated that depending upon which side of this punishment divide one inhabits so also will depend one's attitude towards, for example, the form punishment should take, the gravity of punishment and the relevance of past misconduct. It will also influence one's attitude to substantive issues. For example, from the reductionist point of view there is no inherent reason why criminal liability should be premised upon proof of moral fault. If it could be shown that deaths per thousand of population would be reduced by rendering criminal homicide an offence of absolute liability, an out and out reductionist will find it difficult not to support it. On the other hand, a retributivist could only sanction liability where the killer was found to be morally deserving because he understood his conduct to create a risk of causing death or, in other accounts, because he was culpable in his failure to do so.

WHAT IS PUNISHMENT?

Punishment is usually characterised as the essential distinguishing feature of criminal norms. Distinguishing criminal norms from other parts of society's coercive apparatus is not just an interesting analytical exercise. Much may turn on it. In particular, procedural and evidential safeguards against unjust convictions are normal in criminal trials.[1] These may include procedures designed to ensure that the defendant is able to conduct a proper defence, the right to jury trial, a higher standard of proof, the presumption of innocence, the double jeopardy rule and so on. Clearly, if such safeguards are to be honoured there must first be a cogent means of determining whether the relevant proceedings are criminal or not. This is not simply a question of how the proceedings are labelled, what court they are heard in, or the authority which initiates the proceedings. Because of the inevitable human rights implications attending criminal trials, in particular the stigmatic nature of a criminal conviction and potential loss of freedom, it is clearly necessary that the test is substantive rather than jurisdictional. Accordingly, for the purpose of both the American Model Penal Code and the European Convention on Human Rights, the question whether proceedings are criminal is determined not on the basis of where the proceeding is heard or how a provision is labelled by the relevant jurisdiction but on the basis of whether punishment may result, and fault assigned. The point of this is to ensure that jurisdictions are not allowed to by-pass constitutional challenges prompted by the absence of procedural safeguards by moving cases out of the criminal courts and into specialist tribunals such as mental health tribunals or juvenile care proceedings.[2]

This provokes the question as to how punishment is to be characterised.[3] It is a deceptively difficult concept to pin down. It is inadequate, for example, to describe punishment simply as something unpleasant meted out under the authority of the state in the manner of a set-back to interests.[4] Punishment is both more and less than this. It is less than this in the sense that punishment does not have to be experienced by the recipient as unpleasant to count as punishment. Indeed, it may take the form of an absolute or conditional discharge which has no discernible penal effect on the recipient. It may take the form of something which the recipient craves—as imprisonment may do for the irredeemably institutionalised recidivist.[5] It is more than this in the

---

[1] See generally AJ Ashworth, 'Is the Criminal Law a Lost Cause?' (2000) 116 *LQR* 225–41.

[2] *Ibid* 230–2.

[3] See for example JR Lucas, *On Justice* (Clarendon Press, Oxford, 1980), ch 6; cf Hart, *Punishment and Responsibility: Essays in the Philosophy of Law* (Clarendon Press, Oxford, 1968) 4–5.

[4] For discussion of the relationship between punishment and vengeance see p 74 below.

[5] Though cf JR Lucas, *On Justice*, at 125.

sense that not all instances of state sponsored set-backs of interest count as punishment. It is not punishment to be deprived of unemployment benefit on return to work. It is not punishment to be required to pay taxes. It is not punishment to be required to pay compensation to someone whom one has wronged. It is not punishment to be subjected to forced quarantine, national service, committal under the Mental Health Act, or remand in custody. Each of these unpleasant events may be experienced by the individual as punishment—how often does one hear higher rate tax payers complain that they are being punished for hard work?— and indeed they may prove far more onerous than 'real' punishment, but they are conceptually distinct. Refining our notion of punishment, somewhat, punishment does not appear to have to be unpleasant as long as most people would take it to be so. Imprisonment, then, is punishment for what it symbolises rather than how it is experienced or what it achieves. What it symbolises is a publicly orchestrated response to a wrongful act or omission.[6] It is, at least in core forms of punishment, a stigmatic response.

JUSTIFYING PUNISHMENT

At first sight, punishment may appear relatively unproblematic. The ethic organising our response to wrongdoing, whether in the political arena or in the wider social context of work, sport, school or home, is typically thought to be bound up in the idea that wrongdoing must be paid for. As long as we accept the authority of the punisher the conceptual link between the act of wrongdoing and the punishment appears clear, even to an infant. 'It is against the rules of football to tackle someone from behind. I have tackled someone from behind. Therefore the award of a yellow card is something I deserve.'

The major factors which might be expected to exercise both punished and punisher are not whether the institution of punishment (or reward) itself needs justifying, but whether the individual instance is justified or whether the amount of punishment proposed is fair. Occasionally, however, the punished challenge the authority by which the punisher seeks to impose punishment. To a teacher a child's response may be 'You can't do that. You're not my mummy'. To a parent the response may be 'Don't smack me. If I can't smack you, you can't hit me.' The

---

[6] See generally A Quinton, 'On Punishment' in P Lazlett and D Runciman (eds), *Philosophy, Politics and Society* (Clarendon Press, Oxford, 1956), 83.

challenge is an apt one. Parent and teacher have the law (partly) on their side, and their reasons may be conventionally sound but beyond this it might appear, to the child at least, that they rely on little more other than sheer brute force and the complicity of other adults. What can ever justify one person subjecting another to unpleasant consequences for conduct found to be distasteful? In short, while it may be possible to advance reasons for punishing it is less easy to justify it. The most generally accepted moral foundation of the right to punish children is paternalism. Punishment of children is justified if it is for their good. Few seek to justify punishment on the basis that it is good for the parent or teacher or even the school. It is not generally thought justifiable, for example, to expel a disruptive pupil from school simply to vindicate the interests of the teachers or other children.

If we turn to the political level the same objection can be raised. Once again the basis upon which the state seeks to exert coercive power is a challenge to its authority in the form of wrongdoing. But unlike the parent/teacher/child relationship the foundation of the claim that punishment under such circumstances is morally justified is not one of paternalism. The liberal state has no business doing unpleasant things to us 'for our own good'. As a consequence it is easy to challenge the institution of punishment as doing little other than substituting two harms for one.[7] The key question here, then, is why the state's response to antisocial activity takes the form of **punishment**? Assuming we consent to governance by rules, why does the form in which the state responds to breach of certain rules involve the infliction of suffering? The popular response is 'What else can it do?' After all, most societies have formal institutions of punishment. If norms carry social approval their infraction must be acknowledged else the norm itself will be weakened. Punishment is the signal of the social 'clout' of the norm. As long as norm infringements are punished fairly and consistently, with like cases being treated alike, and there is some form of proportionality between the harm caused and the punishment inflicted, surely that is all we can expect.

But this leaves a lot of questions unanswered. It is by no means obvious why, for example, it is generally considered unjustifiable to imprison an employee for infringing workplace safety regulations but justifiable if the state acts in similar fashion.[8] What gives the state this

---

[7] This is often conceded in the case of severe punishment, for example state execution.
[8] Lacey, (1988) 22.

authority? The root of the problem is providing a cogent basis upon which to square the state institution of punishment with the avowed primacy, in liberal society, of individual autonomy? It should be understood that the state's authority to punish is not logically linked to its tendency to augment human freedom and autonomy. Even in liberal society matters appertaining to the public interests may trump individual freedom and autonomy. In authoritarian systems in which the seat of social wellbeing is the state the criminal law, being the embodiment of the state's will, gains authority and legitimacy by that fact alone, although it should be noted that even here criminal liability will generally be negated where behaviour is involuntary.[9] However, if we accept the premise that we live in a society respectful of individual autonomy, this carries with it the implication that punishment, since it is an assault upon an individual's autonomy, is something which cannot be justified simply in terms of the relative power of the state *vis a vis* the individual.[10] So how else can punishment be justified?

PUNISHMENT AS SOCIAL ENGINEERING

Punishment fulfils a number of functions. Social commentators as diverse as Michel Foucault[11] and Charles Dickens have characterised punishment primarily as a method of social control *'pour encourager les autres'*, in which *'les autres'* means the law-abiding who might otherwise be tempted to cut corners and the means of encouragement is incarceration and in earlier times, execution or transportation. In this respect punishment, as a distinct category of state sponsored coercion, is difficult to separate from non-penal practices such as the incarceration of the insane in asylums, the poor in workhouses, children in orphanages and, as Dickens makes clear in a typically plangent indictment, debtors in debtor's prisons,

> there was a kind of iron cage in the walls of Fleet (debtor's) prison, within which was posted some man of hungry looks who, from time to time, rattled a money box and exclaimed in a mournful voice, 'Pray remember the poor

---

[9] Not always. It is not unknown for members of a family to be victimised for the misdeeds of another. See generally Hart *Punishment and Responsibility*, (1968) 12.

[10] See generally RP Wolff, 'The Conflict between Authority and Autonomy' in J Raz (ed), *Authority* (Blackwell, Oxford, 1990) 20–31.

[11] M Foucault, *Discipline and Punish: The Birth of the Prison* (Penguin, Harmondsworth, 1976).

debtors' . . . We no longer suffer them to appeal at the prison gates to the charity and compassion of the passers-by; but we still leave unblotted in the leaves of our statute book, for the reverence and admiration of succeeding ages, the just and wholesome law which declares that the sturdy felon shall be fed and clothed, and that the penniless debtor shall be left to die of starvation and nakedness.[12]

Punishment, then, has shown itself apt to fulfil a supreme social symbolic function by drawing a line between the socially valuable and the socially valueless members of society. It is the symbolic stick which keeps the rest of us in order.[13] This helps to explain perhaps why the quintessential state response to antisocial behaviour is punishing 'baddies', rather than, say, rewarding 'goodies' a comparably effective form of social engineering.. In some households, by contrast, children are not subjected to a punitive regime because the parents concerned treat bad behaviour as an inevitable by-product of conflicts of interest. Children want fun. Parents want order. Neither desire is more worthy than the other. Punishment, therefore, reduces to a method of advancing one person's interest at the expense of another's which is thought to be unfair and oppressive. Such enlightened parents devise sophisticated mechanisms for reconciling conflicting interests which, in theory, minimises the need for punishment. Why does the state not respond similarly? Instead of stigmatising and repressing prostitutes and incarcerating sex offenders, for example, the state could make virtue of necessity, raise the social and economic status of prostitutes and respond to sex offenders by giving them unlimited access to state-sanctioned sexual services. At one level this would arguably be just as efficient and a more humane method of social control than punishment. On a deeper level, it could divert resources from punishment to the promotion of stable moral and economic communities by creating jobs and rebuilding the housing stock. Common sense tells us that under conditions of full employment fewer people will be on the streets to commit crimes and will have less reason to wish to do so. How can punishment be justified if the state could eradicate the same or more incidents of anti-social behaviour by expanding the range of human choices (through social policy) rather than restricting them (through punishment)? Clearly there is more to state punishment than meets the eye.

[12] Charles Dickens, *Pickwick Papers*, (Randon House, New York, 1943) 607.
[13] A Norrie, *Crime Reason and History* (Weidenfield and Nicolson, London, 1993), ch 10.

The enduring claim informing a variety of different penal strategies over the last century and a half is that through punishment we can engineer a better society in which the advancement of individual interests is understood to be consistent with rather than restricted by respect for the like interests of others. As long as punishment is not too draconian we seem to be collectively better off with state institutions of punishment than without them. Simply speaking, this is the position adopted by the social philosophy of utilitarianism which, in the form usually encountered, holds that the only justification for the exercise of political power is the enhancement of social welfare. It originates in the claim of classical utilitarianism that the purpose of government (and action generally) is the maximisation of human happiness. Punishment, on this view, is an entirely rational political tool in a society committed to maximising social wellbeing. It can be justified as contributing to such wellbeing if, on a cost-benefit analysis of the harm wrought by punishment against the benefits resulting, the latter can be demonstrated to outweigh the former. The harm to be off-set in this utilitarian balancing exercise is not limited to the set-back of interests suffered by the individual offender but also those suffered by his family and the wider community by dint of the (harmful) side effects which punishment typically engenders. This mirrors the approach considered earlier in respect of the criminalisation of wrongdoing which utilitarianism also only supports to the extent that it brings about a net decrease in harm.[14]

In line with its commitment to maximising collective interests the broad thrust of utilitarian penal philosophy is concerned with crime reduction. Indeed, its plausibility is dependent upon its capacity to do so; punishment which leaves crime untouched means harm without corresponding benefit. Punishment offers to reduce crime in a number of ways. Pitched at the right level the threat of punishment offers to deter the individual from offending. Actual punishment may deter the individual from reoffending and others who might be minded to commit a similar offence. Punishment may also fulfil a protective role for society by removing the offender from society and with it his capacity to commit crime. Utilitarian penal strategy typically promotes, in combination with this deterrent and protective effect, the rehabilitative potential of penal techniques. Indeed, for the greater part of the twentieth century

[14] The American example of prohibition is a classic example of how the supposed evils of drink may be outweighed by the evils of prohibiting its consumption.

the rehabilitation of the offender was conceived as a key feature within an overall reductionist strategy, which included deterrence and incapacitation. The rehabilitative ideal shows a humane self-consciousness on the part of the punishing state.[15] Criminal behaviour is not simply an evil to be responded to but a sign that something has gone wrong for the individual as well as for society and the state's humane response is intervention to put this right. It aims both to remodel the offender's personality so as to socialise him, rendering him responsive to normative control, and also to stimulate the kind of talents and skills necessary to encourage a constructive social attitude. Without rehabilitation the penal experience, particularly prison, may conduce to increasing the desire to offend—rather than reducing it.[16]

Of course, social benefits other than crime reduction may form part of a consequence-led analysis such as offered by utilitarianism. For example, one function performed by punishment is affording a proper mechanism for the channelling of public outrage. This does serve an obvious reductive function, since it offers to prevent forms of informal justice such as lynching and vigilantism. Further, it serves to educate the public in the importance of the norms which punishment supports. Less obviously reductive, however, is its function of promoting social cohesion by vindicating the stance of the law abiding.[17] In Emile Durkheim's view punishment is both an expression of the outrage felt by society at offences against core social values and a functional practice, giving support to the moral structure by which a given society is organised and educating its members in those core values. Punishment, in other words, helps the law abiding make sense of the world—one in which order and stability is seen as a good thing in itself rather than to be traded off against personal goals.[18]

The utilitarian approach to punishment neutralises much of the force of objections to state punishment, not least by dint of its own libertarian hostility to excessive use of state coercion for political ends. Its basic premise is that the state has no warrant to punish unless it will have some good effect and even then the amount of punishment should not exceed that necessary to fulfil that good effect. Looked at in the

[15] See generally FR Allen, *The Decline of the Rehabilitative Ideal: Penal Policy and Social Purpose* (New Haven, Connecticut, 1981).

[16] Francis T Cullen and Karen E Gilbert, *Reaffirming Rehabilitation* (University of Ohio Press, Cincinnatti, 1982).

[17] E Durkheim, *The Division of Labour in Society* (Macmillan. London, 1984).

[18] N Walker, 'Punishing, Denouncing or Reducing Crime' in P Glazebrook (ed.) Reshaping the Criminal Law (Stevens, London, 1998) 391, at 394.

round, utilitarianism has inbuilt indicators as to the propriety not only of punishment but of the coercive rules which punishment underpins. For utilitarians (good) rules are both worthy of following and, for the same reason, worthy of enforcing within limits. The corollary is that bad rules may be neither worthy of following nor of enforcing, once again within limits. The same principle which holds that punishment should not be imposed unless and to the extent that it secures some overall benefit to society is the same principle which holds it wrong for society to criminalise simply to satisfy the majority's moral preferences.

If we examine this premise more closely, however, it can be seen to generate some of its own objections. An initial objection is that the utilitarian approach to punishment contains no inbuilt mechanism for ensuring justice in the distribution of punishment. It needs to import such a notion if it is to provide a politically acceptable theory of punishment.[19] This is because it is motivated by a notion of the good which is rooted in collective well-being rather than in any concern for the respect and dignity of the individual. The decision to punish is influenced not by who the individual is or what he has done, but by the good punishing him will achieve for society. In theory, therefore, it can justify draconian exemplary sentences, transportation, or physical incapacitation out of all proportion to the offender's wrong, but also, ironically given its reformist credentials, the punishment of those who have not offended. So it can justify the punishment of political opponents, recidivists, persons with unacted on antisocial tendencies and others who have done 'no wrong' but whose social exclusion will '*encourager les autres*' or will be otherwise socially beneficial.

Utilitarianism has an answer to this objection, namely that it is concern for the dignity of the individual which underpins the theory's rejection of punishment for punishment's sake. In real world contexts the individual's vulnerability to collective goals is more apparent than real. Victimising individuals in the pursuit of collective goals would be self-defeating. Injustices would be found out and breed anxiety and thus feed back into the cost-benefit analysis in a super-magnified form. Nevertheless, to deal with just such dangers in utilitarianism, modern consequentialist theories of punishment have been produced which do not take a utilitarian form. Braithwait and Pettit, for example, explain and justify the gap which exists between that quantum of punishment

---

[19] See RA Duff, Trials and Punishment (CUP, Cambridge, 1996), ch 7.

necessary to discharge its condemnatory function and that which occurs in practice in consequentialist terms. In their account the consequence to be aimed at in a satisfactory penal regime is not maximising society's units of welfare/minimising harm which, as has been explained, renders individuals vulnerable to collective needs and goals. The objective is rather the maximisation of what they term 'dominion'. Dominion refers to that sense of well-being in which the individual is able to count himself as free from unpredictable interference with his mastery of his own life. Crime damages dominion in two ways. It attacks the victim's dominion either by destroying it entirely, as in murder or kidnap, or diminishing it, as in assault, theft or harassment. Crime also attacks the dominion of those not directly affected. At a simple level, knowing that there are burglars in the neighbourhood reduces my sense of control over my own life. Punishing burglars on the other hand enhances that sense of dominion. The loss of dominion caused by such punishment in the offender is paid for by the enhanced sense of control experienced in the population at large.

Of course, harsh punishment also has the capacity to diminish dominion. Perhaps we would not have cause to worry so much if only the lawless among us were affected, but a society characterised by a concentration camp approach to punishment would reduce the dominion of everyone. Loss of dominion under such conditions would result, either through association with the wrongdoer or through the sense of unease which harsh penal regimes engender in law-breakers and law-abiding alike in the real world where miscarriages of justice are an all too familiar fact of life.[20] This steers the authors to the conclusion that the severity of punishment should not exceed the degree necessary to maximise dominion. The ruling assumption is that this will involve a beneficial ratcheting down of conventional levels of punishment, which theorists generally are agreed are too high. The cogency of this assumption is questionable, however. In particular it is very arguable that pitching punishment at the minimum level necessary to enhance general levels of dominion will, in fact, involve increases rather than decreases in the general level of punishment. After all, as von Hirsch and Ashworth have argued, the majority population seem to be unrestrained in their desire to make offenders pay. Ratcheting up levels of punishment seems, then, to reassure the law-abiding rather than decrease the sense of dominion.[21]

[20] Contra A Ashworth and A von Hirsch, *Principled Sentencing* (Hart, Oxford, 1998) 332.

[21] *Ibid* 325.

The jury is still out, therefore, on whether a utilitarian specifically or a consequentialist approach generally to punishment is consistent with justice in the distribution of punishment. A more daunting objection concerns the efficacy of punishment. As explained above the utilitarian approach to punishment is plausible even to its adherents only in so far as punishment conduces to the reduction of anti-social activity. Otherwise it is an evil to be avoided. Does punishment reduce crime? This is less clear than might be supposed. Such research as has been conducted into the deterrent or rehabilitative effect of punishment, for example, is equivocal at best.[22] The rehabilitative ideal has been thwarted, even if not entirely discredited, by the empirical reality of incarceration practices which research indicates is better at inculcating the values and skills of those actually incarcerated rather than those of the law-abiding majority to whom they are destined to be returned. Research also indicates that it is the threat of punishment, rather than the actuality of it which has the greatest deterrent effect.[23] Moreover, there is little evidence to suggest that different types of punishment, such as imprisonment, have a greater deterrent effect than others and yet statistics suggest that the more a defendant has been incarcerated the more likely it is that he will reoffend.[24]

Perhaps for this reason the rhetoric of reductionism in recent years has to a significant extent become more explicitly protectionist, reflected in policies gaining support here and in the United States that confirmed recidivists should receive a life sentence. Indeed, it seems obvious that the more bank robbers, wife beaters, muggers, paedophiles and so on are behind bars the safer our society, and we, will be. Even this conclusion can be challenged, however. An initial objection concerns the global efficacy of incapacitation. Although it is reasonable to suppose that for certain classes of crime such as violence and sex offences, the passing of time may reduce the disposition to offend, for other classes, particularly property crime, the disposition to commit offences may in fact be increased. By incapacitating today's burglars, robbers and shoplifters now, one may therefore be storing up problems for the future. Even allowing for this it is plausible that the

---

[22] SR Brody, *The Effectiveness of Sentencing: A Review of the Literature* (Home Office Research Study No 35, 1976); D Beyleveld, 'Deterrence Research as a Basis for Deterrence Policies' (1979) 18 *Howard Journal of Criminal Justice* 135.

[23] See generally Home Office Paper, 'The Sentence of the Court' 1990.

[24] See eg J Andenaes, 'The General Preventive Effects of Punishment' (1966) 114 *U Pa LR* 949.

general level of offending is not affected by incarcerating wrongdoers. Imprisoning offenders merely transfers anti-social activity to a place where it is less visible. Incapacitation appears, then, to be heavily bound up with the 'them and us' facet of state punishment described earlier. Society can tolerate huge levels of wrongdoing whatever the costs to the victims as long as the law-abiding, and by this we mean simply those who for one reason or another are not incarcerated, are not threatened by it.

Taken in the round, utilitarian penal theory suffers, therefore, the damaging objection that it fails to deliver on its key premise, namely that state punishment can be justified and can only be justified by reference to its capacity to augment social well-being, most notably through crime reduction. While the threat of punishment may have a reductive effect and the imposition of certain forms of punishment such as fines an individual deterrent effect, the major institution of punishment for serious crimes, namely imprisonment, may actually be counterproductive whether conceived in terms of deterrence, incapacitation or rehabilitation. Moreover, over a century of penal reform has done little to improve this general picture.

PUNISHMENT AS DESERT

As HLA Hart, himself an otherwise committed utilitarian, acknowledged even were we to assume that punishment works and is therefore an appropriate state practice for the advancement of collective goals this only sustains political reasons for state punishment. Justifying punishment must go beyond this and give an account of why it is morally justified to subject an individual to the state's will in this way.[25] The retributivist's answer, to which Hart in large part subscribes, is that those who inexcusably and unjustifiably do wrong deserve punishment. As we shall see, Hart's notion of desert is an equivocal one. His notion that punishment must be deserved means deserved only in the limited sense of not being 'undeserved'. In other words punishment which does not address an act of culpable wrongdoing cannot be justified. But the fact that a person deserves to be punished does not create the justification. There must still be some point to it in terms of its tendency to do good. Classical retributivism, by contrast, holds that culpable wrongdoing is sufficient in itself to

[25] Hart *Punishment and Responsibility* (1968), ch 1.

justify state punishment. Thus Kant insisted that whatever good might come of punishing wrongdoing this was not the reason for punishment, which is simply that punishment is deserved.[26] Punishment can be viewed, therefore, as an essential concomitant of criminal justice as an end in itself rather than simply a means to an end. Divergences of approach are still possible, however. For some retributivists punishment is the morally necessary response to culpable wrongdoing. For others culpable wrongdoing is merely the precondition of punishment, appropriate and permitted but not obligatory.

The classical approach reflects an everyday moral intuition which links punishment to wrongdoing as the price to be paid for nonconformity. In the political context this is a price owed to the community whose rules are violated, to the victim whose rights are compromised and not least to the wrongdoer himself to whom we show respect when we denounce and punish his wrongdoing. This has a spiritual as well as a moral dimension. Punishment allows the slate to be wiped clean. It vindicates the right and allows for atonement, expiation and ultimately reconciliation. It allows wrongdoer and victim to move forward. Without punishment there is imbalance—the sense of justice unrequited in the victim and the wider public, the sense of guilt and desire to own up in the normally law-abiding offender, as Raskolnikov's descent into despair and madness in Dostoyeski's *Crime and Punishment* attests.

What makes punishment the wrongdoer's desert? This is not an easy question to answer for desert theorists, for the temptation may be to rely on consequentialist concerns such as the need to prevent lawlessness, respect for the rule of law, moral instruction and so on. Where that temptation is avoided it is easier to argue that condemnation is deserved rather than punishment and indeed the two are often conflated: 'Why should the violator be singled out for blame . . .? The answer must ultimately be that the censure is itself deserved: that someone who is responsible for wrongdoing is blame**worthy** and hence may justly be blamed'.[27]

Exposed by this statement are three basic obstacles which desert-based accounts of punishment must surmount. The first is pinpointing a sense in which individual acts of wrongdoing generate a notion of responsibility which renders individuals deserving of censure and

---

[26] I Kant *The Metaphysical Elements of Justice* (Bobbs-Merrill, Indianapolis, 1965), 100.

[27] A von Hirsh, *Doing Justice—The Choice of Punishments* (Report of the Committee for the Study of Incarceration) (New York) (1976), 45–9.

punishment. Alan Norrie has argued that arriving at such a sense of individualised moral responsibility necessitates an artificial separation of the wrongdoer from his own personal history and his social context.[28] The Kantian notion of desert in punishment is predicated upon the notion of an atomised human subject who bears individual responsibility for what she has done and yet the individual is not atomised but is a social animal. What she is and what she does is socially and historically constructed. She does not/cannot, then, bear **individual** responsibility.[29] In Norrie's view, to make moral sense of the way society visits retribution upon wrongdoers first we must be able to locate the individual in her true context which is poised, dialectically, between the personal and the social. The individual is not an atomised individual but neither is she a human cipher—an empty vessel into which all the trappings but none of the substance of human agency are poured. Rather she is a 'relational being' whose responsibility can similarly only be approached 'relationally'.[30] Hers is a responsibility in short which, real and meaningful in itself, is nevertheless shared with others and with the society which makes her. Occasionally liberal thinking about criminal justice is prepared to confront this notion of relational responsibility when the moral identity of the individual subject is patently too fragile to sustain the weight of responsibility that retributive justice presupposes. A good example occurred after the Jamie Bulger case which prompted a fierce ideological battle between, on the one hand, the protagonists of primitive retributivism and, on the other, those who insisted that responsibility could not be individuated but must be shared and shared out, reflecting the more thoughtful theory and practice of Scandinavian legal systems confronting serious juvenile wrongdoing.

Norrie's point is that the individual's location between the personal and the social is generally ignored, the better to prevent the waters of retribution and all the concomitant aspects of liberal theorising about responsibility being muddied, as the Bulger case attests. There is obviously some cogency in this opinion. However, one should be wary of embracing Norrie's ultimate conclusion that criminal justice is doomed to ultimate remain a mere phantom or simulacra of the real thing.[31]

---

[28] For further discussion see chs 5 and 6

[29] A Norrie, *Punishment Responsibility and Justice* (Clarendon Press, Oxford, 2000), ch 1.

[30] In Bhaskar's terminology. R Bhaskar, *Dialectics: The Pulse of Freedom* (Verso, London, 1993).

[31] ' "Simulacra of Morality"? Beyond the Ideal/Actual Antinomies of Criminal Justice' in RA Duff (ed), *Philosophy and the Criminal Law* (CUP, Cambridge, 1998).

Punishment's retributive nature is challenged but not undone by its inability to do full justice to the relationality of human subjects any more than art is compromised by the inability of artists to measure up to the standards of truthfulness or beauty they or their peers set for themselves. Justice in law, like truth in art, cannot be a counsel of perfection. It is something towards which a civilised society struggles rather than an unreachable goal. It is of course always debatable whether society has achieved an appropriate balance between social and individual justice. What we must aspire to is that the individual is not unfairly victimised, that there is a meaningful sense in which the individual does bear personal moral responsibility for what he has done and that the level of punishment to which he is subject reflects this rather than society's requirements.[32]

The second obstacle is the establishment of a satisfactory link between wrongdoing and rule-infringement such that the latter can be viewed as an appropriate basis for the infliction of (state sponsored) suffering. Retributivism, it has been argued, gives a plausible theory of punishment but is less plausible in justifying it.[33] This was the basic problem posed in our initial ball-playing case study.[34] As this scenario indicates, not all instances of rule breaking involve (independent) wrongdoing in any sense appropriate to justify the allocation of blame. The justification for a punitive reaction in such a case, whether in the political or the family sphere, seems to reduce to 'I told you not to and you disobeyed me. That was naughty.' I know better than to try to convince my eight-year-old son that punishing innocuous activities simply upon the basis that they have been prohibited treats him with the respect and dignity which are his due. A yet more formidable burden of persuasion rests with the state in the case of adults with the intellectual wherewithal for making informed decisions. Not only are many rules—the vast majority perhaps—morally neutral but they may not always, whether in their content or application, be unambiguously for the good. Consider, for example, the case of *Chandler v DPP*.[35] A and B had agreed to demonstrate against nuclear weapons at an airfield. They did so out of concern that the proliferation of nuclear weapons was threatening nuclear catastrophe. They were charged and convicted of acting 'for a purpose prejudicial to the safety or interests of the

---

[32] S Kadish, 'Moral Excess' (2000) *McGeorge Law Review* 1.

[33] See B Williams, 'Moral Responsibility and Political Freedom' [1997] *Camb LJ* 96, at 99.

[34] See ch 1.

[35] (1964) AC 763.

state.' Even if we accept, as the House of Lords did, that A and B were wrong in their contention that their actions were designed to promote rather than prejudice the safety and interests of the state theirs was clearly a tenable point of view. From their own point of view they were acting with the greater good of their society in mind, provoking the question as to why society would deem them deserving condemnation, any more than we would Shindler for saving Jews from concentration camps in Nazi Germany. Should we say then not that A and B got their just deserts in the sense that punishment was in some sense necessary to cancel out an act of culpable wrongdoing, but rather that they got what they bargained for?

Putting the question in this way has the consequence of allowing desert theory to escape from the implausible claim that all offenders deserve punishment as a matter of moral necessity.[36] In effect, however, such a position threatens to deprive desert theory of the moral authority by which it distinguishes itself from utilitarianism.[37] 'You got what you bargained for' may have some moral clout in the context of autonomous participants to a contract but it has no moral clout where, as with the rules of criminal law, one is subject to a unilateral prohibition and afforded no option but to obey. At best it gives support to the contention that punishment without responsibility is not deserved—a sentiment only extreme utilitarians are likely to wish to challenge.[38]

The third obstacle is the need to produce a bridge between condemnation and punishment such that the latter and not just the former can be seen as the wrongdoer's due. While we may be prepared to concede that rule-infringement, at least where it takes the form of moral wrongdoing, properly attracts condemnation, the task for retributivism is to justify **punishment**. Consider the following (hypothetical) rejection of the state's authority to exact punishment by a virtuous anarchist, perhaps the kind of person who would be motivated to do what the defendants in *Chandler v DPP* did[39]:

> Although for the sake of argument I might concede that what I did might be thought inimical to society's best interests and if it were this would entitle those affected to condemn me for putting the nation's security at risk never-

---

[36] Why should the liberal state not legislate, for example, an effective defence of civil disobedience for those who act in good faith in the interests of their fellow human beings?

[37] Norrie, *Punishment Responsibility and Justice* (2000), ch 6.

[38] See RA Duff, *Trials and Punishment*, (1996) ch 7.

[39] RP Wolff, 'The Conflict between Authority and Autonomy', 20–31.

theless I repudiate the right of the state to take upon themselves the mantle of the injured party. If I am to be condemned let those who feel wronged by me condemn me. Indeed I would welcome this because it will give me the opportunity to state my case and, who knows, convince my accusers that their condemnation is unjust. The state cannot presume to speak for everyone. Many, perhaps the majority, might not wish to condemn me, particularly if I were given the chance to put my point across. And the state cannot presume to punish me. I am an adult, not a child in need of correction and I repudiate any suggestion that the state has the authority to make me suffer for doing what I think is right just because it has decided otherwise. After all, my flatmate may concede she deserves censure for taking my milk without permission but she would rightly be outraged if I treated this as justification for locking her in her room or doubling her rent. If the state punishes me, then, it is because, like Mafia chieftains, it is invested with the power to do so not the moral authority.

Neither utilitarianism nor desert theory has a ready answer to the first part of the anarchist's objection. Either one accepts the role of the state as the orchestrator of societal coercion or one does not and both classical theory and utilitarianism is premised upon the fact that the state has the authority to govern and to expect compliance, at least as long as it exercises itself in good faith to further conditions of social justice.[40] Only utilitarianism has a ready answer to the second part of the objection concerning the propriety of punishing wrongdoing, which is that concern for individual autonomy must be subjugated to social well-being and if punishment contributes to this it is justified. Desert theory has no inbuilt response. Is there a way of conceiving state punishment which preserves the individual offender from the partisan claims of the state? An initially persuasive version of retributivism offers such an account in which the moral justification for blame and punishment is the same. Where society organises its social affairs by reference to rules of conduct and those rules are calculated to maximise the choices available to all members of society it must follow that individuals are morally obligated to follow the rules and not take short cuts. The benefits of communal living must be paid for by subjecting oneself to its burdens. Irrespective of whether the rule itself was justified, moreover, the justification for the response of punishment is that by acting in this way social equilibrium is restored, and

---

[40] RA Duff, *Trials and Punishment* (1996), ch 8; cf JG Murphy 'Marxism and Retribution' in Duff and Garland (eds), *A Reader on Punishment* (OUP, Oxford, 1994), 47–65; A Norrie, *Law Ideology and Punishment* (Kluwer, Dordrecht, 1991), ch IX; Duff, *Trials and Punishment*, (1996) ch 6.

the offender is deprived of the unfair advantage he obtained over others. The character of the justification should, however, be noted. The justification for the 'punishment' is not to allow the injured feelings of non-offenders to be vindicated or to take vengeance (not morally justified) but simply to restore society's moral equilibrium.[41] Punishment would be the right thing, therefore, even if no harm resulted and nobody was aware of what had happened. Following this analysis, a person deserves punishing for illegal parking in a restricted zone although the parking takes place in an empty street at dead of night and the nearest legal parking space was in a far distant car park. Correspondingly, if the law-abiding demand more 'punishment' than the £10 on the spot fine due, because the illegal parker was accustomed to flouting the rules in this way this should also be ignored in determining the offender's desert.[42]

The unfair advantage theory of desert in punishment while having a degree of force in connection with those offences, such as parking offenders or tax dodgers, which involve offenders in committing short cuts to personal satisfaction is generally considered to be less satisfactory as a means of justifying punishment.[43] The reason simply is that most criminal offences cannot be conceived in this way. It seems perverse to centre our justification for punishment in the indignant claim 'We desisted from hooliganism/raping/mugging that person and so you should have done' If such offenders do deserve punishment it is surely because their deed demands it rather than the bad faith they display to the law abiding. It is also unsatisfactory in providing a theory of the correct quantum of punishment. Primitive retributive theories do better in this respect. One can understand why, for example, the *lex talionis* requires a wrongdoer to be visited with a punishment equivalent to his wrong and, if retribution were simply a matter of satisfying the blood lust of the community in a measured way, it would no doubt have a certain plausibility. But how does one quantify the unfair advantage obtained by rapists, wife beaters or muggers *vis a vis* the law abiding? What is the link between a rape and eight years imprisonment conceived only in terms of taking short cuts? If punishment is the wrongdoer's due it is necessary not merely to have a basis for holding that punishment is deserved but also that the quantum of punishment

---

[41] N Walker in P Glazebrook (eds), *Reshaping the Criminal Law* 1978, 388.

[42] See JR Lucas, *On Justice*, 130 for an elegantly worked distinction between punishment and revenge.

[43] For criticism see generally RA Duff, *Trials and Punishment*, ch 8.

is not out of proportion to the degree of wrongdoing we attribute to the offender.

PUNISHMENT AS COMMUNICATION

If punishment does not operate to cancel out the unfair advantage gained by wrongdoers over the law abiding, how can punishment be justified as the offender's due? The most plausible answer to this question is also the simplest, and is consistent with much of the structure of criminal liability and rhetoric of punishment. Punishment sends a message that a person has done wrong and is being publicly condemned for that wrongdoing. Punishment is the expression of public censure. The medium is the message. In Kafka's chilling short story *In the Penal Settlement* this simple communicative function was posited with the utmost moral clarity. The judgment of the martial court was communicated to the offender by a terrifying machine which etched the sentence of death onto his body by means of needles, in so doing executing him.

If we examine what judges have to say when sentencing offenders for serious offences we can see that it reduces to one central idea 'We hate what you did and for this you deserve punishment.' That central idea may be qualified in different ways. For example, 'What you did was so extraordinarily evil/dangerous/dishonest that you deserve punishment beyond the usual for offences of this type.' Or, 'Although we disapprove wholeheartedly of the wrong you have committed we understand that these were circumstances not of your making. The wrong you have done does not reflect your true character and so you do not deserve the punishment which is normal for offences of this character.' Punishment expresses then both the fact of censure and the degree of disapproval which a given (wrongful) action excites in the moral audience. It relays this message to the victim, offender and the audience.[44] It tells the offender he has done wrong in terms which he cannot ignore were he minded to. It tells the victim that his rights are respected and that society stands shoulder to shoulder with him against those who would harm him. It tells the wider society that such conduct is not to be tolerated and that the state is steadfast in enforcing the values infringed by the offender's action. Occasionally this expressive account of punishment is registered in the very structure of a criminal offence.

[44] *Ibid* 238.

The crime of manslaughter illustrates this very well. The cut off point between a non-punishable negligent killing and a punishable grossly negligent killing is drawn by the degree of social condemnation provoked by the offender's conduct. 'To amount to (manslaughter) mere negligence is not enough. His conduct must go beyond the question of compensation between citizens and amount to, in (the jury's) view, criminal conduct requiring punishment'.[45]

This account of punishment as society's mechanism for identifying public wrongs and expressing the censure attached thereto goes a long way towards satisfying the objection that condemnation rather than punishment is the natural and morally appropriate response to wrongdoing. Punishment is not a price tag. It is a symbol and as a symbol it must convey meaning. It must give expression to society's condemnation of the offender's behaviour. Punishment expresses how bad we consider the offender's action to be.[46] Correspondingly without degrees of punishment extra or reduced condemnation cannot also be registered. It is the fact that punishment expresses public disapproval of what the offender has done which enables us to differentiate it from the other dues which the state is entitled to levy or enforce, say taxes, debts and most notably compensation. The key feature informing the scope of punishment is the kind of moral arguments which must be marshalled to justify the practice. This facet of penal practice accounts for the way excuses interpose themselves between wrongdoing and punishment. Censure expresses the adverse (moral) judgment which wrongdoing elicits and addresses itself to the wrongdoer.[47] So a friend may say to another 'I told you that stuff in confidence and you go and spread it around all over the place. You're not a good friend. 'Apart from reasserting the standards from which the actor is judged to have deviated, an important function of censure is to give the latter a right of response. That response may take the form of contrition or defiance on the one hand[48] or deflecting censure by offering an excuse or justification on the other, thus indicating one's commitment to the values expressed in the standard allegedly infringed.

RA Duff takes forward some of this analysis, and also some of the functionalist concerns of Emile Durkheim. In so doing he escapes from

---

[45] Lord Atkin *Andrews v DPP* [1937] AC 576

[46] See Lord Mackay in *Adomako*.

[47] PF Strawson, 'Freedom and Resentment' (1974) cited from A Von Hirsch, *Censure and Sanctions* (Clarendon Press, Oxford, 1993), at 9–11.

[48] A Von Hirsch, *Censure and Sanctions*, at 9–11.

the narrow 'You are being punished because you deserve it' approach of classical retributivism, embracing an important normative dimension of the dialogue between punisher and punished, namely its tendency to do good, not least in bringing home to the wrongdoer the unacceptable nature of his behaviour. Punishment's expressive nature allows it to function as a method of communication between society and the offender whose values he has flouted. It looks two ways—to censure for past offence and to discourage future infringement. It declares that the subject should not have done what he has done and that he and others will be subject to like sanction for future infringements. The core concern is to address the commission of a wrong by bringing home that wrong to the wrongdoer not by way of compensating the victim[49] but as an expression of disapproval, a demand that the wrong be atoned for and not be repeated.[50] This enables the offender to understand the nature of his wrongdoing and society's reasons for disapproving it and thus to repent and reform himself.[51] As long as the individual to be punished forms part of the moral community which adopts punishment to communicate its values and realign the offender in terms of these values punishment is a force for moral good.[52]

Duff's analysis may, of course, raise questions about how sincere this process of communication is. A true communicative emphasis in punishment must provide space for the individual offender to challenge the moral values supposedly displayed and instantiated in a criminal prohibition. Real moral communities are not communities in which notions of antisocial behaviour are fixed and unchallengable. There is always room for disagreement as to what the prosecution of a blameless life comprises. As illustrated in the discussion of *Chandler v DPP*, moreover, where there is room for disagreement and we consider ourselves unjustly threatened with moral condemnation for acting in an antisocial fashion, justice requires there to be some way of challenging this false sleight on one's character. The broader question concerns the moral standing of the community to communicate its values in this way

---

[49] This is not invariably the case. Exemplary damages may be awarded in certain civil actions but this is exceptional.

[50] RA Duff, *Trials and Punishment*, final chapter.

[51] *Ibid* 238.

[52] Its essentially public function is manifested in the fact that punishment, including financial penalties, is typically rendered to the state rather than the individual victim. Whereas compensation typically addresses only the harm suffered by the victim, punishment is a product of both the harm suffered by the victim and the culpability of the offender.

given the fact that actual societies are unable to deliver the kind of just relations which would render norm infringements themselves unjust and wrong.[53] Duff's response to this, as in liberal theory generally, is that it is unrealistic to temper penal justice by reference to the unjust context within which offending takes place. As long as the individual is part of a moral community whose values he is able to internalise and honour there is no injustice in holding him answerable and communicating society's condemnation if he flouts those values.[54] Punishment thus conceived discloses something about the rules to which it gives its support. The rules are there not merely to exact compliance with state demands but as authoritative statements of the society's values and guides to good citizenship. The good citizen, knowing that his views of anti-social behaviour may not be shared by his community, will nevertheless wish to be guided by community values as instantiated in law, at least unless it turns on a matter of moral principle. The person addressed, whether law-abiding or otherwise, is treated with the respect owing to one capable of choosing to do right or wrong and is thus enabled using the rule as a standard to choose either to avoid public condemnation by complying with the rule or courting censure through breach. This unites the treatment reserved to those who practise civil disobedience, compassionate euthanasia, bank robbery, corporate fraud or rape. The subject of the criminal law is not then treated as the inhabitant of a concentration camp who is told to 'do X or else'. This is not the form taken by its rules. Rather it takes the following form. 'We have decided that doing X is a public wrong. We attach a sanction to it to express this fact and that if, despite this declaration, you nevertheless do X you will be subject to public condemnation.' Or in its typical formulation 'Any person who does A with consequence B in circumstance C with mental state D is guilty of a criminal offence punishable with (a maximum of) X.'[55]

An expressive account cannot lend moral authority to punishment unless it can generate a coherent set of sentencing norms capable of maintaining a fair balance between effective condemnation and respect for the offender's freedom and autonomy. This proper concern has been persuasively articulated by JR Lucas who insists that the expressive features of punishment must be effectively decoupled from its potentialities as a deterrent: 'Instead of asking the question "How can

[53] See A Norrie, *Punishment Responsibility and Justice*, ch 6.
[54] See also R Dworkin, 'Obligations of Community' in J Raz (ed), *Authority*, 218–22.
[55] For critique see *ibid*.

we best dispose of the individual to secure the enforcement of law and order?" as supporters of (deterrence) do, we ask "In view of what you have done, can we let you off any more lightly without acquiescing in it and encouraging others to follow suit?" '.[56] If punishment is simply the visible manifestation of social disapproval for the offender's action why then is punishment generally so obviously more severe than that necessary to express our wholehearted disapproval of an offender's conduct? Either desert is being unnecessarily sacrificed in the anxiety to instantiate effectively the moral message that murder is wrong or there is more to punishment than this, perhaps consequentialist concerns such as deterrence or incapacitation or emotional concerns such as vengeance.

Andrew von Hirsch's starting point, like that of Feinberg, is that the price of crime cannot be determined only by reference to that necessary to show disapproval. It must incorporate a weighting which acts as an extra 'prudential' reason to the citizen not to offend. A sanction must be able to motivate citizens whatever the circumstances, whatever the individual character, whatever the rewards for non-compliance. Social disapproval cannot be expected to do all this work. He strikes the balance between what is necessary and what is deserved by requiring all punishment to be first anchored to a baseline by which society sets the general limits within which punishment for different offences may be meted out. If life imprisonment for murder, say, is the severest sentence a society will stomach, all other punishments are anchored by that relationship between that (gravest) offence and most severe punishment. Once this baseline has been set the task is to ensure that 'person's convicted of crimes of like gravity . . . receive punishments of like severity . . . and those convicted of crimes of differing gravity . . . receive punishments correspondingly graded in their degree of severity'.[57] The point of hard treatment is then to render compliance easier from the individual's point of view. Crucially, however, it motivates him to do what is right because it is right not because he will be punished. This means that the retributive nature of the theory does not collapse into a utilitarian one.

---

[56] *On Justice* (1980), 144.
[57] *Censure and Sanctions* (1993), ch 2.

That the rhetoric of punishment typically fails to dissociate retributive and consequentialist concerns seems, however, to indicate that neither approach is capable of doing true justice to the phenomenon of punishment. Sometimes, reprehensible cases of murder are a good illustration, the appeal of punishment lies is its retributive features. Sometimes, as is reflected in the broad range of regulatory offences, it is deterrence. Sometimes, as in sex offences and career criminals, it is incapacitation. In constant tension with these essentially punitive responses to wrongdoing is rehabilitation whose rationale often argues against the kind of severe penalties which deterrence and retribution are disposed to supply.

This type of conceptual and functional elision can be identified in the clearest cases of non-secular punishments, for example Shari'ah punishments in Islamic states such as Afghanistan in recent memory. On the face of it the amputation of the hands of petty thieves registers as an extreme example of man's inhumanity to man magnified, as in Kafka's metaphor, rather than diminished by the intervention of the state. As an expressive symbol, however, hand amputation is hard to beat in terms of its internal and external communicative coherence. Internally it creates a compelling conceptual linkage between the punishment and the wrong. The hand that stole is the hand forfeited. Externally it communicates to the offender just how seriously society views his wrongdoing. It forces him to accept the message. He is given no option and will be reminded of it until his dying day. It communicates that same message to the wider moral audience. How indeed could it be done more clearly? It tells the victim that society is united in condemnation of the wrongdoer's action, that it takes his side. The punishment is, moreover, shameful. The offender is forced to carry the insignia of moral condemnation in full view of society.

At the same time, the sheer brutality of the punishment allows us to apprehend that shame and the communication of moral condemnation is not the only nor even, perhaps, the main reason for punishment taking this form. Such punishments demonstrate with the utmost clarity what is to many a constant and inevitable feature within all state institutions of punishment, namely a pragmatic decision to profit from the structural impossibility of discerning whether punishment's essential form is retributive or preventive. If we cannot tell what is or is not deserved it allows punishment's preventive features to play the default role, the more powerfully for being unacknowledged.[58] The punishment's deterrent value for the individual offender and society at large is easy to appreciate. It will no doubt be more so for the individual offender the second time round. One can almost imagine the tingle of apprehension in the fingers as they are stretched forward. And of course, if this punishment does not work as a deterrence it will certainly work as an incapacitant. And, who knows, if thievery becomes a practical impossibility, it may even result in his moral and spiritual redemption.

Consequentialism and retribution are, then, apparently locked in tension and yet, as this latter example indicates, seem to display different aspects of a composite whole. The question demanding an answer is whether there is any cogent reconciliation to be made. Is it ever, for example, justifiable to temper retributive justice by reference to a person's lack of dangerousness or moral blameworthiness on the one hand, or responsiveness to rehabilitation on the other? Is it ever justifiable to punish people to a greater degree of severity than the gravity of their wrongdoing demands say, because, as in the case of terrorism, they, their wrongdoing, or their propensity to do wrong poses a particular threat for society?[59] Is it ever justifiable to detain offenders after the period of (retributive) punishment has expired on grounds of dangerousness?

A number of theorists have sought to combine both retributive and consequentialist approaches to punishment in acknowledgement of the undeniable fact that punishment must both be deserved and, in its practices, be beneficial for society. Two general models can be discerned—what might be termed a weak and a strong consequentialist retributive model. A weak consequentialist model has been essayed by HLA Hart whose position, as we have seen, is that while state institutions of punishment can only be justified on utilitarian grounds—the reduction of antisocial behaviour—given instances of punishment must be deserved. Only culpable wrongdoers deserve punishment and only then in proportion to their wrongdoing. This approach affords utilitarianism a moral escape route from the charge that concern and respect for the individual offender is always susceptible to being trumped by collective goals. On the other hand, with so great an emphasis on desert it

---

[58] P Robinson, 'Punishing Dangerousness' (2001) 114 *Harv LR* 1429.
[59] See generally A von Hirsch, *Censure and Sanctions*, ch 6.

can be seen that Hart's model, unlike say that of Braithwait and Pettit which has no way of ensuring that the concern to maximise dominion does not trump individual fairness, in no significant respect differs from retributivism. For Hart, however, while the state has no business punishing people unless social well being is thereby enhanced the criterion for punishment is desert. Hart's difficulty here, as in retributivism generally, is that his overriding commitment to desert seems to deprive him of the wherewithal to present a unified theory of punishment capable of doing justice to the empirical reality of penal practices. While neither utilitarianism nor retributivism has difficulty in accounting for punishment directed against core crimes involving culpable wrongdoing, only utilitarianism has a ready justification for the vast tract of criminal offences punishable without proof of moral wrongdoing. Clearly desert is not everything. Sometimes it is trumped by utility. And indeed it seems naïve, if not in these troubled times also irresponsible, to insist that desert is the 'bottom line'. We need an account which enables us to understand how desert and utility can legitimately operate to qualify each other over the full range of punishable offences.[60]

Strong consequentialist retributive models allow consequentialist concerns to interact more directly with desert as a basis for punishment. In so doing a problem implicit in retributivism generally, including Hart's version, is obviated, which is only partially addressed in expressive theories of punishment, namely how to produce a sentencing system which can relate a given wrongful act to an appropriate (deserved) form and level of punishment.

Desert theory requires like cases to be punished in like fashion.[61] Although it may be impossible to state what level of punishment a particular crime deserves it is possible to state that more excessive or lenient punishments than that suffered by defendants for committing like harms with like culpability are undeserved.[62] Of course this assumes that we have a stable basis for assessing desert. It is not clear that such a basis exists.[63] For a start, does a person who kills four people by four separate actions on four separate occasions deserve more punishment than a person who kills four people by one act

---

[60] N Lacey (1988) 49

[61] HLA Hart, *Punishment and Responsibility*, ch 1.

[62] A von Hirsch, *Censure and Sanctions*, ch 2.

[63] See for example N Walker, 'Modern Retributivism' in H Gross and R Harrison (eds), *Jurisprudence: Cambridge Essays* (Clarendon Press, Oxford, 1992).

on one occasion? Are a person's previous convictions to be counted in an assessment of desert?[64] Again, in assessing someone's desert do we take into account questions of distributive justice. Does A deserve less punishment than B if A has already suffered, in other ways, as a consequence of what he has done or if the punishment tariff would, because of A's personal circumstances (say she is single mother) affect A more severely than B? Yet again, is desert a function of the rule infringement *per se* or of the moral values which the rule instantiates? Consider in this regard murder. Instances of murder range from, at one extreme, cases such as doctor-sponsored euthanasia, where it is difficult to discern either a wrongful act or a culpable state of mind. At the other extreme are killings where there is no better motive than the pleasure and empowerment it affords the killer. Somewhere in between perhaps are cases where the defendant manifests a distorted sense of priorities where the prospects of redemption and atonement are realistic. A not uncommon example is the person who kills his former spouse and children in impotent reaction to an undesired divorce or separation. Using a purely retributive model it is difficult if not impossible to arrive at a cogent basis for quantifying the level of punishment which is the defendant's desert. Do we punish all the same—the domestic approach—on the basis that all people who intentionally take the life of another deserve equal treatment? Do we punish the psychopath more than the jealous spouse because of the cruel and vicious disposition he displayed or the latter because of the number of victims and his relationship with them?

Using a hybrid model these imponderables can be dismissed to a certain extent by allowing utilitarian concerns to fix the form and quantum of punishment, with desert operating only as a restraint upon the potential range of punishable offenders and level of punishments for a given wrongful act. For example, if we take the expression of moral criticism to be the measure of an offender's desert it is possible to produce a range of punishments anchored in the minimum punishment necessary to convey effectively society's disapproval of the conduct concerned at the lower end, but which offers sufficient flexibility,

---

[64] Von Hirsch has argued elsewhere that they should since repeat offending suggests defiance over and above that implicit in simple rule-breaking (although it now appears he has resiled from this position): A von Hirsch, *Doing Justice—The Choice of Punishments* (Report of the Committee for the Study of Incarceration) (New York) (1976); cf G Fletcher, *Rethinking Criminal Law* (Little Brown and Company, Boston, Toronto, 1978), 461–66.

whether by way of deterrence, rehabilitation or incapacitation, to address any particular problem posed to society by this offender and this offence. The Swedish Code provision on homicide is a good example of a strong consequentialist approach demonstrating how questions of desert and utility combined can determine both the criminal label and the appropriate level of punishment.

> S1. A person, who takes the life of another, shall be sentenced for murder to imprisonment for ten years or for life.
>
> S2. If, in view of the circumstances that led to the act or for other reasons, the crime mentioned in Section 1 is considered to be less grave, imprisonment for manslaughter shall be imposed for at least six and at most ten years.

This provision sets both the top end and bottom end of the range of punishment by reference, one presumes, to desert based criteria. The worst kind of culpable killing deserves no more than life imprisonment. The 'least worst' deserves no less than six years. Between these two desert-based anchoring points there is room, arguably too much room, for sentences to be geared towards the consequentialist concerns which utilitarian approaches to punishment embody.

Paul Robinson has essayed a plausible *via media* between the strong and weak versions.[65] Without contributing answers to the question posed above of how different contextual variables affect desert, he argues that while proportionality in punishment should be the norm there are nevertheless good reasons to depart from this norm where the person or activity concerned poses a particular danger to society. 'Extra' punishment may then be justified to engender a culture of compliance or to address the dangerousness of particular types of offender, say recidivists, paedophiles or psychopaths. While desert normally fixes the appropriate level of response in cases of compelling social need, desert may be trumped exceptionally by say the policy concern of social protection.[66] The idea is that the offender's rights must sometimes be overridden for the good of all, as is uncontroversially the case for people suffering from dangerous communicable diseases who may be subjected to coerced quarantine.[67] In the UK two contemporary concerns, albeit from different ends of the dangerousness spectrum, have provoked such an approach. The first is terrorist activities arising

---

[65] For discussion and criticism see A von Hirsch, *Censure and Sanctions*, ch 6.

[66] R Dworkin, *Taking Rights Seriously* (Duckworth, London, 1978) ch 7.

[67] A von Hirsch, *Censure and Sanctions*, 51.

out of the events of 11 September. The second is mobile phone robbery, whose remorseless ubiquity has led even the more liberal members of the judicial establishment to embrace explicitly the merits of deterrence and preventive detention.[68] While this is not the place to explore it, the argument is that as long as the penal response does not reduce to a simple weighing of individual rights to fair treatment against social wellbeing, the state is morally entitled to direct that certain community claims trump individual fairness. Doubts may justly be raised about the stability of the yardstick by which deviations from individual desert may be justified—can terrorism and mobile phone robbery truly involve commensurable trump claims? Nevertheless it is hard to resist the conclusion that being fair to the individual is sometimes simply beside the point in those exceptional cases where society must take extraordinary measures to protect itself and its members from defined and urgent dangers.

ANCHORING PUNISHMENTS AND PENALTIES:
RESTORATION AND VENGEANCE

It is fashionable to suggest that the criminal law suffers from an incoherent mix of welfare and autonomy derived rules. On this view, the law suffers from the fact that it, supported by the harm principle, must point in two directions at the same time. It must morally justify itself by asserting the priority to be accorded to individual freedom encapsulated in items such as the harm principle, retributive punishment, and notions of subjective fault. At the same time its survival depends upon ensuring that matters crucial to collective wellbeing are pursued at the expense of such individualistic ethics. The way it does so, it is thought, is by pragmatically compromising principles of individual responsibility and accountability wherever necessary to give effect to collective goals.[69] This shows, it is thought, that the philosophy underlying the system of punishing offences is incoherent. Either we should effectively record the differentiated contexts within which individuals make their choices to attack society's collective interests, or we should abandon the pretence that a precondition of coercion is establishing personal moral fault and accountability and create an efficient system capable of

[68] See for example Lord Woolf, *The Times*, 29 January 2002.
[69] See A Norrie, 'Crime Reason and Theory' ch 10; *Punishment Responsibility and Justice* (2000) generally.

effectively ministering to our collective needs. Such a system is already in operation in areas such as health and safety, road traffic and so on. It could be extended to cover all crimes.[70]

The more orthodox view described here agrees that the criminal law reflects sometimes competing rationales and objectives, as the above discussion acknowledges. However, neither in its form nor its content is it as **inherently** contradictory or incoherent as critics invite us to suppose. Sometimes individual rights are and must be trumped by collective needs. This is not a failure of justice. It is rather one of the facts of social life to which criminal justice must pay scrupulous attention if individual rights are not to be dishonoured. More broadly, the law can best be understood as containing complementary paradigms of responsibility which offer different accounts of the proper scope of the criminal laws and principles of punishment pertinent to that paradigm. One is a welfarist paradigm which does not require proof of moral wrongdoing or desert in punishment. In order to live a life of relative autonomy we require certain basic welfare needs to be ministered to. Such needs include the ability to eat, travel, work and so on. If we are to flourish as human beings we need the security of knowing that doing these things is not calculated to cause us harm. Only the criminal law can satisfactorily ensure that these collective needs can be properly catered for and this is only possible if the criminal law requires all citizens to satisfy standards of good rather than simply morally blameless citizenship. The essence of such crimes is to prevent harm rather than to punish a moral wrong. Such crimes must not, however, entitle the loss of liberty unless there has been open defiance of the rule. The trade-off between freedom and welfare is that freedom may be compromised to advance welfare (eg, by restricting driving speed) but not so as to put the defendant at risk of loss of actual freedom (imprisonment) for failing to attain the necessary standard of good citizenship.[71]

The autonomy-based paradigm consists of crimes which involve the defendant acting so as to negate some fundamental (moral) value. In this context we are talking of core offences, ie those whose function it is to enforce consensually agreed values central to the integrity of society. Such crimes do require proof of moral fault since the basis for desert in punishment, taking into account the equal autonomy of all, is that the agent acted **so as to** deny the victim's autonomy and thus his

---

[70] B Wootton, *Crime and the Criminal Law* (Sweet & Maxwell, London, 1981).

[71] 52 See A Brudner 'Agency and Welfare in the Penal Law' in S Shute et al *Action and Value in Criminal Law* (Clarendon Press, Oxford, 1993) 21, at 52.

own right to freedom from punishment. For such crimes then imprisonment may be an appropriate response, but only if the defendant's interference with the (fundamental) interests was advertent or at least in defiance of standards we would expect the actor to meet.

Following this analysis, therefore, the task of scholars and judges is to root out examples of the illegitimate use of one paradigm to serve the function of the other. Thus no point is served by insisting upon proof of personal moral fault in welfare offences since the point of such offences is not to enforce moral values but to advance society's welfare interests. This can be done by punishing even those who do not consciously defy society's primary rules of behaviour so long as punishment is an effective mechanism for securing these interests. At the same time, if the object of a crime is the vindication of a fundamental moral value then it must bear punishments commensurate with other such offences and respect the ethical requirement that those subjected to punishment, as opposed to mere penalty, must be morally blameworthy.[72]

Dan Kahan has recently taken this paradigmatic analysis into the heartland of criminal punishment to reflect more deeply upon the paradox of hard treatment.[73] Why is it, he inquires, that liberal theory is so out of step with public opinion in seeking to eradicate imprisonment except where absolutely necessary for purposes of incapacitating dangerous people? In his view the continued public popularity of imprisonment reflects the fact, as the public more than theorist seems to understand, that punishing moral wrongdoing is a shaming process which alternative punishments such as fines or community service cannot match, at whatever level they may be pitched.[74] Different forms of punishment are incommensurable. They cannot be traded in for each other, as say a £10,000 fine might equate to a month in prison and a £100,000 fine to a year. They have different social meanings. A fine in cases of theft or violence sends a message that such wrongs can be paid for, as speeding and illegal parking can be paid for, which leaves the condemnatory function of punishment largely unfulfilled. Imprisonment by

---

[72] As we shall see, ridding the criminal law of the numerous ways in which crimes against fundamental values can be committed without meaning to defy such values would be an enormous project and would come up against a great deal of resistance. Moreover, how exactly to identify such a state of culpability is not entirely without difficulty.

[73] D Kahan, 'Punishment Incommensurability' (1998) 1 *Buffalo Criminal Law Review* 691.

[74] It is easily dissociated from other non penal losses of freedom such as conscription or quarantine since it is degrading and shaming.

contrast expresses the message 'we do not want you to do it. It is wrong for you to do it. And you will suffer moral condemnation if you do it or even if you try to do it.'[75] In so doing the worth of the crime victim and the core values of society are reaffirmed.

The radical conclusion to be drawn from this is that both retributive and preventive concerns can be combined without fundamentally rupturing the delicate balance between offence gravity and sentence severity, which normally guarantees the just marriage of public and private interests. Kahan argues that the major cause of sentencing instability is that punishment cannot square the circle of retribution and prevention. The twin dangers are too much punishment—protective and retributive penal strategies are typically too punitive—or too little—fines are a good deterrent but a bad signifier of moral condemnation and so unpopular with the public as a form of punishment outside the field of regulatory offences. If the state is to counter the continual public demand for 'more punishment' in the form of ineffective and costly prison sentences it should be encouraged to do so by **combining** shaming punishments such as wearing special clothes, doing shameful jobs, and self-abasement rituals—with fines and other effective (non-shameful) deterrents.

What Kahan tends to under-emphasise, unlike, say, contemporary 'restorative' approaches to punishment, is that showing respect for the victims of crimes and the rest of us whose dominion or whatever we call it, is diminished by crime seems to demand more by way of punishment than this 'book-keepers' approach is designed to afford. Although we may deplore it, the psychic disturbances and imbalances which core crimes provoke in victims, their families and the wider society provoke also a very unmodern psychic response, namely the desire for vengeance. It reflects a political paradox as old as civilised society itself. In the *Eumenides*, the final play in Aeschylus's Oresteian trilogy, one of the most compelling confrontations in the history of drama is played out to its conclusion. Orestes is on trial for having killed his mother, Clytemnestra. He was encouraged to do so by Apollo, the God of the modern order, because Clytemnestra had herself killed his father, Agamemnon, albeit with some degree of justification.[76] The

---

[75] Above n 73, at 693.

[76] Agamemnon had himself first killed their daughter, Iphigenia. For a fascinating account of how this play reflects the cultural impetus behind the rise of modernism, the replacement of matriarchy with patriarchy and with it the modern state see F Engels, *The Origins of the Family, Private Property and the State* (Lawrence and Wishart, London 1972), chs 1 and 2.

Eumenides want vengeance, the terrible, unrelenting vengeance the old order demands for those who have committed matricide. They are disinterested in Orestes' reasons for doing so, in the reasonableness of conceiving matricide (closest blood tie) as of being of a wholly different moral order than the killing of a husband (no blood tie), in the unreasonableness of not balancing Orestes's wrong against an appropriate measure of retribution. Apollo, who speaks for Orestes, demands justice. The justice of which he speaks ties punishment to the true moral enormity of what he has done (killing mother but to avenge father) rather than the blood lust of the outraged victim or her champions. This thirst for vengeance is unreasoned and unsatisfiable. It looks only to the deed—the wrong done them—and not to the context of the deed and its motivation.[77] Orestes has suffered enough. Punishment must be justified. Aeschylus's achievement, through his voice-piece Athena, is to unite the opposing voices of Apollo and the Eumenides, placing the suffering of the wrongdoer within a penal context which, while taking account of the victim, does not relinquish the wrongdoer to the victim's fury.[78] His conclusion, which today is still being rehearsed, refined and tempered in the crucible of penological debate, is that the wrongdoer must suffer and in so doing will learn virtue and justice.[79] But suffering is for the disinterested purpose of atonement and to requite justice rather than for the self-interested satisfaction of the thirst for vengeance.

Although Aeschylus presented vengeance as having been dethroned by the modern preoccupation with justice he does not, however, convince the reader that the voices of unreason have truly acknowledged the error of their ways. Why should they have? Justice may supplant vengeance as the organising template of state sponsored suffering but it cannot silence the inclination. A cursory reading of the daily newspapers is enough to convince us of this. No wonder then perhaps that Aeschylus presents the audience with a change of heart on the part of the Eumenides' as abrupt as it is unexpected.

Contemporary debates within penal theory have sought to revive the significance of the victim's point of view, but only in its positive manifestation as the reverse side of the offender's struggle for forgiveness and atonement. It is the victim after all who, in later confronting his

---

[77] JR Lucas, *On Justice*, 130–1.

[78] 'The furies' is the Eumenides more apt title.

[79] See for example the debate between RA Duff and A Norrie in RA Duff (ed), *Philosophy and the Criminal Law* (CUP, Cambridge, 1998).

attacker, is best placed to stimulate in the latter a spiritually honest sense of shame and desire to atone and, moreover, to benefit therefrom. A restorative approach to criminal punishment is consistent then with both retributive and a consequentialist justification for punishment.[80] As yet, little serious intellectual effort has been made, however, to consider whether the more archaic emotion of vengeance, discredited in the Eumenides and by classical retributivism and underplayed in utilitarian treatments, should play a more prominent role in the construction of a tenable theory of punishment.[81] As Shari'ah punishments so clearly demonstrate it is not only easy to substitute the question 'What is deserved?' with its consequentialist counterpart 'What is necessary?' but also with its (psychological) relative 'What do we want?' If we acknowledge, as restorative approaches do, that the state's punitive response offers something of value both to the victim and the wider society, this perhaps should incline us to take more seriously the present covert role already played by 'blood lust' in the constitution of desert. Modifying the words of JR Lucas we may then wish to ask, in fashioning a workable notion of retributive desert, 'In view of what you have done can we let you off any more lightly without acquiescing in it, encouraging others to follow suit or failing sufficiently to honour the understandable desire of the victim, her family and the wider society that you suffer for what you have done?'[82] At the very least, posing such a question might serve to offer a practical input to resolving the difficulty of fixing the cardinal 'anchoring points' of proportionality in sentencing.[83]

[80] For an overview of the many forms of restorative justice, see A Ashworth and A von Hirsch (1998), ch7.

[81] See B Williams, 'Moral Responsibility and Political Freedom' [1997] *Camb LJ* 96; T Honderich, *Punishment: The Supposed Justifications* (Penguin, Harmondsworth, 1984).

[82] *Ibid* 144.

[83] See von Hirsch in *Censure and Sanctions*, 17–19.

3

Criminal Wrongdoing: Acts and Omissions

IT IS EASY to take the subject matter of the criminal law for granted. The popular press is full of the gory detail of 'real crime'. Today's paper contains details of a married teacher who hit his wife's lover over the head with a metal pipe having lured him in the early hours of the morning to a nearby wood for this very purpose. Another item involves the strange tale of a man who burned down the stand at Doncaster Rovers football ground using several cans of petrol in the process, and he did not even follow football. These might be described as the core cases of criminal activity. If a society did not have crimes of aggravated assault or arson before these outrages took place it would not take long before it felt it appropriate to invent them. They are cases where a fully competent adult inexcusably and unjustifiably acts upon and executes his desire to damage the protected interests (personal or property) of another person.

Within such everyday tales can be identified the basic building block of criminal liability, namely wrongdoing. The paradigm of wrongdoing takes the form of voluntary action. Thus an assassination will typically involve an actor whose goal—death of president—is to be achieved by pressing the trigger of a gun pointed at the person of the president from a position of advantage. Each activity which the assassin undertakes—purchase of gun, stakeout, lifting and aiming the gun, and pressing the trigger—involves bodily movements connected with the assassin's determination to kill the president and, in this sense, attributable to him as a goal-orientated agent.

In 1962 the United States Supreme Court ruled unconstitutional a statute rendering drug addiction a criminal offence.[1] What was wrong with this offence? There were two quite separate injustices attached to it. The first was that punishment did not depend upon the defendant having done anything. The provision punished his status—addict—not

---

[1] *Robinson v California* 370 US 660 (1962).

his behaviour—possessing/taking/supplying drugs. The offence was constituted even though the defendant may have lived out his life entirely reclusively so that his status had no discernible public impact. More importantly punishment was not predicated upon the defendant bearing moral responsibility for his addiction. It could originate in childhood or coerced administration, or be provoked by psychiatric illness but it was still the subject matter of criminal liability. As such the provision bore comparison with the kind of punitive barbarism associated with witch-trials and the leper laws of medieval Europe.[2] It contained no requirement that the accused person's conduct/status be voluntary.

THE ACT REQUIREMENT

The Supreme Court's decision is reflective of a basic premise underpinning criminal liability, commonly referred to as the 'act requirement'. It is wrongdoing that attracts punishment and censure, not immorality or wicked thoughts and it is wrongdoing which is the starting point for the process of holding someone accountable in a criminal trial. Without wrongdoing there is no occasion for inquiring into the mental state of someone who is brought to the attention of society's authorities. Locked up in this notion of wrongdoing is the requirement of some prohibited conduct on the part of the accused for which he bears personal moral responsibility. Criminal liability requires (wrongful) conduct and it requires that conduct to be voluntary. Both facets of the act requirement will now be considered starting, in this chapter, with how the law conceives wrongful conduct. I shall suggest that the constitution of criminal wrongdoing, as can be seen most obviously with regard to the criminalisation of omissions, requires particular attention to be paid to the criminal law's communicative function. As will be seen, this, along with law's well understood concern to uphold autonomy and the principle of legality, is a major reason for circumspection in the criminalisation of omissions.

---

[2] See R Porter, *The Greatest Benefit to Mankind: A Medical History of Humanity from Antiquity to the Present* (Harper Collins, London, 1997), 121, 196.

ACTS AND ACTIONS

Loosely, the criminal law is informed by an 'act' rather than an 'action' requirement. So, we talk of an act of killing or theft. This description tells us nothing about the constituent elements of such acts. Is it simply the bodily movements involved in, say, aiming and pulling the trigger of a gun? Or must we include in our description of an act circumstances, such as the fact that the gun was loaded, and the consequences, namely that the bullet met its target?[3] Much may hang upon the answer to this question. For example, if the basis of our responsibility is our bodily movements *tout court* then further explanations are required as to why we are punished for the consequences of those movements.[4] Sometimes the courts have to consider the constitution of criminal acts in order to make sense of a criminal provision.[5] On these occasions it becomes clear that to the extent that criminal liability may or may not require proof of an act, settling upon the appropriate description of an act is by no means straightforward. In *Fagan*, for example, the Court of Appeal had to decide whether a person who accidentally parked his car on a policeman's foot was acting for the purpose of the crime of assault when, having being informed of this, he refused to remove it. Bridge J thought that he was not since acting implied action or activity and here there was none. On the contrary, Fagan had finished acting. James J for the majority, by contrast, thought the defendant was acting. He was parking his car, an act of no finite duration and which lasted so long as the motorist still had manoeuvres to perform which, given he had come to rest on a policeman's foot, was self-evident.

Because some form of deliberated (voluntary) bodily movement is the normal packaging of action it has prompted some to suppose that this also lies at the core of the act requirement.[6] Acts, on this view, are differentiated from other (harmful) events in the material world only in that they manifest themselves through human rather than animal or

---

[3] J Salmond, *Jurisprudence* (Stevens, London, 1947), 370.

[4] See generally RA Duff, 'Acting, Trying and Criminal Liability' in Shute *et al* (eds), *Action and Value in Criminal Law* (Clarendon Press, Oxford, 1994), 75.

[5] JL Mackie, 'The Grounds of Responsibility' in PMS Hacker and J Raz (eds), *Law, Morality and Society* (Clarendon Press, Oxford, 1977).

[6] See for example M Moore, *Act and Crime: The Philosophy of Action and its Implications for Criminal Law* (OUP, Oxford, 1993), 28; J Austin, *Lectures on Jurisprudence* (John Murray, London, 1869) 290.

natural agency.[7] Both would register on a hypothetical instrument, as earthquakes register on a seismograph, designed to detect when things were happening and when they were not. Thus, when one Monday an earthquake occurs this can be designated as an event. When an earthquake did not occur the previous Wednesday this was, rather, no event.[8] In like fashion, a person who scratches his nose is engaging in action. If he forbears from doing so, he is not engaging in action. This is so even though the desire to remove an itch is overwhelming. So also, the criminal law does not incriminate those who, say, hate members of other racial groups but only those who manifest such hatred in action. The bodily movement manifesting racial hatred may be that involved in plunging a dagger into a victim's heart or the bodily movement undergone by the larynx when its owner incites others to share the same hatred. By virtue of the bodily movements involved speaking satisfies the act requirement. Thinking evil thoughts does not. Thinking and other mental processes do not count as events over which the criminal law has jurisdiction—although it is quite possible to register a mental event using neural imaging techniques. Not only are mental processes unamenable to control but since the content of thought is not made manifest in changes in the material world nothing describable as action is registered on our hypothetical instrument.

Conceiving of acts in this way provokes a number of difficulties however.[9] If acts do reduce to (willed) bodily movements it should be possible to define an act in terms of a given set of bodily movements. After all, what is the point of insisting that acts require bodily movement if one cannot describe what kind of movement a given act involves? In fact, few bodily movements speak to the act which they embody. A person can kill with a kiss and save a life with a knife. Both killers and film actors fire guns at third parties. The bodily movements of neither, in themselves, convey the information necessary to know whether the act of killing has taken place. This suggests that there may be more to acts than voluntary movements.

Perhaps our acts are more appropriately described as 'deeds'. Deeds are not constituted **as deeds** by bodily movements, although of course bodily movement will be the normal form of packaging. Deeds are constituted by context and consequences, the intentions of actors and the

---

[7] *Lectures on Jurisprudence*, 267 et seq.

[8] It is not even an event when every seismologist in the world had predicted it would occur.

[9] See for example H Gross, *A Theory of Criminal Justice* (OUP, New York, 1979), ch 2.

interpretation of others.[10] As such, they are counterposed for the purpose of criminal liability, not to the absence of bodily movements, but to purely mental events such as thoughts, beliefs, desires and ideas which it would clearly be inappropriate to punish if society truly respects the autonomy and freedom of individuals. The major reason William Tell is so lauded in folklore is that his arrow hit the apple and not his son. This fact lends his action a different moral and conceptual character than if the opposite had occurred. Again, consider the old chestnut of Nero fiddling while Rome burns. If we ignore what we know to be the true context and point of the saying it could stand as an instantiation of a number of different act interpretations. One interpretation is neutral. It remarks simply the surprising sense of priorities Nero displayed. He preferred fiddling to fire dousing. A psychologist might advance this interpretation to support his thesis that Nero was an intriguingly complex person not given to doing the expected. A second—perhaps the interpretation of a musicologist—is even a favourable interpretation. Nero showed such commitment to his muse that even the destruction of the city could not deflect him. Clearly, given what we understand of the saying, the physical movements of Nero do not help us to make any moral sense of his conduct. To evaluate the deed the audience needs to know who Nero was and what his functions were. This allows us to unlock the contemporary message locked up in the proverb, which is that Nero, the emperor of Rome, was doing something other than that which he ought to have been doing, namely saving Rome. The saying stands as a metaphor for moral responsibility—the kind of responsibility in other words which allows us to say of wrongdoers 'You're a bad person. You've done wrong and deserve to be punished.' The point of formulating these three interpretations is that on the basis of identical bodily movements undertaken by Nero we can identify three quite separate acts or deeds—a malign deed of omission, a morally neutral deed of commission (fiddling), and a morally creditable deed of commission (prosecuting his muse). The insistence that acts, as a basis for imposing criminal liability, require activity ignores the fact that bodily movement is simply the normal packaging of a deed. And it is our interpretation of Nero's conduct rather than any visible manifestation of it which constitutes such conduct as 'deed' and thus an appropriate object of censure or praise.[11]

[10] Cf R A Duff, *Criminal Attempts* (OUP, Oxford, 1996), 293 *et seq.*
[11] See for example R Shapira, 'Willed Bodily Movement' (1998) *Buffalo Criminal Law Review* 349 at 351. But one can be punished for acting upon and even, rarely, for articulating such an idea, belief or desire.

MORAL RESPONSIBILITY WITHOUT ACTION

A cursory examination of criminal doctrine suggests that the minimum irreducible requirement for criminal liability is not bodily movement but moral responsibility. This replicates our everyday assumptions about how praise and blame are properly allocated also, the basic point of the act requirement which is to affirm that punishment and censure must attend bad **behaviour** rather than bad **thoughts**. It is not a call for some kind of deliberated 'activity'.[12] 'Behaviour' in popular usage tends to refer, unlike action, as much to what one does not do as what one does. An order to 'behave' is apt to prompt, in the obedient subject, a cessation of 'activity'. An order to 'act', on the other hand, is an instruction to engage in some form of visible bodily movement. Action Man does not laze around. The words 'behaviour' and 'action' are not always coterminous but together they capture the full range of human agency. Human beings can influence the material world in one of two ways. They can intervene positively in a fashion comparable to that of a natural event. A building may collapse by virtue of an earthquake or a terrorist bomb. Human beings can also influence the world by what they omit or forbear to do. If we omit to tend the garden it will return to nature. If we omit to water the houseplants they will die. A minute's silence at a football ground trumpets, in its distinctive forbearance, the spectators' respect for the qualities of the honoured deceased. There is no compelling reason, therefore, why we should designate movement as the touchstone of criminal wrongdoing. Movement is not the point. Nero's moral responsibility remains intact however the state of affairs came about. We would challenge it, if it were thought appropriate, only upon the basis that the events took place as they did without him being in a position, by virtue of his authority or otherwise, to do anything about it.

Criminal doctrine contains a great many offences which are or may be constituted in the absence of action, howsoever defined. Possession offences are an obvious example. The wrong in possessing controlled drugs or firearms is not the act of taking possession but that of being in possession. Situational offences form another wide ranging set of offences which penalise persons simply for being in a prohibited situa-

---

[12] See for example G Fletcher, 'On the Moral Irrelevance of Bodily Movements' (1994) 142 *U Pa LR* 1443.

tion.[13] So it is a criminal offence to be drunk on the highway or in charge of a vehicle, to be the owner of a dog which is dangerously out of control in a public place, to live on the earnings of prostitution. In each case susceptibility to criminalisation is not attributable to any specific thing the defendant does, but to the existence of a critical connection between him and the occurrence of an event or state of affairs. This has led critics to conclude that situational liability is an aberration from normal conditions of criminal liability in that it requires no proof of (bad) behaviour. Sometimes cases crop up which seem to demonstrate just such a tendency. *Larsonneur* is the classic example. The defendant was a French woman who had been allowed entry into the United Kingdom. She was later subject to an immigration order requiring her to leave the next day, whereupon she set sail for Ireland whence she was deported back to England. On arrival in England she was charged and convicted with being 'an alien to whom leave to land in the United Kingdom has been refused, (and who) was found in the United Kingdom contrary to the . . . Aliens Order 1920'. Clearly her conviction occurred **despite** the fact that her arrival in England was due to no voluntary act of hers. Cases such as *Larsonneur* have been deployed to show that a criminal justice system which forgets that proof of wrong-**doing** is a precondition of criminal liability is apt to criminalise morally innocent people.[14] Without wishing to approve the actual decision, situational liability in general is not an unacceptable basis for liability, however. It is simply the clearest example of how people may be morally and therefore criminally responsible for things 'which happen to them' if it is reasonable for them to have avoided getting caught up in the relevant state of affairs or event. Such a view was taken in the American case of *Martin*.[15] Police officers took the drunken defendant from his own home and subsequently arrested him for '(appearing) in a public place, (manifesting) a drunken condition . . .' Deciding that the defendant was not guilty, Simpson J held that the statute implicitly presupposed a 'voluntary' appearance and here there obviously was none. The objection to a conviction on these facts is not that Martin had done nothing for which he could be held responsible. The objection is, rather, that the provision could not enable people to remain on the right side of the law if it could be invoked against people who

[13] PR Glazebrook 'Situational Liability' in PR Glazebrook (ed), *Reshaping the Criminal Law* (Stevens, London, 1978), 108, at 109.
[14] For example G Williams, *Textbook of Criminal Law* (Stevens, London, 1983), 158.
[15] *Martin v State* 31 Ala. app. 334 (1944).

conscientiously limited the occasions upon which they became intoxi-cated to when they were in their own home. Martin would have had less obvious grounds for complaint if, say, the police had removed him, at the request of the householder, from a house where he had been invited but had refused to quit and had then arrested him in the street.[16]

The keenest difficulty in locating physical action as the touchstone of criminal wrongdoing concerns the status of so-called omissions. Criminal law the world over punishes not only for what one does but also for what one does not do.

Case 1

Eve deliberately starves Adam, her baby, to death.

It is uncontroversial that Eve would suffer severe moral criticism for her conduct and would also be the subject of criminal liability for homicide. In the face of this conclusion, the American theorist Michael Moore has nevertheless argued that omissions based liability stands outside the natural compass of the criminal law. In his view Case 1 is exceptional and represents a case where the criminal law is forced to abjure a key building block in the construction of criminal liability to ensure that key societal goals are not trumped by moral freedom. Outside such special cases omissions are not a proper subject of crim-inal liability.[17]

Case 2

Cain, a bystander, callously watches while Abel, a baby, drowns in a pond.

Moore's explanation why the state is not entitled to punish is that if we look for some behaviour of Cain's by which to account for the baby's demise we find literally nothing—a non-event. An omission is simply the absence of action, that is of a 'volitionally-caused bodily

---

[16] Lanham, 'Larsonneur Revisited' [1976] *Crim LR* 276; Hart *Punishment and Responsibility: Essays in the Philosophy of Law* (Clarendon Press, Oxford, 1968); cf Norrie, *Crime Reason and History* (Weidenfeld and Nicolson, London, 1993), 120–2; W Wilson, *Criminal Law: Doctrine and Theory* (Longmans, London, 1998), 69–70; cf A Simester, 'Voluntary Action' (1998) *Buffalo Criminal Law Review* 403 at 409 *et seq.*

[17] M Moore, *Act and Crime* (1993), generally for critical discussion see G Fletcher, above n 12.

movement'.[18] The basis upon which we would wish to find him accountable is, therefore, that we disapprove of his attitude—which is contrary to the act requirement. In effect, Moore deduces from the (self-imposed) premise that bodily movement is necessary for action that it is also necessary for criminal liability. A number of possible objections can be posted to this analysis. The first again takes issue with the concept of acts as constituted by (willed) bodily movements. Not scratching one's nose is clearly not the act of scratching one's nose but this does not mean it is not an act. It might be the subject matter of some other act. Bidding activity in auction rooms provides a simple illustration. Professional bidders are sometimes wont to signal their interest in an item secretively, say, by winking their eye or scratching their nose. When the bidding gets too high they withdraw in one of two ways, both effective in alerting the auctioneer to their withdrawal from the transaction. The first is to shake their heads—a bodily movement. The second is to forbear from winking or scratching their nose. Both forms of conduct are equally decisive in fixing the bidder with responsibility. But does such forbearance count as action? The argument holds that it is action if it can be described as such. And so it can. For example, if the bidder later remonstrates with the auctioneer for not knocking down the item to him the auctioneer might well object ' But you withdrew!' If, on the other hand, another customer, who did not engage in bidding for the item, makes a similar complaint, the auctioneer would be more likely to object, before calling for the men in white coats, 'But you did not bid'. Not scratching one's nose will normally be a case of non-action (latter case) but context may constitute it as action (former case).

Forbearance is often described as negative action, or an omission, in contradistinction to positive action. On this view when behaviour takes the form of not doing something its essential nature as action will typically be reflected in the language used to describe it. In the above example the first bidder 'withdrew' from the bidding. The other 'non-scratchers' simply did not bid. Exerting oneself to stay motionless whether for fun or for self-preservation is described as 'playing dead' or 'playing possum'. We have no problem, particularly when these things occur on stage, describing these things as 'acting'. Likewise in cases of homicide, both starving and drowning are properly described as acts of killing. So we would say that Eve 'starved' Adam 'to death'.

---

[18] M Moore, *Act and Crime* (1993), 350.

But we would not use the word 'starve' to describe the conduct of Ruth, Eve's nextdoor neighbour, who also 'failed' to feed the infant even supposing she knew of the latter's plight.[19]

As this last example indicates, designating omissions as forms of action does not address the basis upon which liability in cases of non-action is usually justified. As Fletcher points out, omissions cannot be described simply as cases of inaction. They are special cases of inaction, namely those where, as with affirmative action, the omitter plays some morally significant part of the process by which the relevant criminal harm occurs. It would be wrong indeed to subject to public condemnation all those who failed to do anything to prevent Abel's death but the criminal law, like the morality it is based on, does not presume to do so. Conventional morality does not hold Richard Branson responsible every time a homeless person dies for spending money on balloon trips rather than shelter for the needy.[20] Moral condemnation is restricted to those who bear moral responsibility. And criminal punishment is further restricted by other liability filters so as to ensure a proper balance is effected between individual autonomy and social defence.

With this focus, omissions do not constitute exceptions to a liability paradigm requiring willed bodily movements but are simple instantiations of the way responsibility attends our deeds generally rather than our actions specifically. The act requirement specifies nothing more controversial than that it is wrong for the state to punish in the absence of some wrongful and/or harmful deed. It does not specify the nature or form of such deed, only that there should be one. Reflecting its social counterpart (criminal) wrongdoing consists not only of doing what we should not do but also **not doing what we should do**.[21] A child is at least as likely to be censured for failing to wash her hands before a meal as getting her hands dirty in the first place. A partner is as likely to be censured for failing to put the cat out as dropping toothpaste on the carpet, or offending an in-law. In each case censure finds its basic justification in an unsatisfied expectation that the subject should behave in a particular way. That censure is an acceptable response in cases of culpable omissions can be tested by examining some typical excuses or

---

[19] On the other hand shooting but not starving is an act of violence.

[20] This is not to say that cogent moral positions cannot be advanced in support. J-P Sartre, *Existentialism and Humanism,* ch 3.

[21] The opposite is also true. Credit may be won by omitting to do something confounding normal expectations. Children, and prisoners enduring torture, are routinely praised for not talking, the guards at Buckingham palace for not moving.

other condemnation avoidance strategies. These will not, typically, attempt to deflect censure by relying upon the absence of any positive act. The appropriate strategy will be an attempt to deny authorship as in 'That toothpaste is pink. Mine's white.' Or voluntariness as in 'I removed the top very carefully but the tube was too full. The toothpaste just jumped out at me.' Or causation as in 'I admit I told your father he was an interfering old slime-ball but he didn't hear me. He left the party early because he was bored.' Or fault as in 'I couldn't find the cat. I thought you had put her out.' Only in one case will the conduct's status **as an omission** form the basis of a repudiation of censure. This is when there is no expectation that the subject behave in the prescribed fashion. 'Put the cat out? It's your cat. I've never put that cat out in my life!' In short, the act requirement is not meaningfully contradicted by Eve's liability for the death of Adam. Liability is not imposed **in spite of** Eve having done nothing. Nor indeed would it be if Cain were similarly held liable. It is imposed **because** she has done nothing in violation of a binding social obligation. We hold responsible only those whose conduct, by flouting accepted standards of behaviour, is deemed to make a difference to the unfolding of human events. When this occurs, whether the conduct takes the form of bodily movement or passive inaction, the basic minimum requirement for criminal liability is met.[22]

A job of work still needs to be done, however, before we can account for the widespread tendency in criminal justice systems to punish Eve but not Cain. From a consequentialist point of view since human agency is equally involved in both cases, and since the resulting harm is identical, the impetus to criminalise both forms of wrongdoing should, one would have thought, be comparable. From a retributive point of view both cases seem to evince comparable blameworthiness given that in both cases the accused knew what his/her conduct 'meant' for the victim.[23] There is then no obvious moral basis upon which to differentiate acts from omissions.[24]

Even were we to concede that causing harm by affirmative action is morally worse than permitting harm by passive inaction, there are difficulties attending the analytical separation of acts and omissions. It is

---

[22] See for example R Shapira, 'Willed Bodily Movement' in (1998) *Buffalo Criminal Law Review* 349 at 351. But one can be punished for acting upon and even, rarely, for articulating such an idea, belief or desire.

[23] A Honore, 'Are Omissions Less Culpable?' in P Cane and J Stapleton (eds), *Essays for Patrick Atiyah* (OUP, Oxford 1991), 31 at 40 *et seq*.

[24] For further discussion, see ch 4.

clearly of central importance, if liability may depend upon it, to know whether given conduct constitutes one rather than the other. Consider the following variation of Case 2.

Case 3

Cain, on seeing Abel, at first begins to effect a rescue by dragging Abel towards the side. But then, on realising it is his dreaded neighbour's son, desists so as to let the boy drown.

Is the cause of Abel's death Cain's act—releasing his grip—or his omission—failing to see the project through?[25] On first blush it seems to be his act. Abel met his death via a causal sequence which included the kind of bodily movements which we readily associate with drowning someone. On the other hand, if we ask ourselves what provokes us to condemn Cain's behaviour the obvious answer is what he has **not** done rather than what he has done. Cain's actions clearly form part of the sequence of events by which Abel met his death, but Abel has been left in no worse position than if Cain had done nothing or had simply rubbed his hands in glee.[26] Our outrage may be further stoked by the circumstances surrounding the abandonment of the rescue but it is surely not prompted by it. But other cases are less clear.

Case 4

Beaumont and Fletcher are struggling in open seas following a ship wreck. Fearing for his life Beaumont snatches a life belt just before Fletcher is able to secure it. Fletcher drowns as a consequence.

Clearly lawyers and laypersons alike appreciate that Beaumont is innocent of any homicide. What is less clear is how we account for this. Is it to do with the quality of Beaumont's action, of his motivation, is it to do with the causal insufficiency of his conduct, or perhaps a combination of these? It is possible to present an argument that Beaumont's conduct is not the *actus reus* of murder in so far as his conduct is self rather than other-regarding. Suppose Shakespeare and Marlow are marooned and starving on a desert island, looking for food and that

---

[25] M Moore, *Act and Crime*, 27.
[26] *Ibid* 26–7.

Shakespeare finds the only food on the island—a coconut—and scoffs the lot. Marlow soon after dies of starvation. Would we say that Shakespeare's eating of the coconut is the conduct out of which potential liability for homicide is to be fashioned? I think most people would say not. Eating coconuts is self regarding. It is the kind of thing people do to stay alive not to kill. This kind of pre-theoretical analysis describes an analytical tendency to determine whether conduct is an act or omission by reference to a broader causal inquiry. We ask first what caused the death and then we use our answer to that question to structure our interpretation of the relevant deed. Using this approach Beaumont's conduct in Case 4 can be interpreted as an omission rather than an act which generates the welcome conclusion that he is not liable for homicide because of the absence of any duty to give succour to Fletcher.

The removal of patients from life support is a commonly used illustration of the tenuous nature of the analytical distinction between acts and omissions.[27] If done by appropriate medical personnel, in *bona fide* discharge of their duty, such removal is generally analysed as an omission. Here the reasoning behind this is that the patient is left in no worse position than if he had not been connected in the first place as in Case 3 and the doctors were under no duty to intervene.[28] But there are clear differences to be discerned between such cases and Case 3. What Cain does or does not do adds nothing to the reason why Abel eventually dies. He was drowning, as Marlow was starving, before the aborted rescue and he continues to drown thereafter. This cannot strictly be said, however, of the medical disconnection, where the patient's status has been changed from a (relatively) stable to an unstable state and the instrument of this change is, undoubtedly, a 'calorie burning' activity. Or, in the analysis of Jonathan Bennett, the disconnection is an act because it closes off action-opportunities (eg, going to the movies, having a cup of tea) which would otherwise be present.[29] After all, if the disconnection had been performed by an interloper bent on mischief it would be difficult to argue otherwise than that it was the (act of the) miscreant which killed the patient. In like fashion, if Cain had lifted Abel up and brought him to the side only to threw him back in again on realising Abel's identity we would seem to be correct in

---

[27] I Kennedy, *Treat Me Right* (OUP, Oxford, 1988) 170 *et seq.*
[28] J Thomson, 'A Defense of Abortion' (1971) *1 Phil. and Pub. Aff.* 47; *Airedale NHS Trust v Bland* [1993] AC 369.
[29] J Bennett, *The Act Itself* (OUP, Oxford, 1995).

describing Cain as having drowned Abel rather than as having permitted him to drown.[30] It is certainly puzzling if not downright unsatisfactory, when there is so fragile a moral and analytical basis for differentiating acts and omissions, that so much should depend upon it.[31]

George Fletcher has done much to clarify our thinking as to why criminalising omissions may be a problem.[32] It is not that there is some inherent quality in affirmative action which renders it uniquely appropriate to be the subject matter of criminal wrongdoing. Omissions can cause harm just as actions can and can be accompanied by states of mind comparable to those accompanying action. The common law ensures that these elements are always satisfied in respect of crimes of commission by criminalising omitters only where they stand in a **relationship of responsibility** with the victim. The presence of this relationship provides a cogent basis by which to designate the omitter's act as causal. Clearly, for example, Eve's behaviour 'made the difference' between life and death justifying treating her as if she had wrought her harm by affirmative action.[33] It also is capable of converting various loose states of moral blameworthiness into something approaching the degree of responsibility captured by typical mens rea words such as intention and recklessness. Intending to kill someone, for example, suggests some degree of commitment to the outcome or the process by which the outcome is rendered inevitable for which some form of physical activity is the obvious packaging. In the absence of any duty of intervention Cain, were he to be charged with the murder of Abel, would surely be entitled to object that desiring someone's death is not the same as intending to kill them 'Yes', he might concede. 'I wanted Abel dead, but I drew the line at killing him. It is wrong to kill someone. If I had intended his death I would have smothered him in his pram, but I did not want him dead that much.' Where such duty exists such objection loses potency and we are apt to assign a special normative (goal directed) significance to Cain's disturbing attitude.

---

[30] M Moore, *Act and Crime*, 27. For an interesting discussion of these kind of cases see L Alexander, 'Criminal Liability for Omissions' University of San Diego School of Law, Working Paper 22, 2000–01.

[31] P Singer, *Rethinking Life and Death* (OUP, Oxford, 1995), 195–6; J Bennett, *The Act Itself*.

[32] G Fletcher, *Rethinking Criminal Law* (Little Brown and Company, Boston, Toronto, 1978), ch 8.

[33] See generally A Leavens, ' A Causation Approach to Criminal Omissions' (1988) 76 *Cal LR* 547.

More broadly, sometimes the fact that the defendant has **not done something** is the very reason why we might wish to punish. This is reflected in the routine and uncontroversial raft of crimes of injurious conduct rather than harmful result.[34] The external elements of these statutory crimes of omission take the form of the defendant **not doing something,** say, submit a tax return, or provide a specimen[35] or report a road traffic accident[36] which he is placed under a legal duty to perform. The major objection to such explicit statutory duties is a general objection to omissions-based liability. It questions the propriety of calling people to action in the service of collective or individual interests. A second objection is centred in the propriety of criminalising omissions in cases of core wrongdoing. Unless specifically legislated for, it may be contrary to the legality principle to punish those whose contribution to a harmful occurrence is simply that they did nothing to prevent it.

AUTONOMY-BASED OBJECTIONS TO CRIMINALISING OMISSIONS

The moral legitimacy of state coercion is generally thought to be predicated upon the fact that it is a necessary precondition of human freedom and autonomy. Paradoxically, although the rules of criminal law are experienced as restrictions on autonomy, controlling affirmative action generally enhances our opportunities to be effective authors of our own destiny. When people punch us or steal from us they are seeking to be authors of our destiny as well as their own. It is right then to restrict their ability to do so. Punishing omissions, however, seems to compromise rather than enhance human freedom and autonomy since it makes demands of us which may well require us to subjugate our own interests to those of others. Is this not inconsistent with the point of the criminal law?[37]

The major philosophies of punishment give essentially contradictory responses as one would expect. From the utilitarian tradition, for example, we might expect justifying arguments in favour of the criminalisation of omissions if this would enhance general social welfare.

---

[34] G Fletcher, *Rethinking Criminal Law*, 421.

[35] Section 4 RTA 1988.

[36] Section 170 (4) Road Traffic Act 1988.

[37] Macauley *Introductory Report upon the Indian Penal Code* (Longmans Green & Co, 1898), 113 *et seq.*

And yet within the utilitarian tradition it is generally argued that punishment is not justified as a mechanism for enforcing good behaviour and morality. Although it is generally assumed to support it, utilitarianism affords little guidance therefore as to the propriety of punishing omissions. Is freedom a prior value to utility or is it subjugated to it? The priority given to freedom is more obvious in retributivism.[38] The backward (wrong-addressing) rather than forward-looking (social engineering) aspect of punishment seems inconsistent with the point of statutory omissions. Even here, however, for the reasons canvassed earlier there is no knock-down argument why immoral omissions should not be considered sufficiently blameworthy to deserve punishing.

This returns us full circle to a matter discussed earlier, namely the desirability of conceiving two separate paradigms of criminal liability together with their own specific organisational premises, that is, of prevention and condemnation.[39] In this context it is important to distinguish two types of affirmative duties. The first are the routine social responsibilities which arise out of the structural claims of people living together in a modern community. Such communities need to organise themselves so that collective as well as individual needs are satisfied. Unbridled individualism is inconsistent with society's structural integrity and a strong social structure is a precondition of individual self-fulfilment. Without rules criminalising failures to submit tax returns or wear seat belts the problems posed for society trickle down to compromise the very framework within which individual autonomy can be enjoyed. An autonomy-respecting society may then constitute itself through rules by which welfare routinely trumps autonomy. The only crucial limiting feature is that the proscribing rule operates as a standard capable of enabling the defendant to avoid state coercion and that the trade-off is morally justifiable on an all-things-considered basis. For this reason few are disposed to challenge the propriety of affirmative duties per se. The enforcement of such duties are necessary for society itself to run smoothly and therefore for society's members to flourish as individuals. In this respect they evince no basic dissimilarity with proscriptive rules designed to create the basic framework for communal living. If the requirement to tax one's car or wear a seat belt is an interference with freedom and autonomy, it is no more so

[38] N Lacey, (Routledge, London, 1988), 45–6
[39] See ch 2.

than the duty not to exceed the speed limit or not to park in a restricted area.[40] Indeed, as will be apparent from these illustrations the restrictions on freedom represented by the latter rules may be far more onerous. They are continually in force. They come into play typically when most inconvenient. The duty to tax one's car, by contrast, is exhausted in the time it takes to fill out a form and write out a cheque. Even the duty to file a tax return, onerous as it is in its Byzantine complexities, poses no disrespect to the subject as an author of his own destiny. He is given fair warning and he can take his own time. As a general matter of political morality, there is no reason then why affirmative duties should not be subject to the same criteria of criminalisation as proscriptions .

It is the second type of affirmative duty which poses the greatest challenge to the moral legitimacy of state coercion. These are the duties which fall due unpredictably and which may therefore deprive the duty bearer of one of the fundamentals of the autonomous life, namely the right to choose what to do at any given time.[41] An uncontroversial example of such a duty is that requiring drivers of motor vehicles to report a road accident. This duty demands action and action now. It prohibits keeping that doctor's appointment, attending that meeting, or posting that letter. No action will satisfy it other than making a report. Liability for theft, violence and other crimes of affirmative action, by contrast, leave the actor will a full range of options. The actor may not steal, kill or maim but everything else remains open to her. The justification for imposing such a duty in the eyes of its advocates is the same for imposing any other duty. While the focal case of criminal liability may well involve a lawless villain raising arms against innocent people or threatening them in their home it is the prevention of harm which lies at the heart of liberal political morality. And harm can be prevented by requiring citizens not merely to refrain from active wrongdoing but also putting right that which goes wrong. The real issue is whether it is reasonable to force citizens to do so and the determination of this issue is not foreclosed by the fact that the harm engendering conduct involves no positive intervention in the world of events. Taking parenthood as a benchmark, society would be prosecuting an

---

[40] J Feinberg, *Harm to Others* (OUP, Oxford, 1984), 164; G Fletcher, *Rethinking Criminal Law* 602; G Fletcher, 'On the Moral Irrelevance of Bodily Movements' (1994) 142 *U Pa L Rev* 1443.

[41] AJ Ashworth, 'The Scope of Criminal Liability for Omissions' (1989) 105 *LQR* 424, at 427.

unusual notion of autonomy if enforcing a duty of protection and care of infants was seen as compromising its realisation. Perhaps more significantly, however, the fact that enforcing the duty interferes with the parent's freedom of action does not strike one as any kind of reason for not doing so. Sometimes autonomy is not the point. Sometimes responsibility trumps autonomy. The question for the criminal law is to determine when.[42]

The full implications of what is at stake in criminalising this second type of omission are encountered in discussion concerning the desirability of imposing on all people, not merely on parents, spouses, those who have assumed such a duty, or those who are responsible for first creating a peril, a duty of rescue. Many voices have been raised in support of such a duty.[43] For example, it has been argued that since modern society is increasingly informed by and is dependent for its strength upon communitarian rather than laissez faire ethics, it is time that this was recognised so as to open up the range of duty situations to include all cases where we would expect individuals to fulfil their basic responsibilities as human beings to their fellow citizens, included among which is a general duty of easy rescue.[44] Such a duty is at present unrecognised in many jurisdictions because it is here that the autonomy-based objection really begins to bite. The criminal law's major function on this view is the prevention of wrongdoing not the promotion of good habits. We punish murderers not just because they are wicked but because they attack the victim's interests. The difference, then, between affirmative duties such as the duty to rescue and traditional criminal proscriptions is that enforcing the former is apt to stigmatise the very people which liberal society cherishes—those who go around minding their own business and whose destiny is to leave no kind of mark on society let alone a bloody one.[45] In this context, enforcing a duty which falls due unpredictably renders criminalisation a matter of chance as much as a matter of choice or disposition. The notion of wrongdoing conjured up by a failure to satisfy a duty of rescue is one which is unresponsive to the social desirability of inhabiting a society in which passivity was the only sin.[46] Consistent

---

[42] It is not just that the parent has assumed responsibility for the child although such assumption allows us to take the inference that the parent has chosen responsibility before autonomy and so chooses also the consequences of failure.

[43] AJ Ashworth, above n 41.

[44] Cf N Lacey, (1988) ch 8 .

[45] M Moore, *Act and Crime*, 58–60.

[46] *Ibid.*

with this, it has been argued that the imposition of duties to act based upon well-meaning communitarian ideals could threaten the liberal order. If the basis of individual criminal liability is to be reconstructed in terms of what the ties of community morally require us to do, then the individuals are rendered susceptible to sanction for behaving in the very way that Western capitalism encourages and requires for its survival, namely the rational pursuit of self interest in a community of like-minded individuals.[47]

LEGALITY-BASED OBJECTIONS TO CRIMINALISING OMISSIONS

The discussion so far has emphasised those statutory offences which explicitly designate failures and omissions as the conduct element in a criminal offence. We have considered arguments for and against enforcing such affirmative duties of action. The arguments against reduce to a concern that such duties unduly interfere with individual autonomy. The argument for is that there is nothing inherent in the concept of an omission which make its criminalisation more or less intrusive upon individual liberty than for a comparable proscription. The question in each case is whether the advantages secured are outweighed by the loss of freedom attendant upon enforcing the duty, whether enforcing the duty is necessary and effective in securing these advantages, and whether the enforcement will provoke countervailing social harms. The one case where special caution should be exercised in criminalising omissions is in connection with those affirmative duties which are open-ended and/or fall due unpredictably. Such affirmative duties will typically be more onerous than a negative duty since they do not always specify what must be done to avoid liability and also substantially restrict the duty bearer's range of choices. These considerations do not necessarily argue against criminalisation, however. Rather, they counsel caution in ensuring that the usual conditions for criminalisation are met. In particular, since the burden on liberty is high the countervailing advantages justifying imposing that burden must be correspondingly high.[48]

Distinct problems are raised in respect of core crimes such as murder, wounding and assault, whose conduct element is defined in such a

---

[47] A Norrie, *Crime Reason and History*, 1993, 130–1.

[48] Ie, criminalisation must be effective and necessary and not such as would provoke harmful social side effects.

way as to suggest some form of active wrongdoing. Interpreting actions to include omissions may fall foul of the legality principle outside clear cases, such as starving or neglect by a mother, which is in any event universally treated as an affirmative act of killing, rather than simply a 'letting die'. The objection of legality is rooted in the premise that criminal liability demands a perfect match between the conduct of the accused for which he is subjected to punishment and the conduct element in a (pre-existing) criminal offence.[49] The state has the moral authority to punish only if the wrongdoer has conducted himself in a way which the state has explicitly directed that he should not. People should be punished for offending a legal rule not simply because their behaviour is injurious or offensive. It is important to understand the nature of the potential objection. It is not, as explained earlier, that action and inaction are so conceptually and morally distinct that it is inappropriate to run the two together in the conduct element of criminal offences. This is not the case. Indeed, some core crimes are explicitly constituted as capable of being 'committed' by omission. Gross negligence manslaughter is an obvious example. Its fundamental core of wrongdoing expresses neglect and failure rather than deed. Theft, less obviously, has a conduct element which consists of an appropriation of property belonging to another. Appropriation is defined as 'assuming rights of ownership'. Assuming rights of ownership will, no doubt, normally involve some form of affirmative action. When a shoplifter appropriates property his muscles 'move all over the place'. But appropriation is defined in such a way as to indicate that activity in the form of bodily movement is not of the essence. For instance, it includes cases where a person first comes by property innocently and then 'assumes rights of ownership over the property by keeping or dealing with it as owner'. How might a person commit theft in this way? Jack might find a wallet, decide to hand it to the police and then change his mind and decide to keep it or spend the money. Betty might borrow a book and then decide to sell it or keep it. In each case it is conceptually apt to describe what Jack and Betty have done as theft and also linguistically apt to define the conduct element in terms of an assumption of rights of ownership rather than in terms of some form of affirmative action, such as taking and carrying away.

   Where, on the other hand, an offence is articulated in such a way as to indicate that it is (certain forms of) action which constitutes the rele-

---

[49] G Fletcher, *Rethinking Criminal Law*, 628–30.

vant criminal wrongdoing, criminalising omissions may have a number of undesirable effects. First, it may render liable those who have not been expressly alerted to the prospect that their conduct fell foul of the law. Secondly, it may render unclear, for those who have been alerted, exactly what is necessary to avoid liability. Thirdly, it may result in the attachment of an inappropriate criminal label. These dangers are generally avoided in statutory crimes, particularly those of a regulatory nature. This is due to the principle of strict statutory construction which is still of general application in the regulatory arena. Statutory provisions demand textual clarity so as to act as workable and effective standards of correct behaviour.[50] If a statute instructs me in clear terms not to drop litter I should have no reason to fear a prosecution for not providing litter bins in my park, or not clearing up the litter dropped by visitors. In the case of result crimes articulating forms of moral wrongdoing rather than, as in the litter example, specifying the parameters of prohibited actions these dangers are provoked however. If a statute tells me not to wound or kill another person should I not fear a prosecution for not alerting my infant companion to the barbed wire strewn across his path or removing him from the railway line onto which he had strayed? If things turn out for the worse and he is wounded or killed, given that these events are morally attributable to me, what is the objection, if any, to saying that I have wounded or killed him?[51]

The operational theory of the criminal law structures liability for such omissions via its general rules of attribution, in particular the causation and fault requirements. But moral responsibility, without more, is not enough to ground criminal liability. A liability paradigm riven by the distinction between acts and omissions requires courts to make further judgments as to the type of context within which liability for omissions is permissible. No such judgment is necessary in cases of affirmative action since stabbing, drowning, shooting, and so on speak clearly to the wrong which they embody. With omissions, by contrast, liability is filtered through the requirement that the omitter be under a legal duty to prevent the occurrence of the relevant consequence.[52] Courts have to decide, in other words, who should be labelled a wrong-doer by omission. Between the two extremes of parent and stranger

[50] W Wilson, *Criminal Law: Doctrine and Theory*, 69–70, ch 1 generally.

[51] L Katz, *Bad Acts and Guilty Minds* (Chicago University Press, Chicago, 1987), 143.

[52] 'where acts are made punishable on the ground that they have caused, or have been intended to cause, or have been known to be likely to cause a certain evil effect shall be punishable in the same manner provided that such omissions were on other grounds illegal.'

represented by Cases 1 and 2 lies an enormous range of cases where the existence or otherwise of a duty to prevent harm is subject to the common law's overall process of 'rolling review'.[53] It is here that individuals are particularly vulnerable to omissions-based liability. Certainly it is true that existing case law structures the range of duty situations to a large extent and therefore gives some warning as to who is in the firing line. If I am the infant's parent, or have assumed a duty, or I have led the child into danger I am liable if I do not intervene to save her. If I am a disconnected stranger, I am not. But these are judicially created duties and so are, in effect, judicially-created offences. The courts have taken on the role of filtering cases suitable for the imposition of a duty from those which are not. This includes, in cases falling outside the formal scope of an existing duty but within its moral catchment area, whether one should be recognised. If one spouse owes a duty to prevent the death of another who has taken a drugs overdose, should a similar duty be recognised in the case of unmarried partners, or 'weekend lovers', or emotionally detached flat sharers. Again if A falls asleep smoking a cigarette in B's bed owes a duty to extinguish the resulting fire, does the responsibility extend, if A disdains to bother, to C, A's sleeping partner? Again, does a duty extend to other cases where no fault can be assigned, as where attending responsibly to a fire in a domestic hearth causes burning material to jump out and set furniture alight? Does it extend to liability for manslaughter if death ensues?

These are judgments which must be answered on a casuistic or paradigmatic basis, with other analogous duty situations being used as stepping stones to bridge the gap between old and new. Nevertheless they are made *ex post*, rather than *ex ante* and therefore raise the prospect that the defendant will be punished by a law which was not designed to cover the wrongdoing and was not in existence at the time of the supposed wrongdoing. The justification, such as it is, for resiling from the ethic of non-retroactivity is that in most cases the individual will have done wrong and he will know this. If a particularly radical judge decides then to recognise a limited duty of rescue encompassing such situations, we might properly feel that the omitter is getting his 'just deserts'. Should he be able to rely on the punishing state's possibly eccentric rules of attribution, when he himself has all the necessary moral information to hand to guide him in his choices?[54] As long as

---

[53] G Fletcher, 'On the Moral Irrelevance of Bodily Movements' (1994) 142 *UU Pa LR* 1443.

[54] G Fletcher, *Rethinking Criminal Law*, 631–2.

new duty situations develop incrementally in order to reflect what is generally agreed to be the moral foundations of good citizenship, justice of a sort is done. If there are cogent reasons for society to expect rather than merely hope an individual will take steps to prevent harm, such that the individual will understand the nature and scope of his obligation, the gap between the demands of law and morality can be closed. On this view it would clearly be contrary to legality for the courts to legislate a general duty of easy rescue since there would be no reason, other than a recognition of widely held moral aspirations, for an individual to understand that he, possibly before all others, was the person fixed, say, with the duty of saving this child from drowning.

On the other hand, it is a development perfectly in keeping with existing doctrinal dynamics for new duty situations to emerge from existing doctrinal chrysalises such as the assumption of duty, special relationship and causing of danger categories. Indeed there is arguably room for quite distinct new duty situations. One such, already recognised to a limited degree in the field of tort, is the responsibility owed by occupiers of property to ensure dangers which materialise under their occupation do not endanger others.[55] Without such responsibility, house occupancy is a potential source of danger in societies such as ours where privacy enjoys such rigorous protection, since persons threatened by fires or other hazards on other people's property will have scant ability to protect themselves. There seems every reason why this reasoning should not be applicable in the criminal law. Society as well as individuals is threatened when neighbours are not responsive to the basic minimum requirements of community. The development of such narrowly-defined duties are consistent with maintaining the integrity of a society based upon interdependence and self-interest where duties arise to satisfy social expectations rather than moral aspirations.

COMMUNICATING WRONGDOING

An important concern which remains to be discussed is the propriety of assigning the self-same criminal label to omitters as we do to committers. To analyse this concern some consideration must be given to the nature and constitution of criminal prohibitions. In a later chapter it

---

[55] See W Wilson, *Criminal Law: Doctrine and Theory*, 85–6.

will be contended that criminal prohibitions serve to declare norms rather than simply state the penal consequences of performing certain forms of harmful action. Stabbing someone, for example, is a morally significant way of hurting someone. It provokes a particular public response and addresses itself to particular moral concerns of the population. Suppressing this 'action element' in the notion of 'wounding' by, for example, allowing liability to follow culpable failures to prevent others being wounded seems to sever the link between the moral wrong we perceive in a given action and an offence label. In so doing it confounds a common moral intuition that the 'wrongdoing of causing harm (say, actually drowning someone with your own hands) is greater than or at least different from merely standing by and failing to intervene to prevent it.'[56] Whether or not it is the case that passive acquiescence in the occurrence of harm is worse than taking active steps to produce is a matter for debate. One can quite easily, for example, cite examples of where the opposite is the case. What is morally worse, shooting a child to prevent the agony of her burning to death in a flaming inferno one is powerless to prevent, or failing to save a similar child from a similar fate by the simple mechanism of unlocking the door behind which she is trapped? What is surely undeniable, however, is that they are **different** wrongs, if such they are, and this should be reflected in the way they are treated at the doctrinal level. Where offence labels articulate a particular form of moral wrongdoing as the basis of liability it is for a purpose, namely to set the seal of (dis)approval on a particular social practice, which structures our moral response.

As John Gardner has reminded us, it is important to distinguish between action-reasons and outcome-reasons in the evaluation of conduct.[57] These are often conflated, leaving some to conclude that there is no moral difference worth recording at the level of offence definitions between, say, a stabbing and a poisoning, or between a killing and doing something (including 'nothing') which has death as its consequence.[58] Since in both cases there are reasons to prevent the outcome occurring criminal doctrine should respect, through censure and pun-

---

[56] G Fletcher, 'Fall and Rise of Criminal Theory' (1998) *Buffalo Criminal Law Rreview* 275, at 291.

[57] 'On the General Part of the Criminal Law' in RA Duff (ed), *Philosophy and the Criminal Law* (CUP, Cambridge, 1998), 211–3, 244–9; and see J Raz, *The Morality of Freedom* (Clarendon Press, Oxford, 1986), ch 6.

[58] See for example AJ Ashworth, 'The Scope of Criminal Liability for Omissions' (1989) 105 *LQR* 424. Cf G Williams who follows the Gardner/Raz axis, albeit with less theoretical flamboyance.

ishment, the decision of the actor not to be guided in his behaviour by that reason. Not all ways of bringing about a particular consequence excite the same moral response, however. We discriminate between ways of killing and ways of causing death. So, procuring the death of another, if properly termed murder, is nevertheless doctrinally distinct from murder by killing, reflecting the consideration that there are (action-) reasons not to procure a killing which may be expected to operate independently of the (action-) reasons not to kill. Indeed, in extreme cases, this fact may even serve to block the normal impetus to attribute a consequence to the intentional action of the actor. One example is the offence of perjury. It is uncontentious doctrine that murder cannot be committed by perjury. Why is this? Commentators are wont to account for this as a policy decision.[59] But it may equally simply reflect the gap which sometimes opens up in moral evaluation between action and outcome reasons. Causing someone's death through perjury is just not a case of murder and there is no sense in pretending otherwise. It is entirely appropriate, therefore, given that law seeks to communicate society's value structure, that this fact is reflected in doctrine.

Rather than suppressing the distinction between acts and omissions, we might rather wish to record the distinctiveness of the action-reasons against killing or harming others by formally legislating crimes of omission.[60] Such offences are traditionally constituted as conduct crimes the *actus reus* of which is tied to the failure to rescue (say, a drowning person) rather than the result (say, death). There is no logical impediment however to legislating result crimes of omission. One easy way of doing so is to define result crimes so as to remove any action element. The Law Commission have proposed the replacement of the action element of wounding and inflicting grievous bodily harm with that of 'causing serious injury'.[61] There is then no barrier to convicting those who cause such harm by omission, assuming the relevant fault and causation elements can be established. For the reasons suggested above this smacks of throwing the baby out with the bath water. There is a strong case for retaining the action element in crimes of violence. This could be supplemented, where necessary, with specific result crimes of omission. An advantage accruing from so doing is that

[59] Smith and Hogan (2002), 57.
[60] See Ashworth and Steiner, 'Criminal Omissions and Public Duties: The French Experience' [1990] *LS* 153.
[61] Law Commission No 218, *Legislating the Criminal Code* (1993) Cl 2–4, Draft Bill.

it would ease the inevitable tendency to suppress distinctive features in the fault and causation elements where omissions are concerned. If we examine murder, for example, not only is a different test of causation applicable[62] it involves also, as we shall see in the next chapter, a specially constituted fault element which is sensitive to the basis upon which we blame the omitter, namely an evaluation of her conduct on a balance of reasons. This reflects the fact that we blame the omitter not simply for her failure to prevent harm but rather for her failure to satisfy our expectations. This requires special attention to be paid to the context within which the omission took place. It also demands that attention be paid both to the reasons supporting action and to the reasons given for not acting. What efforts does one need to engage in to satisfy whatever duty has been found owing? What difficulties was the omitter subjected to? What was her perception of the situation, and so on?[63] Such considerations as these are typically peripheral to the proof of guilt in core cases of wrongdoing but are surely central in cases of omission.[64]

---

[62] See ch 6.

[63] CF Norrie, (1993) 130–1,

[64] L Alexander, 'Affirmative Duties and the Limits of Self-Sacrifice' (1996) 15 *Law and Philosophy* 65.

4

Criminal Wrongdoing: Voluntariness

IN THE PREVIOUS chapter we examined the act requirement, the governing premise in the constitution of criminal wrongdoing, and considered the contention that this equated to the requirement that the defendant perform some 'volitionally caused bodily movement'. It was suggested that conceiving of acts simply in terms of bodily movements was not convincing not least because it leaves unexplained and unaccounted for the empirical reality of criminal doctrine which embraces actions, states of affairs, failures and forbearances. In this chapter we shall concentrate upon the other facet of the act requirement, namely what it is about the occurrence of certain events, say the death of Abel or the destruction of Rome, which sponsors the view that we are responsible for them and so properly the subject of moral evaluation.

In traditional commentaries upon the criminal law it is said that the basic minimum of moral responsibility generally and criminal responsibility specifically is voluntariness, whether of action or omission.[1] This is presupposed by the very constitution of liberal society by which the state gains its authority to punish not as a means of subjugating that individual's will to the greater good of society but in order to create the conditions under which individuals may assuredly be authors of their own destiny.[2] The rules function to support the rights of individuals to choose how they wish to live their lives.[3] In a sense then a requirement of voluntariness of action informs the natural scope of the criminal law

[1] See for example GE Moore, *Ethics* (Thornton Butterworth, 1912); JL Austin, 'A Plea for Excuses' *Proceedings of the Aristotelian Society Vol 57* (1956–7) 1; HLA Hart, *Punishment and Responsibility: Essays in the Philosophy of Law* (Clarendon Press, Oxford, 1988), ch 4; AJ Ashworth, *Principles of Criminal Law* (OUP, Oxford, 1999), 100.

[2] Although even in authoritarian systems criminal liability will generally be negated where behaviour is involuntary this is not because it is a core value. It has been known, for example, for members of a family to be victimised for the misdeeds of another. HLA Hart, *Punishment and Responsibility*, 12.

[3] See generally AJ Ashworth, *Principles of Criminal Law*, ch 2; J Raz, *The Morality of Freedom* (Clarendon Press, Oxford, 1986) 148–62.

in liberal society. Informing the constitution of offences into external and mental elements and of all theories of punishment is an assumption about the nature of human beings and the part they play in the world of events. Implicit in each is the assumption of free will and that social harms can be morally attributed to people's choices. It would not only be unjust, no purpose would be served by punishing people if human behaviour was not susceptible to normative or physiological control, say, because our genes predetermined all our moves in the manner of a sophisticated game-boy computer programme.[4]

For crimes of mens rea the voluntariness requirement is normally guaranteed by the definitional elements of intention, knowledge or foresight. If A uses B's resisting hand to hit C or trips B so that he stumbles and falls against C there is no voluntary action of B and no definitional fault upon which to harness responsibility for the outcome. For crimes of strict liability, which do not require proof of a specified attitude of mind accompanying the act in question, the voluntariness requirement plays a crucial role in ensuring that there is some tangible basis upon which it might be supposed that punishment is deserved or serves some useful purpose. At its most basic to act voluntarily—to be an author of a criminal wrong—means that the relevant event can be attributed to something the individual has done rather than, say, to someone else or to a natural occurrence. The state does not punish involuntary conduct for the same reason that it does not punish animals, the insane or children. This would not only be unjust it would be inappropriate, just as it would be inappropriate to hold the runaway train responsible for colliding with the school bus or a dog responsible for biting the postman.[5] The moral claim to avoid punishment involved is, on the face of it, more basic than with other excuses. Since all crimes require proof of an *actus reus* and since an act or omission to act is the basic building block of an *actus reus* conduct which is involuntary does not count as an act (or omission).[6] So if A has a heart attack at the wheel of his car and careers through a red traffic light the basis of his claim to avoid punishment is not simply that that he was not at fault but that he was not even the author of the relevant conduct. He was not, in effect, the 'driver' of the car. Similarly if M fails to save

---

[4] W Wilson, *Criminal Law: Doctrine and Theory* (Longmans, London, 1998), 30–3.

[5] KJM Smith and W Wilson, 'Impaired Voluntariness and Criminal Responsibility' [1993] *OJLS* 69; cf EP Evans, *The Criminal Prosecution and Capital Punishment of Animals* (Faber and Faber, London, 1987).

[6] AJ Ashworth, *Principles of Criminal Law*, 101.

L her drowning child because she is pinioned to the ground by K she has not 'omitted' to save the child. An omission to do something, it goes without saying, presupposes the capacity to do so which here is absent.[7] In this chapter I aim to examine the cogency of this position. After discussion of the notion of voluntariness and its relevance to criminal responsibility, I shall consider whether a meaningful distinction can be drawn between the exculpatory grounds of involuntary behaviour and those of orthodox excuses. The view will be advanced, as can be seen most obviously in connection with omissions, that involuntariness is best understood to embody variable standards according to the context within which it is relied upon.

CHARACTERISING VOLUNTARY BEHAVIOUR

The supposition is then that behaviour which is not intentional, knowing or negligent may nevertheless be voluntary and where it is responsibility must be borne for those crimes which do not require proof of such mental attitudes. It is easy to give examples of when voluntariness is lacking—as during epileptic fits and sleepwalking—but what exactly is it which is lacking?

It is traditional to conceive an action as voluntary where the bodily movements which constitute it as action are intentional or volitional.[8] Thus Lord Diplock in *Sheppard*, noted that 'even in absolute offences . . . the physical act relied upon as constituting the offence must be wilful in the limited sense, for which a synonym in the field of criminal law that has now become the legal term of art is "voluntary" '.[9] In the words of Michael Moore action is a movement of the body which follows the will or 'a volitionally caused bodily movement'.[10] Looked at in this way the voluntariness requirement overlaps with without being reducible to the *mens rea* requirement. If A kicks B an opposing footballer his kick is both voluntary and the resulting contact intentional. If A launches a kick at a football, which kick is intercepted by the ankle

---

[7] W Wilson, *Criminal Law: Doctrine and Theory* 87.

[8] The classic exposition is by J Austin, *Lectures on Jurisprudence* (John Murray, London, 1869) 289 *et seq*. For a modern exposition see M Moore, *Act and Crime* (OUP, Oxford 1993) generally.

[9] [1981] AC 394, at 404.

[10] *Act and Crime*, 350; cf K Saunders, 'Voluntary Acts and the Criminal Law: Justifying Culpability Based on the Existence of Volition' (1988) 49 *U Pitt L Rev* 443.

of B, an opposing tackler, the kicking movement is voluntary but the contact unintended. If C kicks A's ankle which causes A's leg to move and make contact with B's leg the movement of A's leg is neither intentional nor voluntary.

These statements reflect a traditional view which treats mind and body as distinct, with mind operating like an (intelligent) ghost in the (body) machine.[11] Action, like any other event on this view, must be caused by something. In the case of events involving human agency it is caused by an exercise of will.[12] In the typical account the desire to act in a particular way is thought to translate itself via the will into the bodily movements which comprise the throwing. So a child might conceive a desire to throw a cup to the floor and then, as might a dance choreographer to his troupe, send (mental) orders to the muscles in her shoulder, arm and fingers to contract and expand all in their correct sequence so that the projectile is properly launched. It is by dint of this effort of will then or the sending of these mental orders that action can be designated voluntary or willed. Correspondingly, action is involuntary when no such 'exertion of the will' takes place. So, a muscular reflex or nervous tic does not count as action because it is not 'willed'. Its cause is the autonomic nervous system rather than the actor's deliberative processes. In such cases bodily movement does not issue from a decision to act in the relevant fashion so it is not volitional and thus involuntary.

There are a number of well-known difficulties attached to characterising voluntary behaviour in terms of volition or what is willed.[13] Clearly, it cannot account for omissions. When one omits to do something the will is typically not involved at all and yet there is a deep sense in which omissions can be conceived as voluntary.[14]

Most intractable, it might appear, is a part scientific, part philosophical problem. What grounds are there for believing that when our body does something it has its genesis in a mental process separate from the body's own system for delivering bodily movement? If so,

---

[11] G Ryle, *The Concept of Mind* (Hutchinson's University Library, 1949), 81.

[12] See for example M Moore, *Act and Crime*, 104.

[13] HLA Hart, *Punishment and Responsibility*, (1968), 98 *et seq.*

[14] *Ibid* 100. To characterise a voluntary omission as a willed failure to act is conceptually absurd. Why should liability depend upon ourselves 'willing ourself' not to make a bodily movement or even willing ourself not to act? And, of course, it is inconsistent with the numerous crimes where liability for an inadvertant omissions is well recognised. G Fletcher, *Rethinking Criminal Law* (Little Brown and Company, Boston, Toronto, 1978), 421.

does this also hold with dogs, budgies, spiders? If not why not? Equally, if volition is the centrepiece of authentic human action why is it that it is rarely experienced as making a contribution to the movements our bodies make? Most everyday actions are performed on automatic pilot where the 'will' at most is an appreciative onlooker rather than the executor of the actor's ambitions.[15] When I unconsciously swat a mosquito buzzing around my ear while all my powers of concentration are directed towards a chess move we would not designate my conduct as involuntary or, for that matter, unintentional. Unconscious perhaps, but not involuntary in the sense that it is something for which I bear no responsibility. If the mosquito was a crying baby the action, we may be sure, would not have occurred and, if it had, we can be sure just retribution would not be long in coming.

Contemporary supporters of volition as the hallmark of voluntary action insist that cases of automatic pilot are not cases where the will is absent but where it is not manifest. When the bodily movements involved in various actions are learned, that part of the will initially responsible for executing the movement fades out of view ready to be called on when necessary to engage in more complex activity.[16] Infants apparently plumb supreme depths of concentration and effort to achieve the simplest goal—to pick up an object, to deliver food to the mouth. Ask an older child simultaneously to rub her tummy with one hand and pat her head with the other and initially she will find this difficult. The more the child wills the hand to pat, or rub, the more it will rub, or pat. But eventually the will subjugates the body's wrong turnings and the child succeeds. Having done so its job is done. Next time the will does not need to be summoned up to engineer the correct movements. After serious road accidents the semi-paralysed are typically urged to move their toes for both diagnostic and therapeutic purposes. It seems unobjectionable to suppose in each case that **without the effort of will** movement or the appropriate movement would not occur, that is that the action is volitional. It may be argued that the fact that the will may sometimes make a contribution to our actions does not mean that it always does.[17] On the other hand, if the will is

---

[15] Indeed, action more often than not is impeded by the will rather than indebted to it, as any golfer, darts or tennis player will attest.

[16] C Ripley, 'A Theory of Volition' 11 *Am Phil Q* 141 *et seq;* M Moore, *Act and Crime*, 129.

[17] Cf R Shapira, 'Willed Bodily Movement' (1998) *Buffalo Criminal Law Review* 349, 360–6.

involved in producing movement in the case of the paralysed why should it be any less so in the case of the non-paralysed? Does not the example of paralysed people and children and the supreme efforts of will which accompany their attempts to perform actions show that volition, if not always 'efforts of will', is the invariable concomitant of the action?[18]

Even assuming this view is correct and volition is involved in all our actions we are faced with a further problem. If the foundation of moral responsibility is volition then it may be thought that this must be because it has a hand in causing the relevant bodily movement. We hold actors responsible for their wrongdoing, that is, because in furtherance of something they desired, they caused their body to move in that particular way, their volition acting as the executive lever. However, from what we know of the natural world it is difficult to discern, even in the case of the paralysed, how mental processes of any kind can 'cause' bodily movement.[19] Mind and matter are not supposed to interpenetrate. Matter is subject to the laws of physics. There can be no exception.[20] We cannot will a cup to fall off the table because only physical forces can impart movement, whether those forces be a gust of wind or another moving body. It seems to follow that we cannot also will a human arm to move—**even if it is our own arm**—because both cups and arms are subject to the same laws of motion. If our arm moves something physical moves it. It may be force exerted by someone else or, more usually, the body's own biochemical messengers—neurons.[21] The same laws of physics dictate that we cannot will our neurons to move, however much we may try. This is the basic reason why we cannot salivate or urinate simply by operation of will. All we can do is to create the right conditions and hope that the body does its stuff.[22]

Recent advances in particle physics perhaps provide a possible solution to this problem. At the sub-atomic level things happen apparently according to a different set of (quantum) principles than in the world

[18] Moore *Act and Crime*, 161–2.

[19] For discussion and review of the scientific literature see K Saunders, 'Voluntary Acts and the Criminal Law: Justifying Culpability Based on the Existence of Volition', n 10 above.

[20] Cf though SE Toulmin and AN Flew, 'The Logical Status of Psycho-analysis' in *Analysis*, December 1948.

[21] These neurons may reflects our desires, in which case we would say the action is voluntary, or be unresponsive to them, in which case we would say they are involuntary.

[22] See generally G Ryle, *The Concept of Mind*, ch 3.

of everyday experience. Here interactions boast no invariable pattern and indeed can be switched off and on simply through the process of observation. Recent studies at the Massachusetts Institute of Technology have speculated that paranormal activity such as mental telepathy and psycho-kinesis, if such exists and there is no proof it does not, is possibly explainable in quantum terms. By extension, at the neurological level this may mean that mental activity equating to the legal theoretical concept of volition is also possibly involved in causing human action, say by desires operating to stimulate the synapses by which neurons can be directed to fire appropriately.

Of course, it is still necessary to discern the moral relevance of locating the source of action in such a process. Should it mean that proving a causal connection between volition and action should be the invariable basis upon which criminal responsibility is assigned.[23] Suppose you inquire of the child who breaks a cup by throwing it on the floor why she acted thus. The answer, if one is forthcoming, may be of one of the following. First, 'I just wanted to'. Secondly, ' I don't know. I just did it.' Third, 'I don't know. It just happened.' A question with which philosophers, if rarely lawyers, have concerned themselves is whether there is any substantial difference between these three responses.[24] On the face of it there is. Censure seems deserved in the first case. The child's response suggests motivation and behaviour expressing this and so in a loose sense also caused by it. In the second case this is less clear cut, although here too the child's response suggests that her behaviour was the product of a controlling intelligence albeit a destructive one. In the final case, if the child is right and it did 'just happen', censure would seem to be unfair. There is a difference between 'doing something' and 'something happening to one'. The problem posed in all three cases, however, is that in everyday life the responses are effectively interchangeable.[25] If you challenge the first child and ask 'Did you really want to throw that cup?' she may well, with reason, say 'No. I just did it'. If you ask the final child 'Did it just happen or did you do it?' she may well offer the following elaboration 'Well I did it, but I don't know why I did it.' I didn't do it for a reason.' Many parents will therefore feel justified in censuring whatever the explanation, barring a claim of

---

[23] HLA Hart, *Punishment and Responsibility*, 102; see also A Simester 'On the So-called Requirement for Voluntary Action' (1998) *Buffalo Criminal Law Review* 403.

[24] See generally R A Duff, *Criminal Attempts* (OUP, Oxford, 1996) chs 7–11.

[25] L Wittgenstein, *Philosophical Investigations* (Basil Blackwell, Oxford, 1953) 158 *et seq.*

accident.[26] But why? What is it about the child's mental processes which attracts censure given that we are disposed to believe her when she denies any conscious decision to have acted as she did?

A comparable problem faced the High Court of Australia in *Ryan*.[27] The defendant was charged with murder having shot the victim dead in the course of a robbery. Under the rules applicable which rendered participants in a robbery guilty of murder if a death ensues he was guilty, whether he intended the victim harm or not, as long as the action of pulling the trigger was voluntary. His case was that it was not. He was startled by a sudden movement of the victim on whom his gun was trained. His finger depressed the trigger as a 'reflex' action. If his account may have been a correct description of events it is difficult to see how his behaviour could be described as volitional. A reflex action is not something one does. It is something which happens which is unattributable to the actor's volition or decision-making processes. Imagine the following variation in the facts of *Ryan*.

Case 1

A and B take part in a robbery on C's shop. In a fit of spontaneous malevolence A tells B that he intends to kill C. B protests. A tells B that B can save C's life if B stands completely still, 'without moving a muscle', for the duration of the robbery. If he moves he will trigger a mechanism which will cause a rifle trained at C's head to discharge. B does his level best to comply but, in response to A exploding an inflated paper bag behind his back, he makes the fatal movement and C is killed.

Just as it seems clear that B's action is involuntary, however we conceive voluntariness, it must also, assuming Ryan's account to be true, be the case that Ryan's movement was similarly 'unwilled' and so decided Barwick CJ. The majority, however, clearly influenced by the fact that Ryan was the author of his own misfortune by placing himself, gun cocked with the safety catch off, in this perilous situation insisted that there was no cogent basis upon which to argue that Ryan's shooting was involuntary given that he had so primed himself and the ease with which he could have prevented it.

[26] See generally B Williams, 'Moral Responsibility and Political Freedom' [1997] *Camb LJ* 96.
[27] *Ryan v R* (1967) ALR 577.

Since the point of a voluntariness requirement is to chart the basic minimum required for criminal responsibility some theorists prefer to analyse voluntary action as being things which the body does which express a motivation, conscious or unconscious, on the part of the actor[28] or which corresponds with something the actor takes himself to be doing.[29] There is then no ghost in the machine which, in response to a desire to kick a football, hit a golf ball, or throw a cup wills the relevant muscles to stretch and contract in the appropriate fashion. There is the desire to kick, hit, throw. There is the bodily movement executing and/or expressing that desire and there is nothing in between or, more accurately, there is no mental activity **for which an individual bears responsibility** in between. In each case the activity is just the expression or outward embodiment of the intention or desire, owing no more to the metaphysics of volition than is salivating in response to a desire to eat chocolate.[30] Here, however, a loose causal connection sufficient to ground responsibility between the action and the desire which gave rise to it can be established wherever the actor lacked the motivation to behave in a way which did not involve that action.[31] This allows for liability, as in the cases of *Ryan* and the cup-throwing infant, irrespective of a pre-formed decision or intention since, as Mackie has argued 'an unopposed desire may lead directly to appropriate movements. I can just do something without deciding to do it.'[32]

Mackie's analysis reflects a contemporary preoccupation with identifying what is common in those cases where it is uncontroversial to suppose that voluntariness, whatever it may be, is lacking.[33] The reformulated question is then what is it for action to be involuntary? Famously, Hart designated movements as involuntary where the relevant bodily movements occurred 'though the agent had no reason for

---

[28] See generally Fletcher, *Rethinking Criminal Law*, 434–9.

[29] HLA Hart, *Punishment and Responsibility* 105; cf JL Mackie, 'The Grounds of Responsibility' in PMS Hacker and J Raz (eds), *Law, Morality and Society* (Clarendon, Oxford, 1977), 175: 'action is voluntary (if) . . . it incorporates some movement which is . . . appropriate for the fulfilment of a desire which causally brings it about' at 179.

[30] Correspondingly coughing is involuntary if bronchial irritation stimulates the cough as an automatic physical reflex but voluntary if it expresses a desire to clear one's throat, even if unconscious and unconnected with a desire to relieve discomfort. It may be voluntary even if the actor desires not to do so, as where he is trying to kick an annoying habit.

[31] 'What is said to be voluntary is causally dependent upon what the agent wants: it is due to his wanting something or to his not wanting something strongly enough.' *ibid*, 180.

[32] *Ibid* at 178.

[33] See generally RA Duff, *Criminal Attempts*, chs 7–11.

moving his body in that way'.[34] This captures the central truth that action does not become involuntary simply because the reasons for acting in this way becomes less compelling than the reason for not doing so. On the contrary, it is only where the accused has no reasons for acting in this way—he is sleepwalking, he suffers a reflex action—that the claim is substantiated.

A basic difficulty with Hart's approach is that it implies that if the accused had such a reason then he would be unable to claim he was acting involuntarily even though he was unable to prevent it happening.[35] In one case this may well be correct, namely where the actor purposively renders himself intoxicated and incompetent to give himself the (Dutch) courage to do what he would be unable to do if competent. Broadly, however, as a way of cutting action down to a size appropriate for the imputation of criminal responsibility the analysis appears defective. With moral responsibility as a touchstone of voluntary action one can, without difficulty, conceive of cases where, for example, moral responsibility is present although the accused had no reason for moving his body in that way, as where a builder stumbles and drops a hod of bricks from a scaffold onto a pedestrian on the street below having disdained to tie his shoe laces before making his ascent. Again one can conceive of cases where moral responsibility is lacking although the actor's movements exactly mirrored what he wanted to do. Consider the footballer who fends off a ball about to strike his face. He has every reason for moving his muscles in the way he does but nevertheless it seems clear that his action is involuntary since he, like every other person in the world, would have been unable to prevent it happening

This notion of involuntariness as being linked with the actor's capacity for acting otherwise is one which is in fact readily associated with Hart's theory of how excuses operate, which is that the state's moral licence to punish is absent in the cases of those who lack the capacity and fair opportunity of conforming to the law.[36] Hart wished,

---

[34] HLA Hart, *Punishment and Responsibility*, 256. In another formulation he modified this characterisation to 'movements of the body which occurred although they were not appropriate . . . for any action which the agent believed himself to be doing.'

[35] Cf A Simester, 'On the So-called Requirement for Voluntary Action' (1998) *Buffalo Criminal Law Review* 403, 422–3.

[36] At 181; Cf J Dressler, 'Reflections on Excusing Wrongdoers: Moral Theory, New Excuses and the Model Penal Code' (1988) 19 *Rut LJ* 671 at 675; S Kadish, 'Excusing Crime' (1987) 75 *Calif LR* 257, 264–5; P Robinson, *Criminal Law Defences* (St Paul, 1984), 349 *et seq*.

however, to distinguish action which was 'literally' involuntary such as reflexes and sleepwalking from action which was 'metaphorically' involuntary (the arena of excuses) such as coerced action. In this way he sought to identify the irreducible minimum necessary for criminal liability—human agency. By making this separation Hart was trying to avoid a problem which bedevils ethical theory, which is to give an answer to the question whether any action is sufficiently freely chosen to warrant the imputation of moral responsibility. Whatever the answer to that question, Hart asserts, what we can be sure of is that there can be no question of responsibility where an actor's bodily movements 'are not subordinated to the agent's conscious plans of action'.[37]

Glanville Williams grasped the nettle disdained by Hart, in an account which renders the capacity to act otherwise the touchstone of voluntariness. Action is voluntary for the purpose of criminal responsibility 'if the person could have refrained from it if he had so willed; that is, he could have acted otherwise or kept still'.[38] The question to be asked is not whether he had a reason for acting as he did but whether he could have prevented himself from acting in this way reasonable though it may have been.[39] 'Movements that are the result of epilepsy, for example are involuntary . . . because the person cannot by any mental effort avoid them.'[40] Using a metaphor from another age the test applicable is whether the defendant could have acted differently if there had been 'a policeman at his shoulder'? I hope to make clear that it is Williams' approach which is a better guide to criminal doctrine, if not entirely free of its own difficulties. It is no bar to an acquittal that the defendant had reason to move his body as he did. Neither is it a bar to a conviction that he did not. The issue governing criminal liability is whether the defendant could have prevented himself from acting as he did.

VOLUNTARINESS, DEFENCES AND THE COURTS

If we examine the full range of defences we see that each in its own way represents a claim of involuntariness of action. At one end of the

[37] At 105.

[38] G Williams, *Textbook of Criminal Law* (Stevens, London, 1983), 148.

[39] Anglo-American doctrine supports this conclusion. If fending off a swarm of bees is involuntary action, then so also is what the footballer does.

[40] *Ibid.*

spectrum the notion of involuntariness adopted is a literal one. Conduct is involuntary if it was not something the actor chose to do but something which happened to him. At the other end of the spectrum the notion of involuntariness adopted is a wholly metaphorical one. A person whose choice is prompted by coercion makes a choice which may be quintessentially considered and rational. It is involuntary only in the sense that under different circumstances the choice would not have been made. As the philosopher George Moore has made clear, it is perfectly cogent to impute moral responsibility for actions to those, such as the coerced, who could have acted otherwise if only they had chosen to and brave the consequences.[41] In the middle of the spectrum lie excuses such as provocation where we are hard pressed to assess what prompted the defendant to conduct himself as he did and where our disposition to excuse seems as much beholden to our assessment of the character of the defendant's conduct disclosed as whether or not he could have prevented himself from acting otherwise.

The courts draw this distinction between literal and metaphorical involuntariness for a good reason. If the basis of the defendant's claim to avoid censure and punishment is that his admitted action is not blameworthy then it is necessary to subject that claim to critical moral scrutiny so that the range of defences on offer reflect our moral judgments.[42] The courts are reluctant to invent new defences however defective the choice if it does not fit the existing template. The form of these templates will mirror a more general moral claim to avoid censure, as say with duress, that although the actor chose to do wrong it is not realistic to expect the actor to have chosen otherwise or that he did not fall below the standards of character expected of reasonable citizens.[43] But it must be understood that success with the raising of a defence is not simply a matter of arranging this basic theoretical defence DNA but also a matter of more general penal policy. In particular, recognising the defence must be consistent with the maintenance of an effective system of blame and punishment.[44] Even defences such as duress represent, for some critics of excuse theory, the

---

[41] GE Moore, *Ethics* (1912).

[42] S Kadish, 'Excusing Crime' (1987) 75 *Calif LR* 257.

[43] See chs 8, 9 below.

[44] S Kadish, above, n 42 at 257; J Horder, 'On the Irrelevance of Motive in Criminal law' in J Horder (ed), *Oxford Essays in Jurisprudence* (OUP, Oxford, 2000), 173, generally.

thin end of a doctrinally destabilising wedge. For example, if excuses are available, as with duress or provocation, where the choice was determined by the context or life conditions of the chooser, why should the range of excuses not be broadened far beyond the ordinary standards of morality?[45]

Where there is literal involuntariness of action, on the other hand, allowing the defendant to escape liability is not likely to compromise our system of morality or the policies underlying the penal system. Indeed it is central to both. Enforcing rules, in any rule-system, presupposes a basic ability to follow them. Even on the football field it is not considered handball if the ball strikes the hand rather than the hand strikes the ball. It is not surprising then that although the definitions of crimes do not include an explicit requirement that the defendant's conduct be voluntary, the courts treat a requirement of voluntariness as a fundamental ingredient in the constitution of all crimes. Recognition that the conduct element in the *actus reus* must be attributable to the defendant 'acting as a moral agent'[46] has been forthcoming in a number of cases. The defence corresponding to a claim of involuntariness of action is known as automatism and is typically presented as a defence conceptually distinct from the excuses.[47] It requires the defendant to be the author of the criminal wrong. The basis of the claim to avoid censure and punishment under discussion is not then, as with standard excuses, 'Don't blame me. I'm only human', but 'Don't blame me. It was not me who did it. 'Automatism has been authoritatively described as an 'act which is done by the muscles without any control by the mind such as a spasm, a reflex or a convulsion; or an act done by a person who is not conscious of what he is doing, such as an act done while suffering from concussion, or whilst sleepwalking'.[48] It encompasses cases where the physical cause of a person's behaviour is an event outside that person's control or where there is an interference with those mental processes which enable a person to identify and follow rules. This reflects Hart's view of involuntary action as involving cases where the agent's conscious mind is not engaged in what he is doing. It emphasises the absence of a conscious directing intelligence

---

[45] See for example M Kelman, 'Interpretive Construction in the Substantive Criminal Law' (1981) 33 *Stanford LR* 591; A Norrie, *Crime Reason and History* (Weidenfeld and Nicolson, London, 1993), 45–7.

[46] AJ Ashworth, *Principles of Criminal Law*, 93.

[47] In the final analysis even coerced choices are choices of the chooser and, accordingly, are an appropriate subject of moral evaluation.

[48] Lord Denning in *Bratty v AG for NI* [1963] AC 363.

leaving uncatered for those who, perhaps conscious of what they are doing, are nevertheless deprived of the capacity to control what they do.[49]

AUTHORSHIP, POLICY AND MORAL EVALUATION

As a starting point for asserting capacity rather than deliberative control over body movements as the basis of responsibility, consider the following well-worn statement of Lord Goddard CJ in *Hill v Baxter*[50]:

> Suppose a driver had a stroke or an epileptic fit, both instances of . . . Act of God; he might well be in the driver's seat or even with his hands at the wheel, but in such a state of unconsciousness that he could not be said to be driving. A blow from a stone or an attack by a swarm of bees, I think introduces some conception close to novus actus interveniens.[51]

Although on the face of it this statement seems to support the notion that moral responsibility is founded upon an actor being in conscious control of his movements,[52] read as a whole it implies that it is a person's capacity to act otherwise, generally, rather than the presence of a controlling intelligence, specifically, which is fundamental to responsibility. This acknowledgement is both a strength and a weakness since a person's capacity to conform to rules, unlike his state of cognition, is rarely testable as a matter of empirical fact. As a result the court's judgment will be, as likely as not, a normative rather than analytical judgment concerned with whether it would be appropriate to hold an actor to be the author of the relevant deed, rather than whether he is.[53] The result is to compromise the distinction between claims of lack of authorship and ordinary excuses which, as I explained earlier, is treated by the courts as fundamental.

[49] See discussion of *T*, below.

[50] [1958] 1 QB 277.

[51] There are two separate claims here. First, the act of driving does not take place where the actor's conscious mind is not directing the conduct for which he stands accused. Secondly, the use of the terminology of causation underlines the fact that the claim to avoid punishment is more basic than that the defendant is lacking fault. In Lord Goddard's example it was the unprompted dehumanised movements, or the stone or bees.

[52] HLA Hart, *Punishment and Responsibility*, 106.

[53] Many think that this normative question is best addressed by assessing the character the defendant's conduct disclosed rather than attempting the impossible task of deciding whether he could have acted otherwise. See below ch 11.

Consider for instance Lord Goddard's example of being hit by a stone or attacked by a swarm of bees. His use of the language of causation implies that such events negates authorship as a matter of pure cause and effect.[54] In the legal arena, however, whether or not an actor is the 'cause' of a criminal harm is a question of attribution rather than scientific fact. We are disposed to treat the bees as the cause of the accident. And we do so not simply because they represent an abnormal occurrence—not all unexpected interventions remove causal responsibility—but because we do not think the driver could be expected to have acted otherwise. Lord Goddard might have been less disposed to rely upon the language of causation if, say, control of the car had been lost due to the driver being startled by a sudden noise from a passenger, or by a sneeze, or being stung by a single bee. These are the kinds of events which it is generally reckoned responsible, careful drivers should be expected to cope with. Likewise, the criminal law concerns itself not simply with whether the defendant was in control of what he was doing, but whether he should have been. This normative question is the kind of question with which excuse doctrine routinely deals supporting the view that in practice a clear distinction between an excuse and a denial of authorship cannot always be drawn. And if it is not possible to create a cogent demarcation point between the two, doctrine will become unstable and inconsistent.

Another strong indication of the close conceptual links between the notion of involuntariness and excuses is provided by the doctrine of prior fault.[55] Excuses are generally forfeited where the defendant is responsible for creating the conditions of her own defence. So a mistake of fact cannot be relied upon if it is the result of voluntary intoxication. And duress is unavailable if the defendant joins a criminal organisation with a known propensity to use coercion to exact compliance. Likewise, for the purpose of automatism, responsibility is not avoided simply because the accused was temporarily not a mistress of her own body at the moment the *actus reus* began. Intoxication induced automatism does not negate voluntariness any more than it can be used to support duress.[56] More broadly, as *Ryan* illustrates, responsibility is only avoided where, on the basis of a broad interpretation of the time-frame surrounding the fatal event, it is inappropriate to attribute authorship

---

[54] Hart adopts a similar analysis, *Punishment and Responsibility*, 109.

[55] P Robinson, 'Causing the Conditions of One's Own Defence' (1985) 71 *Virg LR* 1.

[56] Lipman [1970] 1 QB 152. This is clearly so where the actor becomes intoxicated to give himself Dutch courage.

of the relevant event to the accused.[57] In *Ryan*, it would clearly not be inappropriate. He could not be heard to argue that 'it was not his doing?' In response to Williams' question 'could he have prevented it if he had so willed?' the answer comes 'Of course. He could have kept the safety catch on.' Similar reasoning accounts for the fact that falling asleep at the wheel of a car does not count against a conviction for careless driving or ignoring a traffic signal. Again if a level crossing keeper falls asleep on the job so that the crossing remains open when a train arrives he is responsible if a fatal accident results therefrom. The suggestion is then that in all cases where the court is called to assess the accused's responsibility, the court's concern is not simply with whether the defendant could control what he was doing but with whether he should have done. This general question turns on whether, Hart elsewhere suggested, in all the circumstances he had the 'capacity and fair opportunity or chance to adjust his behaviour to the law'.[58] In his overall scheme of responsibility this is the principle upon which excuses are and should be recognised, which returns us once again to the question whether a meaningful distinction is to be drawn between denials of fault and denials of voluntariness or, put another way, between cases of literal and metaphorical involuntariness.

AUTHORSHIP AND CONTROL

As explained earlier a key implication of the voluntariness requirement is that, subject to the qualifications made in the previous section, involuntary behaviour cannot form the subject matter of strict liability offences. This is of crucial importance since it offers to provide a mechanism for subverting the point of strict liability offences, namely to secure the efficient disposal of cases by removing questions of fault. For this reason, perhaps, the courts have consistently refused to allow the defence to be built upon evidence of anything less than total control. In so doing, however, they have succeeded in creating a two tier notion of voluntariness. In strict liability offences, to be acting voluntarily approaches the view taken by HLA Hart, namely that the 'controlling agency. . . is the mind of a (person) bent on some conscious action'.[59]

---

[57] Kelman, above n 45.
[58] *Punishment and Responsibility*, 181.
[59] *Ibid* at 105.

Only then, where the activity of the accused cannot be interpreted as goal-directed will the defence of automatism lie. So, in a number of cases involving driving offences defendants have been held to be driving their car for the purpose of careless or dangerous driving despite overwhelming interference with their mental processes or powers of control. In *Broome v Perkins*[60] a driver was charged with driving without due care and attention. His defence was that through diabetic hypoglycaemia he had suffered a partial loss of consciousness leaving him unable to drive the car responsibly. He was able to discharge the mechanical functions—accelerating, braking, swerving to avoid obstacles, changing gear, and so on, but not the normative functions—driving systematically according to rules. The defence was rejected. The court insisted that automatism was only available where the loss of control was total. Consistent with this view in *Sibbles*,[61] a case on causing death by dangerous driving, the legal position was explained thus: 'a conviction is appropriate unless the defendant suddenly and unexpectedly was deprived of all thought and that deprivation was unconnected with any deliberate act of his and arose from a cause which a reasonable man would have no cause to think and the defendant did not think might occur'. Similar conclusions were reached in *Roberts v Ramsbottom*[62] where the driver had suffered a cerebral haemorrhage. In both cases it was conceded that no fault attached to the driver.[63]

These cases indicate that the courts recognise authorship as central to criminal liability but artificially restrict authorship to its central case, presumably for reasons of penal policy. This leaves a great many cases uncatered for where we would hesitate to conclude that the relevant event was the actor's 'doing' rather than something which 'happened to him'. Rules are directed against those human subjects who, unlike the insane, children and animals, have the minimum capacities

---

[60] [1987] *Crim LR* 271.
[61] [1959] *Crim LR* 660.
[62] [1980] 1 All ER 7.
[63] Cf Stripp (1978) 69 Cr App R 318; Budd [1962] *Crim LR* 49. Comparable problems of 'line-drawing' have occurred in cases where control has been lost due to the intervention of external causes. In *Burns v Bidder* unexpected brake failure was held to be a defence to the offence of failing to accord precedence to a pedestrian on a crossing. But in *Neal v Reynolds* a driver was convicted of the same offence where, unforeseeably and outside the driver's powers of control a pedestrian stepped out in front of the driver. See generally I Patient, 'Some Remarks about the Element of Voluntariness in Offences of Absolute Liability' [1968] *Crim LR* 23; HLA Hart, *Punishment and Responsibility*, ch IV.

for effective rule following. Perhaps the most cogent notion of responsibility sufficient to ground liability is one which demands the actor be in possession of these minimum capacities at the time of acting. Included among these is the capacity to understand that one's projected conduct falls within the ambit of a prohibitory rule, to understand how to avoid acting in such a way, and to formulate, and act upon, ways of behaving which will achieve this.[64] On all of these tests the defendants' conduct in the above cases was involuntary.

If we examine the defence of automatism outside the field of strict liability offences the tension between social needs and fairness to the individual is resolved in a different and more morally satisfactorily fashion. Here, voluntariness is understood to be a matter of capacity and control generally rather than cognition specifically. Doctrine sometimes treats those who act purposively (with reasons for so acting) to be treated as acting involuntarily if, say, due to hypnotism, brainwashing, concussion or other external trauma, the defendant was unable systematically to conform his behaviour to control by rules. In *T*, for example, the defendant stabbed the victim in the course of committing a robbery. Weeks previously she had been raped. Medical evidence suggested that at the time of the offence she had entered a dissociative state in which the part of her mind which controlled action and the part which followed rules were separated. Although there was no suggestion that the defendant was unconscious of what she was doing or of its rule-breaking character it was nevertheless accepted that she was not responsible for what she did. One can only assume that the substantive basis for the court's decision was that D may have failed to follow the relevant prohibitory rule since that part of the mind which organises the rule-following response was disactivated.[65] She would have been acting as if in a dream. As in dreams, the mechanism of the mind which allows her (and us) to pitch our actions in accordance with our beliefs, knowledge and ambitions, and therefore in accordance with a system of rules, was absent.

It seems then that on the best interpretation of criminal doctrine available involuntariness of action includes both volitional and cogni-

[64] See M Moore, 'Causation and the Excuses' (1985) 73 *Calif LR* 1091; J Dressler, 'Reflections on Excusing Wrongdoers: Moral Theory, New Excuses and the Model Penal Code (1988) 19 *Rut LJ* 671.

[65] For similar decision see *Quick and Paddison* [1973] QB 910; see generally RF Schopp, *Automatism, Insanity, and the Psychology of Criminal Responsibility* (OUP, Oxford, 1991).

tive impairment on a spectrum of potentially excusing conditions stretching from, say, unconsciousness (stroke, heart attack, sleep walking) to cases of, say, concussion-induced confusion. By defining voluntariness of action in terms of a person's capacity to conform, it becomes clear how close a claim of automatism is to other excuses.[66] Cases such as *T* indicate that it represents the paradigm case of most effective excuses which, in its most plausible unifying theory, holds that 'a moral licence to punish is needed by society and unless a man has the capacity and fair opportunity or chance to adjust his behaviour to the law, its penalties ought not to be applied to him'. Literal involuntariness is simply the extreme case on this spectrum which incorporates also less direct claims of involuntariness such as duress, provocation, diminished responsibility and mistake.

INVOLUNTARY OMISSIONS

Both actions and omissions can meaningfully be described as voluntary or involuntary. In law, as has been seen, an action may be voluntary, even where undesired and even where compelled.[67] Behaviour is involuntary where, under some description or other, the actor lacked the capacity to have acted otherwise either because of an absence of physical control or because of a failure of those cognitive and other processes which enable people to act systematically in accordance with rules.[68] This analysis sits, however, somewhat uncomfortably with omissions-based liability. While bodily movement may be appropriately described as 'automatic', non-movement cannot. The mirror image of reflex, spasm, sleepwalking or convulsion for bodily movements is, for omissions, paralysis or coma, but, as with affirmative action although for different reasons, the appropriate measure of moral responsibility must stretch further than these core cases. The American Model Penal Code describes omissions as voluntary if the defendant is 'physically capable' of acting in the required fashion. Accordingly, involuntary omissions cover failures to act for reasons as diverse as unconsciousness, paralysis, incarceration and third party restraint.

---

[66] KJM Smith and W Wilson, 'Impaired Voluntariness and Criminal Responsibility' [1993] *OJLS* 69.

[67] See A Norrie, *Crime Reason and History*, 114.

[68] See W Wilson, *Criminal Law: Doctrine and Theory* (Longmans, London, 1998), 221–6; cf A Simester, 415.

An examination of case law suggests, however, that a still broader, as yet inchoate, defence of impossibility is the counterpart of automatism as applied to cases of omission.[69] This has long been implicit in criminal law doctrine, albeit imperfectly realised. So, in the nineteenth century it was a defence to manslaughter in cases where the death resulted from the defendant's breach of duty to provide necessaries that he lacked the means to do so.[70] The full scope of such a defence is uncertain but it seems reasonably clear that it is not and cannot be limited to cases of physical incapacity. This is because the basis upon which we bring the omitter to account is rather different from that of the actor. The actor is accountable for his act—for firing the gun, for driving the car, for snatching the bag, for setting light to the building. The voluntariness requirement sustains accountability by requiring that the actor 'fires' the gun, 'drives' the car, 'snatches' the bag, 'sets light' to the building. It is not enough that these things happen, that the gun discharges, the car moves, the building catches fire, and so on. All these things can happen through bodily movements made by the defendant without their being actions of the defendant.

The basis upon which we hold the omitter to account is not, however, the obverse of this—the absence of action. If it were, we would all be accountable for the things we failed to prevent happening, which we are not. It is rather the failure to satisfy a duty. Without this duty we can blame someone all we like but they are not accountable. If accountability derives from the fact that the defendant ought to have acted, it is clear then that the law must take account of many things other than physical capacity pertinent to the question of 'ought'.[71] This has been made explicit in a series of road traffic offences which indicate that liability is strict but not absolute. A basic minimum requirement of moral responsibility must always be present. So in *Harding v Price* the Divisional Court held that the duty to report a road accident applied only where the defendant was aware that there was an accident to report. In *Burns v Bidder* James J said that the motorist's duty to give precedence to a pedestrian does not impose an absolute obligation and there is no breach 'in circumstances where the driver fails to accord precedence to a pedestrian solely because his control of the vehicle is

---

[69] See AJ Ashworth, 'The Scope of Liability for Omissions' (1989) 105 *LQR* 424.

[70] A Smart, 'Criminal Responsibility for Failing to do the Impossible' [1987] 103 *LQR* 532, 535; G Hughes, 'Criminal Omissions ' (1958) 67 *Yale LJ* 590.

[71] HLA Hart, *Punishment and Responsibility*, ' "Ought" implies "can" and a person who could not help what he is doing is not morally guilty' at 158.

taken from him by the occurrence of an event which is outside his possible or reasonable control and in respect of which he is in no way at fault.'[72]

Voluntariness: A Variable Standard?

This statement is notable for the potential breadth of the defence. Liability will be avoided not only where it was impossible for the defendant to comply with his duty but also where it could not reasonably be expected, as where perhaps the pedestrian dashed out unexpectedly. Of further note is the way that the statement is couched in terms which refer to the defendant's own capacities. Is impossibility to be assessed objectively or subjectively? It has been proposed in recent years that excuses should be limited to cases where the defendant's reasons for acting as he did are such as to block an inference of bad character.[73] Central to this thesis is that unless the defendant's claim, as with insanity or automatism, amounts to a denial of physical or mental capacity the defendant must act for reasons consonant with the satisfactory discharge of the role occupied at the time of acting. In short, he must act reasonably and the standards of reasonableness are objective and fixed by the role he was occupying whether specialised, doctor, police officer or motorist or general, parent, spouse, house occupant, and so on. It is not then the absence of a fair opportunity to conform to the law *per se* which excuses but that certain reasons for not conforming are sufficiently compelling to allow us to conclude that an actor is not of bad character. This claim will be examined in due course. At this early stage, however, it suffices to remark that this requires some qualification if it is to advance understanding of the justification offered for restricting the scope of liability for omissions.[74]

The signs are that this is well understood by courts at the highest levels which have often asserted variable standards dependent upon

[72] See *US v Murdock*—it is not a voluntary omission to file a tax return if one fails deliberately believing one has a constitutional right to avoid self incrimination and cases cited in G Hughes, 'Criminal Omissions' and A Smart, above n 70.

[73] See for example G Fletcher, *Rethinking Criminal Law*, ch 10; J Gardner, 'The Gist of Excuses' (1998) *Buffalo Criminal Law Review* 575, 580–6.

[74] Smart argues that a defence must be sensitive to the individual capacities of the defendant (557). On this a comparison should be made with Gardner 'The Gist of Excuses' (1998) *Buffalo Criminal Law Review* 575, 580–6.

individualised capacities rather than constant standards based upon social roles.[75] In *Miller* James LJ in the Court of Appeal said that omissions-based liability for arson must be limited so that the actor is not liable for failing to do the impossible.[76] And in the House of Lords Lord Diplock referred to the necessity of taking 'steps which lie within his power to prevent or minimise the damage'. Again in *Sheppard* the House of Lords held that there could be no liability for wilful neglect where the parties were too stupid to appreciate the risks attending their child.[77] More recently in *Emery* the Court of Appeal ruled that coercion could be relied upon by a mother as a reason for not intervening to prevent her partner's cruelty to her child where the mother's powers of resistance had themselves been subverted below the normal and reasonable by the sustained violence and abuse of her partner.[78]

What is apparent upon examining these cases is that, as with affirmative action, what counts as involuntary behaviour/impossibility is determined contextually and there is no clear line drawn between claims of impossibility and claims of justification and excuse.[79] While this is unsurprising in the case of affirmative action for the reasons already canvassed, it is however arguably inevitable in the case of omissions. The general justification for refusing to impose a general duty to act so as to prevent harm to others is commonly reckoned to be a respect for human autonomy. More tellingly, satisfying such duties would impose unpredictable burdens of uncertain scope. It seems to follow that where a duty does exist the scope of the duty to act is similarly not unlimited but is restricted to the 'things a person has signed up for' by virtue of their relationship with the victim, their occupation, their previous dealings with the victim and so on. Criminal doctrine cannot consistently uphold autonomy by restricting duty situations while at the same time demanding the impossible or unreasonable self-sacrifice in the discharge of such duties as are recognised.

To show true (equal) respect for autonomy the criminal law must, moreover, take the omitter's own weaknesses seriously—including weaknesses which most accounts of the proper scope of criminal

---

[75] See Smart above n 70, at pp. 537–42.
[76] [1983] AC 161, 175–6.
[77] [1981] AC 394.
[78] (1993) 14 Cr App R 394. For further discussion of this point see ch 9.
[79] 'Impossibility may be relative rather than absolute, and the defence may have a stronger flavour of justification than excuse in cases where the person omitted to act in order to avoid harming an even greater interest.' Ashworth, (1989), 440.

defences would not countenance as providing reasons for **action** such as cowardice, stupidity, and acquisitiveness.[80] The mechanism for effecting all these processes is the duty.[81] The duty converts passive acquiescence into wrongdoing on the one hand and on the other provides a conceptual hook upon which to hang causal responsibility and fault. At the extreme a parent who cannot swim is not guilty of murder (or manslaughter) for failing to attempt a rescue. It is tempting to suppose that this is for a formal reason, namely that the case represents the omissions equivalent of the requirement of involuntariness of action. More realistically it is for a substantive reason, namely that it is the clearest example of how agents 'by omission' take on the phenomenal attributes of 'killers' only in extreme cases.[82] If the same parent fails to intervene because she is threatened with serious violence by a brutal partner if she does so, or because she is occupied saving the life of another child it can hardly be supposed that she is liable for her failure although the formal elements of murder are present in each of these cases and no cognate defence is available.[83] None of the decisions made in any of these cases are comparable with a purposive killing. Our moral evaluation of the mother's conduct is unavoidably linked to the context within which she is operating. She is not trying to kill her child. She is not trying to save herself. She simply finds herself unable to act as she would wish. Although she may fail to satisfy the standards of resistance of ordinary mothers or even her own standards it is, however, surely appropriate that she avoid liability on the grounds of her involuntary behaviour. It is a fact of human biology that fear paralyses. It is a fact of morality, by contrast, that fear may provoke us to act against our inclination.

CONCLUSION

For purposes of general criminalisation the minimum level of responsibility in cases of omission points up what has often been denied in the case of affirmative action, namely that it is an agent's failure to live up

[80] Cf J Gardner, 'The Gist of Excuses' (1998) *Buffalo Criminal Law Review* 575, 580–6.

[81] See W Wilson, 'Murder and the Structure of Homicide' in A Ashworth and B Mitchell (eds), *Rethinking English Homicide Law* (Oxford, 2000), 21, 49–52.

[82] A Smart 'Criminal Responsibility for Failing to do the Impossible' [1987] 103 *LQR* 542–44.

[83] In many jusrisdictions, including England, duress is not available to murder.

to our expectations which provokes the punitive response rather than say his level of control or cognition. Given that she has not **acted** against reason, this requires due regard to be paid to what the defendant showed herself capable of doing in the context and her general capacity to appreciate how best to acquit herself as a morally responsible human being. It demands that attention be paid both to the reasons supporting action and to the reasons given for not acting. More often than not these considerations will be accommodated through the fault element of the offence. Crimes of negligence and recklessness require regard to be paid to the reasonableness/justifiability of the defendant's conduct. In cases of omissions the weighing of costs and benefits will be particularly sensitive to the defendant's reasons for not acting. More generally, particularly for crimes of intention such as murder, it seems that such considerations are accommodated by adjectival law and the practices of courts and legal officials, which evince a pragmatic tendency to skate over the paper rules in cases of death following an omission. This is most clearly true in medical cases but extends more widely.[84] In Smith,[85] for example, a husband who failed, out of respect for his wife's wishes, to call a doctor when it was clear to him that she would die without medical attention was charged only with manslaughter when, on the test of fault then applicable, a murder charge was an obvious option . As a result the judge was able to direct the jury that they must give weight to the reasonableness of respecting the wife's autonomy when deciding whether he had acted reasonably in delaying the emergency call.

In cases of affirmative action the line separating acceptable and unacceptable reasons for criminal wrongdoing are, by and large, controlled through defence templates. Duress but not poverty is a defence to theft, although the degree of realistic choice in a given case may well be comparable. Some degree of flexibility is nevertheless provided through the defence of automatism which allows people to escape liability to a very limited extent despite uncoerced wrongdoing where authorship is absent. It has been suggested in this context that the voluntariness requirement in English criminal law is simply the extreme case on a spectrum of excuses incorporating less direct claims of involuntariness. It operates when we are deprived of a fair opportunity to conform our behaviour to the law and for reasons which do not compromise our system of morality and law enforcement.

[84] See for example *Airedale NHST v Bland* (1993) AC 89; *Arthur* (1981) 12 BMLR 1.
[85] [1979] *Crim LR* 251.

In cases of omission the link between involuntariness or impossibility and excuse or justification is even more direct and provokes the question whether cases of impossibility are simply the clearest cases of what might be termed a more general balance of reasons approach to the construction of criminal liability. This is not to endorse the view that a balance of reasons approach is determinative of all matters relating to liability, at least if the calculation is role-centred. On the one hand a generally applicable balance of reasons approach threatens to destabilise a rule and rule enforcement system based upon calculability and authority. On the other it devalues the significance of individual weaknesses in the calculation of fairness in the distribution of punishment. The courts increasingly recognise, in my view rightly, that in extreme cases a person's weaknesses must be taken seriously and if these contribute to a breakdown in the individual's ability to conform his behaviour to the law he should not thereby be deprived of the opportunity to defend himself. This is particularly pertinent in the context of liability for omissions where, at least for non-regulatory crime, a different paradigm of liability operates which subverts the 'paradigm of intentional criminality. . .'[86] and also, at least partially, the paradigm of virtue. Fairness in the distribution of punishment where the defendant has not **acted against reason** requires due regard to be paid to his account of why he was unable to do what society has reason to expect of responsible human beings.[87]

---

[86] J Gardner, 'On the General Part of Criminal Law' in A Duff (ed), *Philosophy and the Criminal Law* (CUP, Cambridge, 1998) at 232.

[87] Cf the Law Commission's most recent proposals on involuntary manslaughter. And see G Fletcher, *Rethinking Criminal Law*, 622–34; cf J Gardner, 'The Gist of Excuses' (1998) *Buffalo Criminal Law Review* 593–7.

5

Intention, Motives and Desert

Motives, it is often said, are irrelevant to criminal liability. This is, in fact, only partly true. Some crimes are only constituted upon proof that the defendant's conduct was actuated by a particular (bad) motive. Blackmail is an obvious example. Liability for most property crimes is premised upon the defendant being dishonest and a person's motive will usually be relevant in determining dishonesty. Again, liability, for crimes of recklessness or negligence requires consideration of a person's reasons for having acted as he did. If those reasons do not show the accused to have departed from the standards of care of reasonable people he will escape liability. Overtaking on a blind corner for reasons of getting to a party on time is more likely to attract criminal liability for, say, the purpose of causing death by dangerous driving, than if the manoeuvre was executed for reasons of getting a failing patient to hospital. Good motives may also provide the defendant with a cognate defence. So defences such as duress or self-defence operate to shield from liability even those who cause harm intentionally. It is not simply the fact that the actor is acting under conditions of duress or unlawful force which provides the defence. It is more specifically the fact that these conditions supply the reasons why he acts as he does. If A, a police officer, shoots B dead just as B is about to throw a hand grenade into a crowded street he will escape liability for murder if his motive was to prevent the commission of a serious crime and loss of life but not if he did so to exercise a grudge against B.[1]

What one should rather say, then, is not that motives are irrelevant to criminal liability, but that they do not supplant the criminal law's own resources for determining whether the fault element for a given

---

[1] There is some disagreement in the case of justifying defences as to whether it is the justifying fact alone or the justifying fact coupled with the justifying reason which creates the defence, J Gardner, 'Justifications and Reasons' in A Simester and ATH Smith (eds), *Harm and Culpability* (Clarendon Press, Oxford, 1996), 103; cf Fletcher, *Rethinking Criminal Law* (Little Brown and Company, Boston, Toronto, 1978), 557.

crime is present. Liability for murder does not vary according to the killer's motive for pulling the trigger unless that motive, as in self-defence, is specially privileged by the offence and defence rules which govern liability. At first sight this may seem odd given that the criminal justice system's own account of itself emphasises the link between punishment and moral desert. If punishment is a matter of moral desert how can a person's reasons or motive not matter? Early in the history of the common law a person's susceptibility to punishment was, in fact, more directly determined by moral blameworthiness. *Mens rea* was first used as a form of words to indicate that criminal liability required moral blameworthiness rather than, simply, an accompanying specified state of mind.[2] Thus Bracton defines 'intentional' homicide as occurring 'where one in anger or hatred or for the sake of gain, deliberately and in premeditated assault, has killed another wickedly and in breach of the King's peace'.[3] Only much later was this global notion of moral blameworthiness translated into individual specific states of mind, for example intention and recklessness, necessary for individual offences. It remains the case, however, that in everyday life our moral response to instances of intentional wrongdoing is sensitive both to the actor's motive and to the context within which his intention was formed. It is not unusual for ordinary, reasonable people to approve morally of instances of mercy killing or those who 'take the law into their own hands' in cases such as sexual abuse or child killing. Those whose motives for killing do not show them in a bad light, it might be assumed, are not widely thought deserving of censure and punishment for homicide.

How can this refusal to allow motives a greater role in the construction of criminal identities be explained? At a basic level it can be understood as reflecting the lack of social unanimity concerning the ethical foundations of appropriate action. Not only do we lack a social culture capable of producing a unified notion of right and wrong, we lack even a dominant vision of what such a unified notion would comprise were we to have such a culture.[4] Just as for example there is no consensus as to whether punishment is a matter of moral desert or whether it can only be justified consequentially, so also there is no consensus as to whether the moral quality of individual action can be determined in

    [2] Sayre, 'The Present Signification of *Mens Rea* in the Criminal Law' (1934) *Harvard Legal Essays* 399.

    [3] Cited in Sayre, n 2.

    [4] See A MacIntyre, *After Virtue* (Duckworth, London, 1981), ch 2, and generally.

abstraction from its context and from the consequences which ensue. The enduring euthanasia or abortion issues are prime examples. People who support the same political party, follow the same religion and football team, enjoy the same books, drink together in the same pubs, and structure their lives around the same moral values may nevertheless disagree fundamentally as to whether abortion/euthanasia is a matter of personal choice, of the best interests of all concerned, or inviolable moral obligation.[5]

The state has an obvious role to play therefore in specifying clearly the rules which govern cases where the balance of reasons for and against action may be misunderstood. Where, as in murder and other crimes of violence, the conduct element embodies a moral proscription, lending an actor's reasons for violence a defining role in the offence would be self-defeating. By relegating motives to the 'realm of supervening defences' the clarity of the moral principle—hurting people is wrong—can be sustained. It is a principle which generates its own reason to conform.[6] So it is generally understood that murder is committed whether the killing is done for personal gain or to put an end to the mortal agony of a dying loved one. It may well appear to an individual on the horns of a dilemma that to kill 'mercifully' is the best option and it is just because it may so appear that criminal offences and defences are structured in the way they are.[7] Criminal prohibitions demand obedience even in the face of compelling reasons for disobedience. They have clarity of purpose, which allow us to know what is the 'right' thing to do without our having to engage in complex moral inquiry. If the motive of the actor is capable of providing a countervailing reason not to conform that reason must first be evaluated from the point of view of the proscribing society rather than that of the actor himself or his immediate moral audience. In this way full moral consideration can be given to it.

The suppression of reasons is by no means unique to the rules of criminal law of course. The rules of golf are even less susceptible to unilateral

---

[5] R Dworkin, *Life's Dominion* (Penguin, London, 1993).

[6] As Horder explains for things which are wrong only if done for one reason rather than another (eg theft, blackmail) one makes naturally the excusability or justifiability of D's conduct a prominent role in the definition of the offence. So theft and blackmail specify the kinds of reasons which may make an otherwise innocuous act wrongful. In such cases criminal definitions are wont to take on much of the burden of distinguishing between good and bad reasons for action. J Horder, 'The Irrelevance of Motive in Criminal Law' in J Horder (ed), *Oxford Essays in Jurisprudence* (OUP, Oxford, 2000), 174.

[7] See J Raz, *The Authority of Law*, ch 1 and generally, (OUP, Oxford, 1979).

negotiation. If a golfer hits the wrong ball or signs for the wrong score her reasons for so doing make no difference to her susceptibility to penalty. So a golfer is penalised if she hits the wrong ball by mistake or unilaterally substitutes a damaged ball with an identically placed undamaged ball. She is penalised whether she signs for a higher or lower score than she in fact secured. She is penalised even where the calculation was done by her partner or opponent, whose calculation she took on trust. No doubt the original reasons for these rules were to penalise and prevent cheating but their clarity and force have been effectively sustained by making the rule absolute. As golfers are wont to point out this is helpful to both golfers and the game of golf as it conduces to a rule-sensitive state of mind in which there is no room for ambiguity or mistrust. It is an attitude which finds its typical expression in two facets of the golfer's morality. The first is the tendency in tournament golf to consult an official concerning whether or not a given shot or procedure is legitimate. The second is the golfer's willingness to 'turn themselves in' for rule violations however unintentional and however trivial. To the world outside, used to professional fouls, 'sledging' at cricket, and the intimidation of referees and umpires this suppression of the internal point of view may appear to be anachronistic 'moral heroism'. Golfers reply that the rules are not negotiable and that golf, unlike everyday life, has no room for competing ideas of acceptable conduct.

This finds its echo in the multifaceted character of criminal prohibitions. The criminal law not only acts as a system of coercion punishing obvious villains who manifest their bad character in action, but also functions to limit and inform the choices of good and reasonable people. In so doing public order is secured and with it the moral structure by which people's ideas of correct and incorrect behaviour are first learned and then maintained. Allow good motives to be defences and the law loses objectivity and will lack the ability to co-ordinate the activities of society's members.[8]

If we compare the criminal law's differentiated response to a revenge killing as opposed to a provoked killing this point can be appreciated. If A kills B 'in just retribution' as it were for the fact that B has raped and killed A's daughter A's reason, while perhaps commanding broad public support, is inconsistent with the maintenance of a system of norms which hold that violence is wrong whatever reason the individ-

---

[8] J Raz, *The Authority of Law*, 14–27; J Raz (ed), *Authority* (Blackwell, Oxford, 1990), 1–19; cf J Finnis, 'Authority' in J Raz (ed), *Authority*, 174–202.

ual may have for thinking otherwise. If a rule against violence is to be effective it must operate within a system of enforcement which disentitles people from substituting their own ideas of acceptable behaviour for those of society's elected representatives. If, on the other hand, A kills B 'in hot blood' having encountered B in the aftermath of the dreadful deed, affording A at least a limited defence is not inconsistent with the maintenance of that same system of norms. This is so as long as it is understood that under conditions of extreme provocation even reasonable people may lose the capacity to conform their behaviour to rules and/or to appreciate that the fact that a proposed course of conduct is unlawful is an overriding reason not to pursue that course of conduct in opposition to one's inclinations. By compartmentalising the fault element into definitional mental element and defences the accused is left in no doubt of his social responsibilities, but is afforded notice, in cases of true defences, that the circumstances in which he acts may, if he acts in good faith, provide the basis upon which the court may find that duty to be cancelled or its breach go unpunished.

This plausible explanation has not gone unchallenged. Life is not a game of golf and suppressing reasons might be indicative of a fatal weakness in criminal justice. Its rules demand punishment as a symbol of moral condemnation of some who are blameless or, at least, no more blameworthy than others who are not punished. A person who robs a bank under a mobster's threat of death to her child if she does not can rely on this reason to escape liability. If she robs the bank to pay for the otherwise unaffordable operation which would save her stricken child's life her reason is ignored. In both cases she robs a bank to save her child's life but she escapes liability only if she acts under extraneous coercion. How can the drawing of such a distinction be justified given that the determinants/causes operating here are comparably effective?[9] On this view, practising such closure over the range of possible excuses allows the criminal law to fulfil its essentially coercive function. Suppressing motives is an inevitable concomitant of a system of social control which, historically, has sought to link the content of criminal doctrine with the needs of a society structured by wealth and power and in which social conflict is therefore endemic. Under such conditions it is inevitable that entrenched interests will locate the 'right' in a context-independent respect for the interests of others.[10]

---

[9] M Kelman, 'Interpretive Construction in the Substantive Criminal Law' (1981) 33 *Stanford LR* 591.

[10] A Norrie, *Crime Reason and History* (Weidenfeld and Nicolson, London, 1993), ch 3.

While property crimes, public order crimes and crimes of violence are addressed for the protection of all, the specific needs of the few and the society their activities maintain are thereby guaranteed. The broader 'rights and wrongs' which may legitimate theft as a response to hunger or, as the Balkan experience attests, the use of violence to escape political tyranny, gives way to a decontextualised notion of right and wrong within which interests in property and personal security are inviolable for whatever reason. Thus the form of criminal liability is structured to render individual fault a matter of what one intends rather than the context within which those intentions become manifest. It is a form whose hard edges are rendered largely invisible by the acceptance of certain defences. These appear to protect blameless individuals from the claims of the state; in fact they offer but a pale reflection of their moral counterparts. Law's coercive function can only be achieved at the expense of justice to morally blameless individuals.

This approach appears to identify a crucial weakness in the construction of criminal identities. Rule breaking rather than moral fault is the basis upon which punishment and censure is allocated. This, in turn, renders it inevitable that mechanisms will arise to reconcile the individual's claim to fair treatment with the fixed certainties of the rule of law. One such mechanism is sentencing discretion—the kind of impetus which sees mercy killers escaping incarceration while contract killers receive a life sentence. In the words of one commentator this is a case of the criminal justice system 'having its cake and eat it'.[11] Legitimacy comes from the system's supposed strict adherence to the rule of law and yet what actually happens to offenders—whether they are imprisoned or fined, and actual levels of punishment—is structured by the discretion of judges. Judges, bastions of orthodoxy and moral rectitude can be trusted, unlike the defendant in the dock or the jury trying him, to decide whether and how far the defendant's motive should allow him to escape punishment.

The second way the common law is thought to have 'its cake and eat it' is through the flexibility afforded by the common law to allow judgments of fault to take account of contingency, context and motive. Since the common law system is a dynamic rather than fixed system, problem cases can be accommodated as part of a process of development—the common law's own voyage of self discovery.[12] As shall be

---

[11] A Norrie, *Crime Reason and History* (1993), at 45–7.

[12] 'A Clear Concept of Intention: Elusive or Illusory' (1993) 56 *MLR* 621; N Lacey, 'In Search of the Responsible Subject' [2001] *MLR* 320.

seen, for example, concepts such as intention are not closed, although they are typically presented as closed. This allows much moral work to be done under cover of the rule of law.[13] Parkinson's law of the common law might well under this approach be reformulated as follows: 'Concepts expand or contract to fit the moral purposes their deployment functions to discharge.' The plausibility of this charge will be examined in succeeding sections.

INTENTION AND RESPONSIBILITY

Rationality in criminal doctrine requires a failsafe doctrinal mechanism for ensuring that censure and punishment are deserved and the degree of censure and punishment is proportionate to the degree of blame we assign to the defendant for his wrongful conduct. It is a basic premise of criminal justice that the vehicle for appropriate censure and punishment must be doctrine rather than, for example, the moral and political response of judge or jury. Most crimes which have denunciation and censure as the object of punishment have intention and recklessness as alternative fault elements. These two mental elements easily capture in the typical case the fundamental moral constant in punishment taking the form of retributive condemnation, namely the requirement that punishment be deserved. They do this job by limiting state punishment to those whose wrongdoing is expressive of their autonomy. Punishment is the state's response to an autonomous agent flouting standards of behaviour binding on him as a member of a society which maximises the autonomy of all members via those same standards. The gap between individual wrongdoing and the problematic case of state punishment is bridged by creating a basis for desert in punishment. If the defendant chooses to conduct his life by norms he chooses also the social consequences of breaching those norms.

If we accept that whatever utility punishment might have it must also be deserved, the centrality of intention in criminal liability will be appreciated. Whether we take the view that responsibility for harmful outcomes depends upon one's capacity to have avoided the outcome or having the kind of (bad) character which disposes to such outcomes, intention creates a linkage between outcome and action which could not create a closer association, making the outcome all the actor's

[13] Norrie, *Crime Reason and History*, ch 3 generally.

own.[14] Intentions are distinct from most other mental elements by their internal linkage to action.[15] Action is the mechanism by which human beings bring about changes in the natural world. Human actions, as opposed to mere bodily movements, are invested with meaning and have meaning for the actor. We associate our actions with ourselves as human beings only to the extent that they have meaning for us, so nervous tics and stammers are irritating for the sufferer precisely because they express no goal he takes himself to have when his body moves in the way it does. It is our intentionality, rather than say our knowledge, foresight or beliefs which invests it with meaning.

The meaning to be attributed to action does not stop, however, at the logical linkage between action and the mind. If say a person raised a gun, aimed it at another and pulled the trigger, these movements, we would properly say, were intentional in the sense that they expressed something the actor took himself to be doing. This would leave unanswered the question, however, whether the meaning to be attributed to the action was a desire to kill the other. Without more we might be disposed to presume that it was, but the actor might wish to offer a different meaning, a different intention, say that he was committing a practical joke on the victim, believing the gun to be unloaded. Again he might say that he meant—the connection between intention and meaning is here made clear in 'meant', a synonym for intended—nothing more than what he did. Without thinking or deliberating about why he was doing it he took up the gun and fired it at the victim. In such a case the question arises as to whether this meaning exhausts all other possible interpretations of the actor's intention. This is pertinent both at the level of meaning and evidence. The evidential question is difficult enough. How can a jury be certain that he did assign a (homicidal) meaning to his action? This will generally be established by reference to circumstantial evidence, including as here the use of a deadly weapon, but also other circumstances, such as his relationship to the victim which may bear upon his inclination to use it. But the substantive question is equally problematic. This comes about because of a tendency to assume that a person only 'intentionally does something' if his action was in some way prompted by a piece of mental furniture

---

[14] See RA Duff, *Intention Agency and Criminal Liability: Philosophy of Action and the Criminal Law* (Basil Blackwell, Oxford, 1990), 112–3.

[15] J Hornsby, 'On What's Intentionally Done' in Shute *et al* (eds), *Action and Value in the Criminal Law*, 55, 55–66; RA Duff, 'Action, Trying and Criminal Liability' *ibid*, 77.

called an intention predating, however closely, the relevant action. Judges as well as academic commentators operate with this assumption. In Moloney, for example, Lord Bridge said that 'the fact that, when the appellant fired the gun, the gun was pointing directly at the stepfather's head at a range of about six feet was not . . . disputed. The sole issue was whether, when he pressed the trigger, this fact and its inevitable consequence were present to the appellant's mind.'[16]

The mind, however, does not seem to work like this. Our actions tend not to be accompanied by mental thought bubbles by which we self-consciously account to ourselves for our actions before embarking upon them.[17] Typically we just 'do'. We swat a fly. We hit a ball. We shoot a person. Whether we intend the results of our actions at the time of acting is something that may never cross our minds. It is a meaning which our audience, and we, may have to assign to our action *ex post*. It may well be for this reason—that intentions express degrees of commitment to the outcome rather than cognate mental states accompanying action—as much as for evidential reasons that the old presumption was that a person intends the natural and probable consequences of his act.[18] It may also be for this reason that, as we shall see, the notion of intention manifests a degree of instability—ranging from negligence to subjective recklessness to purpose. Because the notion of intention is indistinct and may fail in any event to map satisfactorily onto blame-worthiness, tests have been developed which offer to blame people not for what they had in mind but rather the state of mind which a given action represented. Lord Bridge himself seemed unconsciously influenced by this idea. At one stage he said that those who foresee an outcome as the 'natural consequence' of what they do can be taken to intend the consequence. And in the above quotation his peculiar use of the word 'to' in 'were present to' when 'in' would be the more natural word implies he may have thought that requiring the relevant knowledge to be part of the accused's deliberative processes would be too fair to the accused. What should be important is the unmediated inevitability of the consequence, whether or not it was contemplated.

---

[16] [1985] 1 All ER 1025.

[17] H Gross, *A Theory of Criminal Justice* (OUP, New York, 1979), 97–8; For further discussion of this point see W Wilson, *Criminal Law: Doctrine and Theory* (Longmans, London, 1998), 123–4.

[18] OW Holmes, *Lectures on the Common Law* (Little Brown, Boston, 1881), chs 2 and 3. For general discussion see KJM Smith, *Lawyers, Legislators and Theorists* (Clarendon Press, Oxford, 1998), ch 5.

The case of *DPP v Smith* is an infamous example of how the doctrinal waters may be muddied by the interaction of these conceptual and evidential issues. A man who drove his car dangerously in a successful attempt to dislodge a policeman was said to have the malice aforethought for murder if, whether or not he was aware of it, death or grievous bodily harm was the natural and probable consequence of so doing. The case is generally treated as (deplorable) authority for the proposition that for result crimes of intention such as murder a rule of evidence applies which relieves the prosecution of the burden of proving that the accused had the relevant consequence in mind at the time of acting.[19] The case can equally be understood, however, as providing a statement about the content of the fault element in murder and as an oblique method of returning murder to its moral roots.[20] A striker who gets his head to the ball in an instinctive, undeliberated lunge will rightly be lauded if he scores a goal. Equally he will be vilified if, also instinctively, he kicks an opponent and is sent off. Accordingly, even if Mr Smith had nothing in his mind other than to dislodge the policeman it is not obvious as a matter of penal justice that this disqualifies society from designating him a murderer. Is he not a person who has shown, through his actions, contempt or indifference for the value of life? By treating the case as turning on matters of evidence the important substantive issue was left unexposed and unexplored.[21] It has been argued at the highest level that the label of murderer is not inappropriately attached to one who in rage, indifference, panic or other reason kills inexcusably, albeit without conscious appreciation of what he is doing.[22]

INTENTION AS A MEANS OF STRUCTURING LIABILITY

Mental elements such as intention perform more than one function. Most obviously they describe the (fault) conditions which circumscribe the state's right to censure and punish someone for their wrongdoing. If a person harms another's interests—a prima facie wrong—liability is not incurred unless that person is at fault. Intention supplies that fault.

---

[19] See for example, *Kenny's Outlines of the Criminal Law* (ed) JWC Turner (CUP Cambridge, 1962), 164; G Williams, 'Constructive Malice Revived' (1962) 23 *MLR* 605.

[20] See O W Holmes, *Lectures on the Common Law*.

[21] G Fletcher, *Rethinking Criminal Law*, 264–74.

[22] R Goff , 'The Mental Element in the Crime of Murder (1988) 104 *LQR* 30, 56.

Intention is rarely the sole fault element in criminal offences, however. For core crimes, such as crimes of violence, it is more usually an alternate fault element with recklessness. This is because where a criminal wrong speaks to the undesirability of people causing harms to the interests of others and it is a matter of morality or good character for such harm not to be caused, it matters little for the purpose of determining whether public censure and punishment is appropriate whether such harm is committed purposively or advertently.[23] What matters is whether the actor chose to perform the relevant conduct by which the harm was effected.[24] The attendant fault element is conceived in this generalised way to indicate that wherever the particular harm is attributable to something the actor did, and he had sufficient options available to him not to act in this particular fashion, it is appropriate to hold him responsible for that harm.[25]

The use of different *mens rea* words, say intention and recklessness, may also be used to grade different levels of wrongdoing. Examples of offences which are graded by mental element include the hierarchy of offences of violence under the Offences Against the Person Act 1861 where, for example, causing grievous bodily harm intentionally is graded more seriously and so punished more severely than the same harm caused recklessly. The common sense assumption here, which is by no means incontestable, is that intention is a more culpable mental state than recklessness.[26] Although both forms of conduct are wrong, deserving of condemnation and punishment, it seems appropriate to register a more stringent degree of moral criticism and punishment in respect of a person who, say, stabs his victim deliberately than of one who stabs his victim advertently. An actor's degree of commitment to a bad outcome generally, if not invariably, speaks to his overall moral turpitude. Intended (bad) outcomes are less easy to justify or excuse. Some compelling reason must be offered why one may with

---

[23] For a different view see M Moore, *Placing Blame* (OUP, Oxford, 1997) 204–5.

[24] Such choice is present whether or not 'we fault the agents because they prefer doing the actus reus to not doing it . . . and because they deliberately implement that practical preference.' A Simester, 'Why Distinguish Intention from Foresight?' in Simester and Smith (eds), *Harm and Culpability*, 77.

[25] Hart, 'Intention and Punishment' in *Punishment and Responsibility* (Clarendon Press, Oxford, 1968), ch IV.

[26] See for example A Kenny, 'Intention and Purpose in Law' in RS Summers (ed), *Essays in Legal Philosophy* (OUP, Oxford, 1968), 146–63; cf A Simester, above n 24, 73–8; For a robust rejection of this view see L Alexander, 'Insufficient Concern: A Unified Conception of Criminal Culpability' (2000) 88 *Cal LR* 955.

impunity do what would otherwise be impermissible. Indeed it may not be coincidental that grading offences by mental element is (almost) exclusive to crimes of violence. Even in culturally heterogeneous societies such as our own, hurting people is universally considered a bad thing. Because hurting people is presumptively wrong it makes particular sense to signal this core value by singling out those who deliberately flout it for special condemnation while leaving other cases of causing harm inexcusably to be addressed in lesser offences. Stabbing or shooting someone deliberately shows an absence of concern both for the interests of the other and for the values that bind us together. We condemn such wrongdoers because of the unequivocality of their rejection of a core value. But if a wound is effected, without being aimed at, by means of a highly dangerous parry in the course of an informal swordfight our condemnation is grounded in the insufficiency rather than the absence of respect shown for the interests of the other and core values.

There are also reductionist reasons for grading by mental element, although these are probably less cogent.[27] By showing commitment to an outcome it seems to render that outcome more likely to occur and the actor more in need of deterrence as an incentive not to act in the relevant fashion. Suppose Adam is discovered by Eve in the course of burgling Eve's house. If his options, in order to make his escape, are to stab her or push her downstairs it makes penal sense to give Adam an incentive to choose the least dangerous option, namely pushing her downstairs. This can be achieved by grading the former intended *actus reus* more severely than the latter foreseen *actus reus*. In the first case the harm aimed at **will only not occur if** a beneficent fate takes a hand. In the second the harm to be avoided **will occur only if** a malignant fate takes a hand. The problem of cogency referred to takes into account the fact that the actor's degree of commitment may not, in any significant sense, affect the overall likelihood of the harm occurring. For example, in my darts playing career I have probably hit more double twenties when aiming for double one than when aiming for double twenty. Similarly there may well be as many burglars who have caused serious harm by bungling than by design. Be that as it may, it is hard to resist the practical working assumption, mirrored in common perception, that grading offences by mental element is appropriate, whether as a generalised harm-reducing penal strategy or as a mechanism for

[27] Kenny, above n 26, 158–60.

bringing home to the defendant the depth of moral condemnation provoked by his breach of core values.[28]

The hierarchy of offences constituted by the Offences Against the Person Act 1861 is not **simply** a matter of grading. As will be explained below, the intention specified in section 18 constitutes the offence as a different wrong as much as a different grade of wrongdoing than section 20 and section 47. A person who is stabbed by a vicious assailant is wronged in a quite different way than someone who receives an undeliberated wound in the course of an informal sword-fight. It is right to signal this in a separate offence specification which also, incidentally, grades the offence as hierarchically more serious than the lesser offences.[29] Likewise, homicide is differentiated into the offences of murder and manslaughter by mental element. It may be thought that the differentiated mental element serves simply to filter and grade different degrees of the same wrong so that more wicked cases of homicide count as murder and less wicked count as manslaughter. This is the view taken in the United States where murder and manslaughter are conceived as forming different degrees of the same wrong and both offences are typically divided into further degrees allowing for differential punishment according to a person's degree of moral wickedness.

The more analytically robust view taken in England is that the differentiated mental elements serve primarily to distinguish two quite different wrongs—as, say, theft is distinct from fraud—which incidentally have death as part of the meat of the offence. The wrong in murder is causing death by an act of serious violence (attack) while in manslaughter it is causing death by acting dangerously.[30] These wrongs find their counterpart in two quite distinct social obligations, namely the obligation not to endanger others, instantiated most famously in Lord Atkin's neighbour principle, and the obligation not to hurt (or kill) others. Since the wrongs are differentiated, criminal justice demands that the obligation broken should be precisely identified or labelled so that blame and punishment match the wrong. We all take risks, perhaps sometimes even mortal risks, but it is that rare individual who attacks another with such brutality as to cause the other's death.[31]

[28] HLA Hart, *Punishment and Responsibility*, 122, 125–7; J Dressler, 'Does One Mens Rea Fit All? Thoughts on Alexander's Unified Conception of Criminal Culpability' (2000) 88 *Cal LR* 955.

[29] J Horder, 'Rethinking Non-Fatal Offences Against the Person' [1994] 14 *OJLS* 335.

[30] For full consideration see RA Duff, *Intention, Agency and Criminal Liability*.

[31] See W Wilson, 'Murder and the Structure of Homicide' in AJ Ashworth and B Mitchell (eds), *Rethinking English Homicide Law* (OUP, Oxford, 2000), 21, 23–4.

Mental elements may, then, alternatively filter those deserving of punishment from those who do not, grade degrees of blameworthiness and finally actually serve to define what it is that is wrong about what the actor does. In the latter case they help to describe the form of a social prohibition. It is important to be clear, moreover, which one of these functions is being performed. The Law Commission have recently proposed the use of mental elements as a grading mechanism in homicide with a fault element reflected in sentencing differentials degrading from intentional/purposive killing (murder) to (subjective) recklessness (manslaughter) to negligence (negligent killing). It is not clear how doctrinal rationality will be advanced by these proposals. If the offence labels serve to differentiate wrongs then these mental elements are inadequate for the task. In particular, they fail to capture precisely why murder is thought different in kind rather than degree from manslaughter. This is not simply that intentional killings, per se, are morally special. What is special about murder is that it issues from an (intentional) attack.[32] If, as is likely, murder is conceived by the Commission as differentiated from manslaughter only by degrees of blameworthiness it seems that intention is being asked to do more moral work than it is capable of. As is well recognised, while killing someone intentionally appears to represent the most morally depraved instance of culpable killing, it is by no means not necessarily so. Some reckless killings attract more revulsion and indignation than some intentional killings. A callous brute who fires a gun into an occupied railway carriage, not caring whether anyone dies, is generally reckoned to be more blameworthy than a person who in a burst of unprovoked anger kills a rival for her partner's heart.[33]

INTENTION AS A MEANS OF STRUCTURING WRONGS

Intentions existing independently of actions cannot form the basis of criminal liability. Why should they? Who is wronged when a person forms an unrealised intention to kill, or steal from them? What harm is unleashed? From a reductionist point of view there is no necessary linkage between one's future intentions, that is, one's internal state of commitment to a given outcome and the occurrence of that outcome. Future

---

[32] Or comparable activity.
[33] Wilson, above n 31 at 24–6.

intentions may be changed, recanted or may simply come to naught. At least until action is taken in furtherance of them there is no rational basis upon which intentions can be subjected to moral evaluation.

This does not tell the full story, however, since it is through our deeds that we are subjected to moral evaluation and intentions may play a signal role in constituting those deeds. An actor's intention plays a key role in the constitution of wrongs which have their root in individuated moral prohibitions. Theft is a different wrong from fraud which is in turn different from robbery and burglary. Again the reason why we should not punch people (respecting autonomy) is not the same reason why we should not drive our cars dangerously (restricting our capacity to cause harm). There are clearly strong grounds for flagging these distinct reasons so as to enable citizens to form a realistic picture of the structure of moral values which drives the criminal law.

It may well be in fact that intentions, specifically ulterior intentions, should play a yet more substantial role in the construction of criminal identities. Jeremy Horder has put a compelling case in favour of extending the range of crimes of ulterior intent so as to reflect more accurately the moral distinctions between different forms of wrongdoing. If we consider, for example, wounding with intent to cause grievous bodily harm and assault with intent to rape, we find that that they serve to record important moral distinctions between different forms of wrongful action. For example, it would overstate the nature of his wrongdoing to convict a person of attempted rape where he has done nothing more than grab his victim with this ulterior purpose in mind. Equally it would be understating it to charge only an assault. For reasons both of fair labelling and communicative efficacy the wrongdoer should be convicted of a serious **sexual** assault and it is his intention which converts a quite minor wrong into a serious and quite separate wrong.[34]

Without forms of criminal wrongdoing which take full account of the practical significance of intentions accompanying actions the temptation is to force such examples of moral wrongdoing into legal pigeonholes they were not made for, thus destabilising doctrine in other fields. Doctrine in the field of theft illustrates this tendency. At present such conduct as removing car keys to facilitate a later theft of the car can be treated as theft of the car itself in so far as it may be interpreted as an

---

[34] J Horder, 'Crimes of Ulterior Intent' in in A Simester and ATH Smith (eds), *Harm and Culpability* (Clarendon Press, Oxford, 1996), 153, 164–6.

assumption of rights of ownership over the car.[35] This clearly fails to reflect the underlying core of moral wrongdoing which the crime of theft seeks to redress. A better solution, in Horder's view, would be the creation of a separate offence of interfering with property with intent to steal mimicking the manner in which burglary is separated into the wrong of stealing while trespassing in someone else's property and the wrong of trespassing with intent to steal.[36]

Structuring Homicide

An infamous example of how destabilising compensatory doctrines necessarily arise in cases where doctrine fails to reflect the underlying core of moral wrongdoing occurred in *Hyam v DPP*.[37] Here the House of Lords upheld the defendant's conviction for murder after she had set fire to a house to frighten her rival in love, knowing the latter was in occupation but without any desire to cause her any serious injury. We can understand full well why the prosecution chose to charge the defendant with murder rather than manslaughter or committing arson with intent to endanger life. Her conduct was despicable, highly dangerous, and showed her utter contempt for the value of life. For these reasons a conviction would be proper in most common law systems and, indeed, in Scotland where it is degrees of moral heinousness generally rather than intention specifically which police the line between murder and lesser killings. Given that these lesser offences were available the House of Lords treated it as incumbent upon them to reach a decision which honoured the traditional method of distinguishing between murder and manslaughter. They achieved this, as is well known, by designating murder a crime of intention while extending the reach of intention far beyond its core case to include the state of mind of one who acts in the knowledge that a consequence is likely to a specified if uncertain degree of likelihood. The case suffered criticism both for producing an incoherent notion of intention and for destroying the bright line separating murder from manslaughter by allowing foresight to satisfy the fault element in both.

In the opinion of some critical observers *Hyam* represents simply the clearest example of the inherent instability of murder doctrine and those other areas of the criminal law which have intention as their

---

[35] By s 3(1) Theft Act 1968.

[36] Horder, above n 34 at 170–1.

[37] *Hyam v DPP* (1975) AC 55.

[38] A Norrie, *Crime, Reason and History*, 50–2; *Punishment Responsibility and Justice* (Clarendon Press, Oxford, 2000), 177–9; 'Oblique Intention and Legal Politics' [1989] *Crim LR* 793, at 800–07; N Lacey, 'A Clear Concept of Intention: Elusive or Illusory' (1993) 56 *MLR* 621.

constitutive mental element.[38] Criminal doctrine boasts the ability to judge whether a killer is guilty of murder or manslaughter without reference to moral considerations such as context or motivation. The only question for the court is a technical one. Did the defendant intend to kill or cause serious injury. Faced with a case of supremely wicked risk-taking, however, the doctrinal gloves come off and strategies emerge to allow juries to reach a moral rather than a formal evaluation of the defendant's behaviour. In *Hyam* this strategy was blatant. The jury was to be told that consciously running the risk of a consequence would, if the risk were great enough, amount to intending the consequence. In later cases the strategy was no less effective for being covert. Juries were directed that they were entitled to infer intention where they were convinced the actor foresaw the consequence as a moral certainty. The message however was muddled. If foresight of moral certainty is not a special case of intention but a state of mind from which intention may be inferred it still leaves intention undefined. Being conceptually vague it thus leaves open the option for juries, with perhaps a hint of judicial encouragement, to infer it, whatever it is, from foresight of less than moral certainty, for example probability or high probability. It also allows the jury to acquit of murder those whose motives were either too good to warrant condemnation at all or not bad enough to warrant the stigma of murderer.[39] Juries are thus enabled, as is their disposition, to record their moral judgment that the social obligation to which the crime charged offered its support had, whatever the definition might say, been broken.[40]

There is no doubt some cogency in this critique but does it amount to a fatal attack on the capacity of intention to mark stable boundaries between the wrongful and innocent actions and between different criminal wrongs? As far as murder itself is concerned it may be argued that present criminal doctrine is trying too hard anyway to keep the wrongs of murder and manslaughter conceptually distinct. Perhaps juries should be allowed some moral elbowroom, as occurs in Scotland and the USA, to convict on the basis of moral turpitude rather than the morally uninformative 'intention'.[41] In England the jury is already

[39] See *Goodfellow*, considered below.

[40] Woollin appears to have solved this problem while leaving the meaning of intention ambiguous. W Wilson, 'Doctrinal Rationality after Woollin' (1999) *Mod LR* 447; cf A Norrie 'After Woollin' ([1999] *Crim LR* 532; *Punishment Responsibility and Justice* (Clarendon Press, Oxford, 2000), 171–81.

[41] N Lacey, 'A Clear Concept of Intention: Elusive or Illusory' (1993) 56 *MLR* 621; J Horder, 'Intention in the Criminal Law: A Rejoinder' (1995) *MLR* 678.

given a central role in deciding what degree of negligence needs to be displayed to convert ordinary non-punishable negligence into gross negligence, the fault element for manslaughter. It is quite likely that English law would have settled on this were it not for the fact that murder in this country carries a mandatory sentence and so there is understandable reluctance to allow such a flexible concept to do the work. In any event this is not a view which is supported here. Conviction labels are as important as is justice in the distribution of punishments.[42] These labels instantiate and reflect a pre-juridical method of categorising antisocial deeds, which method reflects, more or less precisely, the reality of our moral culture. The aim must be to achieve maximum precision. Whether or not one is a murderer as opposed to a manslayer is not a matter of opinion. It is a matter of satisfying an offence definition with a relatively high degree of specificity. The obvious danger is that a risk-centred approach to the fault element in murder serves simply to allow expression for, rather than refine and focus the jury's moral judgment. While this may be (just) appropriate for manslaughter—there must be some way of registering and measuring society's condemnation of appalling lapses of care leading to death—it cannot be for murder which carries so much symbolic importance.[43]

The task then is to develop an approach capable of doing justice to the idea that murder and manslaughter are distinct wrongs while creating a basis for differentiation, which by and large also satisfies our moral intuition, that murder is the more morally reprehensible offence. Significantly in *Hyam* the glimmerings of such an approach was mapped out by Lord Hailsham who located the wrong in murder in a variety of possible intentions.[44] In his view the wrong in murder is satisfied whether a person intends to kill, intends to cause serious injury or intends, without lawful excuse, to expose his victim to the serious risk of death or serious injury. Those who kill with any of these intentions commit a different wrong from those who cause death knowing that their conduct is likely to kill. This is so, however substantial is the risk foreseen and however 'wicked' we conceive their risk-taking to be.

---

[42] This is why we also have various crimes of reckless endangerment to deal with death caused in the course of acting dangerously rather than simply manslaughter. See further C Clarkson, 'Context and Culpability in Involuntary Manslaughter' in AJ Ashworth and B Mitchell (eds), *Rethinking English Homicide Law* (OUP, Oxford, 2000), 132.

[43] W Wilson, *ibid* (2000) 23–4.

[44] J Horder, 'Varieties of Intention, Criminal Attempts and Endangerment' (1994) 14 *LS* 335, 341–4.

A distinct line must be drawn between crimes of endangerment such as manslaughter and causing death by dangerous driving, and crimes of violence such as murder. The point of crimes of endangerment is to criminalise and punish those who take significant risks with the lives and interests of others while 'doing their own thing'. The point of crimes of violence, by contrast, is to criminalise and punish those who launch attacks against the autonomy and physical security of others. It is through the person's intention that we conceive such attacks to have taken place.

With this as our point of reference what distinguishes Mrs Hyam from other risk-takers is that the object of her action was to expose her victim to the risk of death, which is why she set fire to the house only upon being assured of the presence of the victim.[45] Her action demanded a victim and thus, like murder by intending grievous bodily harm, is victim-centred.[46] Intentionally taking the risk thus structures her conduct[47] and allows us to attribute the death, as with GBH murder, to an intentional attack although the risk foreseen may have been relatively slight.[48] Compare *Goodfellow*, another case of arson which went fatally wrong.[49] Mr Goodfellow's purpose in setting alight his own council house was to be rehoused rather than to act hostilely to the interests of the eventual victims. Indeed, if he had been told the house was uninhabited at the time of firing it would have no doubt strengthened rather than weakened his commitment to the project. Looked at another way, which indicates how distinct the two wrongs are, the (merely) reckless killer, such as dangerous drivers and arsonists, act despite the risk of death. Mrs Hyam and terrorists generally act because of it.[50] If there were no risk to life attending their conduct they would not have planted the bomb/started the fire. They would have changed their behaviour.

While there are cogent grounds for conceiving of Mrs Hyam's conduct as involving a different kind of wrong as well as a more serious

---

[45] The key words here are 'could be'. The analysis is not that the actor intends to bring about the outcome but that he intends to subject the victim to the risk of the outcome, which requires the actor both to believe that acting in the way he intends creates the possibility that the outcome will occur and to act on that belief; J Horder, *ibid*.

[46] W Wilson, 'A Plea for Rationality in the Law of Murder' [1990] *LS* 307 at 317.

[47] RA Duff, *Intention, Agency and Criminal Liability*, 110 *et seq*.

[48] LaFave and Scott, *Criminal Law* (West, St Paul, 1978), 542–3, support this lack of emphasis upon degrees of risk where the defendant's conduct lacks any possible social utility in commenting upon *Banks v State*, above.

[49] (1986) 83 Cr App Rep 23.

[50] See n 43.

wrong than that committed by Mr Goodfellow, this does not commit us to conclude that that wrong is murder, however. It might appear, rather, that her case falls between two stools—the wrong of murder conceived as killing in the course of an act of serious violence—and the wrong of manslaughter conceived as killing in the course of reckless endangerment.[51] Arguably then the problem posed by cases such as *Hyam v DPP* where the accused acts in order to create the risk of death or injury would be better addressed by pinpointing the moral wrong involved in such cases with greater precision. It is not that the accused intended to kill, nor merely that he recklessly exposed his victim to the risk of death. It is that he meant to do so. The simplest way of filling this gap in the structure of criminal liability is through the creation of crimes of intentional endangerment. Arson with intent to endanger life would be a narrow form of such offence which could be broadened to criminalise any form of dangerous activity undertaken with the intention to endanger life. If it were thought necessary, such conduct crimes could be supplemented with result crimes, such as causing death by intentional endangerment to remove the destabilising effect that particularly reprehensible occasions of risk-taking exert on criminal doctrine.

The ramifications of this analysis are potentially far reaching and will be considered again in chapter 9. If, as some have urged, all citizens were given a rule book containing the basic guidance citizens needed to avoid falling foul of the criminal law, such a book should ideally express itself in a way as to demonstrate the overall structure of criminal wrongdoing.[52] This requires attention to be paid to the constitutive effect of intentions on criminal wrongdoing and their connection with underlying moral prohibitions. There are two separate but related issues to be addressed. The first, concerning intention's use as defining a wrong, is determining what it is which has to be intended and has been considered here. The second is concerned with determining what it is to intend an action or consequence so that the right people are subjected to punishment for bringing about a given wrong. This will be considered in the next section.

---

[51] See J Horder, 'Varieties of Intention, Criminal Attempts and Endangerment' (1994) 14 *LS* at 344.

[52] See Meir Dan-Cohen 'Decision Rules and Conduct Rules: On Acoustic Separation in Criminal Law' (1984) 97 *Harv LR* 625; Paul H Robinson, 'Rules of Conduct and Principles of Adjudication' (1990) 57 *Univ of Chicago LR* 729; *Structure and Function of Criminal Law* (OUP, Oxford, 1997).

THE MEANING OF INTENTION

Our everyday usage of intention designates consequences as intended if they were 'meant', desired, aimed at; if they were the reason, purpose or objective of the actor's action.[53] Accordingly, the clearest case of intentional action is acting in furtherance of a pre-existing design. However, as has been explained, impulsive action may be no less intentional nor the consequences which ensue intended. The point about premeditation is not that it is a special state of mind but that it represents the clearest case of what the state of mind represents, namely commitment to the outcome. This everyday meaning is, on the face of it, the perfect vehicle for doing the moral job of attributing particular deeds to actors in criminal doctrine. This is because it is through our intentions that our actions are structured and therefore by which we make contributions, good or bad, to the world and society we inhabit. There is a fundamental moral difference between throwing a coin at a beggar for purposes of charity and throwing the same coin in order to hurt them. The judgments of praise or blame that we would visit on people take account of this and it seems quite appropriate that this response should map directly onto criminal liability.

These rules of usage are reflected in criminal doctrine. By and large, for example, intention has a core, or 'black and white' meaning about which there is little judicial or theoretical argument. A person intends an action or a consequence for the purpose of criminal liability when he acts in order to effect it either for its own sake or because it is a means to or precondition of achieving some other object. So if A shoots at B because he wants to kill him he intends to kill him. Again if A shoots B because B is trapped in a blazing car and is screaming in agony A intends to kill B as a means of saving him from unavoidable pointless pain. If A shoots B intending to kill him where B is standing behind C's plate glass window A intends not merely to kill B but also to break C's window. We say that he intends to break the window because success in A's project demands C's window to be broken. It is a precondition of success. In this sense the commitment shown to the consequence is indistinguishable from the case where A desired the consequence for its

---

[53] See RA Duff, *Intention, Agency and Criminal Liability: Philosophy of Action and the Criminal Law* (Basil Blackwell, Oxford, 1990); AR White, *Misleading Cases* (Clarendon Press, Oxford, 1991), ch 4.

own sake.[54] A would consider his action a failure if the window was not broken and would no doubt redouble his efforts if this occurred. A could hardly protest, for example, that 'he did not mean' to break the 'window' or that he did not mean to kill B, because he committed himself to do just that. They were inseparable parts of the package of things he did aim at', which he would not have forfeited if this meant failure in his purpose.[55] A definition of intention which reflects this idea that intention requires commitment to the outcome was adopted in the case of Mohan: 'a decision to bring about, in so far as it lies within the accused's power . . . the relevant consequence, no matter whether the accused desired the consequence or not'.[56]

The limits of this core meaning can be understood by comparing two cases. In *R v Cox* a doctor was found guilty of attempted murder for administering a fatal dose of drugs to a patient.[57] He did so for reasons of compassion as the patient was suffering the excruciating agony of terminal cancer. In *Adams* a doctor also gave his patient, who was suffering excruciating pain, a dose of painkillers so large that it advanced the death of the patient.[58] Devlin J ruled that as long as the dose was given for clinical reasons (pain relief) the doctor's action, and his intent, was lawful. The difference between the two cases is that in the former the doctor acted for the purpose of killing the patient. If death had not occurred he would, no doubt, have considered his action to be a failure. In the latter the evidence showed that the doctor may have acted for the purpose of relieving pain. If the patient died he was resigned to it, but would have been satisfied if his action had the effect merely of stopping the pain. The latter simply could not have had a (direct) intention to kill if he acted simply to avert pain. Only if he acted so as to relieve pain **by killing** would the two intentions coalesce. How can we reconcile this

---

[54] For a different view, although he does not specifically deal with the case of logically inseparable consequences, see AR White, *ibid*, 51–61.

[55] RA Duff's test for intention, above n 53, 110. There is of course a further conceptual distinction between the two cases. In the second case, by contrast, this degree of commitment is absent or unprovable. Sure A is unwilling to forfeit the consequence if this is a necessary evil attending his purpose but it would not signal the failure of his enterprise if B leapt out of the way and escaped injury. Indeed A would likely be very satisfied with the outcome.

[56] [1975] 2 All ER 193 per James LJ at 200. Notice that this definition does not assert that intention is synonymous with purpose. 'When I go to a meeting intending both to cause trouble and to leave before the end, both of these are aimed at, although only the former is my reason or purpose for going.' AR White, *Misleading Cases*, 61.

[57] (1992) 12 BMLR 38.

[58] [1957] *Crim LR* 365.

point with the proposition that motive is irrelevant to intention? The answer is that motive is evidential. A person's reasons for acting may help us to decide what an actor was aiming at or meant to achieve, but unless they form a defence, they do not form a separate basis upon which to make moral sense of his actions. If a person's intention was to kill, such that he would count his actions a failure if he did not succeed, that intention cannot be displaced by a knowledge of why he came to form that intention.

As will be apparent from these examples, a significant facet of intention as a fault term is that it is formally value neutral. The avowed reason for this is that it is possible for the criminal law to fix in advance the circumstances in which a person can escape liability for intentionally causing harm—say through defences such as self defence or duress. Such persons then have a proper choice whether to act as the rule would have them act, or not do so and face punishment. The criminal law cannot, however, fix in advance what a person should do when, without intending to cause harm, they advert to it as when they are driving cars, playing football, demolishing houses and so on. This must be a question of practical judgment. For this reason people who cause harms by risk-taking have their culpability and desert in punishment assessed according to the reasonableness of their acting as they did. Recklessness or negligence are then value laden. They express a judgment that the actor has acted otherwise than we would expect of responsible citizens and so is blameworthy. No moral gap exists between the attitude (or lack of it) he brings to his actions and the reason why we feel those actions are discreditable.[59]

That a consequence is produced intentionally, by contrast, says relatively little about whether we should morally approve or disapprove its occurrence. Of course, if the consequence, as with death, is to be discouraged intending to bring about that consequence will typically provoke just criticism. But this will not be a consequence of the consequence having been intended. It will be because by dint of such intention the defendant will generally find it hard to convince the moral audience that his deed is inoffensive, his conscience clear and his character unsullied, and that blame would be unjust. But our intentions may sanctify as well as discredit our deeds. A pilot who explodes his stricken aeroplane seconds before it crashes in a heavily populated city

[59] J Gardner and H Jung 'Making Sense of Mens Rea: Antony Duff's Account' [1991] 11 *OJLS* 559, at 574.

location will no doubt receive (posthumous) praise rather than blame, although in destroying the plane he will have killed not only himself but his co-travellers.

This has the obvious potential for injustice in such cases where an intended harm does not reflect badly upon the actor and no defence is available. The case of *Steane*[60] is often used to illustrate the kind of compensatory mechanism which arises to bridge the gap between legal and moral evaluation by allowing a formal concept (intention) to do a moral job of work.[61] The defendant made several propaganda broadcasts for the Nazis during the last war. He was later charged with, and convicted of, 'doing acts likely to assist the enemy with intent to assist the enemy'. He had done so under threats that he and his family would be sent to a concentration camp if he did not. His conviction was quashed on the basis of a narrow form of intention requiring proof that the broadcasts were done for the purpose of assisting the Nazis, which they were clearly not. Rather he decided to help them as a means to an end, namely to protect the interests of his family—a purpose all but the most high minded would accept as beyond moral criticism. But, and here is where fault lines between the demands of law and morality are clearly exposed, this would only be so where, as here, the accused's family's life was on the line. If it were not; if he had made propaganda broadcasts to advance their material well being, moral criticism would be his due and the adoption of so narrow a notion of intention politically untenable. In theory, there-fore, criminal doctrine prefers to avoid such dualities by adopting a motive-independent notion of intention qualified by defences such as duress, necessity and self-defence to accommodate those cases where the defendant's reason for action is sufficiently compelling to override the primary obligation. So, in *Kupfer*,[62] Lord Reading stated that in deciding whether the accused, who had traded with the enemy for the purpose of an offence under the Trading with the Enemy Act 1914, had intended to benefit the enemy the question was not whether trade was entered into **for this purpose** but whether the accused **knew** that the enemy would thereby benefit.[63]

---

[60] [1947] KB 997.

[61] G Williams, *The Mental Element in Crime* (OUP, Oxford, 1965) 21; AJ Ashworth, 'Criminal Liability in a Medical Context: The Treatment of Good Intentions' in A Simester and ATH Smith (eds), *Harm and Culpability*, 173.

[62] [1915] 2 KB 321.

[63] For analysis see KJM Smith, *Lawyers, Legislators and Theorists*, 280.

Cases such as *Steane* would pose less of a problem for doctrinal stability if it could be represented as a one-off failure of rationality. It is not clear that it can be so represented however. It may stand simply as the clearest evidence that our everyday notion of intention is itself unstable and, therefore, is unfit to do the job proposed for it in criminal doctrine.[64] While non-lawyers have no general difficulty grasping the difference between an intention and a motive, lawyers and non-lawyers alike do not always agree on what a person's intention consists of. This is not necessarily due to conceptual fallacy or penological chicanery but because we follow, consciously or unconsciously, rules of usage more nuanced than juridical definitions are apt to instantiate. Sometimes, as in *Steane*, intention cries out to be interpreted as purpose. This is not merely because we feel Mr Steane is not to blame for his wrongdoing but because, on one interpretation of the offence charged, he had committed no such wrongdoing. This was Lord Goddard CJ's interpretation. He distinguished between crimes defined in such a way as to show that the wrong must be effected 'in order to bring' about a particular undesirable consequence (here giving assistance to the enemy), where the accused's motive for acting was central, and other crimes of intention where it was not. In his view, and it seems quite plausible, the use of the words 'with intent' were to limit liability under the regulation to cases where an ulterior purpose were to be proved. One presumes that Lord Goddard would also have held that a pedestrian who amputated the arm of a car crash victim as a means of rescuing her from the wreckage before she died of blood loss would not be guilty of causing grievous bodily harm with intent to cause grievous bodily harm for the purpose of liability under section 18 Offences Against the Person Act 1861. What sets section 18 apart from other cases of violence, on this analysis, is that the action is done for a reason, the reason being to achieve the specific harmful consequence which was in fact achieved. It goes without saying that this is not the pedestrian's reason for acting.[65]

Sometimes, by contrast, popular usage hallows a notion of intention which extends beyond this narrow meaning to include cases where, although an actor neither desired the action or consequence either for its own sake or as a means to another end, he nevertheless foresaw it as a morally or practical certain side effect of what he did desire. A wicked

[64] See Norrie, above n 40.
[65] Cf R A Duff, 'Intentions Legal and Philosophical' (1989) 9 *OJLS* 76.

surgeon who removes her victim's liver for transplant into her dying husband can deny the intention to kill the victim but it is not a claim that we need to take seriously at either the conceptual or the moral level. We would say without fear of criticism for our sloppy or slippery reasoning that she intended/meant to kill because she knew that this is what her conduct meant for the victim. This ambivalent response finds its counterpart in ambivalent doctrine. Lining up against cases such as *Steane* a substantial body of authority stands for the proposition that a person who acts in the knowledge that a consequence is a morally certain side effect of the accused's avowed purpose intends both that purpose and the side effect. The distinction drawn is between cases where a side effect is recognised as practically or morally certain to accompany success, and cases where it is recognised to a lesser degree of probability. The reason for this is to prevent a blurring of the line between intention and recklessness. The Law Commission have proposed a definition of intention intended largely as a restatement of the existing law. It states that a person acts,

(a) 'intentionally' with respect to a result when
(i)   it is his purpose to cause it; or*
(ii) although it is not his purpose to cause that result, he knows that it would occur in the ordinary course of events if he were to succeed in his purpose of causing some other result.

The definition renders it clear, for example, that a person intends to kill both when he wants to kill and also when he recognises that death is a morally certain side effect of what he does want to achieve if things go according to plan. Only where his reason for acting is to prevent the result from occurring will such foresight not constitute an intention to bring that result about.[66] Foresight of virtual certainty is a form of intention not simply a means of proving intention. It designates the wicked surgeon's conduct as intentional with respect to the death of his patient if he removes her liver but not if he removes her kidney. The merit of this approach is both substantive and evidential. Substantively, as the example illustrates, actors who act knowing that a given consequence is inseparable from the consequence aimed at are usually indistinguishable in terms of both culpability and responsibility from those who act for that very purpose. Evidentially, it is easier to

---

[66] As where A throws B from the top of a burning building in a vain attempt to save her life.

prove what an actor knew or believed would happen than what he wanted to occur.

The problem posed by the extended form of intention is that it creates a potential culpability gap, since it converts a person's lawful intention into an unlawful intention not by reference to any mischievous disposition, choice or morally flawed reasoning but simply by reference to the state of his knowledge. Intention, unlike recklessness and negligence, does not filter out liability for actions prompted by good motive.[67] For example, A is driving quite lawfully on a narrow mountain cliff road and encounters, on turning a corner, a bunch of hikers stretched out across the road. If, instead of plunging in heroic self-sacrifice off the cliff, he ploughs through the middle of them he does not act recklessly for, say, the crime of reckless driving if this was his only way of staying alive.[68] Deciding whether he acted recklessly requires a moral evaluation of his conduct. Here his risk-taking would, no doubt, be deemed justified because it is quite reasonable and justifiable for a person to choose to bring about a bad consequence, even death, as a side effect if the alternative is his own death.[69] The general thrust of criminal doctrine supports this conclusion since it recognises no general duty of self-sacrifice in the interests of others.[70] If, on the other hand, a hiker died and he is charged with murder the mental element is satisfied under the broad definition without reference to whether or not his conduct was justified.

This is not to say, of course that A would necessarily be guilty of murder. A's liability would depend upon his being able to raise a justificatory defence. As it happens this is not a foregone conclusion. In English law, for example, there is no such defence at present[71] and a trial judge is in no position to invent one. This problem is seen at its most intractable in the field of accessories.[72] A gunsmith who supplies a gun under licence to a customer is acting lawfully. If, however, he knows that the customer intends to use it to commit a criminal offence

---

[67] See generally AP Simester, 'Why Distinguish Intention from Foresight?' in A Simester and ATH Smith (eds), *Harm and Culpability*.

[68] The modern version of this offence is dangerous driving. The point at issue is not affected.

[69] For discussion of this hypothetical see W Wilson, 'A Plea for Rationality in the Crime of Murder' [1990] 10 *LS* 307; G Williams, 'Rationality in Murder: A Reply' (1991) 11 *LS* 204.

[70] This is particularly clear in the case of omissions.

[71] Duress of circumstances which most nearly covers the case is not available to murder.

[72] See most recently *JF Alford Transport* [1997] 2 Cr App R 326.

he is deemed, under the standard meaning, to intend to assist the commission of the offence. A lawful intention—to ply one's trade—becomes unlawful not by reference to the gunsmith's reasons for acting but by reference to his knowledge—knowledge it should be noted that he has no duty to do anything with. He need not inform the police of the customer's plans. He may sell him a holster, or a ten-gallon hat. His autonomy is respected this far. But no further. He may not sell him the gun. In standard cases such as this we may not scruple to sympathise too much. He is acting antisocially after all. But doctrine must fit the non-standard case as well and when it does, as where say M gives her headstrong underage daughter, contraceptives in a desperate attempt to prevent an unwanted pregnancy, doctrine is placed under strain.[73]

INTENTION, MOTIVE AND DOCTRINAL RATIONALITY

It is easy to see how these different cases and the problems they provoke can be exploited to support the view discussed earlier that doctrinal contradiction and instability are inevitable by-products of a system which seeks to exclude consideration of the accused's motive and context in determining questions of criminal fault.[74] A criminal justice system which permitted punishment and conviction of stigmatic offences such as murder, theft and treason irrespective of whether the actor's conduct was properly censurable would be something of a misnomer. In fact, orthodox criminal theory does not deny that contradiction and instability exist. Rather it seeks to offer an account which denies that this is necessitated by the mismatch between the mechanisms developed by the criminal law to protect individuals from unjust censure and punishment, and those developed to protect society from antisocial or harmful activity. It is quite plausible, for example, that much of the reason for doctrinal instability in this area is attributable to a theoretical rather than a political inclination to keep the meaning of intention a matter for the general part. It might be more appropriate, rather, for it to be replaced by offence-specific definitions tailored

---

[73] Duress of circumstances would not be available here as pregnancy is hardly a life threatening condition. Cf though *Bourne* [1939] 1 KB 687. Under the American Model Penal Code such action would be justified.

[74] Such exclusion is workable only so long as this does not contradict the common sense understandings of moral fault which formal mental elements such as intention only too bluntly reflect.

to the precise form of moral wrongdoing embodied in a given offence as implied in Lord Goddard's approach in *Steane*.[75] As John Gardner has argued, variation rather than uniformity is the key for providing a rational fault element.[76] Or put another way, it is only 'academic over-ambition, coupled with the zeal of utilitarian law reformers, that leads theorists to strain to find or impose order and uniformity on what is naturally a highly variegated set of laws'.[77]

A more typical response to the inconsistent doctrine in *Steane* and *Kupfer* is to portray *Steane* as a failure of rationality in an otherwise rational system rather than an indicator of systemic irrationality. On this view there is indeed, as the decision in the case itself illustrates, no basis upon which to level just moral criticism and therefore state censure and punishment. However, to ensure a proper marriage between the justice of form and the justice of content, the question to be asked of Mr Steane was not the one asked of him, that is, whether he breached his obligation—if he did not then neither did Mr Kupfer and this would effectively destroy the point of wartime defence regulations—but whether he had good reason to. He did, but Mr Kupfer did not. The rationality of the system can be upheld as long as one makes a clear distinction between what the rules state are the conditions for liability and the rules which indicate when those conditions are cancelled. In effect, this is thought to be consistent with our overall method for allocating blame. No doubt Mr Steane knew that he was doing wrong. If he is to avoid blame, therefore, it must be because the conditions under which he chose to do so permitted him to do so or otherwise excused the breach of his primary obligation.[78]

---

[75] Some weak support for this line can be derived from Lord Steyn's opinion in Woollin, 'I approach the issues arising in this appeal on the basis that it does not follow that "intent" necessarily has precisely the same meaning in every context in the criminal law. The focus of the present appeal is the crime of murder'. See W Wilson, 'Doctrinal Rationality after Woollin' (1999) *Mod LR* 447, 459–60.

[76] 'In engaging with the widespread enthusiasm for the general part our attention has to shift away from the demand for rationality and principle per se and onto the supposed connection . . . with generality, ie the alleged desirability of removing idiosyncrasy and diversity.' J Gardner, 'On the General Part of the Criminal Law' in RA Duff (ed), *Philosophy and the Criminal Law* (1998) 205 at 206, 249; cf N Lacey, 'Contingency, Coherence and Conceptualism: Reflections on the Encounter between "Critique" and the Philosophy of the Criminal Law' *ibid.,* Wilson 'Murder and the Structure of Homicide' (2000) 46–53; for support for a differentiated meaning in cases such as complicity, attempt, and crimes of ulterior intent see G Williams, 'Oblique Intention' [1987] *Camb LJ* 417, at 435 *et seq*. RA Duff, 'Intentions Legal and Philosophical' (1989) 9 *OJLS* 76.

[77] J Horder, 'The Irrelevance of Motive in Criminal Law', at 186–7.

[78] *Ibid* 174

Compartmentalising the fault element in this way is not objectionable as long as doctrine punishes wrongdoing as so defined and acquits the morally innocent. How doctrine achieves this—by fault element or by defence—is not set in stone. Rational doctrine requires only a systematic mechanism capable of doing the moral job of work achieved by the concepts of recklessness and negligence in filtering out those deserving punishment and the stigma of conviction from those who do not. Extending the fault element currently designated by the word intention to include consequences known to be certain requires, therefore, a cogent support structure of justificatory defences or else a 'lawful excuse' qualification. Otherwise, something has to give—doctrinal integrity or criminal justice.[79] For purposes of illustration the Indian Code section 81 provides a definition of lawful excuse which might profitably supplement the standard definition without succumbing to undue indeterminacy:

> Nothing is an offence merely by reason of its being done with the knowledge that it (will) cause harm, if it be done without any criminal intention to cause harm, and in good faith for the purpose of preventing or avoiding other harm to person or property.[80]

The unsatisfactory method currently adopted in domestic doctrine requires judges to get along and make do. As a consequence it is no surprise that they have adopted, in the definition of intention, a flexible friend which in appropriate circumstances allows good intentions to take doctrinal precedence over knowledge but otherwise is satisfied by knowledge alone. A more rational structuring process would, say in the manner of the Indian Code, ensure an appropriate moral definitional correspondence between intention and knowledge or else specify precisely whether the fault element requires intention or knowledge, or indeed purpose. This is because while there appears to be no necessary moral difference between acting with the knowledge that a consequence will occur and acting with the desire that it shall there is nevertheless a difference in the ways our reasons for acting bear upon our culpability. If we cannot, as *Cox* illustrates, justify intentionally

---

[79] As it did in *Gillick* [1986] AC 112, *Fretwell* (1862) Le & Ca 161, *Salford Health Authority ex p Janaway* [1988] 2 WLR 442; *Clark* (1984) 80 Cr App Rep 344; for a discussion of the issues see I Dennis, 'The Mental Element for Accessories' in PF Smith (ed), *Criminal law: Essays in Honour of JC Smith* (Butterworths, London, 1987); Sullivan, 'Intent Purpose and Complicity [1988] *Crim LR* 641 and Ian Dennis' reply thereto at 651–3.

[80] Indian Code s 81.

producing bad consequences by reference to the good side effects which will occur we can, as *Adams* illustrates, justify knowingly producing bad side effects by reference to the good reasons for which one acts.[81] Doctrinal flexibility is, therefore, necessary but not inevitable to accommodate the culpability gap which sometimes opens up between those who aim at causing harm and those who cause harms as side effects.[82]

---

[81] A Simester above n. 67 at 92.

[82] See AJ Ashworth, 'Criminal Liability in a Medical Context: The Treatment of Good Intentions' in Simester and Smith (eds), *Harm and Culpability*, 173; W Wilson, *Criminal Law: Doctrine and Theory* (Longmans, London, 1998), 282–99; RF Schopp, *Justification Defences and Just Convictions* (CUP, Cambridge, 1998), ch 2.

6

Causing Harm

Case 1

Eve, a patient, is admitted to hospital unconscious having been stung by a wasp to the venom of which she is intolerant. Adam, a young and inexperienced house surgeon, has been on call for twenty-four hours and is having difficulty concentrating. Instead of administering the prescribed remedy, which is an injection of adrenaline, he administers a sedative intended for another patient. Eve dies as a result.

Eve's death is an occurrence a civilised society takes pains to prevent. Something has gone wrong here. Eve's friends and relatives will want explanations, not simply to satisfy their curiosity, but as a way of coming to terms with an event which for them will be a source of pain and anguish. Not unnaturally they will probably also wish to hold someone or something accountable. But who or what should it be? The wasp? Eve's intolerance? Adam? The health administrator who devised the 24-hour roster? The health authority who administered the budget? The government minister who reduced health service spending? The civil servants who advised her? Or the state of the economy which influenced their advice? Each in their own way is influential on the unfolding of the events. Each participant involved, however remote from the eventual outcome, bears some degree of responsibility for the occurrence. What exactly is meant by 'responsible' and 'responsibility' in this context? HLA Hart has provided an important clarification of the different meanings conveyed by these words.[1] The notion of causal-responsibility will be the focus of this chapter but initially this sense needs to be differentiated from some other senses of responsibility referred to by Hart. These he terms role-responsibility, liability-responsibility, and capacity responsibility.

[1] *Punishment and Responsibility* (Clarendon Press, Oxford, 1968) 211–16.

All of us have responsibilities in our different social roles. We have responsibilities to our families, neighbours, friends, employers and work colleagues. Some of these responsibilities are legal, some moral, some both. People who take their responsibilities seriously are said to be responsible people, and irresponsible if they do not. Each of the actors in the above scenario 'has a responsibility' to ensure that their conduct is appropriate for the role they have assumed or with which they are entrusted. Thus the civil servants have a responsibility both to the public and the minister to ensure the advice they give is cogent. The government minister has a responsibility to the public to consider the public impact which implementing the advice will carry. The health authority has a responsibility to the public to secure the optimal level of health care within the budget provided. The health administrator has a responsibility to ensure that the practices and procedures are the best reasonably to be expected in the circumstances. Adam has a responsibility to ensure that the care he gives to patients is appropriate to the level of expertise expected of a qualified doctor. When a person, fixed with a responsibility, as here Adam is, to acquit himself appropriately for the role he takes on he may be legally responsible, that is liable to pay compensation or to be punished, if he fails in this responsibility and causes harm.

Another usage of the words 'responsible' and 'responsibility' concerns itself with causation. In this respect, without necessarily being **blameable,** it would not be incorrect usage to say that the wasp, Eve's intolerance, the administrator, the minister, the civil servants, or the poor state of the economy as well as Adam were responsible for the tragedy. If Adam had not been tired and under pressure he would not have administered the sedative. If the administrator had not created the roster Adam would not have been tired and under pressure. If the health authority had received a bigger budget Adam would have had better conditions of service. If the economy were strong the minister would not have squeezed the budget. If the wasp had not stung and had Eve not been intolerant none of this would have happened. Each participant involved, in other words, had some (causal) part to play in the unfolding of events whether or not we would also seek to hold them accountable for their contribution. This brings us closer to the point of this chapter. When something goes wrong our inclination is not merely to look for causal explanations but to hold someone or something **accountable.** Such a response is not mirrored in its opposite. When fortune favours us we do not tend to hunt for a good fairy on which to hang the credit.

Accountability for the purpose of a criminal trial requires a special form of connection between the undesired event and the defendant's conduct—the kind which elicits the response not merely that he participated in its occurrence but that it was his 'doing'. If he is also found to be blameworthy for what he has done state censure and punishment is his proper due. Given that this is not a clear case of premeditated purposive wrongdoing the basis upon which it might be appropriate to reach the judgment that the relevant event was 'Adam's doing' is not immediately obvious. The most that we can say is that of the various factors which contribute to Eve's death Adam's conduct provides the most direct and immediate connection. In common sense terms then it may be easier to attribute her death to the conduct of Adam than, say, that of the health administrator. But in truth we know that all three are equally the victims of context. When we look at Adam's conduct in context it may seem that this was an accident 'waiting to happen'. If the victim were not Eve it would have been someone else. If the perpetrator were not Adam it would have been someone else. Does this mean that it would be unfair to single out Adam to bear responsibility? Or is there a meaningful sense in which, despite the contributions of the others, we can say that Eve's death was Adam's doing for which he is justly held accountable? The cogency of society's response to this question requires an investigation of the notion of causation as reflected in criminal doctrine.

UNDERSTANDING CAUSATION

Causation speaks to the relationship between events and phenomena in the material world. At its loosest, the causal relationship may be nothing more than an empirically observable 'constant conjunction' between one phenomenon and another.[2] Whenever one event E1 (billiard ball strikes another billiard ball) occurs, another event E2 (second ball moves in the direction of the force) follows it or, in the reverse case, precedes it. At its most analytical it may entail a description of the full set of conditions whose presence guarantees (or is experienced as guaranteeing) the occurrence of the event.[3] In everyday life such accounts

---

[2] D Hume, *An Enquiry Concerning Human Understanding, Open Court, Illinois (1907)*. Section VII.

[3] So, explaining the occurrence of fire will require enumerating conditions such the presence of oxygen and the absence of wet, wind and so on. JS Mill, *A System of Logic* (Longmans, London, 1843) Book 3, ch 5.

fail to satisfy. They ignore the practical function of causal inquiries which is to make sense of things which happen; specifically to identify what it is among the many different conditions which made so and so event occur when it was unexpected or not occur when it was not.[4] From the earliest age babies witnessing a ball rolling into view or hearing a noise out of vision will search for its source. We look, as Hart and Honore have explained, for the thing which makes the difference.

This impulse to understand events in terms of relations of cause and effect seems to be part of what it is to be a human being. Although we cannot be sure that anything causes anything else as a matter of necessity,[5] relations of cause and effect appear to be 'hardwired' into our brains.[6] At the deepest philosophical or scientific level we seek, therefore, answers to questions as to why we exist, how the universe was created, how order came from chaos, how life began and so on. We look for the causes of disease, of natural disasters, of changes in climate. At a more mundane, practical level we look for the causes of changes in the moods of friends and family, of the failure of the car to function, of seeds to germinate. We also look for ways of generating or preventing consequences. We show courtesy to others; we service our car; we spray our roses.[7]

Causal explanations have no ultimate epistemological status however. There is no way of assessing the relative truth status of, say, the view which holds that AIDS is caused by the HIV virus and the view which holds that it is caused by God as retribution for man's sinful ways. Rather we should say that causal explanations are more or less plausible according to the premises which generate them. From a certain theological point of view the religious explanation is highly plausible. If we believe in a just God who rewards and punishes according to our moral desert we can understand the impetus to visit famine and plague upon the ungodly. After all, it has happened before, or so we are led to believe. In scientific terms the HIV explanation is also highly plausible. It has been shown that all AIDS sufferers carry the HIV virus and the syndrome is not suffered by those who are not infected. This

---

[4] RG Collingwood, 'On the So-Called Idea of Causation' (1938) *Proceedings of the Aristotelian Society*, 85 *et seq*.

[5] D Hume, *An Enquiry Concerning Human Understanding* (1907).

[6] I Kant, *Prolegomena to any Future Metaphysics* (Bobbs Merrill, Indianapolis, 1950) 57 *et seq*.

[7] A MacIntyre, 'A Mistake About Causality in the Social Sciences' in P Lazlett and D Runciman (eds), *Philosophy, Politics and Society* (OUP, Oxford, 1956).

account carries a special scientific plausibility, which derives from the fact that it, by contrast with the theological explanation, is one which can be disproved by the production of falsifying evidence yet has so far proved resilient to the attempt.[8] Equally, reflecting the primary function of causal inquiries and explanation in the scientific arena, it is also more helpful as a means of combating spread of the disease through its attendant admonitions against the dangers of unprotected sex or the use of unsterilised syringes.

Causal inquiries in law, by contrast with philosophical or scientific causal inquiries, are not designed to uncover some basic or empirical truth about the nature or workings of the world.[9] Rather their purpose is to create a just basis upon which a human being may be held accountable for the occurrence of a social harm. The overriding concern is to create a credible distinction between those events which are brought about by human agency and those which are brought about by natural causes. Only the former can properly form the subject matter of a criminal trial, with all that it entails. Because the object of such causal inquiries is to ground accountability rather than provide a general causal explanation, the inevitable focus of the trial is therefore upon those events most directly connected with the event and are prima facie instances of wrongdoing viewed from a legal perspective. Lacking any direct connection with Eve's death, therefore, the responsibility of the minister for example will be determined by reference to matters pertinent to his role as minister. If found wanting this entails the type of treatment typically meted out to incompetent ministers. This may include adverse consequences, including perhaps public condemnation, but not state punishment. The responsibility of Adam, however, entails treatment in accordance with the conventions attached to doctors and other citizens whose actions are thought to be too closely connected to a given harmful consequence for the buck of criminal liability to be passed elsewhere. That the minister, civil servant, and so on, bear some degree of responsibility for Eve's death is significant in law only to the extent that their contribution may have some bearing upon the judgment as to whether this agent (Adam) is responsible and accountable for the death of this woman (Eve).[10]

---

[8] K Popper, *Conjectures and Refutations*. (Routledge, London, 1957)

[9] For a different view see M Moore, 'The Metaphysics of Causal Intervention' (2000) 88 *Calif LR* 827.

[10] For an interesting elaboration of this idea see A Norrie, *Punishment Responsibility and Justice* (Clarendon Press, Oxford, 2000).

In tort pinpointing an accountable agent is a precondition of providing a remedy for an injured plaintiff. Without showing that the defendant 'caused' the plaintiff's harm there would be no fair basis for requiring the defendant to pay compensation. At most we can be expected to put right what we have done wrong. Causation, by contrast, is not intrinsic to the point of criminal liability and not all crimes involve causal inquiries. This is because it sometimes, arguably always, makes moral or practical sense to base criminal liability simply in blameworthy actions regardless of consequences and so regardless of the causal process which brings them about. So, the crime of dangerous driving may be constituted in the absence of any evidence of resulting harm. Moreover, where harm has been sustained in a driving accident it is not fatal to the prosecution's case that they are unable to prove that this was attributable to the defendant's dangerous manner of driving.

Causation is then an offence element only in connection with that class of crimes whose gist is the coming about of a particular (undesired) result. That such crimes exist at all implies that it is thought morally appropriate to punish people not merely for their wrongful actions but for their practical contribution to the occurrence of a particular harm. Assault, malicious wounding, causing grievous bodily harm with intent, manslaughter and murder all require proof of causation. In assault the prosecution must show that it was by the defendant's act that the victim was led to apprehend immediate unlawful force. In manslaughter the prosecution must show that it was by the defendant's act that the victim met his death. The offence of causing death by dangerous driving requires proof of a consequence (death) and so also a causal link between the defendant's (dangerous) driving and the death. George Fletcher makes the point that causal inquiries in the criminal setting and rules sustaining them are only necessary when such consequence may occur otherwise than through a defendant's wrongdoing. Hence we do not need causal inquiries for crimes such as rape or theft since they cannot occur but through an act of wrongdoing. Rape is the act by which another is violated. Theft is the act by which another is dispossessed. One is held accountable for that (wrongful) deed. For homicide and acts of violence, by contrast, causal inquiries are necessary since the harms involved may come about through natural causes or accident, and accountability in the criminal process must necessarily rule this possibility out. In fact, this helpful analysis probably understates the role that causation has to play in construction of criminal liability.[11] Causal problems may surface, for example, in crimes of harmful actions as well as consequences. If A snatches a suitcase from B and B is injured in the process A's liability for robbery—a crime of harmful action in Fletcher's analysis—may depend upon an assessment of how the injury came about. If B slipped and banged his head trying to recover the suitcase there will be no liability for robbery. If, however, B's fingers were hurt through the force of A's tug liability will be assured. Again, most cases of fraud require proof that the relevant benefit was obtained as a result of the relevant deception. As with crimes of violence the inquiry is not limited to a simple yes/no answer. The court may have to consider, for example, how potent a cause the deception was.[12]

HOW DO WE ARRIVE AT A PRINCIPLED APPROACH TO CAUSATION?

In tort causal inquiries usually lie at the heart of the proceedings. They are rarely so central in criminal trials. There is a simple reason for this, namely that most tortious claims arise out of circumstances where it is not possible to show any deliberate or conscious wrongdoing on the part of the defendant. Under such circumstances making a cogent causal connection between what the defendant has done and the plaintiff's harm may be difficult. If A deliberately runs down B on a pedestrian crossing, a paradigm case of criminal wrongdoing, it takes no great analytical effort to attribute B's injury to something which A has done. If on the other hand A, in greasy driving conditions, carelessly allows his car to skid so as to collide with a lamppost dislodging the loose lampholder which falls on C's car, which in turn causes him to swerve and collide with B, a passing pedestrian, we have no ready basis for attributing B's injury to A. There is too much to argue about. From the point of view of the defendant the causal connection is just too tenuous or, as it is termed, 'remote'. From the point of view of the plaintiff, by contrast, the very point of tort law—to compensate those injured through the activities of wrongdoers—sustains a notion of causation at odds with a requirement of a robust causal connection.

---

[11] G Fletcher, *Basic Concepts of Criminal Law* Oxford (OUP, Oxford, 1998), 62.
[12] See for example *King* (1987) 84 Cr App Rep 357.

The law of tort seeks a balance between these two competing stand-points. Tort law is designed to ensure that the burden of loss falls fairly. Somebody has to pay—if not the wrongdoer then the victim or his insurance company. In reaching its decision the court is involved in a judgment, therefore, that it is fair that one party, **rather than the other**, bears this loss. The resulting compromise is an uneasy one. On the one hand the courts have insisted upon a degree of proximity between the defendant's wrongdoing and any resulting harm. On the other they have sometimes questioned the desirability of limiting compensation to those who can prove, on a balance of probabilities, a specific causal connection between harm suffered and the tortious activities of another. From its earliest days evidential devices such as the doctrine of *res ipsa loquitur* has allowed causation sometimes to be presumed where the inference is irresistible in the absence of specific proof. More recently, particularly in cases of industrial activities whose defective processes materially increase the risk of certain harms occurring, the courts have sometimes allowed causation to be presumed where there was insufficient evidence of a causal connection on a balance of prob-abilities standard.[13]

In theory, because the criminal trial is driven by a different criter-ion—punishing wrongdoers rather than compensating victims of wrongdoing—the causal connection must also be constructed some-what more rigorously. If we convict someone of murder the moral mes-sage conveyed is that the accused deserves to be associated with the fact of the victim's death and suffer condemnation and punishment for it. For this retributive aim to be fairly prosecuted, it seems obviously necessary that a clear causal connection must be established. Here, as in tort, the basic scheme is that an agent bears no criminal liability for events unless they are unambiguously his 'doing'.

If we probe more deeply, causal inquiries in the criminal law fre-quently face the difficulty of justifying holding an individual account-able for an event in the face of a broader contextual explanation of how that event occurred. For example, a causal explanation of Adam's conduct—say in the course of a public inquiry—will typically empha-sise the context within which Adam was working and conclude that 'this was an accident waiting to happen'. In the legal arena, however,

---

[13] *Mcghee v NCB* [1973] 1 WLR 1; *Bonnington Castings v Wardlaw* [1956] AC 613; cf *Wilsher v Essex AHA* [1988] AC 1074; cf J Stapleton, 'Damage as the Gist of Negligence' (1988) 104 *LQR* 213 and 389.

this fair-minded contextual explanation is supplanted by a concern to judge whether a given harm can be linked in terms of cause and effect to a preceding wrongful act. Such a decision does not require a finding that Adam was the primary cause among all the different other causes operating. Only that his causal contribution was sufficiently strong to warrant holding him accountable. In *Pagett* the defendant used his girl-friend as a hostage and human shield during a gun battle with police. The police marksmen returned fire, killing the woman. The defend-ant's conviction for manslaughter was upheld on appeal. Liability was fought on the question of causation. There were of course any number of causal explanations. The medical explanation was multiple organ failure. The defendant's explanation was the (precipitous) reaction of the police marksmen. The Court of Appeal, without needing to reject any of these causal explanations, found the defendant's conduct in prompting the defensive fire of the police to be an operative cause of the death. Even if the police had acted improperly in returning fire[14] this causal contribution of the accused justified holding him accountable.[15] *Pagett* illustrates certain key points concerning causal attribution. First, there may be more than one legal cause of death. In the unlikely event that the prosecutor, rather than Pagett, had decided to prosecute the police marksman the court may well have found the latter causally responsible. That they did not was no doubt attributable partly to insti-tutional reluctance to prosecute one of their own and partly due to the unlikelihood, given the defensive context, of securing a conviction. Secondly, causation may survive the causal intervention of a third party or other event. Thirdly, the legal cause of death is the cause of death for the narrow purpose of assigning accountability and is not therefore to be confused with the scientific or other explanation as to why death occurred. Fourthly, causation becomes an issue primarily when harm comes about unexpectedly, or a different kind of harm transpires than that intended or expected. It will be appreciated that these points do not help us to identify any necessary qualifications for assigning causal responsibility. It is to this question we now turn.

---

[14] And there was some suggestion that they may have done,

[15] As Norrie suggests it is unlikely that the court would have reached a similar con-clusion had the boot been on the other foot and a terrorist, say, had shot and killed a police officer under the erroneous belief that the officer was about to unlawfully kill him. Cf *Brown*, cited in Norrie, *Punishment Responsibility and Justice*, 145.

ASSIGNING CAUSAL RESPONSIBILITY

Case 2

Adam, in a hurry to get home to watch a football match on the TV, is spotted by traffic police as he is driving well above the speed limit. Instead of responding to requests to pull over Adam increases his speed, zigzags along the road, and 'jumps' a number of red traffic lights. He is finally intercepted when he collides with Eve, a motorcyclist, joining the carriageway from a side street. Eve dies in the resulting crash.

This scenario presents what might appear to be an open and shut case of one or other of the result crimes known as causing death by dangerous driving or manslaughter. We have an obvious case of dangerous driving. We have a death. And we have a death which is met at the hands of Adam. Result crimes require, however, a causal connection if Adam is to be held accountable for what has happened. The starting point for assigning causal responsibility is the *sine qua non* or 'but for' test.[16] The agent's act or omission (or other event) is the cause of a consequence if it would not have occurred **but for** that act or omission (or that event). Conversely if the consequence would have occurred whether or not the agent had acted as he did the agent is not a cause. A distinction is drawn in this respect between factual (real) causes and mere conditions.[17] The factual cause of an event must be selected from the range of everyday **'but for'** conditions. A 'cause is essentially something which interferes with or intervenes in the course of events which would normally take place'.[18] To be a factual cause an **event** must be something extraordinary or abnormal and 'what is abnormal in this way "makes the difference" between the accident and things going on as usual'.[19] Thus the fact that the lights changed encouraging Eve to join the carriageway does not mean that this is a factual cause of the accident.[20] Only if an event is abnormal and so makes 'a difference' to the unfolding of events does it become a factual cause therein.

[16] The MPC defines factual causation in terms of 'an antecedent but for which the result in question should not have (occurred)'.

[17] ie normal everyday events or circumstances which were a precondition of but not the reason why the consequence happened at the time and in the manner it did.

[18] HLA Hart and AM Honore, *Causation in the Law*, (Clarendon Press, Oxford, 1985) 27.

[19] *Ibid* 33.

[20] cf Mclaughlin,'Proximate Cause' (1921) 39 *Harv LR* 149, 160.

It is not enough, then, to show simply that Eve met her death at Adam's hands **while** Adam was driving dangerously. Rather it must be shown that Eve met her death **because** Adam was driving dangerously. Otherwise the occasion for holding Adam accountable in Case 2 will be the fact of Adam being on the road rather than the inappropriate manner of his driving. As such, the cause of death will be a fortuity—an accident in the true sense of the word—rather than a blameworthy deed for which he bears responsibility. If this is to be avoided the prosecution will need to be able to show, therefore, that the accident would not have occurred if Adam had been driving carefully. If, say, Eve had joined the carriageway without stopping to check for traffic and immediately crossed into the outside lane they would have difficulty discharging such a burden. Careful drivers as well as dangerous ones may fail to avoid collisions in such circumstances.

There are two arguable sources of injustice in cases such as this. The first is substantive. Why should it matter that a careful driver would have fared no better in his attempt to avoid the accident? Is it not enough that the manifest elements of wrongdoing are present—the dangerous driving, the death, Adam's involvement in the death? Whether or not Adam driving carefully would have prevented it, it cannot be denied that Eve met her death while Adam was showing the kind of scant regard for the interests of other road users that generates consequences such as this. It is more by luck—the fluke perhaps of an equally careless motorcyclist—than judgment that Adam would escape liability and a criminal justice system which assigns liability on the basis of luck alone has difficulty living up to its name. Given this fact, and since there is no difference in culpability between a person who kills while acting dangerously and a person who kills on account of his acting dangerously, assigning the more serious criminal label is hardly unjust. This argument is yet more pertinent in cases of intentional wrongdoing. Suppose D poisons V and V dies of a stroke or at the hands of another assassin before the poison has a chance to work. D's liability, at most, will be for attempted murder and yet, given that D got what he wanted, would it really be inappropriate to hold him responsible?[21]

Doing so might, in fact, be expected to pre-empt another form of injustice, this time procedural. Whether or not one approves the role of causation in the fashioning of criminal liability the jury may not convict of a result crime unless causation is properly established. Even

[21] *White*, [1910] 2 KB 124

if they believe that it is more likely than not that driving in the relevant manner was the reason why Eve died they should acquit unless convinced of it. However, proving a causal link in this kind of all or nothing fashion will often be beyond the technical resources of the prosecution. The practical likelihood, therefore, is that successful prosecutions will sometimes be dependent upon the jury's willingness to prefer common sense rather than evidential propriety in convicting those they think deserving. This inherent tension between the substance of the offence, competing notions of moral, causal and legal responsibility and the jury's unsupervised susceptibility to slide between them suggests that it may be better to make virtue of necessity and allow a causal link to be presumed in all cases where a person suffers harm at the hands of a wrongdoer.

A yet more radical suggestion, which will be encountered in a later chapter, is that if luck plays so much a part in the occurrence of events and jury equity in case outcomes, then criminal liability perhaps should not take account of resulting harm at all. Causal inquiries would then likewise become redundant.[22] Punishing people according to what they do achieve may unduly favour the accused where, for example, a subsisting[23] or supervening[24] cause operates to negate a wrongdoer's causal responsibility. It might also unfairly stigmatise the accused. It is common place to hear of doctors such as Adam in Case 1 making bad errors of judgment, under the influence of stress or fatigue. It is also common place for drivers to drive dangerously. Both forms of conduct put lives at risk, yet the accident of death places the individual alone at risk of a manslaughter conviction when he/she is no more culpable that the thousands of ordinary people who escape 'causing death'. If we recognise that luck has selected these individuals to be the instruments of others' deaths, it might be better to punish them for what we apprehend is their real wrong, namely that they have (culpably) endangered someone's life. The criminal law already has in place a number of crimes of endangerment.[25] Should we go further and rid the criminal

---

[22] AJ Ashworth, 'Belief, Intent and Criminal Liability' in J Eekelaar and J Bell (eds), *Oxford Essays in Jurisprudence*, third series (Clarendon Press, Oxford 1989); AJ Ashworth, 'Taking the Consequences' in S Shute, J Gardner and J Horder (eds), *Action and Value in Criminal Law* (Clarendon Press, Oxford, 1993).

[23] For example the intended victim was already dead at the time the 'fatal' blow was delivered.

[24] For example case 3 below.

[25] AJ Ashworth, *Principles of Criminal Law* (OUP, Oxford, 1999), 298–306; cf Fletcher, *Basic Concepts of Criminal Law* 472–83.

law of other crimes, such as manslaughter, which emphasise consequence and causation at the expense of conduct and replace them with crimes of endangerment? One advantage served by such an approach is that it solves at a stroke the major problem which, as we shall see, bedevils causation doctrine, namely the production of coherent principles capable of distinguishing fairly between those to whom causal responsibility is assigned and those to whom it is not.

The argument for requiring a factual causal connection is that in the usual cases it plays a fundamental role in setting the limits of accountability which, as explained earlier, is also central to the reason why we have crimes of harmful consequences.[26] The victim's family, for example, will have no doubt as to who or what is accountable for the death. This may be reflected in relief that V died 'naturally' in his own bed or was spared the drawn out pain and suffering which death by poisoning may provoke.

Limiting the Range of Responsible Agents

In the usual case a 'but for' causal connection will conclusively establish causation in law. So, if A shoots B and medical evidence confirms that B died of loss of blood from the wound this will be enough to hold A causally responsible. The *sine qua non* test is, however, only a starting point because outside these clear cases whether causation is established or not is a matter of legal imputation rather than empirical fact. For example, the factual (but for) cause of an event, say death, will be ignored if it is superseded by an independent cause sufficient in itself to cause that event. Suppose that V in the above example was not killed by a stroke or third party but in an accident as he was being taken to hospital. Here D satisfies the 'but for' test but, unless the poison was effective only because of V's weakened condition, he is not properly selected as the cause of death. In common sense terms the accident is a coincidence and we attribute coincidences to a playful fate rather than the instrumentality of individuals. After all, if D is the legal cause of V's death then he is also the cause of the death of any of the paramedics who die in the same crash which at best would be an odd conclusion to reach.

---

[26] L Katz, 'Why the Successful Assassin is More Wicked than the Unsuccessful One' (2000) 88 *Calif LR* 791.

Again, causal responsibility may survive the absence of the 'but for' condition if there are other ways of constructing an unbroken causal sequence. A commonly discussed example is where two (or more) individuals independently shoot another through the heart causing him to die immediately. Medical evidence shows that either shot would have been capable of causing his immediate demise. Both assailants are causes of death for legal purposes even though because of the action of the other the prosecution would be unable to prove that **but for** the action of **one of them** the death would not have occurred.[27] They are causes because, irrespective of the contributions of the other, each sets in motion a chain of events which has death as an inevitable last link in the chain.[28] This type of analysis can account for a more challenging hypothetical.

Case 3

A, intending to kill B, a prisoner awaiting execution, gives him a fatal dose of a soporific drug for reasons of compassion. When A's action is discovered B is taken to hospital where he dies two hours after the time fixed for his execution.

It should be noted not only that but for A's act B would still have died but, moreover, A's act did not even advance the moment when death occurred.[29] Nevertheless, it seems unarguable that A's act did not cause B's death in fact and will be so attributed in law. Not only did it begin an uninterrupted chain of causation ending with the victim's death, it will be the cause of death identified in the autopsy, and there will be no plausible case for assigning causal responsibility elsewhere, whether to the actions of another or to natural causes.[30]

---

[27] See the analysis of this case in J Dressler, *Understanding Criminal Law* (Matthew Bender, New York, 1988), 161.

[28] Cf the definition of factual causation proposed by L Crocker in 'Harm and Culpability: Which Should be the Organising Principle of the Criminal Law? A Retributive Theory of Criminal Causation' (1994) *J Contemp Leg Issues* 65; and R Wright, 'Causation in Tort Law' (1985) 73 *Cal LR* 1735.

[29] Hart and Honore, *Causation and the Law*, at 220 (1st).

[30] One way of reconciling the requirement of factual causation with the but for rule is to refine it slightly. A person is a factual cause of a consequence, say death, if, but for his conduct, the consequence would not have occurred as and when it did. The Draft Criminal Code Bill sidesteps such artifice by deeming a person to cause 'a result which is an element of an offence . . . when he does an act which makes a more than negligible contribution to its occurrence.' 1989 (Law Com No 177) cl 17.

Satisfying the 'but for' test of factual causation is not all there is to causation, therefore. Even where D is a 'but for' cause it may take a further evaluative judgment to hold that D is answerable for his act. Even where he is not, there are instances where assigning causal responsibility is no more than the defendant's due. To be a cause in law it must be possible to denounce the defendant in terms amounting to 'It was by your act (or omission) that this consequence came about.' Such a judgment must look not only to a generalised causal explanation of the relevant event, it must identify a link between the consequence and the conduct of the accused such that designating the latter as responsible and answerable is an appropriate reaction. It is the setting of cogent parameters for this evaluative judgment which poses the greatest problem for causation doctrine.[31]

An initial difficulty concerns consequences which are not normally associated with conduct of the type practised by the defendant. In such circumstances the question posed is whether the consequence is the defendant's doing or whether it is best treated as a natural event. Suppose A, a burglar, causes B, the occupier of the house burgled, to jump to her death out of an upstairs window or delivers such a shock that B dies of heart failure or sends her into a spiral of anxiety and depression which eventually prompts her to commit suicide. Is A properly described as the cause of B's death in any or all of these cases? Is he, that is, accountable? One's natural inclination is to distinguish between reactions which are normal to people faced with such external crises such as jumping out of a window with a burglar at the door and abnormal, such as committing suicide. Although we can see how one event prompts another, too many things seem to be going on to allow us to conclude that the suicide was A's doing. There is 'too much B' in this deed for us to make this connection. The way this is analysed in law makes much the same point. The fact that a consequence was unforeseen or even unforeseeable does not bear upon the issue of causal responsibility except where, subsequent to the defendant's act, **an independent and sufficient cause** has intervened. This follows on naturally from the idea that 'but for' causation is the usual starting and finishing point for causal attribution. If A sets in motion a causal sequence resulting in a social harm A will normally be treated as the cause of that harm, however unexpected it was. Clearly the fact that the consequence was unexpected may have repercussions upon A's criminal responsibility at

[31]Mclaughlin, 'Proximate Cause' (1921) 39 *Harv LR* 149, 160; S Morse, 'The Moral Metaphysics of Causation and Results' (2000) 88 *Calif LR* 879, 886.

large since it may affect his *mens rea*. However, as we shall see, the ascription of causal responsibility follows a separate route, although it should be noted that some have striven hard to build the infrastructure of criminal causation upon the foundations of intended and foreseen harms.[32] The (dubious) theory behind this is that causation and fault are separate elements in the construction of criminal liability. Causation speaks to the deed. Was it by A's act that the consequence came about? This ought to be to be amenable to a simple factual inquiry—a was it or wasn't it inquiry?[33] Fault speaks to the attitude of mind. Was he to blame for the deed by which this consequence came about? This is an evaluative inquiry.

Typical doctrinal implications of this analysis include the fact that the defendant bears the (causal) risk of injuries exacerbated by the victim's poor state of health, irrespective of foreseeability. Others are that the defendant will be responsible if death ensues for unforeseeable medical reasons as long as those reasons were attributable to the defendant's unlawful act in the sense of not being independent of them.[34] The principle applied here is that the defendant must take the risk of bad luck over the choice of context or victim. An extreme case is *Blaue* where the accused was held to have caused the death of his victim whom he had stabbed, although the victim had refused on religious grounds a life-saving blood transfusion. It was the defendant's bad luck to have chosen a Jehovah's Witness as his victim. Anyone else, and he would have been facing a conviction for wounding rather than manslaughter. *Blaue* reflects the common sense notion of causality in which causes of death are conceived in terms of events such as wounds and blows and not in terms of ideas, however unusual or perverse. How could Blaue not be thought of as the cause of the Witness's death? Any contrary conclusion would have to contend with the unambiguous findings of the autopsy report which was heart failure due to blood loss. He must take his own bad luck.

If *Blaue* represented the most difficult case causation doctrine had to deal with there would be little to become exercised about. But it is not. This is because it is well recognised that in certain circumstances a person who initiates a causal sequence will not be held answerable for

---

[32] See for example S Yeo, 'Blameable Causation' (2000) 24 *Crim LJ* 144.

[33] Ought to be, but clearly isn't. Causal responsibility, like blame, must in all cases be assigned. Fault, however, is often a purely formal determination. Did he or did he not intend this consequence?

[34] See for example *R v Dyson* [1908] 2 KB 454 CCA.

them. As explained above, if Blaue's victim had been killed in an ambulance crash on the way to hospital Blaue would not be accountable for his victim's death, assuming the crash was sufficient in itself to cause death. Similarly if she had refused the transfusion in morbid reaction to what she perceived to be an insufferable affront it is doubtful that the court would have been so anxious to attribute that death to Blaue's initial wrongdoing.[35] Why should it? If a person chooses to kill themselves because of something somebody else does it is their choice not the other's. If the other has done something wrong then the appropriate response is to censure and punish for that wrong rather than use the victim's unusual reaction as an occasion to pile on added criticism and punishment. However culpable an agent's conduct is he cannot be held responsible for all the chance events which issue from such conduct. Tragic coincidences, such as ambulance crashes and committing suicide due to morbid depression, attend the occurrence of innocuous actions as well as dangerous ones. The purpose of a criminal conviction is not simply to pinpoint a convenient wrongdoer upon which to pin responsibility, but to declare a moral truth about an undesired event, namely that it was the wrongdoer's 'doing' for which he is accountable.

It is at this point that we identify the major problem in the construction of causal sequences. How do we construct an objective basis for determining those 'but for' consequences which are the wrongdoer's doing and those which are not? The test proposed in the Draft Criminal Code attempts an answer to this question.

1. A person causes a result when
   a. he does an act which makes a more than merely negligible contribution to its occurrence or
   b. he omits to do an act which might have prevented its occurrence and which he is under a duty to do according to the law relating to the offence.
2. A person does not cause a result where, after he does such an act or makes such an omission, an act or event occurs
   a. which is the immediate and sufficient cause of the result;
   b. which he did not foresee, and
   c. which could not in the circumstances reasonably have been foreseen.

---

[35] *Dalby*, below; cf *Stephenson v State* 54 Tex Cr R 101 This conclusion was resisted of course in *Blaue*. Fletcher sees this as a weakness of the 'voluntariness' approach. When is self-inflicted injury ever truly voluntary?

This provision ensures, as we might expect, that causal responsibility is not made dependent upon the foreseeability of the resultant harm but rather upon the foreseeability of the later act or event from which such harm issues. In this the test coheres with the point of causation which is to attribute causal responsibility not on the basis of what a person might reasonably expect to result from his action. This is something relevant, if at all, to the question of fault. Rather the test seeks to isolate conduct which initiates a causal sequence where it has been superseded by a subsequent (but for) cause. As such it renders causality an exclusionary element in the construction of criminal liability operating, much as a defence might do, to exclude liability where (unrebutted) evidence is adduced that the 'true' cause of the result was some subsequent act or event which the defendant, perhaps because of its unpredictable occurrence, was not in a position to guard against.

The Draft Criminal Code provision points up a constitutional weakness in the construction of causal sequences. In seeking to identify the 'proximate' (blameable) cause of a criminal harm from all the various (unblameable) mere factual causes some measure must be produced. The Draft Criminal Code's measure is that of foreseeability. A later act or event sufficient in itself to cause a criminal harm severs the link between that harm and any earlier act but only if that act or event was unforeseeable. The weakness is the open endedness of the standard chosen.[36] By what criteria do we conclude, for example, that Blaue's victim's refusal was either foreseeable or unforeseeable? Our disposition to hold Blaue accountable seems to be influenced by matters other than foreseeability of response; in particular, the moral conviction that people who do dangerous things must bear the responsibility if the danger materialises.[37] Other tests have been produced which are more effective in conveying this response. One such, implicit in *Blaue*, holds that subject to the liability component of the crime itself, proximate causation requires the risk materialising to be one which the defendant would be expected to have in mind as a reason for refraining from acting in the relevant manner.[38]

---

[36] See G Williams, *Textbook of Criminal Law* (Stevens, London, 1983), 385 *et seq*; A Norrie, *Crime, Reason and History* (Weidenfeld and Nicolson, London, 1993), ch 7.

[37] For an extreme theory of criminal causation which is tied to what the defendant intends or foresees rather than the metaphysics of cause and effect see S Yeo, above n 32.

[38] L Crocker, 'Harm and Culpability: Which Should be the Organising Principle of the Criminal law? A Retributive Theory of Criminal Causation' (1994) *J Contemp Leg Issues* 65.

Case 4

Adam places a loaded gun on the table. His six year old daughter, Eve, climbs on the table and grasps hold of the gun. On attempting to climb down again the barrel gets caught between her ankles and she falls off the table, fatally breaking her neck.

Assuming Adam's conduct involves a gross breach of duty his liability for manslaughter depends upon the existence of a causal link between that breach and the death. The above 'within the risk test' injects a necessary connection between why we would seek to blame D for his conduct and why we would seek to hold him accountable for the consequence. Here there is none. B's death, although factually caused by A's negligent action, is an utter coincidence. B could have fallen to her death as a result of attempting to recover her own toy gun, her father's unloaded shot-gun or a cup of fruit juice left over from breakfast. Answerability, on this view, requires therefore a congruence between the risk-creating activity and the materialised risk.

Large tracts of causation doctrine can be accounted for by either one of these accounts. In particular, as Case 4 illustrates, causal sequences may be broken by the kind of abnormal coincidences which cannot be guarded against. On the other hand they are rarely broken where the victims of assaults injure themselves, say by jumping out of a window, or a moving car in trying to escape.[39] Neither are they broken by the contributory negligence of the victim or grossly incompetent medical treatment.[40] In each case the relevant outcome follows an act or event the risk of whose occurrence was generated by the very act of the defendant for which we would seek to blame him. If we treat this as the basic benchmark for deciding whether the relevant act or event was reasonably foreseeable it is clear that they are.

Contradictions nevertheless appear in causal sequences where later acts or events can be both reasonably foreseeable/within the risk of the initial causal sequence and yet still of a nature to deflect attention from the causal efficacy of the earlier act. An instructive example is *Dalby*. Dalby had supplied controlled drugs to his friend, who had died as a consequence of injecting himself with the drugs. Dalby was indicted for

---

[39] *Roberts* [1971] Cr App Rep 95; *Williams and Davis* [1992] 2 All ER 183.
[40] See n 47

manslaughter.[41] A reasonable foresight/within the risk test easily supplies the necessary causal connection between the defendant's act of supply and the victim's death. It was reasonably foreseeable that a person, supplied with drugs for injection, would use them in this way. The risk of V dying as a result of self-administration was one of the reasons why D should have guarded against supplying V with the drug. On the other hand if anything 'caused' V's death it was surely V's own voluntary act in administering the drug. In the analysis of Hart and Honoré the legal cause of an event, by and large, must be traced back to the last person whose voluntary action 'made a difference' to the unfolding of the causal sequence and no further. The emphasis on 'voluntary' action here is important since in everyday speech we readily use the language of causation wherever A influences B to do something. So if A frightens B into jumping out the window we say that A caused B to jump and so also caused his injuries if he suffers any,[42] By extension it seems to follow that if A frightens or persuades B to kill C A causes C's death. This latter conclusion, of course, runs counter to the notion underpinning criminal liability that we must take responsibility for the results of our own action. To avoid it a distinction is drawn between voluntary and involuntary action. In cases where, subsequent to a wrongful act, the victim or a third party intervenes in the causal sequence the chain of causation is broken where, and only where, the intervention is voluntary and is sufficient in itself to cause the result, but is otherwise at most only a contributing cause.[43]

This emphasis provides seductively clear answers to the question 'whose doing was this' or 'who caused this?' If A gives B a bottle of gin and B drinks it with fatal results the legal cause of B's death is B if B is a sane adult and A if B is a young child. In the former case the last voluntary action causing death is B's. In the latter it is A's. Similarly the criminal law treats Othello rather than Iago as the cause of Desdemona's death, despite Iago's own central (but for) role in provoking Othello to depths of murderous jealousy. Although Iago is himself responsible for inducing Othello to kill Desdemona, Othello's was the last voluntary action preceding the death. It is he, not Iago, who

---

[41] [1982] 1 WLR 425.

[42] RG Collingwood, 'On the So-called Idea of Causation' (1938) *Proceedings of the Aristotelian Society* 85 *et seq.*

[43] Although the Court of Appeal did not identify the voluntary decision of the victim to inject himself as the cause of death this is nevertheless implicit in the reason given for denying D's liability.

killed her. Doctrine designates Othello's act as voluntary since, Iago's devious stratagems notwithstanding, it is an uncompelled exercise of free will. As Williams puts it: 'What a person does (if he has reached adult years, is of sound mind and is not acting under mistake, intimidation or other similar pressure) is his own personal responsibility and is not to be regarded as having been caused by other people.'[44]

As will be appreciated, however, the notion of voluntariness is an equivocal one. The same action may be voluntary for the purpose of initiating causal sequences and involuntary for the purpose of ending them.[45] This can be seen most obviously in cases where death ensues as a result of a combination of a wrongful act of violence and subsequent poor medical care. Typical is *Cheshire* where the deceased died of respiratory failure.[46] The defendant's contribution was gunshot wounds to the leg and abdomen of the deceased which had induced respiratory problems. In attempting to alleviate this doctors had performed a tracheotomy. It was negligently performed and subsequently treated and was the direct cause of the deceased's death. Here it is quite clear that the action of the doctors was voluntary for the purpose of determining their own potential liability, say for gross negligence manslaughter assuming the necessary level of culpability were established. But a significant feature of the court's rationale for finding the causal link between wound and death unbroken was its recognition that doctor's who have emergency surgery thrust upon them cannot be expected to get it right every time. In this case Beldam LJ stated that it would only be in the most extraordinary and unusual case that the accused would not be responsible for injuries or death suffered by medical treatment '**attempting to repair the harm done**'.[47] Strictly speaking then it is the reactive nature of the third party's action rather than its foreseeability, reasonableness or involuntary character which sustains the causal link between consequence and the defendant's initial action. In *Halliday*[48] Lord Coleridge expressed the same principle but here in the context of defendant-motivated self-injury. 'If a man creates in another man's mind an immediate sense of danger which causes such a person to try to escape, and in so doing he injures himself, the person who creates such a state of mind (is the legal cause of the injuries which result).'

[44] G Williams, *Textbook of Criminal Law*, 39.

[45] Norrie, *Crime Reason and History*, ch 7. See also 'A Critique of Criminal Causation' (1991) 54 MLR 685.

[46] [1991] 3 All ER 670.

[47] At 677.

[48] *R v Halliday* 61 LTR 701, at 702.

Both *Cheshire* and *Halliday* operate implicitly within a frame of reference which holds that reactive conduct sustains causal sequences. By contrast, conduct which is opportunistic and not by way of reaction, as where having been knocked over by the defendant, a third party takes his opportunity to beat the victim up, terminates the sequence.[49] This analysis, also apparent in cases such as *Blaue* and *Pagett*, indicates that the courts are looking to identify, as if this were possible, the 'real' cause or, as it is often termed, the most potent cause of the relevant consequence. In cases like *Dalby* the 'real' cause appears to be the victim. Quite simply it is 'his choice' if he chooses to inject himself. We say this although we may appreciate that realistically, given the victim's addiction, he may not have had a real choice at all. As a human being he cannot pass the buck of causal responsibility elsewhere. In *Cheshire* the context was quite different. If it were the medics' choice to act it was not the kind of self-orientated choice which disposes us to draw a causal veil over the reasons why that choice was made. The court's approach was expressed as follows: (negligent medical treatment does not exclude causal responsibility unless it) 'was so independent of (the defendant's) acts, and in itself so potent in causing death that [the jury] could regard the contribution made by his acts as insignificant'.[50]

Where a causal sequence is initiated by an act of violence the potency analogy does all the analytical work which notions such as foreseeability cannot do.[51] It is in the nature of acts of violence that they generate unpredictable causal sequences. They produce risks specific to their particular context at each stage in a typical causal sequence—the risk that the victim might be particularly vulnerable, that medical treatment will be slow arriving, that diagnosis is faulty, that the treatment is incompetent, that the treatment is inappropriate for the constitution of the victim, and so on. In a sense then it is always 'reasonably foreseeable' that things will pan out badly in terms of the sequence of events into which the victim of violence is typically tied. American doctrine uses a compelling metaphor to convey this same idea, namely 'dangerous forces which come to rest'.[52] The idea is that once the danger excited by the defendant's action is spent, any later ensuing harm must be due to some other cause but before this 'anything goes'. Thus, in the

[49] *People v Elder* 59 NW 237 (Mich) 1894.

[50] At 677.

[51] See *Smith* (1959) 2 All ER 193, at 198; *Cheshire* [1991] 3 All ER 670 at 677.

[52] Perkins and Boyce, *Criminal Law* (Foundation Press, New York, 1982), 780; Beale, 'The Proximate Cause of an Act' 33 *Harv LR* 633.

American case of *State v Preslar*[53] a husband's acts of violence forced his wife to flee home in freezing weather. She was found within a few hundred yards of her father's home, having apparently chosen to court exposure rather than wake her father up at a late hour. The court found the husband not to have caused his wife's death. Although he may have contributed to it, the causal effect of his violence had been exhausted by the time his wife reached her father's house and had composed herself sufficiently to reach her own (apparently) voluntary decision not to disturb her father.[54] If, then, we re-examine *Blaue* it can be understood that the causal sequence remained intact not because the victim's act was reasonably foreseeable nor even, as Hart and Honore suggest, that it was involuntary but because Blaue's act was still a major contributing factor in the victim's death. If we ask 'who did this'? there can be only one reply—Blaue did it. The dangerous forces were not spent.

A comparison of these two cases indicates both the strength and the weakness of the potency approach to causation. The strength is its ability to produce case outcomes which, by and large, replicate common sense assumptions about what it is to be accountable for a particular consequence. Blaue was accountable. The death was his doing. He stabbed his victim and she bled to death. Preslar was not. He forced his wife into the cold. Cold can kill without doubt but, where succour is all around, only if you let it, as the wife undoubtedly did. The weakness is the test's open-endedness and flexibility. Preslar's wife was rendered vulnerable by Preslar's conduct. Who knows how powerful an impact on her ability to make rational self-interested choices this sequence of acts and events had? It was not as if she had killed herself deliberately. She simply found herself unable to help herself. And why was this? Using comparable tests American courts have held, significantly, that a defendant can be held causally responsible even where the victim, by contrast with Mrs Preslar, **deliberately** self-inflicts injuries, including suicide, prompted by the defendant's unlawful conduct.[55] In the words of one commentator 'it is criminal homicide to cause a normal adult to commit suicide by creating a situation so cruel and revolting that death is preferred to unavoidable continued submission'.[56]

---

[53] 48 NC 417 (1856). An example of an English case embodying this idea is *Jordan*, below.

[54] Cf *Stephenson*, supra; see also Waters (1834) 6 C & P 328 and Williams's commentary, *Textbook of Criminal Law* 397.

[55] *Stephenson v State* 54 Tex Cr R 101; *Jones*.

[56] J Hall, *General Principles of Criminal Law* (Bobbs-Merrill, Indianapolis, 1960), 274.

These cases imply that whichever test is adopted to test the integrity of a causal sequence the ultimate outcome proceeds from what Norrie has described as a socio-political judgment as to whether a given individual deserves to be held accountable for a given consequence.[57] This judgment cannot be 'read off' from the relevant tests although these tests are clearly designed to lend weight and authority to the judgments once made. No doubt the judgments in *Preslar* and *Blaue* took account of the manner and context within which the deaths occurred. In *Preslar* the context—domestic violence in a freezing world—would be mundane, but for its tragic inevitability. How can such a set of unfocused events and acts be disaggregated so as to allow the finger of accountability to be pointed at Mr Preslar? In *Blaue* a vicious stab wound sets a quite different scene causing the curious observer to rush ahead to view the outcome. A stab wound is just too strong a cause of death to be passed over. It is intentional and it is lethal. It takes a lot to deprive such an act of causal efficacy.

It is yet easier to locate a socio-political basis for the attribution of causal responsibility in cases such as *Cheshire* where the negligent actions of doctors contribute to the final outcome. Here we are faced with a victim whose death is caused by the contribution of one intentional aggressor and the sloppy interventions of people trying to remedy the situation. In such a situation to hold a doctor a *novus actor* is not only to free the original blameworthy actor from accountability— significant enough in itself—it is also to lay the semantic foundations for a judgment that the doctor is the real villain in the piece. Overall then it makes good penal sense to deny doctors the status of a *novus actor* unless they themselves are the subjects of a criminal prosecution. A finding that assailant and doctor are jointly causative is also inappropriate since it threatens to muddy the waters of retribution to describe a death as having been caused by the combined operation of a psychopathological disposition on the part of the attacker and a lack of sleep on the part of the doctor.[58]

The upshot of this discussion is that the kinds of consideration, whether mundane (Cheshire) or exotic (Blaue), which fracture our usually unanimous common sense assumptions as to whether a consequence is attributable to the conduct of the defendant renders case outcomes something of a lottery in which judgments of morality and

---

[57] See for example A Norrie, 'A Critique of Criminal Causation (1991) 54 *MLR* at 685.
[58] Cf *Malcherek* [1981] 2 All ER 422.

policy rather than the neutral application of legal principle play the major role. Few would seek to deny this however. The big question is whether it is unsatisfactory for decisions on accountability to be organised in this way. Arguably it is quite reasonable that juries should be given a role in criminal labelling at least in those cases where, as in *Cheshire*, there is an alternative conviction available, say for an attempt or some lesser harm. One possible option in such cases is to abandon the premise that causation is an all or nothing element in criminal liability and embrace the idea that causal responsibility can be apportioned. This would arguably enable the construction of offence labels with appropriately proportioned punishments to reflect the realities of the defendant's causal contribution.[59] A more radical option proposed by Alan Norrie is for responsibility to be 'relationized' to give voice to the true context within which actions take place and consequences ensue.[60] No doubt there is a case for alerting the punishing society to this context so that condemnation and punishment is not disproportionate to the defendant's wrong. Whether or not it is appropriate to record this context within the architecture of criminal liability is more problematic given the importance of communicative clarity in the setting of accountability.[61]

It is where causation plays the defining role in the constitution of criminal wrongdoing that serious concerns are raised. Nowhere is this better exemplified than in *Kennedy*[62] which, in all material particulars except one, was identical to *Dalby*. The difference was that Kennedy, rather than simply supplying the drug the ingestion of which caused the deceased's death, gave, at the latter's request, a fully prepared syringe of heroin. The Court of Appeal, upholding Kennedy's conviction, concluded that *Dalby* was distinguishable upon the ground that in the instant case the defendant had assisted and encouraged the deceased in his use of the heroin, having supplied the syringe ready primed. It is easy to mark this case down as wrongly decided. As Sir John Smith points out, the ground for distinguishing the two cases is hardly cogent. Bearing responsibility for an occurrence is a different matter from causation. One does not cause a sane adult to act by mere persuasion.

---

[59] P Hassett, 'Absolutism in Causation' (1987) 38 *Syracuse L Rev* 683.

[60] A Norrie in *Punishment, Responsibility and Justice*, ch 9. For discussion of relational responsibility see ch 7.

[61] See discussion above at n 54.

[62] [1999] *Crim LR* 65; See also *Environmental Agency v Empress Car Co (Abertillery) Ltd* (1998) 1 All ER 481 (HL).

A more radical observation perhaps is that *Kennedy* is simply the high water mark of a process by which the courts concern themselves more with the question as to who should be held accountable for a social harm rather than whether there is such a person. This **is** unsatisfactory and raises the question, also provoked by Case 1, whether in the rush to find an accountable defendant, we do not run the risk of destabilising the very basis upon which it is agreed that criminal liability should rest. It returns us to the question whether blameworthy conduct rather than harmful results should form the centrepiece of criminal liability. This question is particularly pertinent in connection with those result crimes capable of commission by omission.

Omissions

The various solutions proposed to determine who is accountable for a given social harm do not, despite what has been said, generally confound social expectations nor amount to a morally insupportable burden of responsibility upon individual defendants. People who raise arms against other people and kill or injure them are, without any need for elaborate metaphysical argument, the (causal) agents of such death or injury. It is proper to hold them accountable on the basis of this causal contribution. Result crimes can, however, be committed also by omission. There are two overlapping problems associated with assigning omissions a causal status. The first is whether it is cogent to suppose that doing nothing can cause anything. The second is how in any event it is possible to isolate those omissions which are causal from those which are not causal given that it is almost axiomatic that something other than the conduct of the omitter will be the 'effective cause of death'.[63]

In the ordinary run of events doing nothing clearly causes nothing.[64] Suppose, for example, one sought the cause of death of a child. If I, the child's neighbour, am asleep, stretched motionless and oblivious on my bed at the time of his death there is no obvious causal linkage which can be made between my behaviour and the child's death. The death, quite literally, has nothing to do with me. Some commentators extrapolate

[63] See generally G Fletcher, *Rethinking Criminal Law* (Little Brown and Company, Boston, Toronto, 1978), 585–610.
[64] See ch 3.

from this common sense reasoning that it is always inappropriate to speak of omissions as causing anything.[65] If a child dies of drowning it is the water that kills him, rather than the failure of a bystander or perhaps even a parent to save him.[66] Why should we impute the death of a baby to the unfeeling bystander, when if he had turned a different corner no question of causal responsibility would have arisen?[67] Such an extrapolation seems to miss the point, however, of the causation requirement which as explained earlier is not to identify in some abstract scientific sense the cause of a given harm but to set the limits of accountability for the occurrence of such harm. It is not, then, that I am lying motionless and oblivious which compels the conclusion that I do not cause my neighbour's death. It is the fact that there is no basis upon which to hold me to account. My behaviour in the scenario described makes no more difference to the outside world than if I were dead or had never existed. If, then, it would make no sense to attribute the death to the infant's long dead ancestors or the malign interventions of big, unfriendly, nocturnal giants from a parallel universe it would be no less absurd to attribute them to me. My doing nothing was the kind of doing nothing which has no tendency to produce undesirable consequences. This conclusion would be no different if, hours before the death, I had stuck a pin into a wax representation of the deceased. Sticking pins into voodoo dolls does not cause people to die (I think).

To be a cause of an event, the kind of conduct identifiable as causal, is conduct which conventional thinking rushes to associate with the occurrence of that event. There is no analytic obstruction to characterising omissions in this way. Indeed, there is an uncomplicated sense in which doing nothing may have consequences for the world at large. People who omit to wash themselves have the capacity to empty rooms of their inhabitants. People who omit to refrigerate food can cause it to putrefy. People who fail to remember their wedding anniversary can cause dramatic mood changes in well-balanced partners. People who fail to feed their babies can cause them to die. Doing nothing sometimes makes the difference between something happening and something not happening. So what is the problem with assigning omissions a causal status? In cases of affirmative acts the starting point for associating a

---

[65] M Moore, *Act and Crime* (Clarendon Press, Oxford, 1993) 267 *et seq.*
[66] *Ibid*; cf J Hall, *General Principles of Criminal Law.*
[67] G Fletcher, *Rethinking Criminal Law*, 588–600.

given item of behaviour with a consequence is, as we have seen, the 'but for' test. The particular difficulty posed by omissions is that this test seems ill-equipped to select those who we feel are accountable for the occurrence of a particular harm. In simple terms it is just too easy to ascribe causal responsibility to an omission using the 'but for' test. Suppose, in an example taken from the American jurisprudence, a neighbourhood is roused from sleep by screaming. Hundreds of people go to their windows to see a woman trying to fend off a rapist. Nobody goes to help and nobody calls the police and the rapist is able to consummate the deed. Since each of the witnesses could have done something to prevent it are they all to be assigned a causal status on the basis of but for their failure the act would not have occurred? If not, where is the line to be drawn between those people who could have prevented a consequence occurring and those who should have done so and are accountable for their failure? Is it a matter of geographical proximity, relational proximity, ease of rescue or what?

One obvious difference between inactivity and positive action in the matter of causation is the former's dependence upon other causal agencies. For this reason more than others our moral intuition hesitates to assign to an omission the kind of causal impact which links a villain with a smoking gun to the death of the victim. When A thrusts B's head under water so that B drowns common sense excludes all but A's action from the sphere of causation. We do not ascribe the cause to B's dependence upon oxygen, or C's failure to pick B up at the appointed time, or D's failure to intervene although these are undoubted preconditions of B's death. As Hart and Honore explain, there are certain things which stand out as making a difference to the unfolding of events and it is these things rather than the background conditions which common sense assigns a causal status. Conventional thinking has more difficulty attributing an event to an omission since omissions rarely 'stand out' in this way. This probably accounts for the fact that omissions, say to provide medical care in the aftermath of violence, generally do not sever chains of causation. Omissions do not register on a post mortem report. If, therefore, another's failure to rescue or failure to provide effective medical care is to override the findings of the post mortem the failure must be special—the kind of failure which encourages sane people to unite in condemnation and say 'this is your doing', although nothing by way of 'doing' can be attributed to the other. It is not simple inaction which generates such a response it is the fact that such conduct is both potent and aberrational, representing a deviation from expected standards of behaviour.[68]

The criminal sphere takes up this approach, allowing result crimes to be committed by omission where intervention would have prevented the result and where the failure to intervene was in breach of society's expectations as reflected in a pre-existing legal duty. Consider, for example, criminal homicide, whose conduct element is defined as an 'unlawful killing'. It is no abuse of language to say that the jailor fixed with the responsibility of feeding a prisoner, or a mother with the care of her infant, causes the death of their charge if death follows a failure to provide nourishment.[69] It is the existence of the responsibility which makes the failure aberrational, inclines us to associate the death with the conduct of the omitter, and justifies our inclination to hold the latter accountable for that death. Again, suppose in the example considered above I was the child's babysitter and I had been asked, on the grounds that she had a susceptibility to cot-death, to make regular checks. Suppose also that I had disdained to do so, preferring the comfort of my own bed. In such circumstances it is a quite proper use of language to say that I caused the infant's death since adopting normal behaviour for people in my position would have prevented it. My abnormal omission made the difference between life and death. It is no category mistake or conceptual error to hold then that omissions, like affirmative action, can cause harmful consequences. Our everyday use of language confirms this and since our concepts, including causation, are linguistic constructs it is this notion of causation which is of greatest use in fixing the limits of criminal accountability.

This analysis has been pursued to its utmost in cases involving the medical withdrawal of life sustaining treatment to the terminally ill. Is this a (potentially unlawful) case of causing death or a case of permitting someone to die (of natural causes)? Following the earlier analysis it might appear that such conduct has no substantial causal potency where the deceased is 'doomed' if not, effectively, dead already. Alternatively, so as not to create doctrinal inconsistency with cases where life support is withdrawn by an interloper, we might say that causal responsibility cannot be assigned to doctors who withdraw treatment if, because of its futility, they are under no duty to provide

---

[68] *Ibid*; Hart and Honore, *Causation in the Law*, 35; A Leavens, 'A Causation Approach to Criminal Omissions' (1988) 76 *CAL LR* 547.

[69] Lord Macauley, *Introductory Report upon the Indian Penal Code* (Longmans Green & Co, London, 1898), 113 *et seq*.

it. This has been the general response of courts in England[70] and America[71] in cases involving patients suffering from the condition known as persistent vegetative syndrome. The effective cause of death, in these circumstances, is what makes the difference.[72] Withdrawing life support in furtherance of the doctor's duty to the patient does not make a difference in the sense that it confounds or alters a natural cause and effect sequence by which injury or disease leads to death[73]. What makes the difference is the original condition or cause which makes it a matter of duty for the doctor to do what he does. It is this condition which kills the patient, since if this doctor had not switched off the machine somebody else would have had to. As Fletcher notes, the moral distinction between 'permitting to die' and causing death is not specious casuistry. If nothing can stem the tide of natural causes and doctors owe no duty to make the attempt, their failure to try is both analytically and morally distinct from those who take active steps, however humane, to try to terminate a comparably doomed life.[74]

The second problem in ascribing causal status to an omission in criminal trials is more taxing. This is the matter of **proving** the causal connection. Because omissions generally take effect in the context of other causal influences, the evidential nexus linking conduct with consequence generally promises to be weaker than for the corresponding affirmative action. We cannot always show that it was A's failure to wash which caused the degree of body odour necessary to empty the room. His odour may be resistant to washing. We cannot always show the food would not have putrefied in the same way notwithstanding refrigeration. We cannot always show a person's rescue attempt would have saved the drowning child. In each of these cases appropriate action would probably have made a difference but we cannot be sure. Is this a reason to close off liability for omissions? In *Morby* the conviction of a parent for manslaughter was overturned for a failure for religious reasons to summon a doctor for his child who was suffering

---

[70] *Airedale NHST v Bland* [1993] 1 All ER 821.

[71] *Quinlan*, 355 A2d 647, at 669–70.

[72] See for example Lord Goff, at p 868. Cf Re J Taylor LCJ 'the court never sanctions steps to terminate life. That would be unlawful. . . . The debate here is not about terminating life but solely whether to withhold treatment designed *to prevent death by natural causes.*'

[73] It is upon such a basis that theorists such as Glanville Williams argue that withdrawing life support from the brain dead and those suffering from pvs and other irreversible comatose conditions (282–3) is not a 'cause of death'.

[74] 606–10.

from smallpox as it could not be shown that the life of the child would have been prolonged if assistance had been sought. On the face of it this decision was inevitable. To have decided otherwise would be contrary to standard causal attribution which requires proof beyond reasonable doubt that 'but for' the defendant's conduct the relevant result would not have occurred. But if we observe such evidential niceties it will circumscribe substantially the scope of liability for omissions in result crimes. This evidential gap is plugged in clause 17(1) of the Draft Code which expresses the basis of causal attribution in the case of omissions as follows: 'A person causes a result which is an element of an offence when . . . he omits to do an act which might prevent its occurrence and which he is under a duty to do according to the law relating to the offence.'

The key word here is 'might'. There is no requirement that the prosecution show that 'but for' the failure to act the relevant consequence 'would' have occurred. Causal liability for omissions, on this test, could be imposed even where intervention might not, as in *Morby*, have made a difference. Is this not further evidence supporting the view that decisions on causation owe more to political concerns such as the desirability of finding a suitable person to bear responsibility than the legal/moral concern to ensure that such person is fairly selected?[75]

A way of accommodating this objection must be fashioned if resulting harm is to be allowed to play so great a part in the construction of criminal identities. A plausible accommodation links liability for omissions with another form of derivative liability, namely accessoryship.[76] As will be explained in the next chapter, it is widely thought that liability as an accomplice requires proof of no 'but for' connection between the act of assistance or encouragement and the commission of the offence by the principal. Accessoryship, like omissions, permits liability on the basis of a person's loose association with a primary causal agent rather than his direct instrumentality. If A supplies the murder weapon to B or incites him to action the conduct element of accessoryship in murder is satisfied whether or not it can be shown to be a *sine qua non* of the successful crime. Here also causation of a kind is required, however. A person cannot be guilty as an accomplice if his conduct **could not** have made a difference—if say the weapon was not

[75] Cf MPC 2.03(1)(a) which requires 'the act **or omission** to be an antecedent but for which the result in question would not have occurred.'

[76] For full discussion of the derivative theory of accessoryship and omissions see G Fletcher, *Rethinking Criminal Law*, ch 8.

used, or if the incitement was not heard. It seems possible, then, that here also the court requires simply a 'might have' rather than a 'but for' test of causation. As we can never know for sure that this weapon or incitement did or did not tip the scales but we are convinced that the 'putative accomplice' is properly answerable for its occurrence it makes sense to presume a causal connection. For similar reasons it may be fair to hold someone accountable for an omission so long as the failure to intervene was abnormal and where it is not an unreasonable presumption that intervention may have prevented the undesired result.

Morby poses then as many questions as it settles.[77] It is much easier to prove that a stabbing caused death than that a timely intervention would have prevented it. But the fact that there is such a gap is arguably a poor reason for refusing to hold someone accountable for a failure which common sense designates as the reason for the occurrence. If liability for result crimes for omissions is to be a practical possibility the rules of attribution must make it possible to impute a given harm to the conduct of the defendant. The major questions demanding answers is whether such a way of attributing 'cause' is any less fair than the corresponding rule for acts and whether, because of this and the special nature of omissions, they should have their own special place within the framework of criminal doctrine with rules of attribution tailored to fit.[78]

With regard to the former question it has been remarked that causation does not have to be established as a matter of observable scientific certainty in the case of affirmative action. It is not always necessary for there to be a 'but for' causal connection. And our pre-theoretical notions of cause and effect allow us to assume that a knife wound is a cause of death even where such a wound was causally effective only because of the decision of the victim to refuse a transfusion or because it predated another's murderous attack by a matter of seconds.[79] Similarly we are allowed to assume, in the case of omissions to act, that the omission to act, if abnormal, is causally effective as long as it probably made the difference between the harmful event occurring and it not occurring. If it makes sense to convict an omitter of a result crime, it must also make sense to devise a workable scheme of attribution. Such a scheme must necessarily embody the truth, writ large in accessoryship as will now be seen and arguably implicit elsewhere, that

---

[77] G Williams, 'What Should the Code Do about Omissions?' (1987) *LS* 92 at 106.

[78] See generally discussion at page, ch 3.

[79] Cf R Fumerton and K Kress, 'Causation and the Law: Pre-emption, Lawful Sufficiency and Causal Sufficiency' (2001) 64 *Law and Contemporary Problems* 83.

while causal responsibility is the 'paradigm' case of legal accountability it is not an unyielding precondition. It serves as a functional demand that the parameters of attribution must be responsive, as far as possible, to the key function of causal inquiries in the law, namely identifying and condemning those whom society has good cause to hold to account for the occurrence of social harms.

7

Attributing Liability to Secondary Parties

THE SUBJECT MATTER of this chapter concerns the basis upon which individuals may become criminally liable for the criminal wrongdoing of others. In this it has something in common with criminal attempts where the basis of incrimination is also some activity falling short of the (personal) commission of a criminal offence. In other respects liability for attempt generally matches the normal model of criminal liability which is that the accused is held accountable for something which he has done with an appropriately constructed mental attitude. Liability as an accomplice departs markedly from this standard model in that the basis of the accomplice's liability is not what he has done but what someone else has done. This is not a form of vicarious liability, however, arising automatically by virtue of the actor standing in a particular relationship to another person. Rather it arises because of something the actor has done or not done for which he bears responsibility and which is of a nature to lead him to be identified with the perpetrator of an offence. Whereas the attempter's liability is personal, deriving from what he has done and from the mental attitude which accompanies his action, the basis of incrimination in accessoryship is derivative. The accomplice's liability derives from what the perpetrator has done and **his** mental attitude.

As a simple illustration of how this alternative basis to incrimination follows through into doctrine it is instructive to compare the construction of personal liability for murder with that for complicity. Personal liability in murder follows the standard model. It depends upon proof of an act (of the defendant) by which the death of the victim is caused, executed with the intention either of killing the victim or of causing him grievous bodily harm. Liability as an accomplice to murder, which is derivative, does not require the actor to intend the victim's death. Neither, it is thought, does it require the actor to cause the death. It requires merely that he intentionally associate himself, by giving acts of assistance or encouragement, with a person who he knows will or may kill with the requisite mental attitude. Significantly, therefore, both his deed and his culpability may fall far short of that necessary to incriminate the perpetrator of either the attempt or the substantive offence. A person may be liable as an accessory to murder by dint of an act as innocuous as driving the getaway car or by attending a lynching with a view to giving the perpetrators her moral support.

How can this state of affairs be explained? Obviously there are procedural and evidential advantages in collapsing the distinction between perpetrators and other participators. In particular, it enables prosecutions to proceed to a conclusion against parties to a joint enterprise without fear of collapse for want of proof as to which of two or more persons pulled the trigger, drove the car, took the money and so on.[1] This does not explain why, however, the wrong for which accessories are accountable is the actual wrong perpetrated by the principal rather than their own wrong, say that of assisting or encouraging murder.

The rationale of treating perpetrators and participators alike takes as its starting point the actuality of crime which is, in contemporary society, largely a co-operative enterprise, whether taking the form of small partnerships or gangs, or substantial criminal organisations. It is then the partnership or gang, first and foremost, which robs, kills, defrauds etc rather than the individual perpetrator. In many such organisations, particularly small partnerships, roles are effectively interchangeable. This accounts for the common law's traditional tendency to distinguish between forms of participation which involve co-operative presence at the scene of the crime and those taking place before or after which were treated more leniently. In the case of larger gangs the organisational structure typically will farm out different roles on a competence and power basis alone. Responding to this actuality by limiting accountability for the crime to those who perpetrate it might show insufficient regard for these structural dynamics which render personal causal participation as much a matter of chance or functional necessity as individuated choice.

Equally it might tend to ignore the concentration of power in certain individuals within the organisation which renders the idea that criminal wrongdoing issues from individuated context-independent choices incoherent. Perpetrators, as is well understood, are often no more than

---

[1] The common law justified treating all those present at the scene of the crime as principals and thus eligible for maximum punishment whether or not they actually perpetrated the offence.

pawns in a complex game of criminal chess in which one organisation seeks to delibilitate or neutralise the other. In the narcotics trade this purely mechanical role is captured by the descriptive epithet 'mules' to describe those organisationally insignificant participants who do all the dangerous work of smuggling drugs across state boundaries. Not surprisingly it is 'Mr Big' rather than 'Ms Mule' who engage the organisational efforts of law enforcement agencies. It is clear to everyone that some people who associate themselves with the criminal actions of others are both as dangerous and as blameworthy as the actual perpetrators, if not more so.[2] As a consequence it seems appropriate to hold them punishable for the same reason, to the same extent as the other, and therefore for the same crime. Derivative liability thus allows a degree of flexibility in setting the parameters of accountability for criminal wrongdoing. If causal agency is the method whereby harmful events may be attributed to individual perpetrators it is by co-operative association that accountability may stretch to include those 'prime movers' without whose skills, efforts, dynamism and influence some criminal activity would not occur. This is no doubt how it should be. As explained earlier, it is a kind of fiction in any event which locates the responsibility for social harms in individual 'causing' actors. This is not how life works, and it is why rules of attribution ascribe causal responsibility to omitters simply on a 'might have' rather than a 'but for' basis.[3]

These considerations no doubt explain the fact of derivative liability but not its applications. For example, in common law systems at least no distinction is drawn between mechanical helpers and prime movers. It is as though a bit actor or the make-up artist in *Gone With The Wind* received an Oscar simply for their association with the film rather than for any particular contribution they made to it or commitment they showed to it. The wrong in accessoryship is showing commitment to the principal in the prosecution of his aims rather than any degree of commitment to the aims themselves. The driver of the getaway car is treated on all fours with both the contract killer and the gangland boss who procures the latter. While it is clear that it is fair to attribute the killing in broad causal terms to both procurer and perpetrator, it is

---

[2] Other examples are instigators of criminal offences, say someone who takes out a contract on another's life, and co-adventurers who set out to commit a criminal offence leaving its execution to one of the others.

[3] See discussion of *Morby* in ch 3, above.

equally clear that attributing the death to the driver requires some other justification.

The common law's traditional theory for explaining the equivalent treatment of principals and secondary parties is not that there is substantive equivalence in terms of deed and culpability but that there is a formal equivalence which is set up by the nature of the relationship existing between the two parties. In effect, this relationship is conceived in terms of the civil law of agency whereby certain deeds of the agent are imputable to the principal. Under the civil law an agency relationship arises when one party (the principal) constitutes another party (the agent) as his legal embodiment, most usually for the purpose of negotiating and executing contracts. The freedom and flexibility thus offered to the principal to change his legal relations is offset by corresponding responsibilities to shoulder the consequences, whatever they may be, of the actions of the agent acting under the principal's express or implied authority. In the criminal law this quasi-agency relationship has been explained as follows: 'Liability turns on contemplation or, putting the same idea in other words authorisation, which may be express but is more usually implied.'[4] This notion of authorisation is consistent with derivative liability.[5] By intentionally assisting or encouraging the action of the principal the accessory implicitly authorises P's commission of an offence, and thus P's liability, thereby in effect manifesting consent to his own liability.[6]

There are of course important distinctions to be drawn between the civil law's notion of agency and accessorial liability. Most significantly agency is predicated upon the control exercised over the agent by the principal. The principal is liable for the agent's acts precisely because he instigates the agent to act for him, and, moreover, benefits from his actions. The agent becomes then little more than a puppet in his economic dealings, which is quite properly replicated in the corresponding legal relations. Although accessories may exercise similar degrees of

---

[4] At 175; see also *Wakely* [1990] *Crim LR* 119.

[5] More recently, however, the requirement of authorisation or tacit agreement has been dispensed with. In *Hyde* Lord Lane CJ said that 'realisation' that the principal may kill or cause serious injury with the requisite intention (to kill or cause GBH) was enough to supply the *mens rea* for the accessory even though the accessory did not agree to such conduct being used. In *Powell*, the House of Lords approved this approach. See below.

[6] S Kadish, 'Complicity, Blame and Cause : A Study in the Interpretation of Doctrine' (1985) 73 *Calif LR* 323 at 354–5.

control over the actions of the principal the reverse is usually true and this is to be seen reflected in the respective nomenclatures.[7] In accessorial liability the person taking executive action is called the principal/perpetrator whereas the person who takes responsibility for the action of the other is termed the accessory/accomplice. In agency it is the agent who takes executive action and the principal who takes the responsibility.

A basis other than control for imputing the actions of the principal to the accessory seems in order then if we are to make some moral sense of the current broad scope of derivative liability. Dressler has suggested a forfeiture basis.[8] What happens when people assist or encourage others in their commission of criminal offences is not so much that they step into the principal's shoes in the way that an agent does. Rather that they step out of their own shoes, relinquishing their right to be treated with the concern and respect due to individual rights-bearers. Those who lend their support to a criminal enterprise lose their right to be treated on the normal attributional basis of criminal doctrine, which require criminal subjects to both choose and cause criminal outcomes. The strength of this latter notion is that it accounts for much of the actual state of criminal doctrine—the unwillingness to distinguish between 'prime movers' and cat's paws and the degraded fault element requiring accessories to manifest commitment to the principal primarily rather than the criminal outcome. In a sense then, as with parliamentary democracy, the principal, like the party member voted for becomes the accessory/voter's representative rather than his delegate or pawn.

As a descriptive account forfeiture theory is very plausible but as a normative account it is less so since it fails adequately to explain why it is appropriate or fair to punish one person for the wrongdoing of another rather than for his own wrongdoing. There is no obvious utilitarian justification for derivative rather than personal liability. As Dressler himself has argued, given the different levels of possible involvement and commitment of accessories it is surely more utile to treat and punish people in accordance with the nature of their involvement. Those who show more commitment/wickedness/control need more by way of punishment/rehabilitation than those standing at the periphery of criminal activity. Similarly there is no obvious reason why

[7] See G Fletcher, *Rethinking Criminal Law* (Little Brown and Company, Boston, Toronto, 1978), 656, and generally.
[8] J Dressler, 'Reassessing the Theoretical Underpinnings of Accomplice Liability: New Solutions to an Old problem' (1985) 37 *Hastings LJ* 111.

the principles governing the imputation of one financial transaction from a master to a servant should be hijacked for the entirely unrelated purpose of attributing one person's wrongdoing to another. Sometimes no doubt this may be morally appropriate. It is easy to see why, say, Iago (or any other procurer of another's crime) forfeits the right to be condemned and punished on his own account for the murder of Desdemona by Othello. Truly, principles of causation notwithstanding, this killing is Iago's doing. But equally, it is not easy to see what moral principle is being prosecuted when mere mechanical helpers whose assistance may make no ultimate difference to the course of events are condemned via the same doctrine.[9] If it is thought right to condemn and punish a secondary party for his involvement in the commission of an offence this can be done without subduing the accessory's own individual involvement.

ACCESSORIES AS CAUSES OR PRIME MOVERS

Of course most of these objections wither away if it is possible to conceive of both mechanical helpers and instigators as bearing causal responsibility. Looked at in isolation from other features within the construction of criminal liability this is at least to a limited extent quite plausible. Judges and commentators often imply a causal basis for liability[10] and sometimes go further and insist upon it, as in the following statement of CS Greaves, the draftsperson of the 1861 Accessories and Abettor's Act:

> Jurors . . . understand that he who causes a thing to be done by another is just as responsible as if he did the thing himself—*qui facit per alium facit per se*[11]—and there is no more difficulty in satisfying them that a man ought to be convicted of a murder who causes it to be done by another in his absence, than in satisfying them that, where one man inflicts a mortal wound in the presence of another, that wound is as much his wound as if he had inflicted it, if they were both concurring in the act that caused it. In both cases a jury must be satisfied that the act of the killer was caused by the other. . .[12]

---

[9] As when Emilia, Desdemona's maid, delivers to Iago her mistress's handkerchief the principal means by which Iago intends to provoke Othello to murderous jealousy.

[10] See for example Devlin J in *NCB v Gamble* [1959] 1 QB 11, 20 and discussion thereon in KJM Smith *A Modern Treatise on the Law of Criminal Complicity*, (Clarendon Press, Oxford, 1991), 56–7; cf D Lanham, 'Primary and Derivative Liability' [2000] *Crim LR* 707; 'Accomplices and Withdrawal' (1981) 97 *LQR* 575.

[11] He who does something through another does it himself.

[12] CS Greaves, *The Criminal Law Consolidation and Amendment Acts of the 24 & 25 Vict.* (2nd edn, London, 1862), 21–2. See also JF Stephen, *A Digest of the Criminal Law of England* (London, 1877), 24.

Liability as an accessory for procuring the commission of an offence by a person innocent of *mens rea,* as where A spikes P's drink so as to induce P to drive a motor vehicle with excess alcohol, already requires causation.[13] It might seem to follow that a causal connection also grounds liability in the case of **inciting** someone to commit a crime given that the inchoate offence is still available for (non-causal) encouragement.[14] After all, accessorial liability is dependent upon the offence having been committed. What better explanation for this than that A has incited P **to** commit the offence, that is, has caused P's commission of it?[15] There are, however, a number of objections which can be posted to this reasoning. Most obviously the theory does not seem to fit the doctrinal facts. For example, although accessorial liability for encouraging the commission of the offence requires the encouragement to be communicated to the principal thus supporting the causal thesis it does not require him to be influenced by it. In *Giannetto* it was said that where A had encouraged P to commit a killing A was complicit although P had already planned to execute it.[16] And in the American case of *State v Tally* it was stated that accessorial liability for acts of assistance is not negated by the absence of the most tenuous 'but for' connection.[17] It is enough that the assistance made the principal's job easier.

A second objection is raised by Professor Kadish who, adopting the analysis of Hart and Honore, argues it is fundamental to the notion of moral responsibility upon which criminal liability is predicated that individual action is not caused but chosen. When Iago, by deceitful stratagem, provokes Othello to murderous jealousy it is not by Iago's deed that Desdemona meets her cruel fate but by Othello's. A dupe he may be, but not a robot or cipher. Once we concede the opposite the whole basis upon which punishment and condemnation are justified, that individuals have free will and therefore bear responsibility for what they do, is attacked.[18] Sir John Smith echoes this point in his critical commentary on the case of *Kennedy* arguing that 'to be responsible for the death of another is not the same, for legal purposes, as being the

---

[13] Attorney-General's Reference (No 1 of 1975) [1975] 2 All ER 684.

[14] Cf *A-G v Able* [1984] QB 795, and see G Williams, 'Complicity, Purpose and the Draft Code [1990] *Crim LR* 4.

[15] Where the secondary party has instigated the commission of an offence, treating the latter on all fours with the perpetrator is morally appropriate as in such cases there will often be a clear 'but for' causal connection.

[16] (1997) 1 Cr App R 1.

[17] 102 Ala 25 (1894).

[18] Kant, *Prolegomena to any Future Metaphysics* (Bobbs Merrill, Indianapolis, 1950), 93–4.

cause. Otherwise we would have no need for a separate structure of liability for accessories.'[19] The law of accessoryship is necessary, in other words, precisely because, while it is not possible to impute causal responsibility for a criminal harm to anyone other than its perpetrator, it may nevertheless be appropriate to attribute responsibility for that harm to some, such as accessories, who are not causally responsible.

On the other hand there is an important sense in which one person may cause another to commit an offence which survives Hart and Honore's insistence that human action is chosen not caused, and for this reason renders a person susceptible to moral condemnation and punishment. In Dressler's analysis what we do, if not cause the actions of others, may nevertheless trigger or induce such actions and in so doing make them as much a matter of the inducer's responsibility as the perpetrator. It is upon such a basis that certain theorists account for the suppression of the distinction between perpetrators and accessories. It is not that their conduct is just as bad as the principal or that they participate but rather that they are sufficiently causal, in a broad undoctrinaire sense, to merit treating them as contributing to and therefore for that reason responsible for the result. Establishing this causal relation is central to explaining the key requirement in accessorial liability that the substantive offence actually be committed and that, unlike with inchoate offences, the secondary party merits equal punishment and stigma.

KJM Smith, who advocates a causal basis for accessorial liability, explains how it is possible to derive a causal explanation of accessoryship even from cases which seem to reject one.[20] An instructive example is *Calhaem*, which is generally exploited to illustrate the non-causal basis to liability as an accessory.[21] W was charged with counselling (by instigation) P to murder T, her rival in love. There was evidence that P may have killed T as a result of losing his self-control upon meeting T for this purpose and thus was not acting in execution of W's counsel. W was convicted of murder and appealed on the basis that there was no proof that her actions had caused P to kill T. While this argument was apparently rejected, Parker LJ hinted at some loose causal requirement, stating that it was enough that 'there was some connection' between the counsel of the defendant and the act done and that he was acting within the scope of his authority.' Smith and Hogan insist that

[19] [1999] *Crim LR* 65, at 67–8.
[20] KJM Smith, (1991), ch 3.
[21] [1985] QB 808.

the connection referred to is not a 'causal connection'.[22] But the facts of *Calhaem* nevertheless support the causal connection thesis. W's counselling was clearly a **but for** cause of the killing. H would never have met, let alone killed T, unless he had been asked to kill her.[23] Nowhere does any indication appear that this may not have been central to the court's reasoning. Indeed the only case the court considered of (successfully) counselling a killing which would not attract accessorial liability involved a hypothetical in which no form of causal responsibility could be established. Parker LJ said that 'if the principal offender happened to be involved in a football riot in the course of which he laid about him with a weapon of some sort and killed someone who, unknown to him, was the person whom he had been counselled to kill, he would not in our view have been acting within the scope of his.'[24] A quite plausible reason for denying the instigator's accessorial liability in these circumstances is that he would not, unlike *Calhaem*, be **a factual cause** of death.

DERIVATIVE LIABILITY: TENSIONS AND INSTABILITY

There are many other examples of doctrinal tensions arising when the basis of liability is not the blameworthy deed of the actor himself but the culpable assistance or encouragement given to someone else in their wrongdoing. One such is reflected in the ambiguous fault element in accessoryship. Derivative liability for accessoryship as opposed to that characterising vicarious or omissions-based liability seems to call attention to some form of unity of purpose or joint enterprise. After all, if A is to be liable because P is liable this is best explained on the basis that the nature of the relationship between A and P renders punishing the one for the misdeeds of another appropriate. This relationship, one would assume, must be constructed out of the criminal wrongdoing itself rather than say A's ability to influence P's behaviour as in the case of parent and child, or employer and employee. Significantly, this is not carried though into doctrine, however, where the general principle is that liability as an accessory requires nothing other than a knowing act of assistance. If liability here is derivative it derives not so much from any community of purpose between P and A as from the fact that A, being in a position to thwart P's criminal endeavour, failed culpably to do so. In short, it appears to be an adjunct to omissions-based liability, placed in a separate doctrinal category so as not to necessitate the

[22] Smith and Hogan, (2002) 132.
[23] Cf KJM Smith, (1991) at 59.
[24] [1985] 2 All ER 269 per Parker LJ.

delivery of a new duty situation capable of over-incriminating those who get caught up in the misdeeds of others.[25] So whereas a gunsmith who supplies a gun to a customer knowing it is to be used to commit murder bears responsibility if this event occurs, he bears no responsibility if his knowledge of the criminal purpose post-dates the act of supply and he fails to inform the authorities.[26] A reconciliation between social responsibility and individual autonomy is made, but at a price, the price being an irrational doctrinal sledgehammer to crack an anti-social nut in the former case and an equally irrational failure to support the most basic social responsibilities with matching legal duties in the latter.

Another instance of the tensions existing between a derivative and inchoate basis for accessorial liability concerns the doctrinal implications of a criminal enterprise miscarrying in some way. In the usual case if A agrees with P that P should commit C (a criminal wrong) then A's liability tracks P's in its entirety. So if the agreement is to beat up Y and Y, contrary to the expectations and desires of P (and A), dies then P is liable for manslaughter and so, derivatively, is A. The corollary of this is that if A and P agree that P should commit C (a criminal wrong) and P deliberately deviates from this joint enterprise and commits D (a different criminal wrong) A's liability tracks P's only up to the point where P deviates from the common purpose. So if A and P agree to steal property from X and P deviates from the plan and kills X, A is liable for the theft, assuming it occurs, but not the homicide. The doctrinal tensions emerge when there is an alternative basis for attributing responsibility for a criminal harm other than that agreed upon and so for which the accessory is derivatively liable. A common case is where the principal commits a crime other than that for which assistance or encouragement were provided for the purpose of executing that offence or escaping detection or apprehension. So, in the last example if P kills X in order to make his escape or to prevent X identifying him, the question arises as to the ingredients necessary to hold A also liable. Two strains are evident in the case law. The first, consistent with derivative liability, requires the accessory's assistance or encouragement to have been given on the understanding that such a deviation may occur or where the possibility of such events occurring are implicit in the enterprise itself: The position was expressed by Lord Parker in *Anderson and Morris* as follows:

[25] AJ Ashworth 'The Scope of Criminal Liability for Omissions' (1989) 105 LQR 424.
[26] See ch 6.

where two persons embark on a joint enterprise, each is liable for the acts done in pursuance of that joint enterprise . . . (including) liability for unusual consequences if they arise from the execution of the joint enterprise.[27]

So, in *Dunbar* the liability of the accessory was expressed to be dependent upon P executing a term of an agreement between A and P. If the facts were such that A could be construed to say 'Yes I agree that you may commit serious injury if contingency X occurs' it would be fair that A takes responsibility for the consequences of that agreement. He could not meaningfully claim 'this is not my killing.'[28] Again, in *Baldessare*[29] the accomplice of a joyrider was held jointly liable with his principal for manslaughter when the joy ride ended in the death of a pedestrian. Liability hinged not upon the mere fact of complicity in the joy riding but complicity in a particularly dangerous instance of it. The principal was driving without proper lights and at an excessive speed. The Court of Criminal Appeal held, dismissing the appeal, that the jury were entitled to take the inference from all these facts that the principal did not exceed the terms upon which A agreed to accompany him on the trip.

This notion of authorisation is consistent with derivative liability. By intentionally assisting or encouraging the action of the principal the accessory implicitly authorises P's commission of an offence, and thus P's liability, thereby in effect manifesting consent to his own liability.[30] More recently, however, the requirement of authorisation or tacit agreement has been dispensed with. The first indication came in *Chan-Wing-Siu*, in which Sir Robin Cooke stated that 'a secondary party is criminally liable for acts by the primary offender of a type which the former foresees but does not necessarily intend . . . (Liability) turns on contemplation or, putting the same idea in other words authorisation, which may be express but is more usually implied.'[31] Current orthodoxy holds that it is enough that the parties contemplated that the principal may commit the relevant offence, say murder, as a possible incident of the successful execution of the joint enterprise, say robbery. Liability here is based in the fact of participation in a joint unlawful enterprise which carries risks of additional harms for which parties

---

[27] *Anderson and Morris* [1966] 2 QB 110, at 118.

[28] *Dunbar* [1988] *Crim LR* 693.

[29] (1930) 144 LT 185.

[30] Kadish, 'Complicity, Blame and Cause : A Study in the Interpretation of Doctrine' (1985) 73 *Calif LR* 323 at 354–5.

[31] At 175; see also *Wakely* [1990] *Crim LR* 119.

must bear responsibility.[32] Strangely that same orthodoxy holds that it is authorisation rather than contemplation where the principal departs from the common purpose but nevertheless commits the offence agreed. So if A and P agree to cause T grievous bodily harm by hitting him with a baseball bat but P, unforeseen by A, stabs him fatally with a knife, A is not complicit in the murder.[33] These kinds of tensions between a derivative and inchoate form of liability for an accessory are endemic in the case law. Sometimes secondary parties are judged on the basis of their own fault and deeds; sometimes on the basis of others.

The derivative theory of liability is also unable to account for another recent doctrinal development, namely that an accessory may be liable for an offence greater than that of the principal offender. Suppose, for example, it is Iago's (successful) plan that Othello will kill Desdemona but that Othello is able to avail himself of the partial defence of provocation. Does this limit Iago's responsibility also to voluntary manslaughter? On the derivative theory of liability the correct position seems to be that **accessories** are **incapable** of bearing greater liability than that of the principal. The accessory should be punished for what has happened rather than for what has not. Once again, how else can we explain the requirement for accessorial liability, not merely that A has given P assistance and encouragement towards committing the primary offence but also that that offence be committed? This argument was accepted in *R v Richards*. Mrs Richards procured P and P1 to cause Mr Richards, her husband, serious injury. P and P1 only partially executed this charge inflicting a minor wound upon him. Mrs Richards, P and P1 were charged under section 18 OAPA with wounding with intent to cause grievous bodily harm. Mrs Richards was convicted but P and P1 were acquitted of this offence and convicted of the lesser offence of malicious wounding under section 20. On appeal Mrs Richards' conviction was reduced to malicious wounding. In *Howe* this approach was disapproved. Lord Mackay, in the House of Lords, ruled that it was no objection to the conviction of a secondary party for a graver offence that the secondary party had the *mens rea* only for a lesser offence.[34] There is, however, a very strong objection,

---

[32] In *Hui Chi-ming v R*, the Privy Council approved this approach and interpreted Sir Robin Cooke's use of the word 'authorisation' to mean only that foresight of death or serious injury was not enough [1991] 3 All ER 897.

[33] *Powell and English* [1997] 4 All ER 545.

[34] Smith and Hogan, (1999) 149–51; G Williams, *Textbook of Criminal Law* (Stevens, London, 1983), 373–4.

namely that *Howe* serves to elide two separate areas of law, namely incitement and complicity. Returning to *Richards* it is clear that Mrs Richards committed two separate wrongs, namely inciting the section 18 offence and being an accomplice to the section 20 offence. Both of these could properly have sustained convictions for Mrs Richards. 'Topping up' her liability for one offence by reference to some other wrong she may have committed ruptures the ordinary structure of liability which matches a criminal wrong with its appropriate mental element, in the process creating broader doctrinal incoherence.

A related testing ground for the plausibility of the derivative theory of accessorial liability concerns those cases where, for some reason, the principal has dropped out of the picture. The position originally taken by the common law was that accessorial liability was dependent upon a convicted principal and that the accessory's liability shadows, in its entirety, that of the principal. The common law has moved on from this rather strict position. The derivative theory of liability requires, as a minimum, only that a crime has been committed. If it has, and the secondary party's participation can be proved, then there is no objection in principle to his conviction if, for example, the principal cannot be detected or if he is acquitted for lack of evidence. The true theoretical problems emerge when the principal is not acquitted for lack of evidence but because the things she has done do not amount to the criminal offence charged. In one situation it is clear that accessorial liability is not possible. This is where no *actus reus* can be identified. So, in *Thornton v Mitchell* a bus conductor negligently gave the all clear to his driver who was reversing his bus when in fact there was a pedestrian behind the bus. The bus reversed into the pedestrian, injuring him. The driver was charged with careless driving with the conductor as an accessory. The charge against the driver was dismissed on the ground that he had not been careless in relying upon his conductor's signals. The conductor was, therefore, also acquitted on the ground that there was no offence to abet.[35] Again in the Australian case of *Demirian* the deceased together with D conspired to blow up a consulate.[36] Unfortunately for the deceased he managed to blow himself up instead. D was charged as accessory to murder. The full court of Victoria held that he could not be found guilty as an accessory to murder since the

[35] Cf RD Taylor, 'Complicity and Excuses' [1983] *Crim LR* 656.
[36] [1989] VR 97. For discussion see D Lanham, 'Primary and Derivative Liability' [2000] *Crim LR* 707.

deceased had not committed murder. Clearly in such situations there is a temptation to punish a participant on the basis of their blameworthy deed rather than the non-existent criminal wrongdoing of the principal but equally clearly the derivative theory of liability disallows this.

A different situation is where there is criminal wrongdoing but the mechanism for effecting this wrongdoing takes an unusual course. If P wishing to kill B puts poison in her whisky P is criminally liable for the resulting death whether B pours out her own fatal draft or if it is effected by the unknowing T. In this latter case P is liable not as a secondary party to T's innocent act of perpetration but as a principal in his own right. He has performed the *actus reus* of murder with the relevant *mens rea* which act is the legal cause of B's death,[37] Similar conclusions account for the liability of P if he uses a child, monkey or robot to effect a burglarious theft. In this latter case, however, it is necessary to rely on a specific doctrine of the criminal law to secure P's liability. Burglary requires the principal to have 'entered premises as a trespasser'. Since P does not himself 'enter' the premises his liability requires that he be able to commit this crime 'by proxy' through the instrumentality of an 'innocent agent'. And so the law provides. As long as the crime itself does not envisage personal participation, as say with the crimes of bigamy and rape, the doctrine of innocent agency enables the actual perpetrator of criminal wrongdoing to drop out of the picture leaving the instigator as the principal.

The core cases of innocent agency are those where P is enabled to commit the relevant offence through the (blameless) instrumentality of another. Blameless instrumentality may arise due to infancy, insanity, or lack of *mens rea* as where P secretes drugs in A's luggage without the latter's knowledge so as to procure their unlawful importation.[38] More problematic is the case where P has a cognate defence. Say P threatens A with grievous bodily harm unless he administers a beating to T. Assuming A is acquitted on grounds of duress is it permissible to invoke the doctrine of innocent agency to justify convicting P as principal?[39] The courts have answered in the affirmative. Indeed, the usefulness of this doctrine in obviating the theoretical problems of

---

[37] P Alldridge, 'The Doctrine of Innocent Agency' (1990) 2 *Crim LF* 45.

[38] *White v Ridley* (1978) 140 CLR 342. Lanham argues that the defendant in *Thornton v Mitchell* could have decided on this ground, namely that P drove 'carelessly by means of an innocent agent', driving being an activity which can naturally occur by 'remote control', above n 36 at 711.

[39] It should be understood that P cannot be liable as perpetrator as he is not deemed to 'cause' A's action.

attributing liability to a secondary party in the absence of a punishable principal have encouraged the courts to stretch it beyond its natural boundaries. In *Cogan and Leak*[40] L encouraged C to have intercourse with L's wife. As a result of what L told him C believed the wife was consenting when in fact L was coercing her. C was acquitted of rape for lack of *mens rea*. The Court of Appeal ruled that this was not fatal to L's conviction. First L could have been convicted as the principal offender. He had raped his wife though the agency of another. The problem, of course, was that he had not raped his wife.[41] This is not the kind of crime, unlike say theft or murder, that one can commit by proxy.[42] The Court's alternative ground was that the husband could be found guilty as accessory to rape although the other was acquitted for lack of *mens rea*. The decision in effect abandons the requirement that A's liability derive from the liability of P. What is important is that criminal wrongdoing takes place not that C was liable for it. Indeed, derivative liability is premised upon the fact that A encourages or helps P to commit an offence, which clearly he does not if, in the case of crimes of *mens rea*, he knows that the other lacks a criminal intent. Less problematic in this regard is *R v Bourne*[43] in which H forced his wife W to submit to buggery with a dog. W was not charged with the offence, but H's conviction as an accessory was upheld on appeal. The decision can be explained on the basis that the prosecution were able to establish all the elements of the principal offence. H's conviction can then be justified as an orthodox case of derivative liability. He had, in effect, procured through duress the commission of the offence. Although W had a defence this, being an excuse only, was personal to her and could not therefore be relied upon by H.

On the basis of these two cases we can see therefore that there are two separate strains in case law involving criminal wrongs procured by the culpable act of another. The first, consistent with derivative liability, justifies conviction on the basis that as long as the elements of an offence are established it is no bar to convicting a secondary party that

---

[40] [1976] 1 QB 217.

[41] Cf *People v Hernandez* (1971) 96 Cal Rept 71; indeed it might mean that a man (or woman) could commit rape on another using the 'innocent instrumentality' of a broom handle (something other than a penetrating perpetrator); see generally Williams, *Textbook of Criminal Law*, 371; KJM Smith, (1991), 107–10.

[42] And if it were, women could commit it, which is inconsistent with rape's statutory definition section 1(2) Sexual Offences Act 1956, 'a man commits rape if he "has sexual intercourse with a person who . . . does not consent".'

[43] (1952) 36 Cr App R 125.

the perpetrator escapes liability on the basis of a defence personal to him. The second, which is inconsistent with derivative liability and indicates an inchoate basis to liability, requires only that the secondary party procure the *actus reus* of the offence or, on another analysis 'causes' the *actus reus* to take place.[44] Onto this *actus reus* the secondary party's own *mens rea* is grafted, *mens rea*, it should be noted, that appertains to the substantive offence itself rather than to participation in the perpetrator's commission of it. Liability here is premised on the secondary party's own personal wrongdoing rather than that of the principal.[45'] Both strains are pragmatic responses to the doctrinal gap opened up by the derivative theory of liability. As such they are supportable because, as these cases illustrate, there is no substantive reason for the gap in the first place.[46]

A further problem arises, however, where the principal, as in *Bourne*, has a defence but it is a justification rather than an excuse or, more precisely, it is not a defence personal to the principal.

Case 1

A comes upon P in the course of attacking V, A's enemy. A natural opportunist, A gives P a gun, which P duly uses on V to shoot him dead. Suppose that P was justified in using fatal force because he was in turn seeking to repel V's murderous attack.

Here the position changes in a number of different ways. First, A does not procure the killing. She merely assists and encourages it. Second, the killing is, in any event, not wrongful which means that A, although she may think she is assisting P's commission of murder, is in fact assisting and encouraging P to do something lawful. Note also that this is a different case from that where A acts on her own account to kill V and unknown to her the conditions are such as to justify her doing so.[47] In such circumstances A's action is not justified since she does not act for the reason of self-defence, which reason alone affords her the

---

[44] See Lanham, 'Primary and Derivative Liability' [2000] *Crim LR*, 712–3.

[45] 'C had sexual intercourse with (the wife) without her consent. The fact that C was innocent of rape because he believed that she was consenting does not affect the position that she was raped'. Not a cogent ground for the decision. Rape only occurs where both mr and ar occurs. Lawton LJ thought that it had, at 223.

[46] Neither is the gap entirely closed in Fletcher's account of the two cases, *Rethinking Criminal Law* at 667.

[47] See ch 9 for discussion.

privilege of using force against another.[48] Here, however, the action taken by P against V is uncontroversially lawful. The problem we are faced with is A's motivation, which may incline us to the view that A must be guilty of something if not murder. Is there any means to convert the common sense intuition that A deserves to be associated with a wrongful killing into a reality? The first possibility is that P may be guilty of incitement to murder by virtue of the encouragement implicit in offering A the gun. There are two objections to this. A practical objection is that it is not difficult to imagine cases where no encouragement could be inferred as where the gun was delivered into P's presence surreptitiously. In such a situation incitement would not lie. Another objection is that a conviction for incitement does not adequately record the wrong which we attribute to A which is wrongful participation in an actual death rather than the inchoate offence. For similar reasons convicting A for attempting to aid and abet a murder does not quite 'hit the spot'[49] even were such an inchoate offence to exist.[50] It seems to mistake the true nature of A's role. She has the *mens rea* for the substantive offence—she acts in order to kill. Moreover, she plausibly can be considered also the legal, not merely factual, cause of H's death because of the substantiality of her 'but for' contribution. This argues for principal offenders to be defined so as to incriminate **all those** who have control over whether or not the *actus reus* takes place whether or not they participate in its execution.[51]

The second possibility is to convict A of murder by means of the doctrine of innocent agency. The obvious objection to this strategy is that it flies in the face of what we apprehend to be the point of the doctrine, which is to loosen the doctrinal strictures concerning what it is to be a perpetrator. A perpetrator on this view is someone who performs the *actus reus* part of a (result) crime by means of his own 'hands on' participation or is someone who 'causes' the result in some other way. Clearly one can cause a result by programming a robot or manipulating

---

[48] For discussion see ch 9.

[49] Charging the attempt here reflects the fact that A thought and hoped he was assisting P to murder V but was mistaken due to the justificatory context.

[50] The common law does not recognise an offence of attempting to aid and abet. Either the substantive offence is committed in which case such participation is real rather than attempted or it is not, in which case there is no offence from which complicity and *a fortiori* attempted complicity can derive. The MPC takes a different approach. See G Fletcher, *Rethinking Criminal Law*, 198.

[51] For further discussion of this 'causation' approach to secondary party liability see Lanham, generally.

the behaviour of a child or insane person. Equally, with only a slightly loosened notion of causal influence, one can 'cause' a result by coercion. It is less easy to analyse a secondary party to a justified killing as having caused the death without ultimately subverting the point of complicity doctrine which, rather than challenging the notion of individual causal responsibility upon which criminal liability is premised, allows a limited complementary model of attribution to operate where criminal harms issue from collaborative enterprises. If A could be liable as principal in the case where P's action is justified there seems no reason in principle why, in any case where Mr Big sets up the mechanisms whereby his minions commit crimes to his order, Mr Big should not be treated as perpetrator. While this does not seem objectionable in itself it diminishes the basic moral distinctions separating participation in crime as perpetrator and as assister, encourager or instigator in no less significant a fashion than in the former analysis.[52] Both responses to Case 1 are too much influenced by A's wicked motivation, too little influenced by the fact that P's conduct was quite lawful and too little concerned with matching what is wrong with A's behaviour with an appropriate criminal label. If A has committed a wrong it seems quite clear that that wrong is not murder, whether as accomplice or principal. It is better designated as intentionally procuring the killing of V, or some such, which signals the undeniable fact that A's wrong is a wrong personal to her rather than derived from P's (non existent) liability. Similarly constructed offences could serve to fill the culpability gaps left uncovered by derivative liability and unsatisfactorily plugged by the doctrinal devices offered in cases such as *Bourne* and *Cogan and Leak*.

WITHDRAWAL FROM PARTICIPATION

As a general rule, where the actor repents of his wrongdoing subsequent to its commission this goes to mitigation rather than liability. A renunciation of a criminal purpose exculpates only if it occurs before sufficient steps are taken to constitute either the substantive crime, if

---

[52] See generally J Gardner, 'On the General Part of the Criminal Law' in R A Duff (ed), *Philosophy and the Criminal Law* (CUP, Cambridge, 1998), 211–3, 244–9; Cf P Glazebrook, 'Structuring the Criminal Code: Functional Approaches to Complicity, Incomplete Offences and General Defences' in A Simester and ATH Smith (eds), *Harm and Culpability* (Clarendon Press, Oxford, 1996), 195. And see *Assisting and Encouraging Crime, Consultation Paper*, Law Com. Report No 131 (1993).

applicable, or an attempt if it is not. While there is some doubt as to the existence of a defence of withdrawal in connection with criminal attempts, there is no doubt that such a defence exists in relation to accessorial liability.[53] This will, however, leave any inchoate offence already accruing untouched. For the reason why withdrawal is uncontroversially accepted as a defence for complicity but not for attempt it is necessary to isolate their distinctive features. As has been explained, the derivative nature of accessorial liability means that it is no part of the prosecution's case to prove any commitment to the criminal purpose. With attempts, by contrast, this is central to the prosecution's case. It is because (and only because) of A's commitment to the criminal outcome that his actions are deemed wrongful. The upshot is that with attempts it is far easier to subsume the defence in the wider requirement that the prosecution prove any steps taken were accompanied by a settled intention to bring about the *actus reus* of the consummated offence. As in attempts withdrawing from a criminal enterprise may signal an initial absence of *mens rea*, most notably in cases of joint enterprise where the principal goes beyond what is agreed and the secondary party's withdrawal is circumstantial evidence of the scope of that agreed purpose.[54] Such withdrawal may equally serve to negate the *actus reus*, as where a secondary party having first proffered his support for the criminal enterprise later withdraws it before the offence is consummated, or where having given practical assistance, say in the form of a weapon, this is later revoked by retaking the weapon.[55]

Beyond such cases, withdrawing from a complicitous relationship may also serve to exculpate the secondary party rather than preventing his initial inculpation. Typically this will occur where the latter has done enough with the necessary mental element to incur liability as an accessory but he then repents his action and his involvement and takes steps to renounce his complicity. As with attempts it is not immediately obvious why this should be the case, given that the elements of complicity are satisfied.[56] Withdrawal, it should be noted, cannot easily be presented as a defence in the same way as duress or self-defence can be presented. First, it cannot be decanted into one of the usual defence

[53] See ch 8.
[54] *Perman* [1996] 1 Cr App Rep 24.
[55] D Lanham, 'Accomplices and Withdrawal' (1981) 97 *LQR* 575.
[56] See generally KJM Smith, 'Withdrawal in Complicity' [2001] *Crim LR* 769; D Lanham, 'Accomplices and Withdrawal' (1981) 97 *LQR* 575.

templates. It is not a defence of 'reasonable reaction'. Neither is it a defence of impaired voluntariness.[57] Perhaps as a consequence withdrawal is not easy to conceive in terms of its aptitude to excuse or justify what the accessory has done. The usual effect of both excuses and justifications is to denature a definitional element prior to its constitution as an offence element. The cake is put in the oven but because of the presence or absence of a special ingredient it fails to rise. So duress negates the culpability the accused's intention would normally presuppose. Likewise self-defence negates the wrongdoing the accused's conduct would normally manifest.[58] In both cases the defence prevents a criminal offence from having come about. Withdrawal, by contrast, does no such thing. The cake rises—the ingredients are sound—but it collapses before consumption; some other explanation is necessary for the failure. And so it is with withdrawal in complicity. The party does not claim that it would be wrong to punish him because external events or his internal constitution rendered his conduct blameless or innocuous. So what is his claim to avoid liability?

There are two obvious possibilities. The first is a claim from policy, namely that it is desirable to afford a defence to those who have committed themselves to a criminal enterprise for the purposes of discouraging crime, and for creating an incentive to withdraw.[59] If there is no incentive to withdraw why would the secondary party ever wish to do so, let alone bring the matter to the attention of the authorities. The second is that the accused's change of heart expunges the culpability and/or dangerousness which his initial involvement presupposes. This argument is more compelling here than in the context of attempt liability where the constitution of the attempt, unlike that of the complicitous association, seems to require something by way of manifest wrongdoing or dangerousness to have occurred before any need to rely upon a renunciation would arise. As explained earlier complicity requires no proximity between the conduct of the secondary party and the consummated offence. It requires only an act or assistance or encouragement, perhaps entirely innocuous in itself, in an enterprise which at some later, possibly much later stage, bears fruit. The lack of any requirement of proximity or manifest dangerousness demands, it might be thought, some avenue to be open to the secondary party to

[57] See chs 10 and 11

[58] For general discussion see ch 9.

[59] KJM Smith, (1991) 255; Law Commission Consultation Paper 131 *Assisting and Encouraging Crime* (1993) 4.133.

turn back the clock to enable the latter to redeem himself, as his change of heart would suggest he deserves.

The failure to settle on an agreed theory of withdrawal leads to inevitable ambiguities as to the form withdrawal must take. On the one hand the derivative basis to liability might lead one to suppose that if the basis of inculpation is voluntary association with the principal through the giving of encouragement or help then factual withdrawal, possibly coupled with communication of an intention to withdraw,[60] should be sufficient to effect a dissociation. This does not satisfactorily address the issue as to what withdrawal consists of. Is it simply a matter of **retracting** what one has offered or is it, rather, the **negating** of whatever that offer has produced? Case law is ambiguous, although overall it seems more supportive of the latter analysis. It tells us that the form withdrawal has to take to be effective depends upon both the form of accessoryship and how far advanced the principal's actions are. The more directly and actively involved the participation, the more direct and active the steps necessary to withdraw. Significantly, however, what counts as direct and active steps must vary according to the nature of the participation. In some cases the most direct and active participation is consistent with withdrawal by the scantiest of actions. Thus if A procures P to kill C it seems to be enough simply for A to communicate the countermanding of his instruction.[61] On the other hand if A has merely given encouragement, prior to the offence taking place, A must again serve unequivocal notice that the commission of the offence is no longer assented to. However, this time it may perhaps be necessary to seek to dissuade the principal from committing the offence if the countermand is to bear a comparable potential to neutralise the initial encouragement. In both cases A withdraws exactly that which he has given thus neutralising any noxious consequence of his initial wrongdoing. The difference is that where advice or other assistance is given it cannot usually be neutralised by simple countermand.

It is here that we are most in need of a clear theoretical rationale. Retracting assent is a fish from a different kettle than neutralising assistance. In *Grundy* A gave details to burglars concerning the premises to be burgled and the habits of the occupants.[62] Two weeks before the offence was due to take place A told them that he did not want the

[60] *Becccara and Cooper* (1975) 62 Cr App R 212.
[61] Croft [1944] KB 295.
[62] [1977] *Crim LR* 543 CA.

offence to take place and sought to dissuade them from proceeding. The Court of Appeal held that this was sufficient evidence of withdrawal to be put to the jury.[63] Given that the information was influential and helpful to the burglars it may be surprising that more was not required in the way of withdrawal. It seems to provide accessories with an easy and undeserved escape route from accessorial liability. The message seems to be that you can give your assistance, get paid for it, and then on the day after make an earnest plea that the offence not be committed. The decision can be supported on the ground that it may have been asking too much by way of heroism to require A to have informed the police or the householder unless, perhaps, the crime embarked upon was a very serious one or his involvement substantial. On the other hand it may stand as the clearest possible evidence of the judiciary's understanding that the derivative theory of liability has no justified application outside accessoryship's paradigm cases of co-operative criminal enterprise. Applied to all cases of 'lending support' it is, as suggested above, a doctrinal sledgehammer to crack a pretty fragile nut, namely the inclination natural to large proportions of the citizenry to prioritise their own interests and turn a blind eye to the dubious activities of their paymaster.

In such cases it is understandable then that effective withdrawal requires something more than 'unequivocal notice' of an intention to abandon the common purpose'. Once the mortar is set it may indeed take a sledgehammer rather than a gentle tap to bring down the wall of co-operative criminal enterprise although what this involves will clearly vary. In *Becccara and Cooper*[64] A, B and C broke into a house in order to steal. A gave B a knife to use on anyone who interrupted them. However, when V did interrupt them A said 'come on, let's go' and then immediately left the house. Deciding that the withdrawal was ineffective, it was stated:

> Where practicable and reasonable there must be timely communication of the intention to abandon the common purpose from those who wish to dissociate from the crime to those who desire to continue in it. What is timely communication must be determined by the facts of each case but where practicable and reasonable it ought to be such comunication, verbal or otherwise, that will serve unequivocal notice upon the other party . . . that if he proceeds . . . he does so without the further aid and assistance of those who withdraw.[65]

[63] See also Whitefield (1983) 79 Cr App R 36.
[64] (1975) 62 Cr App R 212.
[65] Per Roskill LJ at 218.

Here, something 'vastly more effective was necessary'. Although adopting a language consonant with derivative liability one assumes the Court of Appeal were looking for some form of positive intervention to prevent the offence taking place. What else could A have said to make his withdrawal clear? Arguably the requirement of some form of positive intervention goes to show what common purpose cases already disclose, namely that the true basis of accessorial liability is not assent or authorisation but 'lending support'. Withdrawing 'support' as opposed to 'authorisation' does seem to imply a requirement of some form of counter-action. On the other hand this analysis is difficult to reconcile with the widely held belief that complicity requires neither causation nor commitment to the criminal outcome, but simply a willingness to align oneself with the principal's project. If this is the case there are clearly arguments for differentiating accessories according to whether they are co-adventurers, where there are strong grounds for requiring accessories to take all reasonable steps to prevent the commission of the offence, and mechanical assisters where the grounds are less strong.[66]

One question so far left undiscussed is whether, as in attempt, a cogent withdrawal defence implies good motivation. Is a purported withdrawal prompted by fear of apprehension, for example, effective? Once again this would seem to depend upon the theoretical basis to the defence. If we allow the defence for its incentive value good motivation seems to be beside the point. Conceived purely in terms of public policy, as long as the defendant takes effective steps to undo what he has done society profits, whatever his motivation in so doing. It may be then that the defence has a quasi-justificatory character, differing from self-defence and necessity only in so far as it is not dependent upon the defendant's (good) reasons for acting.[68] It is, however, hard to square such a poorly motivated decision with the assumption that withdrawals must have either exculpatory or justificatory significance. If the basis of the defence is to enrich the notion of culpability and dangerousness which participation in crime expresses, good motivation is arguably as important as it is in criminal attempts. Here, as will be seen, the defendant's withdrawal serves as an indication that the values his initial action was

---

[66] KJM Smith, 'Withdrawal in Complicity' [2001] *Crim LR*, 779–82; Law Commission Consultation Paper 131, *Assisting and Encouraging Crime* (1993) 4.135.

[68] For general discussion of the reasons approach to defences see ch 7.

challenging were also the explanatory reason for the renunciation. On this approach it is only where the accessory's explanatory reasons for withdrawing match the guiding reasons why he should not have become complicit in the first place that we can say that the flame of culpability and/or dangerousness has been truly doused.

Withdrawal due to fear of detection might then be effective if such fear was prompted by a prudential recognition that the wages of crime weighed heavier than its rewards rather than externally prompted anxiety that the 'cops were closing in'. In this latter case the would-be withdrawer has his own reasons for withdrawal (fear of detection). We blame him, change of heart notwithstanding, because he should be guided not by his own reasons but by the exclusionary reasons contained within the prohibition itself. Plausible in theory, such a motive-sensitive approach is probably too impractical to be workable in practice. Not only is the cut off point between genuine repentance and opportunistic changes of heart conceptually vague, proving that the withdrawal is prompted by the one rather than the other is also likely to prove troublesome. Even if such problems could be resolved it is unlikely, moreover, that it could be done so in a manner which advanced the more general reductionist goals subscribed to by a defence of withdrawal in complicity. All these factors combined probably argue in favour of a relatively generous approach to the problem of motivation by contrast with that operating in the field of criminal attempts.

COMPLICITY AND CAUSATION: A RATIONAL APPROACH TO CRIMINAL ATTRIBUTION?

The gradual adoption of a causal rather than participatory basis to liability in the case of non-perpetrators as evidenced in some of these cases instantiates what Norrie has termed in another context one of the antinomies of criminal theory.[69] A cogent morally-based notion of accessorial liability seems both to necessitate and yet be challenged by a causal account. Little wonder then that no obvious consensus has been reached as to the basis upon which liability is ordered, and that doctrine reflects this absence of consensus in ambiguous and inconsist-

---

[69] See also Goodrich.

ent doctrine.[70] The causal account appears necessary to justify punishing A for something P has done and to explain why liability is premised upon that crime actually having been committed. Indeed, the least controversial cases of derivative liability are cases where P is little more than a compliant pawn in A's hands. And yet it is also challenged by it. Resting accessorial liability on a causal basis raises questions as to why we need a separate structure of liability for secondary parties. Why do we not rather pull in all those, not simply perpetrators, who make a substantial contribution to the coming about of a criminal wrong?[71]

Those critical of the structure of criminal liability do not need to search deeply for a plausible response. The law of accessoryship can be analysed as a necessary adjunct to a notion of criminal responsibility centred in individual causing actors separated from their social and historical context. Returning again to the hypothetical with which we started the chapter on causation, although Adam's conduct proves the most direct and immediate connection with Eve's death, her death is in truth no more Adam's doing than it is that of the health administrator, civil servant or government minister. All three are equally the victims of context. The law of causation, on this view, fulfils the socially important function of rendering invisible the real reason for the occurrence of social harms. This is necessary if society is to be enabled to organise itself in a way which makes both moral sense to its citizens and which appear to be ordered in a context-independent even handed fashion. For this reason the assignment of criminal responsibility necessarily operates in a different way from the way responsibility is assigned elsewhere in political and social life. Historians are not wont to account for the Russian Revolution in terms of the political ambitions of Lenin and Trotsky but rather in terms of historical forces which these individuals were motivated to serve and foment. Even criminologists search far beyond the narrow frame of reference provided by the criminal law for the 'causes' of crime. Yet the criminal law seeks to locate individual 'causing' actors upon whom to place the whole burden of responsibility.

---

[70] Notice also the antinomial character of the two competing notions of accessoryship—derivative and inchoate. Does this not mirror the necessary ambiguities instantiated in doctrine at large that there is no single way of ensuring a method of constructing liability for secondary parties which does not also threaten to expose the social context within which individuals cause their harms?

[71] Cf Glazebrook 'Structuring the Criminal Code' in A Simester and ATH Smith (eds) (1996), 195, 196.

Clearly something has to 'give'. We want individual causal agency to be at the heart of criminal responsibility but individual causal agency cannot be allowed to exhaust the full range of responsibility relationships. We need it both ways. The law must practice dual standards if it is to convict Mr Big for the drug trafficking activities of his 'mules', Iago for the murder of Desdemona but not convict the health administrator, civil servant and health minister all of whom make their very influential contributions to the death of Eve. This can be achieved via the rules of complicity. The rules of causation coupled with the rules of attribution for complicity circumscribe very precisely the range of people who are properly subject to criminal liability. It restricts liability in the case of those who do not themselves perpetrate in a direct and immediate fashion a criminal harm to those who act **with the intention of assisting or encouraging** a blameworthy perpetrator in his. The rules of accessorial liability, as with liability for omissions, are designed to make questions of attribution more sensitive to historically and politically rooted moral judgments concerning who is fairly held accountable for crime.

The criminal law treats the accessory as if he had committed the wrong himself because whether or not he can be deemed causally responsible it is not unfair to hold him accountable. It is for this reason that the accessory is usually punishable within the full range of punishments available for that offence. This is not necessarily so. Under the German system, for example, punishment for secondary parties is formally discounted to reflect their participatory rather than executory status. There is no such formal discounting in common law systems. This reflects the common law's more pragmatic approach which permits much theoretical rubbish to be swept under the carpet. It allows punishment and condemnation of all those who are associated with the offence, which is a good thing. It does not necessitate rules capable of distinguishing fairly and consistently between different levels and forms of participation, which is a bad thing, on the presumed ground that the creation of such rules would pose a serious legislative headache. The absence of such rules, however, means that differentiating degrees and forms of involvement still goes on but becomes a matter of prosecutorial and judicial discretion tailored to questions of individual fault and participatory role. So it allows for the kind of sentencing flexibility which can punish the (non-perpetrating) instigators of crime as severely, or more severely, than their hired-hands, while also allowing the more typical accessory to be punished less severely than the perpetrator. The theoretical problem thus posed is that this undermines the notion that the accessory's liability derives from what the perpetrator, rather than what he himself has done.

The range of problems left uncatered for by this fudging of the theoretical basis to accessorial liability spreads across the whole field of doctrine. Given that some cases of participation are equivalent under one analysis or another to perpetration while others are not, how can this best be instantiated in consistent doctrine? If liability is derivative, how do we deal with those cases where a co-adventurer goes beyond the common purpose if not what was contemplated? How do we deal with those cases where the principal commits a lesser/greater offence than that to which encouragement and assistance are offered? On what basis is it proper to deem a non-perpetrator to be guilty of the primary offence if for one reason or another it is not possible to convict the perpetrator, and so on?

A number of possible solutions may be mooted. An obvious solution is to abandon altogether the derivative basis to accessorial liability, already much disregarded, and render participation in crime an inchoate offence. This is the position adopted by the Law Commission which recommends replacing accessorial liability with two separate inchoate offences, namely assisting and encouraging crime.[72] The advantage is that an inchoate basis to liability attacks the fiction that there is a necessary moral congruence between those who perpetrate crime and those who help or encourage its commission or that the principal was somehow acting as the secondary party's executive agent. It would, however, require complementary provisions for dealing with cases where, as in *Cogan and Leak* or *Bourne*, the secondary party procures the commission of the *actus reus* of the offence by an otherwise innocent or semi-innocent principal. The strong disadvantage of this proposal is that it ignores the intuition that it is often appropriate to ascribe authorship of a crime to someone other than the perpetrator.[73] Such people should not labelled, along with mere mechanical assisters and encouragers, as mere facilitators, but as principals. As Sir John Smith has argued in the context of murder,

---

[72] Law Commission No 131 *'Assisting and Encouraging Crime'*; see K J M Smith, 'The Law Commission Consultation Paper on Complicity: (1) A Blueprint for Rationalism' [1994] *Crim LR* 239.

[73] For example, Case 1.

those who are instrumental in bringing about a killing should not have their responsibility set apart from those who directly perpetrate it because . . . (we) feel strongly that D is responsible for those deaths. If we are going to punish him because he bears that responsibility, we are going to punish him for the homicide; and if we are going to punish him for the homicide, then he ought to be charged with, and convicted of, homicide.[74]

Another possible solution is to retain a form of derivative liability but to tie liability as an accessory not to the principal's mental attitude but to that of the secondary party. Somebody who acts for the purpose of effecting a criminal wrong arguably commits a different wrong from someone who acts for the purpose only of assisting or encouraging another to commit such wrong. This is so although in given instances culpability may be comparable. The wrong most obviously attributable to the uncaring supplier of a murder weapon, whether a private individual or a state licensed corporate arms dealer, is that of being a killer's 'armourer' rather than a party to a killing/murder.[75] So those who help or encourage because they want the substantive offence to take place could be treated as principal offenders.[76] Those who help or encourage because they merely wish to be helpful or encourage the principal offender in the commission of the offence could be treated as facilitators. The problem with this latter approach is that the distinction between these two states of mind will often be paper-thin and certainly sufficiently insubstantial to make for easy prosecutions.[77] Another response would be to hang accessorial liability upon the notion of control. Both instigator and 'principal in the second degree' are prime movers and so easy to associate with the principal's deed. So where A procures P to kill T, A is the prime mover since, although C pulled the trigger on the gun, it was W who pulled the trigger on H's life. Such an analysis is consistent with the rationale for the doctrine of innocent agency. In the former case we have a conscious, purposive agent. In the latter we have an innocent pawn. But both involve, as executor, an agent who does his principal's bidding[78] which should be enough to warrant equal treatment and punishment. The objection to

---

[74] JC Smith, 'Criminal Liability of Accessories: Law and Law Reform' (1997) 113 *LQR* 453 at 461.

[75] See generally J Gardner, 'On the General Part of the Criminal Law', 211–3, 244–9.

[76] Cf Giannetto, supra.

[77] Cf I Dennis, 'The Mental Element for Accessories' in PF Smith (ed), *Criminal Law Essays in Honour of JC Smith* (Butterworths, London, 1987).

[78] G Fletcher, *Rethinking Criminal Law*, 657–9.

both *mens rea* and control tests is that they do not cover the case of those who, without being in a position to influence the commission of an offence, nevertheless provide crucial assistance so as to put them on an equivalent causal footing with the perpetrator. If a secondary party, say by providing crucial information or supplying an otherwise unobtainable tool necessary for the commission of the crime, is a *sine qua non* of the crime's successful commission should he not, along with the perpetrator be held accountable for the commission of that offence?

An altogether more satisfactory way of dealing with the problem of different degrees of causal influence might be to create a structure of offences reflecting such difference. It seems extraordinary that the common law, unlike say the German system, makes no formal distinction between a person who successfully incites another person to kill her husband and an ordinary retailer who knowingly supplies the murder weapon. This can be done by drawing a distinction between causal and non-causal participation in crime with the former punishable upon an accessorial basis and the latter, involving lesser acts of assistance and encouragement, upon an inchoate basis. It makes obvious sense to require a causal connection in the case of **inciting** someone to commit a crime, given that the inchoate offence is still available for (non-causal) encouragement.[79] Cases of assistance might though be treated differently since charging an inchoate offence is not an option for (non-causal) acts of assistance and, as explained above, proving even a minimal **but for** causal connection would be next to impossible in most cases.

---

[79] G Williams, 'Complicity, Purpose and the Draft Code, [1990] *Crim LR* 4.

8

Criminal Attempts

CRIMINAL LIABILITY AND susceptibility to punishment requires, in the paradigm case, proof of wrongdoing. It will normally be of the essence of core crimes that those subject to criminal liability are found responsible for causing harm to the interests of other individuals. These harms may take various forms including most obviously physical injury, as in homicide or wounding, or damage to property interests, as in theft or fraud. This basic model of criminal liability explains why both the act requirement and the harm principle forms part of the basic theoretical landscape of criminal law. Individuals are subjected to liability for their acts or, more precisely, their deeds rather than their thoughts. And deeds which are innocuous in that they cause no harm to others are not considered meet for condemnation and punishment.

Against this theoretical backdrop there are a raft of offences whose purpose is primarily pre-emptive rather than retributive in nature. Such offences typically allow law enforcement authorities to intervene for the purpose of preventing harm rather than reacting to it by allowing arrest and conviction for acts directed towards, or preparatory, to the commission of a substantive offence. The essence of each is that liability attaches for activities which fall short of the commission of another offence. Many such offences are constituted as offences in their own right. Examples include most offences of possession including possessing articles for use in burglary, theft or 'cheat' and carrying an offensive weapon, burglary and other crimes of ulterior intent.[1] Attempts likewise criminalise activities falling short of the commission of direct harm but are not offences in their own right. Rather they form a step towards the commission of another offence, and being thus parasitic on that offence exhibit no liability elements intrinsic to the offence charged. For this reason problems of definition and scope may arise.

---

[1] Theft Act s 25(1) and (2); Prevention of Crime Act 1953 s 1. Possessing controlled drugs contrary to s 5 Misuse of Drugs Act 1971 is not an inchoate offence however since the possession is not criminalised for its preparatory quality.

Punishing attempts to cause harm raises a number of troubling questions, the resolution of which demands a secure theoretical basis for liability,[2] namely, what is the threshold at which lesser (non-criminal) forms of engagement in criminal wrongdoing become criminal attempts? Can attempts be abandoned once this threshold is reached? What state of mind does an attempt imply?[3] What is the appropriate basis for punishing attempts relative to the consummated offence? What is the conceptual link between attempts and consummated offences—are attempts truly inchoate versions of consummated offences or are the consummated offences rather aggravated versions of the more basic attempt?

CONCEIVING ATTEMPTS

Although the basis for incrimination is the attempter's criminal intention—his desire to kill, to steal, to injure and so on—liability for attempt does not run counter to the act requirement. One is held responsible not for one's having formed an intention to commit crime but rather for acting upon that intention. This is reflected in the universal requirement that there be some 'overt' deed, present since the earliest beginnings in medieval law of criminal liability for attempts.[4] This began, as Sayre has described, not as a generalised form of criminal liability but as an occasional response to certain attempts to commit crimes of a particularly serious nature, which were readily viewable as encompassing their own harm.[5] It appears, for example, that by contrast with the civil law criminal assault was originally conceived as an attempted battery and thus punishable irrespective of any alarm suffered by the victim.[6] In the seventeenth century any number of offences were created which criminalised actions dangerous for what they foreshadowed rather than what they achieved. Typical examples included lying in wait and going armed with a pistol. The notorious Waltham Black Acts rendered any number of apparently innocuous deeds capital

---

[2] See R A Duff, *Criminal Attempts* (OUP, Oxford, 1996) generally.

[3] See AR White, *Misleading Cases* (Clarendon Press, Oxford, 1991), p 15 *et seq.*

[4] Sayre, 'Criminal Attempts' 41 (1928) *Harv LR* 821.

[5] *Ibid.*

[6] Perkins and Boyce, *Criminal Law* (Foundation Press, New York, 1982), 615; J Dressler, *Understanding Criminal Law* (Matthew Bender, New York, 1988) 332–3.

offences on the basis that they were inchoate forms of deer poaching.[7] It is not surprising, given this opportunistic, coercive pedigree that some commentators have argued that liability for attempts is undesirable, lacking sufficient conceptual precision to sustain moral authority.[8] A better strategy may be to expand those substantive offences, such as burglary, which are both conceptually precise and morally communicative.[9]

The modern law of attempts is generally agreed to begin with *R v Scofield*, in which it was confirmed that liability depended upon both act and harm, including the harm to public interests encompassed by any attempt to commit a crime.[10] This recognition was of crucial importance to the development of generalised liability for attempts because of the requirement imposed that there should be a harmful deed upon which to graft the relevant criminal intention. The harmful essence of the activities constituting the *actus reus* of criminal attempts is now recognised as anchored not merely in the alarm which may be experienced by victims or witnesses but in the myriad ways that collective and individual interests can be 'set-back', in Feinberg's analysis, or individual 'dominion' impaired, in that of Braithwait and Pettit.[11]

This 'layering' of affected interests explains the ambiguous character of many offences. Is assault, for example, still properly to be understood as an inchoate form of the crime of battery or is it a crime in its own right? In principle if it is a step towards the commission of a battery and, by virtue of this fact, a set-back to individual or collective interests or dominion, then it is an inchoate offence. If on the other hand it is conceived as a direct violation of the interests of the individual victim, then it is a crime in its own right. This invites the conclusion that assault is primarily an offence in its own right constituting part of the family of crimes which seek to vindicate individual interests in autonomy. A person is guilty of attempted battery rather than assault, therefore, if he aims a punch at a person who is oblivious to the action

[7] Such as going around blacked up after dark—a common method adopted by poachers to avoid detection. See EP Thompson, *Whigs and Hunters: The Origins of the Black Acts* (Allen Lane, London, 1975) generally.

[8] See generally P Glazebrook, 'Should We Have a Law of Attempted Crime?' [1969] 85 *LQR* 28.

[9] J Horder, 'Crimes of Ulterior Intent' in A Simester and ATH Smith (eds), *Harm and Culpability* (Clarendon Press, Oxford, 1996), 153.

[10] Here the misdemeanour of arson. Cald 397 (1784).

[11] J Feinberg, *Harm to Others* (OUP, Oxford, 1984), ch 1. J Braithwait and P Pettit, *Not Just Deserts* (OUP, Oxford, 1990). And see ch 2.

taken.[12] As Fletcher explains 'we need a clear idea 'of the interests which an offence seeks to vindicate (before) we can know whether the offence is inchoate or consummated[13].'

Although it appears historically rooted in a more sinister state enterprise, namely the control of those deemed socially dangerous, the more politically neutral contemporary function of the law of criminal attempts, and its limiting principle, can be construed as the prevention of harm. But harm is conceived in a non-material sense of set-back to public or private interests or loss of dominion. When levels of preparation are such that a substantial threat is posed to the security of society it may, therefore, be reasonable and necessary for law enforcement agencies to engage in pre-emptive action. It is at this point that unresolved inconsistencies in theory and doctrine in the field of criminal attempts begin to surface. If material harm is not necessary, is punishment to be ordered on the ground of the actor's wrongdoing? If so, what is the measure?[14] Or is it to be ordered on the ground of the actor's dangerousness/blameworthiness?[15] If so, the danger is that this mode of incrimination is liable to fall foul of the legality principle—that people should be punished for having done something (legally) prohibited rather than for being an immoral/dangerous person.

It is understandable, therefore, that much of the theoretical interest in criminal attempts stems from the linkage which must be shown between a given substantive offence and the kinds of activities which will incriminate those who take (unsuccessful) steps towards bringing it about. This interest derives, in the main part, from certain unresolved questions informing criminal theory at large which, in the context of liability for attempts, take on a particularly acute character. Foremost among these is whether the basis for liability as an attempter is arrived at subjectively or objectively, whether a successful accommodation can be made between a notion of attempt based in harm prevention and one based in wrongdoing, and how far luck should be a factor pertinent to criminal liability.[16] So as to foreshadow the kinds of

---

[12] But see Perkins and Boyce, *Criminal Law*, 159 for a different analysis.

[13] G Fletcher, *Rethinking Criminal Law* (Little Brown and Company, Boston, Toronto, 1978), at 133.

[14] For discussion of the doctrinal arguments which can be attributed to this disjunction see KJM Smith, *Lawyers, Legislators and Theorists* (Clarendon Press, Oxford 1998), ch 11.

[15] For discussion see RA Duff, *Criminal Attempts*, 134–5.

[16] *Ibid*, ch 8.

difficulties which may arise, suppose that Adam has decided to kill Eve by lacing an after dinner mint chocolate with cyanide sufficient to kill intending to give it to Eve after completing a meal together. Clearly if he successfully executes his plan and Eve dies he will be liable for murder. If he does not, liability for an attempt may arise. But what must Adam do before punishment is in order? Consider the following possibilities:

Case 1

Eve falls ill during the meal before Adam has a chance to hand her the adulterated chocolate and Adam misses his opportunity.

Case 2

As before except that Eve completes her meal but Adam, by mistake, gives Eve an (unadulterated) orange cream.

Case 3

As before except that Eve refuses the adulterated after dinner mint and takes the unadulterated orange cream.

Case 4

As before except that Adam, by mistake, adulterates the chocolate with castor sugar rather than the intended cyanide, which chocolate Eve scoffs with relish.

Case 5

As before except that Adam, repenting of his action, retakes the poisoned chocolate and substitutes it with a harmless chocolate before Eve has a chance to eat it.

Finally consider three further unrelated hypotheticals:

Case 6

Adam takes a large quantity of sugar through customs believing it to be heroin and so subject to import restrictions.

Case 7

Adam, in execution of his desire to kill Eve, sticks pins into a voodoo doll which he believes will be effective in causing her death.

Case 8

Adam takes a large quantity of sugar through customs believing it, erroneously, to be dutiable in such large quantities.

As will be appreciated if dangerousness/culpability of **actor** is the basis upon which punishment is ordered an attempt should lie in all cases except perhaps Cases 7 and 8. These latter cases, involving utterly innocuous activities, bespeak perhaps a person whose notions of doing wrong are too far removed from the real world to indicate that he has any special disposition to do harm or otherwise perform antisocial acts.[17] Even here, however, it may be thought that a person's dangerousness/culpability stems not from what he does or does not do but rather from his attitude towards rules and the interests, individual and collective, that these rules sustain. In one case Adam shows, by his actions, that he lacks consideration for the legally protected interests of others. In the other he manifests an unwillingness to pitch his behaviour in accordance with rules. If in both cases this has resulted in the execution of innocuous acts the next time it may not do.

If on the other hand it is dangerousness/wrongfulness of **action** which grounds punishment there is only one case, namely Case 3, which is an unequivocally antisocial act. Here Adam 'did his best' to bring about the prohibited result. Cases 1, 4 and 6 no doubt disclose a dangerous/blameworthy character but Adam has done nothing to endanger Eve's life in the former cases and nothing which the law prohibits in Case 6. Case 1, of course, can be analysed differently from the

---

[17] Cf R A Duff, *Criminal Attempts*, at 380.

other cases since Adam did not get to the point of trying to kill Eve but in each case, given Adam's determination, it is more by luck than by judgment that Adam did not succeed in bringing about the substantive offence.

In order to address the range of situations in which liability for an attempt might properly arise it is helpful to distinguish three different kinds of attempt. The first, of which Case 1 is an example or where the attempter is apprehended before achieving his criminal purpose, is an incomplete attempt. The special feature of an incomplete attempt is that things still need to be done before the attempter can be said to have got to the point of trying to commit a criminal offence. The relevance of this is twofold. First, from the point of view of the criminal law's preventive function there is a case for allowing the intervention of law enforcement agencies, although there is still time for Adam to change his mind and do the right thing. Penal policy must in such cases be able to reconcile its retributive and preventive functions. Clearly it is better for harm to be prevented but there must nevertheless be a critical point before which official intervention is discounted to reflect the law's overriding commitment to freedom and autonomy, displayed in such features as the presumption of innocence and the act requirement. The overriding concern here, therefore, is to devise a secure benchmark for when the criminal attempt actually begins.

The second is a failed attempt, of which Cases 2 and 3 are examples. Failed attempts refer to those cases where the attempter has done every-thing he wants to do to bring about the substantive offence but the pro-scribed result is not forthcoming. An attempt may fail for a number of reasons. The intended victim may move. The gun may jam or miss its target. The owner of the wallet to be stolen may resist its appropriation. On the face of it there can be little objection to attempt liability in cases of failed criminal attempts. Not only has the attempter disclosed his antisocial intentions, he has acted upon them. If the substantive offence has not been committed it is not then because he lacks commitment to the enterprise, but by reason of a fortuity lying outside his control. However, attempts sometimes fail because the method adopted to bring about the substantive offence is entirely inapt for the purpose or because the steps taken do not form part of a sequence of steps capable of bring-ing it about. These factually or legally 'impossible' attempts constitute the third type of criminal attempt. In such a situation criminalisation may pose a problem because action which is incapable of setting back interests is not easily categorisable as wrongdoing or, from another point, harmful. If the actor is to be punished therefore it seems to be because of his mental attitude rather than the quality of his deed. The relevance of having performed the (doomed-to-fail) action is evidential rather than substantive. He is punished because he is wicked rather than because he has done a wicked thing.

CRIMINAL ATTEMPTS: THE MENTAL ELEMENT

In chapter 5 I discussed how the mental element of intention can play a number of different roles in the constitution of criminal offences. Intention fulfils a defining role for criminal attempts, as encapsulated in its use in the Criminal Attempts Act 1981. Section 1 provides as follows:

> If with intent to commit an offence to which this section applies a person does an act which is more than merely preparatory to the commission of the offence, he is guilty of attempting to commit the offence.

This section makes clear that the wrongdoing struck at by the section are people who act in furtherance of an intention, under some description or other, to bring about a criminal offence. So a person is guilty of attempted murder if he (unsuccessfully) fires a gun at a person because he wants to kill him but not if he does so in an attempt to prove to their sceptical friend that the victim is wearing a bullet-proof vest. This is so even though the shooter is aware that he may be mistaken. The proper means of dealing with the latter case is by fashioning offences such as intentional or reckless endangerment tailored specifically for that form of wrongdoing.

This begs the question posed in chapter 5 as to what mental state intention describes. In particular, does the constitution of a criminal attempt require proof of direct intention or will foresight of virtual certainty suffice? A related question posed but not resolved in chapter 5 concerned the possibility of variable meanings of intention. Are there grounds, for example, for differentiated meanings according to whether a person is charged with murder or attempted murder. The traditional systematisation of criminal law into the general and special part argues against this.[18] But there are clearly grounds for giving *mens*

---

[18] For critique see cf N Lacey, 'Contingency, Coherence and Conceptualism: Reflections on the Encounter between "Critique" and the Philosophy of the Criminal Law' in RA Duff (ed), *Philosophy and the Criminal Law* (CUP, Cambridge, 1998); cf J Gardner, *ibid.*

rea words such as intention context specific meanings depending upon
the functional role played by intention in the constitution of the
offence. Crimes of ulterior intent, of which criminal attempts are an
example, are obvious candidates for a narrow notion of intent.[19] This
is because the definition of such crimes is explicitly constructed with a
view to the defendant having something 'in mind' at the time of performing the external elements of the offence. As was there suggested,
this was the view evidently taken by Goddard LCJ in *Steane*.

Taking an ordinary language view to the notion of an attempt it is
clear that what an actor knows or believes is in no way constitutive of
the deed we describe as attempting or trying. This ordinary language
approach identifies an attempt or a trying as something which is done
'by doing something else'.[20] So we attempt to score a goal by kicking
the ball towards the goal. We attempt to kill by aiming the gun and
pulling the trigger. This means that to know what it is which F or A is
attempting we have to understand his reasons for acting, what he has
in mind, what his objective is 'by doing what he does'. If F pulls S's
loose tooth out because it is irritating and painful to S, F does not try
to hurt S although he knows this to be inevitable, and this is because
hurting S is no part of reasons for doing what he does. If A's route home
is intersected by a stream he does not attempt to get his feet wet when
he wades across for the self-same reason.

Such an ordinary language approach seems unobjectionable when
applied to much of the criminal law. If A is charged with attempting to
violate the speed limit it would seem to require him to take steps
towards so doing with this objective in mind. If A was found to be driving a vehicle with a speedometer which he knew under-recorded his
travelling speed but not the extent, it goes without saying he has done
wrong. However, that wrong is not the wrong of attempting a speeding violation. He has done no such thing, although he knows it is a certainty this will happen. It is the wrong of careless driving, or driving an
unfit motor car or something of that description. On the other hand
restricting the fault element in criminal attempts in this way rather than
say following that of the substantive offence leaves uncatered for the
myriad ways in which actors can unjustifiably attack the interests of
others without this being their objective.[21]

---

[19] RA Duff, *Criminal Attempts* at p 75.
[20] AR White, *Misleading Cases*, 15.
[21] RA Duff, *Criminal Attempts*, 30 *et seq*.

Case 9

Adam, a wicked doctor, whose wife Eve is dying of liver failure, kidnaps Jane and surgically removes her liver for transplant into his wife.

If Jane survives the operation, through, say, the miraculous intervention of another surgeon with a spare liver, it is hardly open to Adam to deny that he did not attempt to kill Jane. If this consequence admittedly did not form part of the reasons for which he acted he nevertheless knew that this is what his action meant for Jane and he did everything in his power to bring that consequence about. The common law gives voice to this contextualised meaning of intention in criminal attempts. In the leading case on the mental element in criminal attempts intention is defined as 'a decision to bring about, in so far as it lies within the accused's power . . . (the relevant consequence) whether the accused desired the consequence or not.' This definition, which is clearer than any other produced over the last few years including *Woollin*,[22] means that the question to be asked is whether the accused 'meant to bring about the consequence he did' rather than 'did he try to bring it about?' or 'did he know it would happen?'

In cases such as this, where the consequence has some intrinsic moral significance, the notion of an attempt appears to take on a richer significance than that more usually accorded to it in everyday speech. The problem we are left with, however, is that this significance is not easily systematised. It is not simply the inevitability of death which makes Case 9 an easy one to decide the way it is. It is that there is no better way of characterising the significance of what Adam has done. Everyday usage is unlikely to reach a comparable conclusion where, for example, the actor's motivation was unequivocally good, as where he throws his wife off the top of a burning skyscraper in an attempt to save her life.[23] Or where, although bad, the relevant consequence is easy to dissociate from the actor's purpose. Consider, for example, attempting to cause criminal damage. It is not difficult to imagine cases where everyday usage will affirm the existence of an attempt, although damaging property is the last thing on the actor's mind. Say Adam throws an egg at Eve for the purpose of humiliating her. Since the prospect of the egg breaking structures his action and so also part of his reasons for

[22] For discussion, see ch 6.

[23] See W Wilson, *Criminal Law: Doctrine and Theory* (Longmans, London, 1998), 534–5.

acting, the unavoidable conclusion is that he intends the egg to break and attempts to break it. But can one effect such an attempt without any commitment to that outcome? Suppose Adam had thrown a plate at the back of Eve's head intending to hit her. He knows that whether or not he succeeds in hitting her the plate will be damaged, barring a miracle. Does this fact alone mean that he is attempting to damage the plate? Our everyday use of the word suggests not. He is not trying/exercising himself to break the plate, only to hurt or scare Eve. But suppose Adam threw what he knew was Eve's priceless Ming vase chosen, like the plate, merely for its weight and proximity. Here the moral significance of what Adam has done is coloured by the enormity of the potential consequences and it seems plausible that, whatever might be the position in everyday usage, criminal doctrine should register his act primarily as a serious offence against property rather than a minor offence against the person. Although he is only trying to hurt Eve he also 'succeeds' in attempting to damage Eve's property because this is what his action means both for Eve and her property and he knows it. Of course there are other ways of accommodating such wrongdoing, namely through extensions to existing crimes of endangerment, but the fact that Adam did not throw the vase in order to break it seems a feeble reason not to punish him for the uncompromising steps he took in the direction of doing just that.

INCOMPLETE ATTEMPTS

If criminal liability follows a failure to see a criminal project through to its conclusion two areas of potential difficulty assert themselves. The first is how far along the criminal path an attempter must proceed before his conduct is meet for criminalisation. The second is whether it may be possible, once this critical point has been reached, for a putative attempter effectively to withdraw so as to preclude the liability which would otherwise arise. Two contrasting approaches have been adopted in determining when the attempt begins—a subjectivist and an objectivist approach.[24] The former holds the attempt to be constituted when the actor performs an act which substantiates a blameworthy or dangerous disposition. Since he has such an attitude or disposition it is appropriate to isolate and confine him on harm-preventing grounds or

[24] See generally R A Duff, *Criminal Attempts*; G Fletcher, *Rethinking Criminal Law*, ch 3.

punish him on retributive grounds, depending upon one's theoretical inclinations. Under this approach the attempt can begin no earlier than when the defendant's *mens rea* becomes visible in the performance of some act indicating the defendant's commitment to the criminal project. It thus supports intervention at an early stage. By contrast with objectivism the act is not demanded for substantive reasons, say because it bespeaks an inchoate harm manifested in the outside world. Rather it is required for evidential reasons—to substantiate the fact of the attempter's blameworthy/dangerous inclinations, which subjectivists hold to be the cornerstone of attempt liability.

Subjectivist responses to liability for attempts are, however, faced with a problem. If it is a person's criminal intention rather than his deed which dictates the law's coercive response then there is no secure basis for ensuring that the law of criminal attempts remains consistent with the underlying ethic of minimal criminalisation and certainty vouchsafed by the harm principle. The point about harm is that it gives society a signal as to when a coercive response is warranted. In the case of consummated offences that signal could not be clearer. A victim lies bleeding or dead. A wallet has been appropriated, a house burnt down. In the case of attempted crime, by contrast, no such harm is necessary. Sure, there may well be a victim terrorised by his close shave but equally the victim may, as in Case 1, be entirely oblivious and the crime hardly advanced beyond the drawing board. As long as the focus for incrimination is the accused's intention rather than his deed there is a danger that law enforcement agencies will too easily be able to manipulate evidence to substantiate the former and to intervene oppressively against those whose deeds are too equivocal to incriminate. Any commitment to civil liberties and minimal criminalisation entertained by a subjectivist will, therefore, require him to temper his subjectivist inclinations by reference to some secure freedom-sustaining benchmark for intervention.[25] In other words the subjectivist seems to be forced onto the territory of the objectivist. As will be explained, this requires both that the attempter acts for the sake of bringing about the substantive offence and that his actions, independently from his mental state, manifests the conduct of someone 'attempting' or 'trying' to bring it about. Indicative of the kind of reconciliation which can be made is the American Model Penal Code which describes the conduct element in attempted crime as the taking of 'substantial steps' towards commis-

[25] G Fletcher, *Rethinking Criminal Law*, 47.

sion of the substantive offence. Requiring 'substantial steps' is clearly more than that necessary simply to evidence a commitment to bring about the substantive offence.[26] Further, the establishment of such 'substantial steps' requires conduct which 'strongly corroborates' the actor's criminal purpose to effect the substantive crime and the Code specifies a number of activities capable, 'if strongly corroborative of the actor's criminal purpose' of constituting an attempt, so as to avoid indeterminacy.[27]

In principle, the difference between subjectivist and objectivists in their attitude towards the conduct element in criminal attempts is that subjectivists require the relevant acts to manifest an intention to commit the substantive offence whereas objectivists require the relevant acts to manifest the actual attempt. The subjectivist is concerned with what has already been done—has the victim/object been located, the weapon primed and so on. The objectivist is concerned with what the defendant still has to do.[28] Has he done enough to enable us to say that he is 'attempting' to commit the offence, enough to warrant condemnation for his deed alone? There are a number of different formulations for marking this requirement that the accused's acts must be sufficiently proximate to the commission of the substantive offence for us to recognise it, objectively, as an attempt to commit that offence. In truth none of these formulations are able to serve up any precise rule capable of determining in a once and for all fashion whether a given act or series of acts go to perpetration or merely preparation. It would be surprising if such a rule could be produced although clearly a just penal policy surely requires it.[29] If from a philosophical perspective a person attempts to do something 'by doing something else' as when one attempts to open a door by turning the handle and pushing,[30] such a narrow notion of attempt seems incapable of satisfying the point of

---

[26] Art 5.01(1)(c).

[27] Art 5.01(2). These include: (a) lying in wait, searching for or following the contemplated victim of the crime; (b) enticing or seeking to entice the contemplated victim of the crime to go to the place contemplated for its commission; (c) reconnoitering the place contemplated for the commission of the crime; (d) unlawful entry of a structure, vehicle or enclosure in which it is contemplated that the crime will be committed; (e) possession of materials to be employed in the commisssion of the crime, which are specifically designed for unlawful use or which can serve no lawful purpose of the actor under the circumstances; (g) soliciting an innocent agent to engage in conduct constituting an element of the crime'section 5.01(2).

[28] G Williams, 'Wrong Turnings on the Law of Attempt' [1991] *Crim LR* 416.

[29] RA Duff, *Criminal Attempts*, 62.

[30] AR White, *Misleading Cases*, 15.

attempt liability from either objectivist or subjectivist perspectives.[31] Indeed, the courts have rejected a last-act test, that is, one which holds that an attempt lies when the defendant performs the last act necessarily performed by him to constitute the offence. This is clearly inappropriate as a general limiting test if the law of criminal attempts is to advance the cause of social defence. Many acts in furtherance of a substantive offence manifest both dangerousness and criminality before the defendant's last act is completed. In *R v Jones*, for example,[32] the Court of Appeal rejected, surely rightly, the defendant's argument that buying and preparing a gun, donning a disguise, lying in wait for the intended victim, jumping into the latter's car and taking out the gun were, given that the safety catch had still to be removed, mere acts of preparation rather than perpetration and affirmed a conviction for attempted murder.[33]

Once one abandons a conceptual approach to criminal attempts, however, one is forced to rely upon common sense approaches which, like any other perceptual characterisations, are likely to be indebted to the frame of reference of the beholder. No doubt this accounts for the general failure of judges and commentators to agree a general formula capable of reconciling effective social defence with the need to protect individuals against precipitate and oppressive intervention, and which can act as a secure guide both for citizens and law enforcement agencies as to the cut-off point between (lawful) acts of preparation and (unlawful) acts of perpetration. Standard (objectivist) versions of the proximity test embrace, for example, not only the defendant's last act but also those earlier acts which are 'immediately and not merely remotely connected with the completed offence'.[34] Whether or not the requisite proximity is established is a question of fact and degree, which inevitably deprives the test of desirable certainty. Domestic law instantiates this indeterminacy in a typically loose formulation which records the attempt as constituted by some act occurring at some indistinct point between the final consummation of the offence and acts of mere preparation: 'If with intent to commit an offence to which this section applied, a person does an act which is more than merely

---

[31]   There are other and stronger arguments in favour of adopting such a conceptual approach, however. See below.

[32]   *Jones* [1990] 3 All ER 886.

[33]   G Williams, 'Wrong Turnings on the law of Attempt' [1991] *Crim LR* 416.

[34]   *R v Eagelton* (1855) Dears CC 515 at 538.

preparatory to the commission of the offence, he is guilty of attempting to commit the offence.'[35]

Different fact situations have spawned different versions of the proximity test. An early attempt to put some flesh on the bones of the test was essayed by Salmond. Because it is easy and harmless to plan a criminal endeavour, but less easy (and more harmful) to execute it, the state's moral authority to condemn and punish demands at the very least an act of 'manifest criminality', that is, an act which 'shows criminal intent on the face of it'.[36] This gives the appearance of a simple and effective test for distinguishing acts of perpetration from acts of preparation. The former, by their very nature, must surely speak to the consequence in furtherance of which they are performed. In fact, however, this does not follow at all because in the absence of material harm even proximate acts may be too equivocal to be describable as harmful or wrongful on their face. Suppose, for example, A in furtherance of an intention to kill B lies in wait outside his house with a length of rope with which he intends to execute the killing by strangling when B next leaves the house. A subjectivist approach, which concerns itself with what the accused has already done rather than what remains still to do, will view this as an attempt upon proof of the relevant criminal intention. An objectivist approach by contrast requires proof of an act of 'manifest' wrongdoing. Does lying in wait with a length of rope supply this? If we ignore what we know to be A's intention his actions are entirely innocuous. There are any number of (lawful) reasons why A should hang around in a public street with a length of rope. Suppose then B had left the house and A was walking quickly towards him rope in hand. A's action is no less equivocal than before. If we eschew evidence of A's purpose he could be intending to give B the piece of rope, or tie him up with it, or perhaps ignore him entirely and walk on down the street. It seems then that constructing a notion of manifest wrongdoing without reference to the actor's intention disables us from identifying any but the most obvious forms of inchoate wrongdoing.

Although there are clear dangers for civil liberties in constructing a notion of attempt around the accused's criminal purpose there are good reasons, therefore, for allowing evidence of this purpose to provide the kind of contextual information necessary to decide whether the acts of the accused are harmful or innocuous. This is, after all, why

[35] Criminal Attempts Act 1981. S.1 (1).

[36] J Salmond, *Jurisprudence* (Stevens, London, 1947), 404. See generally G Fletcher, *Rethinking Criminal Law*, 139–57.

criminal attempts are considered offensive. Certain acts are alarming and cause public disquiet although they do not involve material harm. To know what these acts are we must first assign them a meaning which we are unable to do, absent information about their motivation and context. The problem for the unequivocal act approach however is that once it allows this information in, there is no obvious reason why it should not, in like fashion to the Model Penal Code, fasten upon acts at some stage removed from the commission of the substantive offence.[37] Like all but the most extreme subjectivist approaches then it is constitutionally unstable.

More theoretically engaged with what makes action taken in furtherance of a criminal objective meet for preventive or retributive reaction is the 'Rubicon test'. This holds that a person is not adjudged to be beginning his attempt until he has 'burnt his boats' and he cannot turn back.[38] The Rubicon test appears to effect a neat reconciliation between principle and policy, the policy being social defence and the principle being no criminal liability in the absence of culpable wrongdoing. It reflects an appropriate ethical attachment towards punishing only those who show a clear disposition to flout authority and commit a criminal harm. Until one has 'burnt one's boats' everyone can be counted, for both moral and practical purposes, as law-abiding or, from another point of view, as a law-breaker. For moral purposes it is antisocial endeavour rather than antisocial inclinations which separate the worthy from the unworthy members of society and which renders us susceptible to moral criticism. It also potentially marks the point at which the actor's intentions are sufficiently clear to highlight, say, the need for a potential victim to use force in self-defence.[39] The test then offers to create a conceptual bridge between what the law says is the point at which prospective victims of crime may consider action to be sufficiently hostile to their interests to permit a defensive response, and the point when previously putative criminals become real ones.[40] For practical purposes 'burning one's boats' is necessary to show that a law-breaking disposition exists as opposed to that of the harmless fantasist who will always draw back within touching distance of the precipice. Nevertheless, the Rubicon test has attracted criticism. First,

---

[37] For discussion see G Fletcher, *ibid*, 139–46.

[38] *DPP v Stonehouse* [1977] 2 All ER 909.

[39] This is RA Duff's reason for supporting the test, *Criminal Attempts*, 390.

[40] An incomplete bridge, however, given the flexibility of the imminence requirement in self-defence. See ch 8.

it has not been clearly established which of two versions is the ruling test. Is the Rubicon to be analysed in a psychologistic way so that the relevant acts, considered from the actor's own internal point of view, are of a nature to override any inclination to withdraw he might otherwise have had? Or is it to be considered from the external point of view so that the Rubicon constitutes the point at which the putative attempter 'comes out', displaying his anti-social inclinations and thus depriving himself of the option of crawling back into the woodwork? If the former, it collapses into the substantial steps test. If the latter it collapses into the unequivocal act test discussed above. On both versions, critically, there is no obvious way of determining when the critical point is reached when a person has passed the Rubicon—the point at which it is reasonable to assume from either the actor's internal or objective point of view that there is no turning back. Moreover, both versions make it difficult for law enforcement agencies to intervene when the defendant is 'on the job';[41] but has not yet embarked upon the final steps which will bring him to effect the consummated offence.[42]

Such an indeterminate notion of the conduct element in attempt seems to contradict what is after all the major point behind the objectivist approach, namely that there should be some observable, empirically-based benchmark for intervention enabling the putative attempter to know when to draw back from the brink and law enforcement agencies when to intervene. Domestic law has refused to adopt such an ambiguous approach preferring to steer its own equally indeterminate 'midway course' between the last act or Rubicon requirement and preparatory acts.[43] The view taken is that no one test is likely to accommodate the various factual nuances which can enable us to state with precision and conviction when what the accused is doing is 'trying' to commit the offence rather than simply preparing for it.[44] The substantive offence of murder may be formulated and executed in the blinking of an eye. The attempt may then be so proximate to the commission of the offence that no legal formulation could serve as a preventive as opposed to a reactive measure. Some criminal frauds, however, take so long to set up and execute that one can envisage justified intervention well before the point when any individual interest was threatened and well before any

---

[41] That is, the second version of the Rubicon test.

[42] See for example, *Gullefer* [1990] 3 All ER 882.

[43] KJM Smith, 'Proximity in Attempt: Lord Lane's Midway Course' [1991] *Crim LR* 576.

[44] See H Gross, *A Theory of Punishment* (OUP, Oxford, 1979), 127–8.

objective 'danger signals' are apparent. It follows that only sometimes will close geographical and temporal proximity be of the essence. For other crimes, rape is an obvious example, case law supports the intuition that an attempt requires an act not only requiring such proximity but also unequivocally directed towards that criminal purpose. This state of affairs indicates, more perhaps than any other feature within the criminal justice system, how the attempt to reconcile social defence with a principled respect for individual autonomy demands a degree of compromise with traditional rule of law values. Determinacy is not possible and given the multifarious behaviours which may be adopted in furtherance of different criminal objects, it may not even be desirable.

That there is no objective means of concluding whether an attempt has begun outside last act cases may not mean, however, that such decisions as are made, necessarily compromise the rights of individuals to fair treatment. Indeterminacy may sometimes be morally justified to combat determined efforts to pursue activities known to be at the margins of criminality.[45] As it is commonly argued in connection with other examples of penal indeterminacy, those who for no better reason than self-advancement skate at the margins of legality have no compelling ground for complaint if they are not given precise warning as to when they are about to fall in.[46] Likewise, for the purpose of criminal attempts, why should those who take substantial steps in furtherance of a criminal objective have any cause for complaint if they are adjudged to have passed the point of no return?

On this view society's highest aspiration is to have in place an adjudicative framework in which respect for individual freedom and autonomy creates the lens through which individuals are measured for state coercion rather than being simply a matter against which collective goals are weighed. This aspiration, if it is to be prosecuted effectively, must influence not only the doctrinal rules themselves but also criminal procedure. In this regard it can be seen clearly in operation in domestic law where trial judges are invested with a wide power to withdraw cases from the jury where the latter may be otherwise too quick to convict on the basis of the defendant's dangerous inclination.[47] It is a

---

[45] See generally AJ Ashworth, *Principles of Criminal Law* (OUP, Oxford, 1999), ch 3.

[46] 'Overly precise statutes invite the criminally inclined to frustrate the intent of legislation by skirting the inflexibly precise language. As a result fairness only requires that a statute put law-abiding non-lawyers on reasonable notice that their intended conduct runs a reasonable risk of violating the statute.' J Dressler, *Understanding Criminal Law* (Matthew Bender, New York, 1987), 28.

[47] I Dennis, 'The Elements of Attempt' [1980] *Crim LR* 758.

power, moreover, rigorously policed by the appellate courts. Yet more strenuous attempts to ensure collective needs do not trump individual rights to fair treatment are made in the United States where explicit factual models have been created to guide both individual and law enforcement authorities as to where the line is drawn between acts of preparation and acts of perpetration.[48] Here, as elsewhere, the liberal's response to the critical accusation that criminal justice cannot accommodate the inevitable tensions between public interests and individual rights is that criminal justice is an achievement of civilised societies rather than an unwinnable cultural abstraction.[49] It is hard to find fault with the view, however, that some other method, more conducive to providing clear guidance as to the boundaries of permissible action, is a structural and moral imperative.[50]

VOLUNTARY ABANDONMENT

As a general principle repenting a crime, once consummated, does not affect liability. This can generally be accounted for by reference to the constituent elements of typical offences. Most crimes cannot be rubbed out by repentance, even where the defendant is able and willing to make good his wrong. That the actor repents and seeks to undo what he has done is obviously in his favour since it discloses a character of greater virtue and less in need of deterrence, incapacitation and rehabilitation than others who perform similar deeds. It may be appropriate therefore to reflect these facts in the punishment he is given. But since the actor has done wrong and he has caused harm he is nevertheless appropriately brought to account.

Not all substantive offences can be accounted for in this way of course. Crimes of endangerment, for example, require merely that the dangerous action takes place, not that it is sustained, since it is the presence of the danger which constitutes the set-back of interest upon which liability is premised rather than its materialisation. Less easy to account for is the non-relevance of voluntary abandonment in crimes such as theft where the conduct element is not necessarily premised

[48] The Model Penal Code provides a basic template for judging whether given acts of the defendant are sufficient to corroborate the accused's determination to commit a criminal offence See above n 27.

[49] See for example RA Duff, *Criminal Attempts*, 390.

[50] See below for further discussion.

upon an act of manifest wrongdoing. Taking up goods in a supermarket with theftuous intent may be punishable although the shopper changes his mind almost immediately and replaces the goods and so no meaningful harm has come of it. This raises the question of the relevance of voluntary abandonment to attempt liability where there is also no material harm requirement and there are obvious grounds for incorporating some doctrinal incentive to encourage would-be attempters not to convert the harm of endangerment into the harm of consummation. If punishing the consummated offence acts as an added incentive not to do the wrong thing, then not punishing abandoned attempts may counteract the ('in for a penny, in for a pound') disincentive which punishing both attempts and consummated offences may bring about. This time, however, by adding to the attempter's own moral or prudential reasons to desist from the behaviour in question.[51]

Of course, in the ordinary run of events the very constitution of a criminal attempt must have in mind the possibility that the putative attempter may desist from the consummated offence. It is for this reason that the Rubicon test is initially so persuasive and why the 'more than merely preparatory' formula is, as exemplified in *Jones*, typically interpreted restrictively . If criminal intervention is premised upon dangerousness and moral blameworthiness then until the would-be attempter shows his true colours as action man rather than mere fantasist there is no ground for linking him to the substantive offence. There is all the difference in the world between a person who performs a series of acts because he is going to effect a given harm and one who performs such acts simply because he would like to. If society, notwithstanding the absence of such a credible link, nevertheless feels his conduct constitutes a threat to its security this is a reason to punish him for that which he has already done rather than for what we do not know he is still to do.[52] Accordingly, in traditional domestic commentaries, withdrawing from an attempt is treated as of no greater relevance than in its propensity to substantiate the actor's absence of commitment and therefore the inappropriateness of pre-emptive intervention.[53] Sufficient flexibility is built into the 'more than merely preparatory'

[51] See generally A von Hirsch, *Censure and Sanctions* (OUP, Oxford, 1993), ch 2.

[52] Such a credible link is established where the accused has performed his last act or where, notwithstanding the absence of such an act, he is sufficiently close to doing so that a hypothetical observer, knowing what he does of him, would apprehend his criminal purpose.

[53] Smith and Hogan, (1999), 327; Glanville Williams *Textbook of Criminal Law* (Stevens, London, 1983), 410.

formula to allow evidence of voluntary withdrawal to colour the courts view of whether or not the attempt had actually begun. An actor's change of mind, say in desisting from killing or robbing a bank, is used to indicate the necessary commitment to go through with the offence was never formed, reflected by the ease with which the project was ultimately abandoned. As Fletcher puts it: 'Whether the actor has an intent of (the required) degree of firmness can be determined only by waiting to see whether in fact he carries out the plan.'[54]

It takes on far greater momentum, however, in those jurisdictions such as the United States which favour a subjectivist approach to criminal attempts and thus substantially extend the time frame within which criminal intentions may be concretised or abandoned.[55] It is not surprising, therefore, that compared with the ten lines in Smith and Hogan and two lines in Glanville Williams, the American commentators Perkins and Boyce devote four, and LaFave and Scott, five, pages to the subject.[56] A cognate defence of voluntary withdrawal is an important antidote to a test for attempts drawn so widely.[57]

Are there grounds, or indeed is there a need, for such a defence in domestic doctrine to deal with those cases where, for example, acts of perpetration have commenced and/or the Rubicon has been crossed and yet the defendant desists from further consummation? Once again, this depends very much upon the way we view punishing attempts; whether, in particular, attempt liability is forward-looking and preventive, or backward-looking and retributive. If it is the latter, the view taken in domestic doctrine, then irrespective of whether social harm becomes visible, it should be enough that the attempt should have begun since, change of heart notwithstanding, condemnation and punishment justly attends the actor's antisocial conduct.[58] If it is the former, there are grounds for allowing such a defence at least up and until the point is reached where social harm becomes visible. At that stage the dangerousness of both act and actor crystallises and with it the reductive features in punishment are brought into play.[59]

---

[54] G Fletcher, *Rethinking Criminal Law*, at 188; cf RA Duff, *Criminal Attempts*, 65–75.

[55] See generally D Stuart, 'The *Actus Reus* in Attempts' [1970] *Crim LR* 505, at 519 and see note.

[56] I note with concern that I devote only a short footnote to the matter in *Criminal Law: Doctrine and Theory*.

[57] And so it is recognised by the MPC s 5.01 (4).

[58] R Perkins, 'Criminal Attempt and Related Problems' (1955) 2 *UCLA L Rev* 319, at 354.

[59] This is the view adopted by the German Supreme Court. See G Fletcher, *Rethinking Criminal Law*, 193.

On some accounts a defence of voluntary abandonment may, however, serve to undo a harm already done.[60] If the act is dangerous and/or blameworthy the defendant's renunciation of it shows that he is not and neither, since the flame of fault is doused, is he deserving of punishment. As Duff puts it:

> Conduct takes its character as a criminal attempt from its relationship to the complete offence which she intends to commit: it counts as an attempt because it is directed towards that offence. Once she abandons that attempt, though, it ceases to be one . . . (she embarked on the attempt): but in the end she did not try (but fail) to commit it.[61]

The cogency of this approach hangs largely upon the production of a stable and workable notion of voluntariness. Is this possible? As already remarked action is presumed to be voluntary for the purposes of inculpation. We must take responsibility for our choices even though the context makes such choices hard to resist. With regard to abandoning a criminal course of conduct, however, it is easy to see how the opposite presumption should be the rule. If a person is so committed to a criminal project that he goes almost to the brink of bringing it about, why would he then desist? The natural presumption must be that he would desist only because of external intervention or failure of nerve. It is not clear that either should serve as a basis for a discrete defence. Abandonment caused by external events challenges the notion that the defendant freely chose to abandon his criminal objective. It will be appreciated that this notion of voluntariness is quite at odds with that operating for the purposes of exculpation where external determinants are treated as capable of informing but not **causing** a human, and therefore free, choice. Voluntary renunciation, at least if this is to deflect an inference of bad character, must arguably manifest the accused's commitment to the very values to which the steps already taken will normally suggest he was unresponsive. Consistent with this analysis the American Model Penal Code designates a renunciation of a criminal purpose involuntary if it comes about through a change of circumstances such as increased probability of detection or apprehension, or which make more difficult the accomplishment of the criminal purpose. The operational parameters of the defence can be sketched by comparing two cases. In *Le Barron v State*[62] a conviction for attempted

---

[60] M Wasik, 'Abandoning Criminal Intent' [1980] *Crim LR* 785, at 788.
[61] *Criminal Attempts*, 395.
[62] 32, Wis.2d 294, 145 N.W.2d 79 (1966).

rape was confirmed although the would-be rapist had desisted upon being convinced by his victim that she was pregnant and fearful for the survival of the pregnancy. Similar decisions have been reached where the would-be rapist desisted because the woman screamed, or because of the intervention by stranger. In *People v Graham* the court allowed that a defence to attempted arson may obtain where, having poured petrol onto a bed, the defendant failed to follow through his criminal purpose, telling his son that God had 'stayed my hand'.[63] These cases can be reconciled. In *Le Barron* the defendant's change of heart affords no indication that the values his action was challenging (respect for sexual autonomy) were the guiding reason for the renunciation. The indication is that he now has his own reasons for desisting (compassion). We blame him, change of heart notwithstanding, because he should be guided not by his own reasons but by the exclusionary reasons contained within the prohibition itself.[64] In *Graham*, however, it is evident that his reasons for desisting were attributable to his ultimate enlightenment (better late than never) that it was wrong to commit arson. Both cases then are attuned with the point of attempts liability which is to allow individual actors maximum freedom of action consonant with showing respect for the interests of others. Where before the point is reached that material harm is caused a person **is able** to repent his harm-causing action because it is wrong and not because of some external cause, there are cogent grounds for allowing a defence of withdrawal. Either society's interests in security and safety have been compromised or they have not. If there is still room for a change of heart and a drawing back from the brink there must be room for a defence which gives voice to this key fact of 'no harm done' and which, incidentally, can act as an incentive to abandon the criminal purpose.[65]

Such an analysis is not the only possible notion of voluntariness fit to substantiate the defence, however. Fletcher notes, for example, that German case law allows the defence wherever renunciation is free and informed, that is where the actor is still 'master of his own decision'. This allows fine, perhaps too fine, distinctions to be drawn between

---

[63] 176 App. Div. 38, 162 N.Y.S. 334 (1916).

[64] For discussion see J Raz, *The Authority of Law* (OUP, Oxford, 1979), 16–26; J Gardner, 'Justifications and Reasons' in A Simester and ATH Smith (eds), *Harm and Culpability*, ch 5.

[65] Cf D Stuart, above n 55, for a sceptical response to the notion that the defence operates as an incentive.

desisting due to failures of nerve, crises of conscience or victim persuasion where the defence would be allowed, and desisting because of non-conscience led factors such as the intervention of strangers which would not.[66] This objection is most apt in connection with those crimes such as rape and robbery where attempt liability, as reflected in the on the job/unequivocal act tests most commonly characterising such attempts,[67] is closely related to the reason why the substantive crime itself is thought harmful. There is, for example, a very close moral connection between the wrong of attempted rape and that of the consummated offence, which is that in its paradigm form the former is unlikely to take place without a loss of autonomy and associated feelings of alarm and anxiety. If then a defence of voluntary abandonment is to be recognised it seems to operate in defiance both of the harm principle and the retributive principle that wrongdoers should pay for the wrong done to others. Perhaps this is another example of how the generalist credentials of a defence are incompatible with the just disposal of decisions across a broad range of different fact situations. Rather than having a hole in the structure of attempt liability, itself lacking conceptual precision, which can only be plugged by a defence ambiguous both in its moral pertinence and its application, should we not rather redraw the whole map of inchoate offences so as to map more clearly the different moral connections which can be made between substantive offences and acts performed in furtherance of such offences. Only in respect of completed attempts are there uncontroversial grounds for making a direct moral connection between what the accused has done and the consummated offence. That ground is that if condemnation is warranted for commission of the substantive offence then it is also equally warranted for trying to commit that offence. The wrong which demands addressing is that the actor has tried to do what he is forbidden to do. But where the defendant has not done all the acts necessary on his part to bring about that offence, the moral connection between the two is not so clear since until that point is reached he has tried nothing.[68] It is surely because of this that so little headway has been made in reaching some form of unanimity as to whether the appropriate test

[66] At 192–4.

[67] See discussion at n 43.

[68] 'When successful the attempt to do so and so becomes the doing of so and so; the turning of the handle and pushing is opening the door . . . So the orders "Try to do this" and "Do this" are obeyed in the same way.' AR White, *Misleading Cases*, at 15.

should be a subjective or objective one, whether it is harm prevention or moral condemnation which best captures this form of liability.

A plausible way forward to deal with those wrongs currently desig-nated incomplete attempts is through the more systematic deployment of possession offences, crimes of endangerment and crimes of ulterior intent. These are able to pinpoint in a more precise fashion the nature of the moral connection which can be made between an activity possi-bly innocuous in its own right and a given substantive offence. In Case 1, 2 and 5 it is arguable, for example, that the kind of moral connection which can be made between the consummated offence and what the accused has done is misrepresented by the use of the word attempt given the enormous gap existing between what has occurred and what would have to occur for the action to be successful. We would be on stronger analytical ground if, rather, we characterised Adam's wrong-doing and his dangerousness, in terms say which emphasised his involvement in the preparation of a noxious substance with intent to kill. Attempts liability, because of the necessary compromises which social defence must make with rule of law values, allows many wicked and dangerous people to escape liability. At the same time, as this last example illustrates, it seems to afford too broad a basis for condemna-tion and punishment by contrast with the moral precision capable of being offered by offences of ulterior intent.[69]

PUNISHING ATTEMPTS: THE SIGNIFICANCE OF RESULTING HARM

Should an attempt be punished as the consummated offence?[70] The answer to this question depends on the basis upon which one seeks to justify punishment in the first place. From the utilitarian point of view it can be argued that the appropriate level of punishment would, on general utilitarian grounds, be the same as that for the completed offence since attempters show themselves as much in need of incapa-citation and rehabilitation as achievers. Moreover, the deterrent func-tion of the criminal law is arguably as well advanced by punishing attempters as achievers. Public interests are advanced if the public are

[69] P Glazebrook, 'Should We Have a Law of Attempted Crime?' [1969] 85 *LQR* 28; J Horder, 'Crimes of Ulterior Intent' in A Simester and ATH Smith (eds), *Harm and Culpability*, 153. And see discussion in ch 6, above.
[70] See generally M Davies, 'Why Attempts Deserve Less Punishment Than Complete Crimes' (1986) 5 *Law and Philosophy* 1.

aware that people will be punished whether or not they succeed with their plan. On the other hand there are good utilitarian reasons for reducing punishment for a failed attempt although there may be grounds for treating complete and incomplete attempts differently. The latter arguably should be treated as less serious than the former since the defendant did not get to the point of 'trying' to commit the offence. This may mean that the defendant is both less culpable and less dangerous than a complete attempter, justifying less serious consequences.[71] Second, with respect to complete attempts, utilitarianism has a bias towards minimalism in punishment. Punishment should be no more than is necessary to fulfil society's purposes. If it appears draconian, as it will to the majority of retributivists, the institution of punishment will lose support as well as creating unnecessary suffering to the attempter.

If we favour retributivism the level of punishment again varies according to whether one takes a harm-centred or a culpability approach. If the latter, it may be argued that the criminal justice system should reflect the manner in which God's justice is meted out, namely upon the basis of what we try to achieve rather than what we do achieve.[72] Indeed some have argued that the division between attempts and consummated offences should be collapsed entirely[73] and replaced by the more morally informative division between complete (Cases 3 and 4) and incomplete attempts (Case 2). If we take murder as an example, this would justify not only **punishing** attempters and achievers similarly, but even punishing them for **the same offence** since their wrong is the same, namely that of 'trying to kill'. It is down to good or bad luck rather than anything intrinsic to the defendant's conduct whether the actual death occurs. The defendant can only 'try'. It is certainly true that punishing people according to what they achieve may unduly favour the accused where, for example, a subsisting[74] or supervening[75] cause operates to negate a wrongdoer's causal responsibility. It might

---

[71] AJ Ashworth, 'Belief, Intent and Criminal Liability' in J Eekelaar and J Bell (eds), *Oxford Essays in Jurisprudence*, Third series (OUP, Oxford, 1989); Ashworth, 'Taking the Consequences' in S Shute, J Gardner and J Horder (eds), *Action and Value in Criminal Law* (Clarendon Press, Oxford, 1993).

[72] For a different view see M Davies, above n 70, 28–9.

[73] AJ Ashworth, 'Sharpening the Subjective Element in Criminal Liability' in RA Duff and N Simmonds (ed), *Philosophy and the Criminal Law* (Wiesbaden, 1984), 79.

[74] For example, the intended victim was already dead at the time the 'fatal' blow was delivered .

[75] For example Case 3, above.

also unfairly stigmatise the accused. It is common place for drivers to drive dangerously putting lives at risk, yet the accident of death places the individual alone at risk of a manslaughter conviction when he/she is no more culpable that the thousands of ordinary people who escape 'causing death'. If we recognise that luck has selected these individuals to be the instruments of others' deaths, it might be better to punish them for what we apprehend is their real wrong namely that they have (culpably) endangered someone's life. The criminal law already has in place a number of crimes of endangerment.[76] Should we go further and rid the criminal law of other crimes, such as manslaughter, which emphasise consequence and causation at the expense of conduct and replace them with crimes of endangerment? One advantage served by such an approach is that it solves at a stroke the major problem which, as we have seen, bedevils causation doctrine, namely the production of coherent principles capable of distinguishing fairly between those to whom causal responsibility is assigned and those to whom it is not.

An assessment of the cogency of this position requires deeper consideration of the philosophy of punishment. It is premised upon the idea that what an actor deserves by way of punishment is a matter of his culpability alone and one can be blamed only for what one has tried to do.[77] If this is the case it is hard to counter it. An attempting murderer is as wicked as a murderer. Of course he will often be more so.[78] Desert, however, is not surely a simple matter of culpability. The centrality of resulting harm for assessing desert in punishment is but one manifestation of a much broader social phenomenon, namely that judgments of praise and blame and attendant rewards and penalties are responsive not only to what we do, the way we do it and the attitudes which accompany our actions but also the consequences which ensue. We are praised and blamed for our achievements rather than our exertions. As human beings we are made who we are by our successes and our failures, by our good deeds and our bad. In sport playing well or in a sporting fashion attracts praise, or condemnation in the opposite case. But ultimately reward follows success. One has to score more

---

[76] AJ Ashworth, *Principles of Criminal Law*, 298–306; cf Fletcher, *Rethinking Criminal Law*, 472–83.

[77] P Winch, *Ethics and Action* (London 1972), 160 and discussion in AJ Ashworth, (1984), 82–4; for critique see RA Duff, 'Acting, Trying and Criminal Liability' in Shute et al (eds), *Action and Value in Criminal Law*, 75, 77–90.

[78] AJ Ashworth, 'Criminal Attempts and the Role of Resulting Harm under the Code and under the Common Law' (1988) 19 *Rutgers LJ* 725.

runs, take more wickets, sink more putts, hit more greens, swim or run more quickly to win the prize. Even here, desert is of pivotal importance in determining the propriety of allocating reward or penalty. The referee or umpire will have many occasions to adjudicate upon whether some event is attributable to something a player did. In football, did the striker trip or was he tripped? In cricket, was it the ball which dislodged the bails or was it the wicket-keeper's gloves? If she makes an error of judgment, dissatisfaction, even anguish, is experienced by all affected, including (partisan) spectators. This anguish will take the form not merely of disappointment but of justice denied.[79]

Correspondingly, resulting harm is a key element in setting accountability. It is basic to the wrongdoing which desert in punishment addresses.[80] Those who kill, maim, or set fire to buildings change the world for the worse and the criminal justice system is in place to render those who wreak such change accountable. The wrong of killing, maiming or arson, in short, is not trying but rather achieving these consequences. This is the wrong that the victim, the victim's family and the wider society demands to be identified, set right and for which the defendant must pay his dues and the (morally responsive) defendant will wish to atone. It is appropriate, therefore, to declare these facts of moral life in corresponding criminal prohibitions and attendant levels of punishment according to the success or failure of the actor's criminal purpose.

IMPOSSIBLE ATTEMPTS

The above discussion has explored the central tension which exists both in criminal doctrine and theory between a conception of liability built around the dangerousness of the individual actor and one based in the dangerousness/manifest criminality of the act. This tension manifests itself most obviously where the actor still has some way to go before actually trying to do what the *actus reus* of the consummated offence requires to be done for criminal liability to follow. The actions taken may be innocuous in themselves or they may be equivocal, show-

---

[79] J Dressler, *Understanding Criminal Law*, 338.
[80] See generally M Moore, *Placing Blame* (1997), 218–46; cf S Morse, 'Moral Metaphysics' [2000] *Cal LR* 886–9.

ing the actor to be up to no good but disclosing no clear link to the relevant substantive offence.[81]

In the case of completed attempts the tensions are of a different order. Completed attempts manifest their purpose and are as closely connected to the *actus reus* of the consummated offence as it is possible to get bar success. Even here, however, problems of legality may be posed which require resort to an underlying theory of liability. These occur in respect of what are known as impossible attempts, examples of which include Cases 2, 4, 6, 7 and 8. In each case Adam has tried to commit the offence in the sense of doing everything he had deliberated upon to bring about the *actus reus* of the consummated crime and yet his action was doomed to be harmless. In Cases 2, 4 and 6 and arguably 7 we have a dangerous/ blameworthy actor but no dangerous action. In Cases 7 and 8 on a generous view of Adam's conduct we seem to have neither. The issue to be settled, therefore, is whether liability is engaged according to what Adam has done—the objectivist approach or according to what he believed himself to be doing—the subjectivist approach. On the latter approach Adam is guilty in all cases, save perhaps, Case 8. Following the former approach Adam is not guilty of an attempt in any of these situations. He has done nothing which the law forbids and has caused no harm, material or otherwise. No one's interests have been harmed by what Adam has done. Not all cases of impossible attempts can be analysed in this way. Some actions look to be wrongful/harmful although they are objectively incapable of bringing about the consummated offence. Suppose, for example, Adam, in furtherance of his plan to kill Eve, enters her bedroom and fires a gun at what he supposes is her sleeping form but is in fact a bolster. Again suppose Adam dips his hand into Eve's (empty) pocket with the intention of stealing therefrom. Most objectivist accounts inevitably overlay their analysis with certain necessary premises, in particular the practical need to inform the hypothetical viewer of what the actor has in mind to provide a secure footing for evaluating his conduct. If Adam, for example, had shot a dummy in a shop window this would manifest criminality only upon proof that Adam thought it was his deadly enemy. Without this information there would no cause for the observer

---

[81] Cf *Davey v Lee*. What the defendants had done (cutting through a perimeter fence) no more supported a conclusion that they intended to steal from the hut within than that they intended to set fire to the hut or rape the inhabitant of the hut, if any [1967] 2 All ER 423.

to suffer the alarm and anxiety which the theory of manifest criminality requirement presupposes is essential to criminal liability.[82]

This does not entirely eradicate the distinction between objective and subjective approaches, however, since certain actions are calculated to be innocuous however badly motivated they may be. A pure objectivist approach could, therefore, arrive at a decision as to whether an action portrayed manifest criminality independently from the beliefs which gave rise to it. An easy example is Case 7. However ill-intentioned the accused's action is, the conclusion cannot be escaped that this is a neither dangerous nor wrongful act. If the hypothetical observer were to be told Adam's motivation and asked for his reaction he would no doubt say 'Let him get on with it. It's better than trying the real thing.' Characterising this hypothetical is the fact that the actions taken were, in Fletcher's words 'inapt for the purpose' and in Duff's lacking any connection 'with the real world'.[83] To be guilty of any crime it is generally thought there must be some empirically-based causal connection between the deed done and the result intended. Here there is none. Black magic is not a way of killing people.[84] Neither, it would seem, is there such a connection in Cases 2 and 4. Giving people delicious chocolates is not a way of killing them. A distinction may be drawn between this case and other cases of (factually) impossible attempts, where the accused's cardinal error was ineptness rather than inaptness. So, attempting to kill someone with an unloaded gun or an amount of poison too small to cause harm do not fall foul of Fletcher's aptness test of impossibility. As will no doubt be appreciated, while drawing such distinctions may make a lot of common sense there is no substantial theoretical basis for distinguishing between inapt and inept attempts. Either we punish on the basis of the accused's beliefs, in which case we punish the person who believed that death could be caused through black magic, the person who believed his chocolate was laced with cyanide and the person who believed his gun to be loaded. Or we disregard the constitutive effect of beliefs and punish only those, like the person who shoots and misses, whose actions instantiate the very risk against which the law of criminal attempts is pitted. Favouring the former approach, which is the stance now taken in

---

[82]   T Weigend, 'Why Lady Eldon Should be Acquitted: The Social Harm in Attempting the Impossible' (1978) 27 *DePaul L Rev* 231; cf Strahorn, 'The Effect of Impossibility on Criminal Attempts' (1930) 78 *UPA L Rev* 962.

[83]   At 380.

[84]   RCL (1978) 165–6.

domestic doctrine, corresponds moreover to what we apprehend to be the conceptually correct sense of attempting to do something. As White puts it: 'The fact that I cannot kill a man who is already dead, pick a pocket which is empty, take what is not there or scale a mountain which is unscalable is no reason why one cannot attempt to do these.'[85] However, it is apt to emphasise the accused's wicked intentions as opposed to his dangerous deeds. Favouring the latter approach is apt to emphasise the dangerousness of deeds as opposed to intentions.[86] This may have the unfortunate consequence of removing the criminal sanction from someone who is clearly culpable and dangerous.[87]

The stance taken in domestic law and the United States is uniformly a subjectivist stance homing in upon the dangerousness of the actor rather than his action. It renders him guilty of a criminal attempt if, on the facts as he believed them to be, the steps he has taken would have involved him in the commission of an offence. So on the facts of Cases 2, 4, 6 and 7, Adam would be guilty of a criminal attempt since if the facts were as he believed them to be the offence would have been constituted. This leads to the discomforting possibility of liability even for the kind of inapt attempt which signify both an objectively non-dangerous act and actor as in Case 7. These kinds of problems are left to be dealt with by prosecutorial discretion. This stance poses one further problem, however. To address it we will examine Case 8. Here what the accused is trying (and succeeding in doing) is not a criminal offence. The steps taken by the accused are not steps taken, proximate or otherwise, in the constitution of the *actus reus* of an offence. It is clear then that if there is no offence of evading duties on the import of sugar there can be no (criminal) attempt to do so either.[88] As Lord Hailsham in another context put it 'steps on the way to the doing of something which is thereafter done, and which is no crime, cannot be regarded as attempts to commit a crime.'[89] This would be a clear case of liability detached from legality, and indeed both objectivists and subjectivists hold that attempts to commit illusory crimes are incapable of forming the subject matter of a criminal attempt.[90] Lord Hailsham

---

[85] AR White, *Misleading Cases*, at 28.

[86] Fletcher, *Rethinking Criminal Law*, 170–4, White, *ibid*, 29.

[87] See Perkins and Boyce, *Criminal Law*, 622–4, for an extended discussion.

[88] For a real life version of this see *Taafe* [1984] 1 AC 539 where the thing imported was currency which the accused mistakenly believed was prohibited.

[89] *Haughton v Smith* [1975] AC 746.

[90] Fletcher, *Rethinking Criminal Law*, ch 3 generally; RA Duff, *Criminal Attempts*, 380.

in fact formulated this statement in a quite different context, namely where the thing the actor thought he was doing did form part of the *actus reus* of a genuine criminal offence, although because the accused's belief was mistaken, the offence attempted was incapable of being committed. As a result, the House of Lords concluded that defendants who took possession of a consignment of corned beef, believing them to be stolen when in fact they were not, could not be guilty of an attempt to handle stolen goods. What the defendant did was lawful by any other measure than his state of mind. Criminalising his behaviour, therefore, would impose criminal liability for intention alone.[91]

There is clearly some degree of (perverse) deductive logic in this position which can be uncovered if we substitute for an attempt to commit a crime an attempt to reach a destination, say Edinburgh. Suppose A gets on what he supposes is the plane to Edinburgh but it is in fact the wrong plane and he is taken to Berlin. Can we say that A has attempted to go to Edinburgh when at no stage did he commit acts capable of leading him to such destination? The weakness in the analysis is that it asserts a meaning for criminal attempts whose conceptual basis is at best controversial. The point of the law of criminal attempts is to incriminate those who try unsuccessfully to commit crimes. If we then ask the question, 'Did Adam in Cases 2, 4 and 6 try to commit a crime?' the answer is clearly yes. It is only if we ask a different question, namely 'Did Adam try to do something which was a criminal offence?' that the answer is no. Which of these questions we prefer to ask depends of course on whether we wish to punish Adam for his dangerous and culpable inclinations manifested in action or whether we wish to punish him for his dangerous and culpable action reflecting a corresponding attitude of mind.

This does not fully the problems associated with *Haughton v Smith*, however, since the question, 'was the actor trying to commit an offence (of handling)?' elicits an equivocal reply. In Fletcher's view it depends upon whether it was a necessary part of success in the actor's project, in other words, that the offence would have been committed. Duff's similar response asks whether the interests protected by the offence of handling are subject to attack (the normative core of attempts) or merely endangered, for which an appropriate criminal wrong must be

---

[91] The reasoning is disclosed in the following statement of Lord Reid. 'The crime is impossible in the circumstances, so no acts could be proximate to it . . . he took no step towards the commission of a crime because there was no crime to commit.' Lord Reid in *Haughton v Smith* 499–500.

fashioned.[92] This in turn requires some assessment of what it would take for the defendant's plan to be successful.[93] Reflecting this reasoning, the House of Lords found in *Anderton v Ryan*, in the face of the express wording of the Criminal Attempts Act, that a person who handled goods believing them, erroneously, to be stolen, was not guilty of attempting to handle stolen goods (video recorder).[94] The difference between this case and say Case 7 is that success in Adam's project requires the sugar to be heroin. It was a matter of complete irrelevance to Ryan who would have kept the video recorder whatever its status. So he was not attempting to handle stolen goods because it was not intrinsic to his plan that the goods should be stolen.[95] Given that nothing manifestly criminal or even harmful has occurred there are clearly strong grounds for concluding that the use of the criminal sanction would be both oppressive and unnecessary, even say for a crime of endangerment, where the defendant is not motivated to defy the law.[96]

---

[92] RA Duff, *Criminal Attempts*, 364.

[93] In *Haughton v Smith*, success in their plan requires the goods to be stolen.

[94] They quickly overruled this decision in *Shivpuri*, to the evident relief of a great many commentators.

[95] See for an extended treatment of this approach Fletcher, *Rethinking Criminal Law*, 152–66; cf RA Duff, *Criminal Attempts*, 378 et seq.

[96] The majority of their Lordships in *Shivpuri* felt that *Anderton v Ryan* was distinguishable on this ground. For a contrary opinion see JC Smith [1986] *Crim LR* 539.

9

Packaging Criminal Liability

Wrongdoing and Harm

Criminal liability and susceptibility to punishment requires, in the paradigm case, proof of wrongdoing. It will normally be of the essence of core crimes that those subject to criminal liability are found responsible for causing harm to the interests of other individuals. In this way the actor shows his contempt for the victim which state punishment seeks to address by subjecting the wrongdoer to the state's will just as he has done to his victim. By shaming the wrongdoer the victim's worth is reaffirmed.

There is no single template governing the constitution of criminal wrongdoing. An offence may define the conduct element by reference to the seriousness of the harm as in causing grievous bodily harm, or by reference to the way the harm is delivered as in wounding or poisoning, or by reference to the nature or consequences of the harm inflicted as in blinding and castration. Specifying the manner and/or consequences of causing harm typifies common law crimes which are juridical representations of wider moral prohibitions. The structure of criminal doctrine was fashioned from these wrongs, which reflect deep moral distinctions operating at the social level. As explained in chapter 5, there are important moral distinctions to be drawn between stealing and borrowing, between stealing and fraud, between murder and manslaughter, between rape and inflicting grievous bodily harm, between assault, battery and false imprisonment, between assault and attempted rape and so on.

George Fletcher has usefully explained the distinctive form of doctrinal development for crimes which articulate forms of wrongdoing as paradigmatic in nature. The fact of being rooted in the common law presupposes a degree of judicial creativity to keep the nature of the criminal wrong largely congruent with the underlying social prohibition. Just as the ways of hurting people, for example, are not closed so also crimes of violence rooted in the moral precept that hurting people is wrong, are open and responsive to these new ways.[1] Recent notable examples of paradigmatic doctrinal development in this field include *Ireland* in which the traditional notion of an assault as proscribing physical confrontation was replaced by one proscribing actions provoking apprehension of future harm.[2] Again in *Burstow*, inflicting grievous bodily harm was reconceptualised so as to require neither physical injury—psychological injury will do—nor, in consequence, any form of blow by which such grievous bodily harm was delivered.[3]

Outside paradigmatic wrongs, criminal wrongdoing is necessarily constituted through the legislative text which alone controls its field of application. An example, which bears useful comparison with the above offences, is section 30 Offences Against the Person Act 1861 which provides that 'whosoever shall unlawfully and maliciously place or throw in, into, upon, against or near any building, ship or vessel any gunpowder or other explosive substance, with intent to do any bodily injury to any person . . . shall be guilty of an offence.' Section 30 is constituted in terms which requires action and, moreover, action which takes a specific form, namely 'placing' or 'throwing' in connection with 'explosives'. So liability is not incurred by, say placing burning material against a building or placing a bomb in a public square. Again, an omission to remove an explosive is implicitly excluded by the words 'place' and 'throw' and so would not support liability for say failing to remove a stick of dynamite from a building. In each case the wrongdoer may deserve to be punished but he does not deserve to be punished for **this offence** since the wrong is expressly constituted through the offence definition.

Increasingly, the basic form of criminal law takes as its basic point of departure the social desirability of preventing harm, howsoever it may be occasioned, rather than identifying and articulating forms of moral wrongdoing meet for criminalisation. This emphasis can be seen in the proliferation of regulatory conduct crimes such as driving offences, and health and safety regulations which penalise conduct conducive to the creation of social harm and which bear, at best, only a contingent relationship with an underlying moral precept. By contrast with core crimes, where punishment is largely retributive, punishing regulatory crime is quintessentially, if not exclusively, utilitarian in nature. It is also to be

---

[1] Fletcher, *Rethinking Criminal Law* (Little Brown and Company, Boston, Toronto, 1978), ch 2.
[2] [1998] AC 147.
[3] *Ibid.*

seen in the tendency to designate the conduct element in result crimes as the causing of the relevant result cut loose from any specific deed of wrongdoing. This is particularly apparent in initiatives to codify the criminal law. For example, the Law Commission's proposals for crimes of violence[4] envisage a ladder of seriousness leading from intentionally or recklessly causing injury to another, leading to recklessly causing serious injury to another, to intentionally causing serious injury to another and so on upwards to homicide also graded by fault element.[5] The idea behind this manner of confronting violent wrongdoing is to create textual clarity (to satisfy fair warning) and to differentiate on grounds of seriousness of harm and culpability alone (to foster fair labelling).

There are important things at stake in choosing between a harm-orientated rather than a wrong-articulating approach to criminal prohibitions. Foremost among these, as section 30 illustrates, is the need to reconcile the defensive purpose underlying a prohibition with the restricted focus that such rule-generated prohibitions engender. Of no less significance is the fact that criminal prohibitions serve to declare norms rather than simply the penal consequences of performing certain forms of harmful action. A criminal code is possibly better able to communicate the boundaries of socially acceptable behaviour if it packages crimes in morally significant ways. And certainly moral criticism is best communicated by means of a criminal label which embodies a socially meaningful moral wrong. As Gardner has argued, the Law Commission's approach to crimes of violence ignores this communicative function. While there may be little textual clarity in offences such as malicious wounding/infliction of grievous bodily harm and grading precision (what counts worse malicious infliction of grievous bodily harm or wounding with intent to cause grievous bodily harm?) this is more than made up for by moral clarity. Stabbing someone, for example, is a morally significant way of hurting someone. It addresses itself to moral concerns of the population. Causing someone injury/ serious injury does not do so in anything like as effective a fashion.[6]

---

[4] Law Com No 218, *Legislating the Criminal Code: Offences Against the Person and General Principles* ; Home Office, *Violence: Reforming the Offences Against the Person Act 1861* (1998). Law Commission in Report No 237, *Legislating the Criminal Code: Involuntary Manslaughter* (1996).

[5] See M Wasik, 'Form and Function in the Law of Involuntary Manslaughter' [1994] *Crim LR* 883.

[6] For a full consideration see J Horder 'Rethinking Non-Fatal Offences Against the Person' [1994] 14 *OJLS* 335; *cf* J Gardner in 'Rationality and the Rule of Law in Offences Against the Person' [1994] *Camb LJ* 502.

Structural tensions are exposed when criminal norms may alternatively be conceived in terms of articulating wrongs or in terms of harm prevention. An example has been met already in the field of omissions regarding crimes whose conduct elements imply some form of action without specifying precisely what form such action must take. This is the problem of liability for omissions in respect of crimes of commission. Can one commit murder, by omitting to prevent death, arson, by omitting to put out a fire, wounding, by omitting to deactivate a booby trap? The common law met this problem by the kind of paradigmatic legal development described by George Fletcher. Historically omissions were permitted to form the subject matter of certain crimes of affirmative wrongdoing, notably homicide,[7] but only, as in the case of the neglect of an infant by its parent or of a patient by a doctor, surgeon or midwife, where the context rendered the omission directly analogous to affirmative action.[8]

Originally doctrinal development proceeded largely by means of extensions to the range of duty situations. More recently, judges have shown themselves increasingly willing to suppress the action elements in forms of criminal wrongdoing in favour of a more expansive approach which looks to the harm to be prevented rather than its mode of delivery. In the specific field of omissions, criminal liability has been incurred not merely where the relevant provision envisages action but action of a particular kind. Moreover, it has been deployed not only both in respect of common law wrongs but also wrongs whose originating source is legislation. So, in *Speck* the failure of the accused to remove a child's hand from his penis was interpreted as an **act** of gross indecency.[9] In *Miller* the failure of the accused to put out his own carelessly started fire was interpreted as arson[10]. In *Shama* a person who failed to fill out a form necessary to display his tax liability was interpreted as 'falsifying' a document.[11] In each case the defendant had 'done wrong' it goes without saying but was there an **act** of gross indecency; was there **arson**; was a document **falsified**?

This kind of development tends to be presented in criminal law textbooks as a doctrinal error or at least pressing against the boundaries of

---

[7] Homicide is a common law crime. Its boundaries are not controlled in the same way as statutory crimes and can develop incrementally by analogy with other cases.

[8] Stephen, article 233 of the Digest.

[9] (1977) 2 All ER 859.

[10] *Miller* [1983] 1 All ER 978.

[11] [1990] 2 All ER 602.

legitimate interpretation.[12] In fact, such cases reflect current interpretative orthodoxy over the broad expanse of criminal doctrine. Another look at *Ireland* confirms this impression. Here the issue facing the House of Lords was whether an infliction of injury (here psychiatric injury) could occur in the absence of any harm-delivering blow. Lord Steyn, holding that it could, said that the 'problem is one of construction. The question is whether as a matter of current usage the contextual interpretation of 'inflict' can embrace the idea of one person inflicting psychiatric injury on another. One can without straining the language in any way answer that question in the affirmative. I am not saying that the words cause and inflict are synonymous. They are not. What I am saying is that in the context of the Act of 1861 one can nowadays quite naturally speak of inflicting psychiatric injury.'[13]).

Inflicting harm or wounding, in this context, is now interpreted to mean simply that a given harm has been caused when there was a duty not to cause it. If liability for 'infliction' is simply 'a matter of current usage' it would seem that there can be no objection to liability for an infliction by omission either, although hitherto section 20 has been understood not to be capable of commission by omission. The questions, which the criminal law has to work out, are micro rather than macro questions. What statuses or contexts generate the duty of intervention? What must one do to discharge these duties, and so on? In both cases the wider communicative function of decanting wrongdoing into morally informative packages of information seems to have been ignored.

PACKAGING CRIME

Mens Rea and Actus Reus

Case 1

Adam raises a rifle, looks through the viewfinder and presses the trigger. Almost instantaneously Eve, who is standing in the direction the gun was pointing, falls down dead, a bullet through her heart.

Has Adam committed a crime? It might well appear so. We might even be so bold as to name that crime and call it murder. But the matter

---

[12] See for example Smith and Hogan, (1999) 49–50.
[13] At 189.

of Adam's criminal liability is not that simple. The general conceptual framework governing criminal liability limits liability to occasions where the accused has perpetrated a given social 'harm' in circumstances disclosing moral fault. Following this framework, the general model for criminal offence definitions is a statement of some prohibited conduct, with or without some designated result, and an accompanying mental attitude. This combination of elements is traditionally summed up by the Latin maxim *actus non facit reum nisi mens sit rea* which is usually translated as 'an act is not criminal in the absence of a guilty mind'. So as to establish criminal liability the prosecution must here establish a number of things which are not made explicit. On a conviction for murder, they have to show, for example, that it was by Adam's bullet that Eve met her death and not, for example, the coincidence of a simultaneous heart attack or a bullet from another assassin. Even were that condition to be satisfied Adam would not be criminally liable if, for example, he shot Eve in order to prevent her immediately shooting to kill him, or if he was entirely unaware of her presence as when he is shooting a rabbit and Eve unexpectedly pops up in the line of fire.

In theory the *actus reus* and *mens rea* elements of criminal offences are doing different jobs. The **external** or conduct elements of the offence *(actus reus)* supposedly reproduce the substance of a society's 'rules of conduct'—the rules which tell all of us what we can and cannot do. Such rules exist without the sphere of criminal law. In the law of tort, for example, rules of conduct declare that citizens should avoid intentional interference with, or invasions of a person's autonomy, freedom of movement, or property, real or personal.

As explained earlier, law is not unique in creating rules which govern our conduct in this way. Clubs, professions, games and sport all have conduct rules breach of which typically involve the imposition of some penalty. For instance, using golf again as our comparator, rules operate to constitute the game as one in which the players use clubs to hit small balls into less small holes in a particular order in the minimum number of shots. They also co-ordinate playing practice, being designed to ensure that the integrity of the game is proof against a player's natural desire to use (or declare) as few shots as possible. A typical rule, therefore, makes the moving or picking up of balls, which a player might otherwise wish to do in order to avoid an obstruction, subject to a one stroke penalty. The attachment of the penalty does not imply any discredit attaches to rule violations. It is simply a logical feature of the rule which has the structuring of the game and how it is played as its major function. It specifies the unpleasant consequences which attach for acting otherwise than the rules recommend.

Some of the conduct rules of criminal law also serve in regulating and co-ordinating the game of life. They tell you how fast you can drive your car, where you can park, what safety measures your factory must deploy and so on. Like the rules of golf, penalty for non-compliance is not dependent upon the presence of any culpable attitude. But there is a difference. Golfers tend to self apply these rules even where the infringement was unintentional, there was no prospect of detection and where the consequences in terms of status and money are severe. If on the other hand a sporting golfer found himself unknowingly speeding on his way home from that exciting round it is fair to hazard that he would not turn himself in at his nearest police station. Why is this? The facetious answer would be that the golfer treats golf rules more seriously than the rules of criminal law. And so in a sense he does. What distinguishes his attitude towards the two sets of rules is that he seems to have internalised the standards which the golf rules embody. They become his rules and his standards just because they are rules. Speeding rules, by contrast, while he may be disposed to obey them because he knows they conduce to a safer society or because he wishes to avoid the penalty, make no other mark upon his practical reasoning, that is, his reasoning about what he ought to do. There would be no point in turning himself in, he would reason. The game of life is in no way diminished by my failure to do so. The speeding rules are there to guide my behaviour and to give disincentives for making the wrong choices. If on one occasion they are not effective in this way this is a reason to do better in the future rather than make a pointless personal sacrifice.

Other criminal rules have a deeper function. They embody obligations (unlike golf rules) which depend for their authority not upon the existence of the rule itself and their internalisation but upon a generalised acceptance of the truth of the standards concerned. Murder and other crimes of violence, theft and fraud, for example, embody social obligations which are easily understood and articulated. Do not kill. Do not steal. Do not deceive. Do not hurt. What is special about the embodiment of these obligations in the rules of criminal law is that their presence there serves to declare society's core values. People who kill, hurt, steal and deceive are subject to moral condemnation and punishment because doing so is inherently discreditable and not simply because they have flouted authority. For all these reasons susceptibility to punishment which, unlike golf penalties, are stigmatic in character requires proof of fault. It is simply not fair to denounce and punish someone who has committed harm unless they are at fault in so doing.

The **mental** (mens rea) element is, in theory therefore, something quite distinct from the relevant rule of conduct. It operates to filter those deserving censure and punishment for their wrong from those who do not and to grade liability according to their degree of fault.[14] The premise here is that the criminal law has a function to perform over and above declaring wrongs or compensating victims. That function is to limit punishment to those who defy the values embodied in criminal norms and thus deserve to have their conduct denounced as a public wrong. This filtering role is clearly expressed in the classic statement of Lord Hewart CJ in *Bateman* in which he distinguishes the fault necessary for criminal liability in manslaughter from that sufficient for liability in tort. As manslaughter is a criminal offence ('It must be shown that) . . . the negligence of the accused went beyond a mere matter of compensation and showed such a disregard for the life and safety of others as to amount a crime against the state and conduct deserving of punishment.'[15]

As explained in chapter 5, however, this account ignores how the mental element in crime may actually serve to constitute the wrongdoing of which the defendant stands accused, rather than simply serve as a filtering or grading mechanism. Separating the elements of liability into *actus reus* and *mens rea* nevertheless serves to advance understanding of how crimes are constituted. Criminal law lecturers typically preface their lectures on individual crimes with an account of standard criminal law methodology. It will go something like this: 'Now boys and girls, each of the crimes we are going to look at will be approached in the same way. First we will look at the substance of the crime itself. Then we will look at the mental element. When you are answering questions analyse them in the same way. Establish the *actus reus* first. Only when you've done that turn to the *mens rea*.' This helps to convey the (partly informative) message that criminal liability, say for theft, involves some form of conduct (the defendant must have appropriated property belonging to another) which is essentially a matter of empirical fact and is separable from the conditions of liability

---

[14] Paul H Robinson 'Should the Criminal Law Abandon the *Actus Reus-Mens Rea* Distinction?' in S Shute, J Gardner, J Horder (eds), *Action and Value in Criminal Law* (Clarendon Press, Oxford, 1993), 187, at 206: Paul H Robinson, 'Rules of Conduct and Principles of Adjudication' (1990) 57 *Univ of Chicago LR* 279.

[15] (1925) 19 Cr App R 8, 11.

(was the appropriation made with dishonest intent) which is essentially a matter of moral evaluation.

The fact that both wrongdoing and its associated culpability requirement needs to be established independently also clarifies thinking about who should be punished, and for what and affords a handle for analysing what might otherwise be problem cases for criminal liability. Consider, for example, the crime of rape, the *actus reus* of which is having intercourse with a person who does not consent. Under traditional theory this provides a corresponding fault element, namely an intention to have intercourse and an absence of a positive belief that the other is consenting. If then A has intercourse with V mistakenly believing her not to be consenting he has not committed the *actus reus* of rape and so cannot be guilty of rape even though the requisite mental state can be proved. This is not to say that A has not done wrong, nor that A does not deserve punishment. There is no doubt that A has and does, but the wrong that he has done and the wrong for which he deserves punishment is not the wrong of rape. It is the wrong of acting upon the intention to rape another person. Gratifyingly for potential victims and the law abiding among us, and unluckily for A, there is a criminal definition which corresponds to this wrong, namely attempted rape.

In the corresponding case where A has intercourse with V, who does not consent, but where A believes her to be consenting criminal liability is also avoided. This time, however, it is not because there is no wrongdoing but because A lacks the blameworthy attitude which has been designated as necessary to render that wrongdoing punishable.[16] We might be forgiven for concluding that there is no structural difference to be made of the *mens rea* and *actus reus* elements in criminal liability. This would be a mistake. In the second case, as far as the victim is concerned she has been raped. A wrong has been done even if, in legal-analytical terms, that wrong is not (the crime of) rape. This carries implications for the parties themselves. Because A is perpetrating a wrong on V, V is entitled to defend herself by using force to resist A's unjustified attack notwithstanding the fact that A lacks the fault necessary to convict him. It also carries certain implications for third parties. If, in the first example, T were to assist A in his project of having intercourse with V he, like A, would not be guilty of rape as

---

[16] Criminal fault normally, if not invariably, requires the relevant wrongdoing to be reflected in A's conscious mind. This is not to deny there are equally grounds for possible conviction for rape on the basis of an alternative fault element (such as negligence as to the fact of consent).

accomplice since no rape has occurred. In the second, by contrast, T may, in similar circumstances, be appropriately convicted as an accomplice to rape if he, unlike A, was aware that V was not consenting, since he would be acting with the fault element for a criminal wrong to procure that wrong.

Offences and Defences

Of course, something is left out of this account of the structure of criminal liability, namely the matter of criminal defences. Our teacher will typically follow up his explanation of the *actus reus* and *mens rea* elements as follows: 'Finally we will see what defences, if any, may be raised by those who have performed the substance of the offence with the relevant state of mind. When you are answering problem questions don't consider defences until you've first established the *actus reus* and *mens rea*.' Our teacher's analysis assumes, of course, that it is not possible to account for criminal defences within the *actus reus/mens rea* equation—that they are truly a third and independent element in the construction of criminal liability. This is not uncontroversially the case. It may simply make for ease of exposition and analysis to be able to explain, for example, that murder is an intentional killing liability for which may be excluded by the presence of certain circumstances serving to negate wrongdoing (justifications) or culpability (excuses).[17] That these circumstances are common to all crimes allows textbooks to separate these general issues from the specifics of individual offences.[18]

Some defences, clearly, can be subsumed within the *actus reus/mens rea* equation.[19] For example, both insanity and intoxication, even involuntary intoxication, can be conceived as operating within the parameters of the offence as particular doctrinal manifestations of the principle that it is for the prosecution to prove the mental element explicit or implicit in the offence definition. If they are unable to do so due to the defendant's intoxication or insanity they fail to discharge

[17] Smith and Hogan, (1999) 35.

[18] For discussion of the cogency of separating analysis of criminal doctrine into the general part (matters supposedly common to offences generally, eg defences, the meaning of intention etc.) and the special part (matters specific to individual defences) see J Gardner, 'On the General Part of the Criminal Law' in RA Duff (ed), *Philosophy and the Criminal Law* (CUP, Cambridge, 1998), 205, 244–9.

[19] For general discussion see P Robinson, *Criminal Law Defences* (West, St Paul, 1984); cf M Moore, *Placing Blame* (1997).

that burden. However, even with those defences an element of moral evaluation—'Does this person deserve censure?' enters into the analysis when a purely cognitive approach to *mens rea*—'Is the definitional mental element established or not?'—does not. This can be seen most starkly in connection with voluntary intoxication where, in most jurisdictions, the defendant may escape liability where *mens rea* is negated in respect of those crimes where intention is the mental element but not for crimes where only foresight must be established. The view taken is that drunken offenders do not deserve to be able to rely on their lack of foresight if such foresight was absent only because they were drunk. Other defences, notably self defence and necessity, strike to the very heart of criminal wrongdoing and can be understood both as opposing the *actus reus*, in so far as *actus reus* refers to the conduct prohibited in the definition of a given offence, and as opposing *mens rea*, involving the claim that the defendant lacked criminal intent. Still others, however, are less easily categorised as negating either *mens rea* or *actus reus*. Duress, for example, is generally and best understood as operating to confess and avoid liability rather than as negating the relevant criminal wrongdoing or definitional mental element.

Does conceiving of defences as a third element in the construction of criminal liability rather than operating within the definitional contours of the offence entail anything important? From a procedural and phenomenological point of view it probably does. Fletcher explains the analytical division historically as a concomitant of a criminal process in which prosecution and defence bore separate burdens.[20] The prosecution bore the burden of proving the basic (inculpatory) elements of the offence, and the defence those matters which, like self-defence, operated to exculpate the defendant from liability for that offence. In the majority of contemporary jurisdictions, although the prosecution bears the burden of proving the offence elements and disproving such defences as the defendant is minded to raise, the defence still retains an evidential burden in respect of the latter. The prosecution's burden of persuasion does not kick in, in other words, unless the defence is first able to raise sufficient evidence to substantiate the possibility that the defence claim may be true.[21] Offences inculpate. Defences exculpate. This sustains the desirable state of affairs that the parameters of offences are static and certain while the grounds of excuse and justification have a degree of

[20] G Fletcher, *Rethinking Criminal Law*, ch 7.
[21] Cf A Stein, 'Criminal Defences and the Burden of Proof' (1990) *Coexistence* 26: 70, 82–6.

flexibility reflecting the inevitably context-driven plausibility of excul-patory claims.[22] Approached in this way the elements of criminal offences can be viewed as fact configurations of prima facie culpable wrongdoing for which the defendant may account by a credible denial of moral blame or wrongful action. Keeping the conditions under which an offence is committed separate from the conditions under which lia-bility for that offence may be avoided sustains this idea to a certain extent. The offence/defence distinction serves as a formal reminder that people are expected to give an account of themselves when they violate a primary prohibition.[23] At the societal level this allows the criminal law to present itself in a way which can best communicate the moral message which a given offence definition embodies while at the same time ensuring that the state's authority to condemn and punish is vouch-safed by its conformity with society's practices of blaming. In this regard defence doctrine has an inbuilt teleological dynamic which offence doctrine has all but lost. As Richard Tur has put it, the 'heads of excuse are never closed and justice is not beyond the age of childbirth even where the criminal law is codified.'[24]

Whether it fulfils any substantive function is more questionable. Glanville Williams has argued that it conceals more than it discloses.[25] He takes *actus reus* to comprise not only the conduct/result/circum-stance referred to in the offence definition but also the absence of any ground of justification which would render an otherwise unlawful act lawful. There is no substantive distinction to be made between what goes in the offence definition and what is left outside it to mop up those problem cases for which the definition fails to make explicit provision. A person who kills another in (reasonable) self-defence is not guilty in Williams' analysis because killings in such circumstances are lawful and if they are lawful this means the *actus reus* is not established. Indeed, it would be quite possible in theory to define say murder so as to include all intentional killings otherwise than under conditions of self defence, provocation, insanity, necessity, and so on. There are, however, difficulties attached to suppressing the distinction between offence and defence in this way. Clearly some defences, infancy is a

---

[22] R Tur, 'Objectivism and Subjectivism' in Shute *et al*, *Action and Value in Criminal Law*, 213, at 214.

[23] G Fletcher, *Rethinking Criminal Law*, ch 7; A Simester, 'Mistakes in Defence' [1992] 12 *OJLS* 295.

[24] R Tur, above n 22, at 215.

[25] See also M Moore, *Placing Blame*, 170.

good example, do indeed seem to operate in the same way as an offence element, liability being a matter of the existence or otherwise of certain external facts. So, if a person is under the age of ten and commits what would otherwise be theft he cannot be criminally liable. The fact of not being an infant is thus implicit in the notion of liability which the offence definition supplies. Theft could quite easily and logically be defined as follows: 'anybody over the age of ten who dishonestly appropriates property belonging to another with the intention of permanently depriving the other of it is guilty of an offence.' Other defences do not seem to operate in this all or nothing fashion. An important function of criminal defences is that they allow, unlike offence definitions, for contingency and context in the construction of criminal liability. Typically they invite consideration of matters, such as motivation, which are central to assessments of moral desert but peripheral to the kind of empirical yes/no questions in which criminal definitions are typically expressed.

Case 2

A shoots B, the leader of his own gang, just as B was himself (unlawfully) about to shoot C, a member of a rival gang.

The Williams approach holds that A's action is always lawful, being necessary and proportionate in the defence of C. A's personal motivation does not affect this equation. But suppose the action taken was not to defend C but for the selfish reason of killing a rival so as to take over leadership of the gang. Intuitively A's motivation makes all the difference to whether we describe A's action as a murderous killing or defensive action.[26] How is it possible to be acting 'in self-defence' unless the action is undertaken for **defensive** purposes? Equally clearly, A's (exculpatory) reasons do not form part of the substance of what is prohibited nor of the mental element which accompanies it and yet they form a necessary object of the court's inquiry into the presence of culpable wrongdoing.

Criminal doctrine embodies this regrettably all too subtle differentiation between *actus reus,* whose existence may be discerned without reference to personal good or bad motivation, and defence where

---

[26] Cf Macauley Works (ed Trevelyan 1866) vii 552 quoted by Williams *Criminal Law: the General Part*, 22.

appropriate motivation may be of central constitutive importance. In *Dadson*[27] D, a constable, wounded P, an escaping poacher, with a shotgun. He was charged with unlawful wounding, as one might expect. However, unknown to D, P was an escaping felon and the law of that time permitted the shooting of escaping felons. Could D rely on this unknown fact to escape liability? The court held that he could not and that he was properly convicted of unlawful wounding. Where a defendant was seeking to justify what would otherwise be a case of criminal wrongdoing it was necessary that he be aware of the facts which would render his action justified. Glanville Williams has insisted that the decision is patently wrong as he had done nothing which the criminal law had 'interdicted'.[28] If a person cannot be guilty of rape if, unknown to him, the other is consenting he can no more be guilty of unlawful wounding if unknown to him the other is an escaping felon. As Dadson had shot someone he was legally permitted to shoot there was no *actus reus* and so no criminal liability.[29] Of course, it sticks in the throat a bit to allow a person who has acted as Dadson did to escape liability. He was morally as guilty as any other person who shoots another for no good reason. In the rape example the mistaken rapist remains, as explained earlier, guilty of an attempt on the basis of having acted in furtherance of an unlawful intent. This is a neat and quite logical response to a case where, as here, the prosecution were unable to establish an element in the offence definition. The would-be rapist tried to commit the offence and, for reasons beyond his control, failed in his endeavour. Williams' solution to the law's inability to convict Dadson of unlawful wounding is to punish him also for attempted unlawful wounding.[30] Here, however, the strategy is less plausible. Whereas consensual sexual intercourse is a normal facet of human behaviour, and therefore in need of no justification, wounding is not. If a wounding is to be lawful it can only be because the special conditions under which it took place rendered it normal and therefore justified. What are these special conditions? Simply that it was undertaken **for the reason of** deflecting an attack. Where these conditions do not apply the correct offence to charge, therefore, must be the offence corresponding to the norm infringed, which in *Dadson* is a wounding rather than an

---

[27] (1850) 2 Den 35.
[28] Williams above n 26, 24; P Robinson, 'A Theory of Justification: Societal Harm as a Prerequisite to Criminal Liability' (1975) 23 *UCLA LR* 266.
[29] G Williams, above n 26, 23
[30] Since he had the intention to wound and performed acts in execution of this intention.

attempted wounding. As Smith and Hogan argue, if his action is truly justified how come he is still guilty of the attempt?[31] Suppressing the distinction between offence and defence seems then to sever the link established earlier between punishment and desert.[32]

The relationship between offence and defence has been usefully reassessed in recent years.[33] In its most cogent presentation[34] the criminal offence definition gives citizens reasons not to act in the prohibited fashion. Put simply, those reasons are that acting in the relevant way is authoritatively adjudged to be wrong and liable to render the actor accountable if he chooses to infringe the prohibition. These reasons defeat the actor's own reasons for acting otherwise than the rule requires.[35] So if the actor says I stabbed this person for a good reason, namely that we were fighting a duel which family honour required us to prosecute to its ultimate conclusion, this reason is defeated. The state's response may well be, for example, 'this is the very reason why we declare these rules, namely to inform you that if you do have a reason for stabbing someone it is a reason you should not act upon however compelling it may appear as a reason to you.'

Criminal doctrine does not close the door entirely upon a person's reasons for acting in violation of the rule. In John Gardner's analysis, justificatory defences refer to that class of defence where the defendant's reasons for acting are specially privileged, being effective **not** to cancel the reasons informing the rule itself—these remain intact—but to cancel the obligation not to act for one's own reasons.[36] They are privileged if two conditions are satisfied. First, the context must require or permit the action as a matter of objective fact **and** second, the actor must perform the action for that reason. As he puts it 'No action is justified unless it is true both that there was an applicable guiding reason

---

[31] G Williams, above n 26, 37.

[32] For an overview of response to the *Dadson* 'problem' see RL Christopher, 'Unknowing Justification and the Logical necessity of the Dadson Principle in Self-Defence' (1995) 15 *OJLS* 229.

[33] See G Fletcher, 'The Right Deed for the Wrong Reason: A Reply to Mr Robinson' (1975) 23 *UCLA LR* 293. J Gardner. See n 38.

[34] G Fletcher, *Rethinking Criminal Law*, 552–69.

[35] This analysis follows that of J Raz who explains in *The Authority of Law* (OUP, Oxford, 1979) that legitimate authority turns upon the acceptance of exclusionary rules. Accepting authority involves 'giving up one's right to act on one's judgement on the balance of reasons (26).' The justification for so doing is that it is likely that an individual subject will act for the right reasons if he accepts the 'directives of the alleged authority as . . . binding and tries to follow them rather than by trying to follow the reasons which apply to him directly.' (19); cf JR Lucas, *On Justice* (OUP, Oxford, 1980), 40–3.

[36] At 117. See n 38

(moral justification) for so acting or so believing and that this corresponds with the explanatory reason why the act was performed or the belief held.'[37] Self-defence, necessity and consent of the justificatory defences and (possibly) duress of the excuses operate in this way. They require there to be a reason why the defendant is permitted to act as he does—for example the threat of imminent force—and for the defendant to have acted for this reason. Gardner's position helps explain both why *Dadson* is rightly decided and why it is proper to invoke the offence/defence disjunction.[38] The gangster in Case 2 will be guilty of murder therefore if he kills his leader for the reason of taking over leadership (not a guiding reason/moral justification) but guilty of no crime if he does so to defend the life of the rival gangster (guiding reason). This clearly conforms to our moral intuition. The option to convict of attempted murder in the former eventuality makes even less sense—given his cold-blooded success—than would a similar legal outcome in *Dadson*.

Alan Norrie in a recent critique of this approach argues that Gardner[39] is ultimately unable to account coherently for the offence/defence division. It is clear that the latter has to conclude that criminal wrongdoing must be separated into offence and defence elements if law is to guarantee that those, and only those, who are blameworthy get their just deserts. Whereas justice requires criminal wrongdoing to be describable in terms of objective facts, law's formal logic is in need of supplement if some who are undeserving (e.g. Dadson) are not to evade the reach of the relevant criminal prohibition. Unfortunately, as Gardner is forced to concede, the separation between offence and defence is artificial since ultimately there is no secure analytical test for whether an aspect of wrongdoing forms part of offence definition or goes to justification. As will now be explained, *Dadson* could just as easily have been acquitted without the need to impugn the offence/defence distinction by which his conviction was justified.

Consent offers a useful illustration of the thrust of Norrie's critique as it records this artificial status graphically, sometimes operating definitionally as constitutive of the wrong and sometimes extra-definitionally

---

[37] Consistent with this view, Ashworth proposes a general defence of 'law enforcement'. See 'Testing Fidelity to Legal Values' (2000) 63 *MLR*.

[38] Cf Smith and Hogan, (1999) 34 and ATH Smith, 'On *Actus Reus*' 97–103, footnote 9 supra; J Gardner, 'Justifications and Reasons' in Simester and Smith (eds), *Harm and Culpability* (Clarendon Press, Oxford, 1996), 103; cf Fletcher, *Rethinking Criminal Law*, 557.

[39] Also Fletcher whose approach is comparable.

as 'defeasing' an otherwise prima facie wrong.[40] Domestic criminal law has adopted the historically contingent stance that crimes of violence such as murder and malicious wounding are qualitatively distinct from crimes such as rape, assault and battery and false imprisonment. Only the latter are constituted definitionally by the absence of consent. Where consent negates wrongdoing for the former class of crimes, as it does in the case of lawful sports, surgery and horseplay, it does so extra-definitionally by means of a justification. This enables the context to be filtered for social acceptability. Duelling and fisticuffs are wrongful, consent notwithstanding. On the other hand boxers are legally permitted to inflict serious injury on other boxers in the course of their sport. Their reasons for acting attract a special privilege.[41] If (absence of) consent was an invariable offence element the law could not operate these dual standards which fulfil important social functions. We need a law which allows doctors to perform life-saving surgery at the same time as prohibiting duelling.[42] The law's technique for squaring this circle and allowing a moral/political evaluation ultimately to determine lawfulness is to render all cases of intentional harm-causing 'prima facie wrongdoing' subject to defeasance in cases of justificatory reasons.

Further examination of consent points up another difficulty, namely the requirement insisted upon by both Fletcher and Gardner that to negate wrongdoing through a justification rather than through the offence definition D must act for the (protected) reason. Is this naturally so? One can easily conceive of many cases which fit the model. So if a doctor, envious of a concert pianist's gifts, amputates the latter's hand following a car crash for reasons of malice and not because he believes it is clinically necessary he would be acting unlawfully although it subsequently transpired the procedure was in fact necessary.[43] Equally, however, one can conceive of cases where appropriate motivation seems to be entirely beside the point of the exculpatory

---

[40] The term 'defeasibility' is Richard Tur's.

[41] Another way of saying this is that absence of consent, for assault is inculpatory. For assault occasioning ABH the presence of consent may be exculpatory (Fletcher, 553–4).

[42] But we cannot generally tolerate a law whose **offence elements** require the court to decide on moral or political grounds whether a person's action is lawful or not. This must be a technical determination, as it is in rape. Exceptionally however it will not be as with dishonesty in theft.

[43] This seems to cohere with the point of distinguishing between offence and defence which is to allow norms of prohibition (do not hurt other people) to be off-set by norms of justification (unless it is consented to as an act of therapeutic surgery) subject to the actor being appropriately motivated.

claim which is, as Williams argues, that one has done nothing which the law has 'interdicted'.

Case 3

Cain, a professional boxer, animated by hatred of Abel, a rival, decides that the least troublesome way to inflict grievous bodily harm upon the latter would be in the ring. In furtherance of this plan he procures his manager to stage the fight whereupon the consequence he desires duly transpires when he knocks Abel out causing permanent brain damage.

Common sense suggests that Cain's personal *animus* can have no relevance to the essential lawfulness of what he has done. He does what he signs up to do and what he signs up to do is perfectly lawful. Why, however, if consent in boxing competitions operates extra-definitionally as a justification for something which would otherwise be wrongful[44] can Cain's motivation be ignored? Is it simply a matter of 'policy' rather than impartial application of principle as to whether a defence carries a mental element just as it seems to be a matter of policy as to whether an aspect of wrongdoing goes to defence rather than definition?[45] More generally are there no overarching principles governing when the actor's reasons matter and when they do not? Is it all a matter of the 'shifting sands of historico-political judgement'?[46]

The short answer is a qualified yes.[47] There is clearly a necessary fluidity governing when law allows moral or political judgments to determine criminal liability. The division of law into offence and defence makes this possible, in the process no doubt giving unwonted authority to the manner in which these judgments are being made. This is not necessarily to concede, however, that criminal justice is thereby compromised representing some covert 'fixing' operation enabling law to pass off moral and political determinations of guilt as the impartial application of rules. We require only that such historico-political judgments as are made chime with the publicly declared values by which our society structures its notion of criminal wrongdoing. As has been suggested criminal justice is aspirational rather than an absolute. It is

---

[44] Ie, rather than structuring the wrong comprehended by causing grievous bodily harm with intent.

[45] Smith and Hogan (1999) 36.

[46] A Norrie, *Punishment, Responsibility and Justice*, 164.

[47] As both Gardner and Fletcher concede.

something, like truth or beauty, to be pursued rather than 'something-which-can-never-be-achieved'. In JR Lucas's clear analysis this aspiration finds its basic ethical template in the notion of universalisability by which like cases are treated alike within an overall context of critical reasonableness. The reconcilation of individual justice, doctrinal rationality and social needs is effected by ensuring that the legal reasons applicable can be individualised (that is) based in facts about (the defendant), sufficient to justify, even to him if he is reasonable, not simply our reaching an adverse decision, but its being adverse to him.'[48]

Understood in this way, there is a job of work to be done which the analytical separation of criminal liability into *actus reus*, *mens rea* and defence does quite satisfactorily. This is to posit certain norms of behaviour articulated with maximum moral clarity by which citizens may apprehend that, for example, hurting people is wrong. Likewise law is also enabled to articulate the norms whereby citizens are permitted to infringe a given norm of behaviour. In this way the moral landscape of crime can best be communicated and appreciated the better to guide our behaviour if not, admittedly, our opinions. That the landscape itself changes in accordance with society's changing ideas of acceptable or unacceptable behaviour demands a degree of fluidity which can be filtered through the form of law. Consent, for example, discloses a clear moral logic in the apparently 'hokey-cokey' way that the *actus reus* of rape (or common assault) requires consent to be absent, whereas that of unlawful wounding is made out even where it is present. This logic is only discernible by reference to the forms of moral wrongdoing which certain criminal definitions express.[49] In rape this is uncontroversial. It is wrong to have intercourse without the other's consent. And it is wrong because it constitutes an attack on the victim's autonomy. This explains why assaults, batteries and false imprisonment are constituted as crimes, and torts also, in the absence of proof of harm. Such wrongs may be aggravated by harm but they are not constituted by it. The wrong in wounding or inflicting grievous bodily harm, by contrast, is the wrong of hurting people. This is compounded no doubt where the hurt is unwelcome but the wrong may be constituted notwithstanding. Good human beings do not stab each other, shoot each other, or beat each other to a pulp. Hurting people is

[48] JR Lucas, *On Justice*, 45.
[49] See K Campbell, 'Offences and Defences' in I Dennis (ed), *Criminal Law and Criminal Justice* (Butterworth, London, 1987).

wrong and it does not automatically become desirable, even permissible, if it is consented to. A similar analysis can be marshalled to account for the extra-definitional nature of self-defence. We do not say that no human value is challenged when citizens use violence to counter violence—something 'untoward' still happens when a person injures or kills another in self-defence.[50] We say rather that while the value is challenged the context permits the resort to force as a necessary evil in a society which values individual autonomy. Whether or not the victim was consenting or was defending himself the moral principle articulated by rules governing crimes of violence is not contradicted but it may be still be appropriate to exempt persons from the critical judgment that they have acted wrongly. We can deplore the event without condemning the act which produced it.

Wrongdoing and Attribution

In recent years a number of attempts have been made to examine the conditions of liability without the categories of *actus reus, mens rea* and defence into which they are traditionally decanted.[51] Even if we accept the tripartite nature of criminal liability—*actus reus, mens rea*, and defence—it does not assist in producing any overall conceptual harmony.[52] The important analytical point made in each attempt is that not all of the doctrines comprehended by the phrase *actus reus* refer to the objective state of affairs proscribed by a criminal prohibition. The voluntary act requirement, for example, describes, in a similar manner to excuses, the circumstances under which a person is fairly answerable for a harmful occurrence. Correspondingly, the definitional mental element sometimes helps define the wrongdoing rather than what makes the actor responsible for it.[53] Again, not all questions of fault or responsibility are settled by the *mens rea* doctrines but require resort to the principles governing defences and causation, for example.

George Fletcher has made considerable progress along the road to reconceptualising the conditions of criminal liability. In preference to the *actus reus/mens rea/*defence separation, he separates the conditions

---

[50] See Fletcher, *Rethinking Criminal Law*, ch 6.

[51] Cf AJ Ashworth, *Principles of Criminal Law*; P Robinson (1993) infra.

[52] Paul H Robinson, 'Should the Criminal Law Abandon the *Actus Reus-Mens Rea* Distinction?' in Shute *et al* (eds), *Action and Value in Criminal Law*, 187, at 206.

[53] The intention to deprive permanently in theft is an illustration.

of liability into those of wrongdoing and attribution. Other theorists, using comparable models, have sought to distinguish rules of conduct (directed at citizens to guide their conduct) from rules of adjudication (directed at judges to guide determinations of responsibility).[54] The distinction drawn in each case is between what the wrongdoing is and the features which make a person responsible for it. Under Fletcher's model defences operate according to whether they can be categorised as excuses or justifications. If the former they are relevant to **attribution**, that is whether the defendant is responsible for his wrongdoing. If the latter they are relevant to **wrongdoing**, that is whether his admitted violation of the rules is in fact an instance of wrongdoing for which he must account.

There are a number of helpful analytical consequences attached to structuring criminal liability around a wrongdoing/attribution rather than the traditional *mens rea/actus* reus/defence separation. These will be outlined now before suffering elaboration in later chapters. They follow from the separation of defences into justifications and excuses. The first consequence is that it helps account for the fact that those who assist a person acting in a justified fashion, say in self-defence, also escape criminal liability. If it is not wrongful for B to resist C's unjustified threat or throw overboard C's cargo to prevent the sinking of a ship it can no more be wrongful for A to assist him.[55] On the other hand, if B's action is only excused, say on the grounds of coercion, B's action remains wrongful, although he may not be blameworthy. If A then lends his assistance he is assisting the commission of a wrongful act for which he will properly be held to account. Again, the scope of the law on self-defence is rendered intelligible by distinguishing between the use of justified force (no wrongdoing and cannot lawfully be resisted) and excused force (wrongdoing without responsibility and can lawfully be resisted). This allows us to explain why a person can use force in self-defence not only against those who act unlawfully but also against aggressors such as the criminally insane or infants, whose actions are excused. The point of self-defence is to vindicate the right of individuals to remain free from unjustified interference or attack. This remains the point whether or not the attacker is to blame for what he does.

---

[54] See also Meir Dan-Cohen, 'Decision Rules and Conduct Rules: On Acoustic Separation in Criminal Law' ((1984) 97 *Harv* LR 625; Paul H Robinson, 'Rules of Conduct and Principles of Adjudication' (1990) 57 *Univ of Chicago LR* 729.

[55] See ch 10.

Apart from the greater analytical rigour attached to this formulation there are other advantages which accrue. At present there is much academic and judicial enthusiasm for a criminal code so that the elements and limits of criminal liability can be ascertained with a relative degree of certainty. This is widely acknowledged to be a good thing because by means of such a code citizens can realistically be expected to appreciate what it is they must or must not do in order to avoid state punishment. A code for citizens would serve therefore the basic principle of criminal justice that people should not suffer conviction and punishment except for breach of an obligation capable of being ascertained upon reasonable inquiry and existing at the time of action.[56] If a code is to be effective in this regard it is moreover probably important that it should be structured according to function with one part for citizens and officials declaring the conduct rules by which their society is organised.[57] The other part can then be directed at legal officials uniquely, directing them how to decide whether a person bears responsibility for a given infringement, how it should be graded, or otherwise when it would be inappropriate to prosecute, convict or punish notwithstanding the infringement of a given rule. Although Fletcher's wrongdoing/attribution distinction is unable to help with all these questions it seems to provide a basic template for what should appear in either code. Justificatory defences, since these serve to qualify the notion of wrongdoing, are properly contained in the code for citizens. Doctors need to know, for example, when they can legitimately perform surgery, or when it is lawful to administer drugs which will accelerate the death of a patient. On the other hand matters going to attribution such as excuses, including true excuses and capacity based exemptions, should be in the officials' code but seem to fall outside the scope of an operational citizen's code. The fact that one is provoked, or is insane or under-age should not form part of one's practical reasoning process concerning what one ought to do, if only because it might alert say infants to the full range of antisocial behaviour society is prepared to tolerate from them. Another compelling advantage of such separation is that it allows the conduct rules of a given society to be articulated with maximum clarity. The Swedish Code provisions on murder considered in chapter 2 illustrate the ease with which such a functional

---

[56] Particularly in previous epochs the state has used the inbuilt ambiguity and indeterminacy of the common law system to criminalise activities ex post facto.

[57] See Meir Dan-Cohen, above n 54.

separation can be achieved. If a Swedish citizen were to desire to know how he would need to act in order to avoid a conviction for murder the Code, in effect, tells him that he will avoid conviction if he does not kill anyone. If he inquires 'Does this mean I will be guilty of murder if I kill someone by driving dangerously on the road?' the answer is 'You may be unless the judge takes the view that the circumstances of your killing justifies the imposition of a lesser offence label and punishment.'

A Swedish citizen does not need a degree in law to know how to avoid a conviction for murder. He does not need to know and indeed perhaps should not know, for example, that he may be excused in whole or in part if he is insane or acted under duress or provocation or acted for altruistic reasons such as euthanasia. These are matters pertaining to the culpability of the actor for the wrong he has committed and thus to the reaction it is appropriate for society to marshal. They are matters which a judge must consider in deciding whether and how much a person is to blame. This provokes the more general question as to the precise content of the respective codes. The Swedish Code provision offers a minimalist account offering little by way of guidance as to the kind of considerations a person should have in mind as a reason for acting or not acting in a particular way.[58] Paul Robinson has argued for a yet more minimalist account in which matters such as results and causation do not figure. What citizens should be told not to do is to hurt people. If then death occurs following an act of violence this is a matter to which a judge can attend in grading the offence. His own adjudicative rules will designate a breach of a conduct rule as particularly serious where it produces a particular consequence (here death) and the actor is adjudged causally responsible for that consequence. On the face of it there is much to be said for this approach. To act as guidance conduct rules must limit themselves to the things which we can control. We can control what we do but not the consequences of what we do. On the other hand, and for the same reason, Robinson's citizen's code will not help the person become a better citizen and it is this objective before all others which should surely inform such a project in liberal democracies. A richer solution to the problem of the content of a citizen's code is offered by RA Duff who notes that the rules of criminal law fulfil the important role of communicating values rather than offering a list of 'do's and don'ts' with attendant penalties.[59] The law

---

[58] P Robinson, *Structure and Function of Criminal Law* (OUP, Oxford, 1997).

[59] RA Duff 'Rule violations and wrongdoings' in S Shute and A Simester (eds). Criminal Law Theory: Doctrines of the General Part (OUP, Oxford, 2002) 47, 51–6.

of murder, for example, does not simply prohibit killing people; it declares the scope of the wrong in murder, thereby creating a division between murder and non-culpable or less culpable homicides. Part of the function of a code must therefore be to effect and perfect this declaratory function so that citizens are able to make moral sense of criminal rules and effectively attend to the normative structure of the society as embodied in criminal prohibitions.[60] Any matter, therefore, to which a citizen properly should or may attend when deciding how to conduct him or herself is a matter for the code of conduct. This will include mental elements where these serve to define a criminal prohibition and defences in so far as they enshrine norms of behaviour capable of offering guiding reasons for and against action.

Two points need to be made, however, in connection with the placement of defences. The first concerns the difficulty of pinpointing an uncontroversial dividing line between excuses and justifications. The second concerns the cogency of drawing the line between rules of conduct and rules of adjudication at the interface between excuses and justifications.

Separating Excuses and Justifications

The point of defences in the criminal law is to underwrite the principle that (only) culpable wrongdoing is punishable. As such defences 'refine the wording of (offence definitions)'[61] and operate in tandem with the *actus reus* and *mens rea* requirement to ensure that liability turns on both fault and wrongdoing.[62] The criminal law boasts a range of defences stretching from justifications such as necessity and self-defence through complete excuses such as involuntary behaviour and duress to partial excuses such as provocation. In this, defences mirror how in discourse generally individuals offer reasons for their conduct as a means of avoiding moral condemnation and informal sanctions. Justifying reasons involve the claim that the actor's conduct was not an instance of wrongdoing but was a morally permissible or even desirable thing to do. Excuses concede the actor's conduct to be wrongful but claim, in recognition of the fact that the actor is only human,

---

[60] See J Gardner, 'Rationality and the Rule of Law in Offences Against the Person' 502, 514 *et seq*.

[61] P Robinson, 'Criminal Law Defences: A Systematic Analysis' (1982) *Col L Rev* 199, at 209.

[62] See generally G Williams, 'Offences and Defences' (1982) 2 *LS* 233.

that no blame or, in the case of partial excuses, only qualified blame, attaches to him. In short, justifications negate wrongdoing; excuses negate blame.

Once upon a time, whether a defence was categorised as an excuse or justification was potentially of great moment. A killer excused of homicide nevertheless forfeited his possessions to the Crown. A justified killer did not. Formal consequences no longer attach to categorising defences in this way. Perhaps they should do. As Robinson has argued, suppressing the distinction serves to suppress important moral and penological functions of defence doctrine. One such is the provision of secure labels for different forms of wrongdoing. For example, a person who kills another under the mistaken belief the other was about to commit serious violence, or robs a bank under conditions of duress presently receives an unqualified acquittal. In a sense this is undeserved. After all in each case the actor has done something which, while understandable and excusable, is nevertheless to be deplored. It might make more sense then to register excused wrongdoing with a special verdict, say 'not guilty by reason of excuse.'[63] It might also justify different evidential or procedural conventions such as a reversal of the burden of persuasion coupled perhaps with a lower standard of proof.[64] Not only would such outcomes chime better with the equivocal moral response which excused wrongdoing tends to elicit, it is possible that there would be a greater readiness to accept marginal excuses such as killing for reasons of compassion, if the consequence was not an outright acquittal. It could also serve as a basis for grafting onto the not guilty verdict enforceable conditions designed to reduce the likelihood that such wrongdoing would be repeated. The defence of automatism is an obvious case in point. In England the courts, largely for reasons of social defence, have often strained to implement the special verdict of not guilty by reason of insanity or even convict in cases where, although lacking definitional fault, the wrongdoer shows himself in need of treatment, supervision or other corrective measures.[65] Clearly the impetus to engage in such practices would be lessened if a different form of acquittal were available which gave courts the powers necessary to minimise the dangers posed by a given excused wrongdoer. Such reasoning

[63] P Robinson, above n 61.

[64] See A Stein, 'Criminal Defences and the Burden of Proof' (1990) *Coexistence* 26: 70, 82–6.

[65] *Lipman* [1969] 3 All ER 410; *R v Sullivan* [1984] AC 156; *Burgess* [1991] 2 All ER 386.

clearly does not apply in cases where the defendant's conduct is justified in the sense of being socially desirable or acceptable. Here an unqualified acquittal is appropriate reflecting the fact that no wrongdoing is attributable to the defendant.

Assuming it is a worthwhile task to formalise this separation of defences into justifications and excuses, can such separation be achieved? What makes conduct justified as opposed to merely excused? This is not an easy question to answer with any great precision, although certain general distinguishing features can be advanced. It is fairly clear, for example, that the normative structure of justificatory defences generally tends to complement and support that of the offences themselves. Certain defences operating as justifications are therefore rendered necessary and perhaps inevitable. A simplified analysis of crimes of violence, for example, illustrates why a system of prohibitions grounded in moral norms presupposes also a systematic means of justifying infringements. Crimes of violence fulfil the dual function of vindicating and supporting individual autonomy and also upholding the moral principle that hurting people is wrong. The former function plays the major structuring role in the make up of the offences. They are illegal largely, though not entirely, because they represent an unjustified attack upon individual autonomy. Where autonomy is not unjustly compromised violence itself is easier to justify. Accordingly, consent, self-defence and medical necessity usually negate the wrongdoing implicit in acts of violence, cancelling as one might expect the duty to be guided by the reasons informing the rule. The same reason—respect for autonomy—explains the reason not to use force against another and also the reason why that reason is defeated when the other consents, or is incapable of consenting where the use of force is in his best interests, or is himself subjecting the other to unjustified force. The moral force of the offences would make no sense without their corresponding justifications.

More broadly, however, the conditions under which derogation from a prohibitory norm is permitted or desirable is less obvious. Consider again the case of Mr Steane, charged with treason for assistance given to the enemy under the threat of the concentration camp for himself and his family.[66] Assuming we would wish to grant him a defence is it one awarded to him as a concession to his humanity (an excuse) or because the context is such as to render his conduct socially

---

[66] See ch 5.

permissible (justification)? The standard answer is that his action is justified if it advances collective interests as the lesser of two evils but excused at best if it advances the interests of Steane and his family at the expense of such interests. This answer, however, conceals as much as it reveals. We have no problem with understanding that it is in society's **collective** interests to permit a person to use (self-serving) force in self-defence even as against a blameless aggressor or a number of aggressors. Capitulating to unjust threats is a sacrifice a person ought not to be required to make. What is it then which makes treachery a worse evil from the collective point of view than the death of an individual's family members? What value is being advanced? What manner of cost-benefit or other analysis of the good is capable of providing the kind of hard evidence which will make Steane's decision look simply self serving? In any event, in deciding whether a person was justified in acting as he did do we not need to look at things from the actor's perspective?[67] If Steane and others like him thought, as they probably did, that (minor) acts of betrayal were small beer compared with the consequences of non compliance should society not, given the profoundly human values motivating their decision, accord significance to this?[68]

Comparable questions are provoked where the actor believes in the existence of facts which would warrant the use of force, say in self defence or necessity or under conditions of consent, but he is mistaken. The would-be aggressor is in fact a citizen free from any inclination to do harm. The youth who appears to be consenting to rough and undisciplined horseplay is in fact too frightened to display his true intolerance of the situation.[69] The person appearing to require emergency surgery is in fact fit and well. Do we treat the actor's action as justified because the reasons he took himself to have for the actions he undertook were acceptable in the eyes of the law? Or, assuming the mistake is a reasonable one, only excused because although the law does not permit people to use force in self defence/etc unless the actor was the subject of an unjust attack etc, it also understands that citizens are not to blame if the reasons they took themselves to have for acting in this way are well-founded?[70]

There are a number of different possible responses. A view already discussed holds that whether action is justified is a matter of objective

---

[67] For discussion see J Raz, *The Morality of Freedom* (Clarendon Press, Oxford, 1986), 314.

[68] JR Lucas *On Justice*, 42–3.

[69] *Aitken* (1992) 95 Cr App R 304.

[70] J Gardner, 'The Gist of Excuses' (1998) *Buffalo Criminal Law Review* 575.

empirical fact in much the same way as whether someone has performed the conduct element in an offence definition. Action is not justified unless it is justified.[71] The merit of this analysis is that it coheres with what we intuit to be the main point of making the distinction between justifications and excuses. It explains why those whose interests are threatened by people who mistakenly believe their conduct to be justified may lawfully resist the action taken and a third party intervening to defend the latter's interests is himself justified in so doing.[72] Since the person is not an aggressor/consenter/ill patient the action taken against him is unjustified and so can justifiably be resisted. Mr Steane's action was also not justified but this time because society, in the form of *ex ante* guidance in the form precedents, had so declared it. The reasons why he failed to follow society's guidance might excuse him from blame but it did not make his action acceptable. This objectivist theory of justified action as explained earlier poses significant difficulties. If the question whether action is justified is a matter of objective fact alone it seems to follow that actors may be acting lawfully although they were entirely unaware of or indifferent to the beneficial consequences which would attach to their action. Such consequences are counter-intuitive. The actor's reason for acting appears to make a difference not only to our assessment of his responsibility for his action but also to the quality of that action.

The opposing subjectivist approach to justificatory defences treats the actor's (appropriate) motivation or reasons for acting as a necessary, perhaps even sufficient, ingredient of justified action. The American Model Penal Code, for example, states that force used against another 'is justifiable when the actor believes that such force is immediately necessary for the purpose of protecting himself against the use of unlawful force by such other person. . . .'[73] Of key significance here is that force used for defensive purposes does not require the defender to be the subject of aggression, only that he believes himself so to be. Believing one's action to be justified means that it is justified. A similar stance is adopted in relation to justificatory necessity.[74] The obvious objection is that it renders perfectly lawful what is, both from

---

[71] P Robinson, 'A Theory of Justification: Societal Harm as a Prerequisite to Criminal Liability' (1975) 23 *UCLA LR* 266.

[72] For further discussion see J Waldron, 'Self Defense, Agent-Neutral and Agent-Relative Accounts' (2000) 88 *Cal LR* 711.

[73] MPC s 3.05(1).

[74] S 3.02 (1).

an objective point of view and from the point of view of the person against whom the 'justified action' is taken, an unjust attack. Moreover, since it is the actor's beliefs rather than the objective state of affairs which render his action justified it seems to imply that resisting such action is itself unlawful. Such a state of affairs, if anything, is more counter-intuitive than the objectivist approach to the unknowingly justified actor.[75] The reasons-based analysis of justified action, discussed earlier, neatly avoids both difficulties. Action is justified only if the conditions are such as to defeat the reasons to act as the prohibitory norm requires and one acts for those reasons.[76] This follows our intuition that police officers and others who kill, as they see it, in self defence or to prevent the commission of crime have at best an excuse for their actions if it later transpires that they were mistaken.

Excuses, as has been explained, are traditionally thought to operate in a different fashion from justifications. They negate the blame normally associated with performing criminal wrongdoing rather than the fact of wrongdoing. The standard view holds that wrongdoing is excusable if an actor lacks the rational capacity to conform his behaviour to the law or otherwise if it would be unfair to hold him accountable or fully accountable. Falling into one or other of these categories are the defences of insanity, automatism, diminished responsibility, provocation, infancy, duress of threats, duress of circumstances, mistake and provocation. Defences of either type fit in here in recognition of the fact that obedience to a primary rule of conduct is not always to be expected or even to be desired.[77] From this point of view there is no systemic impetus governing the recognition of excuses corresponding to that of justifications, where the system of prohibitory norms is capable of generating its own support system of norms of justification. Rather the impetus is extrinsic to the system of prohibitory norms. Excuses are demanded in any coercive system whose authority is predicated upon respect for the humanity of the governed.[78]

From another perspective, excuses form part of a package of defences including justifications, which kick in to negate liability, offence definition notwithstanding, where the actor's conduct does not

[75] See discussion on *Dadson*, above.
[76] G Fletcher, 'The Right Deed for the Wrong Reason: A Reply to Mr Robinson' (1975) 23 *UCLA LR* 293; Fletcher, *Rethinking Criminal Law*, 557.
[77] See later discussion on duress.
[78] HLA Hart, *Punishment and Responsibility* (Clarendon Press, Oxford, 1968), ch 2; JR Lucas, *On Justice*, 137–8.

deviate markedly from what is generally accepted to be the standards of good citizenship. In this it has been argued that there is no fundamental structural difference between justifications and excuses. Both depend upon the actor being appropriately motivated. Excuses differ from justifications only in that there is something 'suspect about the reasons for which one acts'. It is for this reason that excused action can be lawfully resisted but not assisted. In the words of John Gardner, the structure of excuses depends upon the structure of justifications, requiring a union of 'guiding' and 'explanatory' reasons. The need to establish an excuse only arises if one cannot claim a justification. Excuses such as duress, provocation and mistake operate in a similar fashion to justifications such as self defence and necessity to exculpate those who acted upon reasons which manifest no hostility to the values underpinning criminal doctrine. While appropriate beliefs and motivation are **necessary** features of all defences they are not sufficient in themselves to constitute **justified** action. One has an excuse if there is no valid reason for acting as one did but the person acting nevertheless takes there to be valid reasons, and there are objective grounds for so taking.[79] Returning to our analysis of *Steane*, Mr Steane's claim to avoid liability takes exactly the same form whether he is successful in raising a justification or is (relatively) unsuccessful in raising only an excuse. In each case he is presenting the claim that what he did was nothing that other responsible citizens might equally have done in the same circumstances. Whether his claim to avoid liability takes the form of a justification depends upon the court's determination that other responsible citizens might equally have done the same because it was **the right thing to do** or was otherwise **permitted** as a means of securing the actor's autonomy

It is central to this thesis that true excuses (eg duress, mistaken belief) are analytically separate from exemptions (insanity, infancy, diminished responsibility). Excuses rely upon the defendant's reasonable, if morally suspect, response to external events. Exemptions presuppose the absence of reasonableness. Punishing those lacking the capacity to follow rules is inappropriate rather than simply unfair. As will be argued later, this division into excuses and exemptions imposes a rather unforgiving straitjacket on criminal defences and for most practical purposes they are probably best served by treating them as one. For example, some excuses straddle the line dividing exemptions and

---

[79] J Gardner 'Justifications and Reasons' (1996) 119.

excuses. Automatism and involuntary intoxication are cases in point. Both rely upon the defendant's irrationality without implying in any way, as do insanity and diminished responsibility, that he is not a fit subject for moral evaluation. Other claims to avoid liability which Gardner dubs excuses may also be founded upon the absence of reason rather than a suspect reason. Duress is a case in point. Finally, while exemptions do not operate to give people guiding reasons for acting otherwise than the relevant rule would recommend, it is not at clear that the same can be said of all excuses. The distinction would not help therefore to determine the proper limits of a citizens' code. Once again, duress is a case in point and one to which we now turn.

Duress and the Citizen's Code

Earlier it was remarked that the cogency of a workable separation of defences into excuses and justifications is open to question. The defence of duress is a useful illustration of a number of difficulties surrounding this division. A person who robs a bank under threat of death escapes liability but this is not because coerced robbery is not wrongful. Doctrine does not hold robbery to be unlawful 'unless performed under threats of death'. What the robber does is personally justified— no one can be expected to sacrifice her own life for the sake of obedience to a prohibition of at most medium gravity—but it is not objectively justified. No moral values are advanced or vindicated by her participation in the robbery. The robber has at best an excuse, therefore.[80] The coercion to which she is subject negates responsibility not wrongdoing. Unlike other defences, however, duress covers a broad terrain. At one extreme it involves a form of moral involuntariness where the defendant acts upon fear alone.[81] Perhaps this was the case with our robber. So incapacitated was she by the gun placed against her head that she just 'does' regardless of the circumstances. This is a paradigm case of duress as an excuse. There is no question that the citizen does wrong but it would be more than can reasonably be demanded to expect her to do 'the right thing'. She is excused but her action is not justified. At the other extreme are cases where the coercive

---

[80] J Horder, 'Self Defence, Necessity and Duress [1998] *Can J of Law and Juris* 143, at 159.

[81] KJM Smith, 'Duress and Steadfastness' (1999) *Crim LR* 363, 373–4.

circumstances to which the actor is subjected appears to render his action objectively justified on any theory of justification.[82]

Case 4

Adam, who is driving his car on a motorway is subject to intimidation by a lorry driver who is 'tailgating' him at high speed. The only way Adam can avoid the threat of an accident is to break the speed limit and avoid his tormentor.

If anything can justify breaking the speed limit this can. The speed limit is in place to protect us from the risk of injury, not to subject us to such risks. For the same reason that the citizen could not properly be convicted of reckless driving (gravity of potential harm to driver justifies the risks which avoiding action will entail for others) so also Adam should not be guilty of breaking a speed restriction. He is not, unlike the first defendant, acting upon fear alone which might excuse him. He is not even claiming a mere personal justification grounded in the fact that speeding is a reasonable choice to make where the alternative is subjection to a mortal risk. Rather he is claiming that he is acting as reason would have him act and that his reasons are guiding reasons, that is true for all people at all times rather than personal to him in his emergency.[83] It seems that this may have been the view taken by Goddard LCJ in Steane. His reluctance to approve the idea that Steane's personal motivation counted as a criminal intention for the purpose of liability implies that he took the view that there was no criminal wrongdoing to be excused. This raises questions about whether we should stake so much upon the excuse/justification division.

In the middle of the spectrum the coercive event may not be such as to deprive the defendant of the ability to act according to the reasons upon which the criminal law would have us base our actions, and yet she may nevertheless be granted a defence although she chooses not to act on such reasons. In *Hussain*, for example, duress was thought by the Court of Appeal to be available as a defence to hijacking an aeroplane where the hijackers had done so to avoid deportation and its likely consequence, namely death or serious injury at the hands of the

---

[82] Action is justified under utilitarianism theory since conduct is the lesser of two evils. Action is justified as a vindication of autonomy because his action is self-defensive allowing him to defeat the rights of another as means to that end.

[83] JR Lucas, *On Justice*, 42–3.

Iraqi authorities.[84] Here the defendants acted for a reason rather than without reason. The reason was not one which the law would have them act—fear for one's life does not justify hijacking any more than it does murder—and doubtless they knew this. This is one of those occasions where there are reasons for the good citizen to act as he did[85] but not justifying reasons since there is something 'suspect about the reasons for which he acts'.

Significantly, whether we denote such cases as justifications or excuses, mid-spectrum cases of coercion seem to be at odds with Fletcher's thesis that excuses go to attribution rather than wrongdoing. Adopting the words of Fletcher, 'the question (is) whether a particular wrongful act (hijacking) is attributable either to the actor's character or to the circumstances that overwhelmed his capacity for choice'.[86] In neither *Steane* nor *Hussain* can we say that the defendant's act was attributable to circumstances which overwhelmed the capacity to choose. Rather, the circumstances simply made choosing to do the right thing, whatever that might happen to be, more difficult. This elicits the perhaps surprising conclusion that the coercive event under such circumstances does not prevent the attribution of wrongdoing to the defendant. Neither does it negate wrongdoing. Rather, in Duff's plausible argument, it translates one (punishable) form of wrongdoing (say hijacking) into another form (say hijacking under duress) for which punishment is not warranted, either because it would be futile, or since moral heroism is more than can be reasonably expected of ordinary people, because it would be excessive.[87]

The significance of this analysis is that it renders questionable certain assumptions to which the excuse/justification/ wrongdoing/attribution division subscribes. Consider for example the proposition that assisting those acting under conditions of justification is lawful but unlawful where only excused. If it is true that certain coerced choices straddle the boundaries between these two oppositions then what are to make of the legality of a third party giving acts of assistance in such a case?

---

[84] [1999] *Crim LR* 570.

[85] Even this is not controversial. See V Tadros, 'The Characters of Excuse' (2001) *OJLS* 517.

[86] G Fletcher, *Rethinking Criminal Law*, 801.

[87] RA Duff (2002), 61–8.

Case 5

X, a bank cashier, is instructed by Y, a bank robber to empty her till, under pain of serious injury, and deliver the contents to Y. X complies, reasoning that it is better to do so than face the consequences. Z, X's colleague, helps X to empty her till not because he is fearful for her own life nor because he thinks his action will save X's life, but because he wants to ensure a speedy end to the proceedings deciding, quite understandably, that no harm will come of it.

It goes without saying that X will escape liability as an accomplice to robbery but probably not on the grounds that her conduct is justified, although she clearly has good reasons in her own eyes for acting as she does.[88] An orthodox analysis of this scenario supposes that X escapes liability as an accomplice on grounds of an excuse. Z, however, will not, being unable to avail himself either of duress by threats—he was under none, or of circumstances—there were no circumstances which compelled him to act as he did. He reasons simply, as X does but without her incentives, that it is better to help than not help. Given that both viewpoints are equally reasonable and well-founded, it seems plausible that if X escapes liability than so should Z whether we choose to designate X's action as excused or justified.

Consider finally the contention, articulated by Paul Robinson, that rules of attribution should be excluded from the citizen's code since citizens have no reason to be made aware of the circumstances when their wrongdoing may be excused. If as Duff argues, surely correctly, the coercive circumstance does not go to attribution alone but rather qualifies the wrongdoing against which punishment is directed, then it is arguable that certain reasons for acting, whether or not they are designated as justifications or excuses, must appear in the citizen's code. Faced with the kind of emergency X and Z are faced with it is not enough for them to be told that their action is not justified since they will rightly respond 'Yes, but does that mean I will be punished if I go ahead and do it?' Given that neither of them are relieved of their capacity to make reasoned choices, a liberal polity owes it to them and citizens generally that they are not left in the dark as to the penal consequences of acting according to their inclinations. Both are in need of practical guidance about what they ought to do and also what they may do, norms of prohibition and norms of justification notwithstanding.

[88] See J Raz, *The Morality of Freedom*, 146.

10

Criminal Defences: Setting Limits to Justifications

MOST CRIMINAL DEFENCES share a common template. The template helps structure defences according to shared moral organising themes. Not infrequently the basic elements in the template are subjected to strain when there is a lack of agreement as to the moral claim to avoid punishment which a given defence embodies. For example, provocation and duress are particularly difficult to place. Is the general claim to avoid responsibility for these defences, like self defence, 'because of the circumstances in which I was placed I acted reasonably according to the relevant social standards applicable'.' Or is it, like diminished responsibility, 'because of matters outside my control I experienced the rule as less easy to follow than other people'.[1] This is not simply a theoretical teaser. It has very practical ramifications. If, for example, provocation amounts to a simple denial of capacity it is clear why it should be necessary for the accused to be able to adduce evidence that he was provoked to lose his self-control, but it is not so clear why it should be necessary that the prompt to which he responded was objectively provocative. In this chapter I aim to examine the defences of duress, self defence and necessity with a view to exposing how a common template sustains their individual internal moral ordering and also creates a framework by which to account for other cases of excused or justified protective action left unprovided for by these defences.

DURESS, NECESSITY AND SELF-DEFENCE: THE BASIC TEMPLATE

The template common to duress, necessity and self-defence is that the actor reacted reasonably to allay the unjust threat of harm. As will now be explained, the notions of reasonable reaction underpinning them are

[1] See generally J Horder, 'Provocation and Diminished Responsibility' (1999) *Kings College Law Review*.

configured in similar fashion. In each case the response must be necessary and reasonable. A further requirement for two, certainly, and one,
arguably, the necessity must be for immediate action.

The Necessity to React

The requirement, that the reaction be necessary is, of course, axiomatic
in necessity. The claim to avoid liability is that the actor was uniquely
placed to prevent harm befalling individual and/or collective interests
through action which would necessitate the infringement of a primary
rule of behaviour. So, for example, he was standing behind a person
about to be hit by a car and could prevent this by pushing him out of
the way. For self-defence the force deployed is a matter of privilege
rather than the moral imperative implicit in the foregoing example and
is restricted to cases where it is necessary to repel the attack.

For duress the actor's response must also be necessary. Unlike self-
defence, where the erstwhile duty to retreat requirement[2] has been
translocated into the more generalised inquiry as to whether the defendant's resort to force was reasonable,[3] the fact that there are ways open
to the actor of retreating from or otherwise avoiding the threat is of
potentially greater consequence. The defendant relying upon duress is
after all asking to be excused, which would seem to require as a minimum that he has left no reasonable stone unturned in attempting to
meet his legal obligations.[4] With self-defence, by contrast, the defendant does not seek to excuse his conduct but insists that he is permitted
to meet unjustified force with (reasonable) resistance. Human beings
cannot be expected always to retreat in the face of threats to their autonomy.[5] A comparison of two cases may be instructive. In *Field*
the defendant was warned that some men were on their way to attack
him. Rather than retreat he stood his ground until they arrived. The
promised attack duly transpired, during the course of which the defend-

---

[2] Until fairly recently a person threatened with an unlawful attack would not act lawfully in resisting it by force unless he had availed himself of any opportunity he may have
had to retreat. The existence of such a duty of retreat reflected the idea that the use of
force was presumptively wrong and therefore to be avoided at all costs. See G Fletcher,
Rethinking Criminal Law (Little Brown and Company, Boston, Toronto, 1978), 864–8.

[3] See *Bird* [1985] 2 All ER 513; Draft Criminal Law Bill 1993, cl 28(8).

[4] See generally J Horder, 'Occupying the Moral High Ground/ The Law Commission
on Duress' [1994] *Crim LR* 334, at 337–8.

[5] Fletcher concludes that this sentiment weighs particularly heavy with the American
public.

ant stabbed one of the attackers fatally. The court concluded that the defendant had no duty to quit premises he was lawfully inhabiting simply to avoid attack. It followed that he was entitled to defend himself using reasonable force when the attack occurred. By contrast, in *Gill*, on a charge of theft of his employer's lorry, the defendant was unable to avail himself of the defence of duress where he had been left alone after the threats had been issued and prior to the theft and thus been afforded a good opportunity to raise the alarm and escape the threat.[6] No doubt if Gill instead of capitulating had met coercion with defensive force his conduct would have been considered exemplary notwithstanding similar opportunities being available to raise the alarm'.[7]

Immediacy

The requirement that the reaction be necessary can be taken to imply that an immediate response is called for in the case of self defence and duress. The defences are rooted in the predicament of the accused, namely an emergency which compels him to act now. Without this emergency why should we not expect the defendant to act like all other reasonable people and seek help? In *Gill*, for example, the major reason why the defendant was unable to plead duress successfully was that the threat to which he was subjected could not immediately be carried out. Given this fact it was natural for the court to conclude that it was not necessary for him to capitulate to the threat. Such a conclusion cannot always be drawn. Sometimes an imminent threat no less than an immediate one may be expected to undermine the fortitude of the recipient. In *Hudson v Taylor* the defendants were teenage girls who had committed perjury having been threatened with violence if they did not do so. The trial judge refused to allow their defence of duress since the threat could hardly have been carried out there and then in open court. The Court of Appeal, allowing the appeal, said that whether or not this was true, the jury should be allowed to take into account the impact such threats are likely to have on young girls, who might naturally be fearful of the risks involved in seeking police protection.[8]

---

[6] [1963] 2 All ER 688.

[7] Cf *Cousins* [1982] QB 26.

[8] Cf *State v Green*, 470 S.W. 2d 565 (1971) (SC Missouri) for a less realistic response. The Law Commission's Draft Criminal Law Bill, 1993 cl 29.6 'would allow the defence even where the defendant had ample recourse to official protection as long as he believes, however unreasonably, that the protection would prove ineffective'.

An immediacy requirement, albeit interpreted with a degree of generosity, appears then to be intrinsic to the moral underpinnings of duress. The political and moral underpinnings of self defence also imply immediacy. At the moral level we distinguish between action taken in response to an attack, or threatened attack, and angry aggression.[9] At the political level the privilege afforded by self defence to 'take the law into our own hands' must be a privilege which is consistent with the generalised subjection of individuals to governance by rules. It would not be if respect for autonomy allowed us to take strategic decisions to oppose non-existent or uncrystallised threats with violence or engage in angry retaliation.

Restricting the parameters of self defence in this way exposes a problem for criminal justice comparable to that obtaining for duress, in that it leaves something of a moral hole in the structure of defences. The way we react, and can be expected to react, to danger is heavily determined by context and sometimes context may explode the easy distinction between retaliation and defensive action and between pre-emptive-defensive and aggressive action. This is most apparent in cases involving domestic cumulative violence where rules governing immediacy in self defence have come under particular strain. Numerous studies of the realities of domestic abuse indicate that victims may find themselves in positions where they cannot escape or where escape would be dangerous and that this inability to escape may affect what is realistic to expect of the victim by way of self protection.[10] In such circumstances the victim 'may have to strike when the chance arises, rather than waiting until it is too late'.[11] It may thus be 'necessary' to attack an abuser who is asleep or drunk,[12] but who has threatened violence when he awakes.[13]

---

[9] Aileen McColgan, 'In Defence of Battered Women who Kill' (1993) 13 *OJLS* 508, 517–8; id (2000) *Women Under the Law. The False Promise of Human Rights* (Pearson, Essex, 2000), 200 contends for a less rigid application of the proximity requirement.

[10] See for example M Mahoney 'Legal Images of Battered Women: Redefining the Issue of Separation', 90 *Mich L Rev* 1; M Wilson and M Daly, 'Till Death Do Us Part' in J Radford and DEH Russell (eds), *Femicide. The Politics of Woman Killing* (Open University Press, Buckingham, 1992); and generally F Kaganas, 'Domestic Homicide, Gender and the Expert' in A Bainham, S Day Sclater and M Richards (eds), *Body Lore and Laws* (Hart Publishing, Oxford, 2001).

[11] A McColgan, *Women Under the Law. The False Promise of Human Rights*, 200.

[12] See *People v Diaz* 2714 Supreme Ct Bronx Co New York (1983) cited in McColgan, 'In Defence of Battered Women who Kill'.

[13] McColgan, 'In Defence of Battered Women who Kill', 519; McColgan, *Women Under the Law*, 205. See also *State of Arizona v Buggs* 167 Ariz 333, 806 P 2d 1381 (1991).

Canadian courts, in particular, showing a realistic understanding of the realities of domestic abuse have interpreted the immediacy requirement with a substantial degree of flexibility. In one case the judge observed that to require a battered woman to 'wait until the physical attack is "underway" before her apprehensions can be validated by law would be . . . tantamount to sentencing her to "murder by instalment" '.[14] In England there are also indications that doctrine has been loosened up so as to allow imminence rather than immediacy of threat to ground legitimate defensive action, but so far there has been no suggestion that it will permit the kind of pre-emptive attacks just suggested. Domestic courts have shown flexibility in two distinct situations. First, where pre-emptive action is taken which falls short of the actual deployment of force. So arming oneself with petrol bombs[15] or threatening to kill someone[16] may be legitimate defensive action in the face of a future threat of violence. Second, in cases of law enforcement where aggressive action is taken to prevent the probable commission of future offences.[17] Such cases illustrate the crucial organisational role played by the defence templates in keeping the defences themselves 'honest'. Given the obvious potential for abuse in contexts involving agents of the state collective interests are unlikely to be advanced by a general weakening of the immediacy requirement. If this leaves undeniable moral gaps in areas such as domestic violence these can be appropriately plugged by creating discrete defences of impaired rule-following capacity for those who 'take the law into their own hands' in the face of will-sapping cumulative abuse.[18]

Self-defence no less than duress requires then the 'one-off' emergency taking place in circumstances where we cannot rely upon the state to protect us and where no threat to the rule of law is posed by the defendant taking unilateral action.[19] Does the same reasoning hold for necessity? It is notable that the American Model Penal Code has no immediacy or imminent risk requirement. Except where the legislative

[14] *Lavallee v The Queen* (1990) 55 CCC (3d) 97 at 883.

[15] *A-G's Reference (no 2 of 1983)* [1984] 1 All ER 988; *Fegan* [1972] NI 80.

[16] *Cousins*, above n 7.

[17] For elaboration see AJ Ashworth, 'The European Convention and the Criminal Law' in *The Human Rights Act and the Criminal Justice and Regulatory Process* (1999) Cambridge Centre for Public Law.

[18] For example defences of temporary mental instability. For discussion see S Morse, 'Diminished Capacity' in Shute *et al* (eds), *Action and Value in Criminal Law* (Clarendon Press, Oxford, 1993), 239.

[19] J Horder, 'The Irrelevance of Motive in Criminal Law' in J Horder (ed), *Oxford Essays in Jurisprudence* (Clarendon Press, Oxford, 2000), 174 179–80.

context indicates otherwise conduct which the actor believes to be necessary to avoid a harm or evil to himself or to another is justifiable, provided that the harm or evil sought to be avoided by such conduct is greater than that sought to be prevented by the law defining the offence charged.[20] The obvious problem posed by this formulation , which is compounded by the priority given to the actor's own beliefs, is the threat it offers to basic rule of law values—be guided by what the law requires and not one's own personal assessment of what the situation demands. No one can blame the victims of emergencies acting in the best way possible to allay the threat of harm. But where there is no immediate necessity the individual must allow himself to be guided by society's *ex ante* collective decisions. These tell us, for example, that being homeless is neither justification nor excuse for trespassing in an unoccupied house.[21] We may disagree, as we may well be disposed to if we are homeless ourselves, but we must be guided by the law's rather than our own ideas of the guiding principles obtaining in a given predicament. In cases of immediate necessity, however, say being lost in a blizzard on a deserted mountain, the nature of the emergency sets necessary moral and political limits on the applicability of the defence. The individual reacting to a one-off emergency does not appoint himself as a legislator in his own cause, his conduct has no implications for future cases, nor indeed is he morally blameworthy if he acts reasonably to allay an imminent threat of death from exposure.[22]

It is inevitable, then, that necessity's core cases do involve one-off emergencies of a character similar to private defence. The actor pushes the victim out of the way of the oncoming car, breaks the speed limit to get a pregnant wife to hospital, throws cargo from a ship which would otherwise sink, moors his boat in another's dock in the teeth of a storm. In domestic doctrine, subject to one exception, conditions of necessity have been recognised as a defence only within the somewhat artificial limits imposed by duress of circumstances which requires, as in the lost mountaineer example, the actor to act to avoid an immediate threat of death or serious bodily harm. The exception is in medical cases. Of central importance here, at least in theory, is that the person acted against is a beneficiary rather than a victim of the action which renders less problematic the fact that the action is in notional violation of a rule designed

---

[20] By Article 3.02.
[21] *Southwark LBC v Williams* [1971] Ch 734.
[22] J Horder, above n 19.

to protect and vindicate individual interests.[23] Moreover, in such cases doctors have the opportunity of seeking declarations of legality in cases where a proposed course of action is not unambiguously in the patient's interests.' Unfortunately, perhaps, although doctors have the opportunity to seek *ex ante* guidance they are not bound to. This may not be unduly troubling in the standard case of doctors acting in their patient's clinical interests. But outside such core cases there is reason to be less sanguine where medical interventions have the capacity to compromise a patients fundamental rights, say to privacy and/or autonomy. Even judges are not immune from the tendency sometimes to view a patient's best interests through the evaluative lens of the carer.[24]

Proportionality

Having concluded that the defendant was or may been acting under conditions of self-defence, duress or necessity the template requires consideration of whether the amount of force used was or may have been reasonable in the sense of being proportionate to the interests threatened.[25] The proportionality requirement in necessity is once again intrinsic to its function which is the advancement of collective interests. This is most obvious in necessity's classical utilitarian form which balances on a cost/benefit basis the social harm which will result if the rule were honoured against that which will result if it were not. However, it should be noted that while proportionality on a lesser of two evils basis is necessary it is not in itself enough to constitute the justification. This is because of the manner in which the pursuit of utility inevitably comes into conflict with respect for individual rights.[26] A cost/benefit analysis can be used to justify killing, harming or torturing innocent human beings if this would advance collective interests. This is compatible neither with the principle of the sanctity of human life nor with a respect for individual autonomy. Versions have therefore

[23] This qualification, though central to the normal justificatory rationale of necessity, has recently been sidestepped. See *Re A (conjoined twins)* [2000] 4 All ER 961.

[24] Cf *F v W. Berkshire Health Authority* [1989] 2 All ER 545; *R v Bournewood Community and Mental Health NHS Trust* [1998] 3 All ER 28; *Re Y (Mental Patient Bone Marrow Donation)* [1997] *Fam* 110 for examples of how the best interests of the patient can be reconstructed in this way. These issues are explored in Cicca, 'Sterilising the Intellectually Disabled: The Approach of the High Court of Australia in *Department of Health v JWB and SMB*' (1993) *Med LR* 186.

[25] See G Fletcher, *Rethinking Criminal Law*, 870–5.

[26] S Gardner, 'Necessity's Newest Inventions' [1991] 11 *OJLS* 125.

been produced to counter such excesses. In particular, a qualification may be introduced to ensure that the cost/benefit calculation cannot operate to trade off (unequal) harms, for example one death to save two lives, but only to trade off unequal interests, say minor injury to prevent major injury. Even with this qualification, however, a utilitarian calculation is capable of justifying the victimisation of innocent people. It could justify, for example, coerced blood transfusions or kidney transplants to save a patient's life.[27] One way of meeting this objection in cases involving direct action taken against the interests of another is to require the interest attacked to be both hierarchically inferior and of a different nature than that advanced. Requiring all inferior interests to yield to superior interests in cases of conflict would, arguably, be quite consistent with a deep commitment to individual rights and well-being. Property rights, for example, should arguably yield to personal rights since they are only there in the first place to make 'life worth living'. Their purpose is not to provide absolute protection to property, but to allow us to live our lives free from a potentially devastating obstacle to living an autonomous life, namely the denial or usurpation of the fruits of ownership by others. Under this approach, it would be justifiable to infringe A's property interest to advance B's personal interest but not vice versa. Neither would it be justifiable to infringe a personal interest to advance another personal interest, say to kill or torture one person, to save the life of ten.

As I will later suggest where direct attacks are not involved but harm prevention is the reason for acting a proportionality requirement does not need to be couched so restrictively. This is because action is easier to justify where its purpose is good and the harm wrought is incidental to rather than constitutive of the act concerned. A commitment to proportionality may possibly allow then third party interests of a similar nature to that advanced to be set back, as long as the set-back is an unavoidable **side effect** of that action rather than a direct attack on the autonomy of another using that other as means. In this latter respect the proposal shows some structural affinities with self-defence where the harm occasioned is incidental to rather than constitutive of the act and where, possibly in consequence, although proportionality of a kind is necessary it is not thought proper to insist upon a lesser of two evils

[27] See A Brudner, 'A Theory of Necessity' [1987] 7 *OJLS* 339, 358–65. It also ignores the fact that, sometimes, less harm may be done by sacrificing the **superior** interest. Cf A von Hirsch and N Jareborg, 'Gauging Criminal Harms: A Living Standards Analysis' (1991) 11 *OJLS* 1; A von Hirsch, *Censure and Criminal Sanctions* (Clarendon Press, Oxford, 1993), 30–2.

measure. So while the defender is generally permitted to kill if fatal force is necessary to prevent being killed herself, or raped or maimed she may not kill to defend her possessions, her home, or less serious interference with her physical interests even supposing this was the only means available to her.

What has not yet been considered is why self-defence carries any kind of proportionality requirement.[28] If, as seems likely, the defence is so constituted as to vindicate a general right to autonomy and freedom from unwarranted interference it is not immediately obvious why the victim of attack should need to look beyond that which is necessary to fulfil that aim. The necessary supposition here, reflected also in the organisational bifurcation of criminal law into regulatory (harm-preventing) and core (autonomy-sustaining) offences, is that autonomy is one among many interests protected by the criminal law. Accordingly, self-defence like other justificatory defences which accord individuals the permission to take 'the law into their own hands' must instantiate and give voice to the overall structure of values by which our system of criminal offences is ordered.[29] Those values include the respect accorded individual autonomy but also ultimately the sanctity of life,[30] and the general moral principle that hurting people is wrong. If consent is no defence to murder or duelling it is because society's moral values do not ultimately reduce to an uncomplicated respect for individual auto-nomy.[31] Likewise, what would it tell us about the hierarchy of values supporting criminal doctrine if fatal force could be used to repel an attack on property if not that property rights took priority over the value of human life? A defender must, therefore, look to matters other than her understandable desire to protect her interests against unjustified attack in settling upon the appropriate mode of response. She must balance the threat to her own autonomy and physical interests against the setback to the other's interests were that threat to be successfully repelled. An aggressor does not forfeit the protection of the criminal law entirely. His interests in life and bodily security are valued as highly as those of the

---

[28] For discussion see AJ Ashworth, 'Self Defence and the Right to Life' [1975] *Camb LJ* 272, 295 *et seq*; S Uniacke, *Permissible Killing: The Self-Defense Justification of Homicide* (CUP, Cambridge, 1994), 32–4.

[29] See discussion at p 136.

[30] This structuring is evident in the European Convention on Human Rights. For discussion see AJ Ashworth, 'The European Convention and the Criminal Law' in *The Human Rights Act and the Criminal Justice and Regulatory Process* (1999) Cambridge Centre for Public Law.

[31] W WIlson 'Consenting to Personal Injury: How Far Can You Go?' (1995) 1 *Contemporary Issues in Law* 45–65.

victim, but if all else fails, respect for his victim's interests permits the victim to put his interests before those who pose an unjust threat to the limited degree necessary to sustain the moral credentials of the criminal law—to support both the welfare and the autonomy of its members.[32]

In theory, therefore, proportionality of response is as central to justifying self defence as it is to action undertaken under conditions of necessity. What level of response is permitted is a question of balance rather than absolutes and self defence, like necessity, strikes that balance in a manner appropriate for its own specialised moral agenda, here supporting individual autonomy. Perhaps it is understandable then that the balance of convenience in establishing the defence generally tends to favour the defender.[33]

Duress has no explicit proportionality requirement.[34] Recent statements both in duress by threats and in the developing field of duress of circumstances, however, confirm the view that proportionality of response is central to duress and that the death or serious injury requirement marks the limits of proportionality in domestic law. In *Harris* it was said that duress of circumstances requires the court 'to look at all the circumstances in deciding if the respondent had acted reasonably and proportionately to avoid threat of death or serious injury . . . The potential evil of the suspected robbers escaping had to be balanced against the evil of a serious collision.'[35] Lord Hailsham in *Howe* said that duress by threats requires the coerced choice to be such that the defendant 'may reasonably regard as the lesser of two evils'.[36] Coercion works in other words not because the choice taken is the

---

[32] See G Fletcher, *Rethinking Criminal Law*, 870–5; For versions of the forfeiture analysis of self defence see Judith Jarvis Thomson , 'Self-Defense' (1991) 20 *Phil & Pub Aff* 283; S Uniacke, (1994), ch 6.

[33] The Model Penal Code states that the use of force is justifiable when the actor believes that such force is immediately necessary for the purpose of protecting himself against the use of unlawful force. See generally G Fletcher, *Rethinking Criminal Law*, ch 10. In England the test is less defender-friendly way but nevertheless the question of reasonableness of response is determined with some sensitivity to the defender's own assessment of his predicament.

[34] KJM Smith, 'Duress and Steadfastness' (1999) *Crim LR* 363, 373–4. A balancing of harms approach which would allow the defendant a defence wherever the harm avoided was greater than the harm inflicted has been repeatedly rejected. See *Graham; Hudson and Taylor* [1971] 2 QB 202: *Lynch*; See Law Commission Working Paper No 55, Defences of General Application (1974), paras 16–17. The Model Penal Code explicitly adopts a balance of harms approach. s 2.09 1. Some American cases do not always adhere strictly to the approach. cf LaFave and Scott, *Criminal Law* (West, St Pauls, 1978), 379.

[35] *Harris* [1995] 1 Cr App R 170; KJM Smith above n 34 at 368.

[36] *Howe* (1987) 1 ALL ER 771, at 782, per Lord Hailsham.

lesser of two evils—if it were we would be dealing with a case of necessity—but because from the defendant's point of view and others who may be caught in his predicament it certainly seems to be. The apparent basis to the defendant's claim to escape liability is that since reasonable people would have acted similarly, it does not merit blame. However, this analysis might be questioned in the light of the widespread death or serious injury requirement in duress. After all, it may be thought that any harm is proportionate if the threat is enough to make the reasonable person do as the accused did. This adds some substance to the competing view that it is not the reasonableness of the defendant's reaction to coercion which excuses but rather the sheer futility and/or moral impropriety of demanding an impossible sacrifice.[37]

DIFFERENTIATING DURESS, NECESSITY AND SELF-DEFENCE

With harm prevention at their core and a common template it may perhaps be assumed that wherever a person acts reasonably and proportionately to prevent the set-back of interests a defence is available and it does not much matter which one. But this is incorrect. The defences are driven by different moral agendas. Horder, adopting an analysis proposed by Suzanne Uniacke, describes these as follows: In duress the cost of conformity to law is having to make an unreasonable personal sacrifice. In necessity the cost of not acting in a way which may involve wrongdoing is a yet greater evil or harm, rendering it morally imperative to act in that fashion. In self defence legal permission is granted to a person to take necessary and proportionate steps to resist, repel or ward off an unjust threat posed by another person.[38]

Specifying these agendas allows us some insight into the potential scope of each defence, and also its limits, since they dictate the doctrinal differences bounded by the overall template. So, the supposed absence of an immediacy requirement in necessity is no doctrinal aberration. This is most apparent in the specialised context of medicine, where doctors acting in their patients' best interests are required to minister to their patients' clinical interests on a pre-emptive as well as

---

[37] See J Dressler, 'Exegesis of the Law of Duress: Justifying the Excuse and Searching for its Proper Limits' (1989) 62 *S Cal L Rev* 1331.

[38] S Uniacke, *Permissible Killing*, 177–89; J Horder, 'Self Defence, Necessity and Duress' [1998] *Can J of Law and Juris* 143.

reactive basis. It reflects the broad moral agenda of necessity which is to underwrite the desirability that individuals do what they can to prevent harm befalling others. Again while proportionality of response is central to all three defences the level of response permitted varies with the moral agenda of the respective defences. Necessity requires that action taken must be unambiguously for the best if society's *ex ante* normative guidance is to be overridden and if individual rights are to be protected from the routine claims of social utility. Duress requires the sacrifice demanded of the victim (typically death or serious injury) be of such a high order that expecting obedience would be futile before the rights of innocent people can excusably be compromised. Moreover, if the undesirability of people having to make such an unwonted sacrifice lies at the heart of the defence it makes (some) sense that any sacrifice demanded of the innocent third party be unambiguously less than that demanded of the equally innocent victim of coercion. Self defence strikes the balance in a manner appropriate for its moral agenda which is the permissibility of resisting an unjustified attack. By posing an unjust threat the aggressor forfeits his right to be treated with concern and respect equal to that of the defender.[39] A notable effect of this is that by contrast with the other two defences, self-defence is **universally** recognised as capable of justifying the use of lethal force.[40]

At a broad theoretical level, while self defence and necessity operate as justifications, duress paradigmatically operates as an excuse. This bears witness to the moral premise that taking direct action against the interests of an innocent person for reasons unconnected with the advancement of goods we all have in common cannot be justified, even if it may be excused. So, if A threatens B with death unless B stabs C any reaction by B involving the use of force can only be justified if it is force used to disable the threat (ie force used against A) and can be excused at best if it is in capitulation to the threat (ie force used against C).[41] This is, at a common sense level, because C is an innocent as regards B and at a more analytical level it is because B's use of force is not adopted for the purpose of neutralising the threat (a socially

---

[39] Judith Jarvis Thomson, 'Self-Defense' (1991) 20 *Phil & Pub Aff* 283; S Uniacke, *ibid*, 206 *et seq*.

[40] Although some qualification must be offered to this in the light of Article 2 of the European Convention. For elaboration see AJ Ashworth, 'The European Convention and the Criminal Law' in *The Human Rights Act and the Criminal Justice and Regulatory Process* (1999) Cambridge Centre for Public Law.

[41] Cf J Horder, above n 38, 149–50.

acceptable and valued reaction) but is a capitulation to it (an unacceptable but possibly excusable reaction). Neutralising unjust threats are rightly permitted. Capitulating to them rightly are discouraged. As we say, 'two wrongs do not make a right'.

Important doctrinal consequences for the three defences attend their separation into justifications and excuses. Since any assistance given to a person acting in a justified fashion is also justified A can lawfully help B to resist C's unjustified threat or throw overboard C's cargo to prevent the sinking of a ship. In theory, A would not be acting lawfully if B's action against C in both cases was the result of coercion.[42] Again, it is generally supposed that resisting justified action must itself be unjustified. So B cannot, with justification, resist A's use of (reasonable) force, although he may be excused if he was acting under a well-grounded belief that A was acting unlawfully. Fletcher argues that the same principle applies to action taken under conditions of necessity so that if jettisoning A's cargo to lighten a sinking vessel is justified then it must follow that such action cannot lawfully be resisted.[43] He cites cases in the field of tort in support. In *Ploof v Putnam*, for example, the owner of a dock was held liable in damages for the loss of a ship which he had refused a licence to moor during a storm.[44] The evident basis for the decision is that the dock owner was not justified in resisting a necessary intrusion. It is, however, possible to mount an argument against this decision and the logic underpinning it. Self-defence, by contrast with necessity, is centred in the actor being legally permitted to use force against unjust attacks. The corollary of this is that by dint of his unjustified conduct an aggressor forfeits his usual rights to remain free from interference and thus to defend himself through resistance. The defence would make no sense without such a corollary. It would in effect legislate an indefinite escalation of violence. Such reasoning does not apply under conditions of necessity where the basis of the justification is the desirability that the other's interest should be **overridden**, which carries no necessary implication that those rights are **forfeited**. Another American case supports this analysis. In *Vincent v Lake Eyrie Trans. Co* a dock owner was able to recover damages

---

[42] In theory, because it is not universally accepted that the lawfulness of rendering assistance to another performing the *actus reus* of an offence hangs upon whether performing the *actus reus* is itself lawful by virtue of being justified. For an alternative view see ch 7.

[43] G Fletcher, *Rethinking Criminal Law*, 759–62.

[44] 81 VT. 471, 71 A. 188 (1908).

against the owner of a boat which had been permitted to moor and which subsequently had caused damage to the dock.[45] Fletcher prefers to analyse the case simply as a qualification of the (in his view correct) decision in *Ploof v Putnam* entitling properly compliant dock owners to compensation if the sacrifice demanded of them causes damage.[46] Another and more plausible way of understanding *Vincent* is that it underlines the fact that the dock owners' rights are not forfeited, merely capable of being overridden. It is a natural corollary of the fact that the dock owner's rights are (lawfully) overridden that the person who benefits restores to the owner what the latter loses as a consequence. While it may be morally undesirable to defend personal interests under conditions of necessity those conditions do not strip the resister of his legal rights, whether to resist the intrusion or claim damages if his interests are thereby harmed.

Such differentiated doctrinal consequences renders it important to be able to chart with precision the respective contours of the defences of reasonable reaction. Once again, these are not self-evident.

NECESSITY AND SELF-DEFENCE

The origins of self-defence were based in an early recognition that executing someone for murder was unfair if the killer was acting to save his own life.[47] The well understood human inclination to fight for survival later came to be seen as excusing homicide although the action taken was against an innocent rather than an aggressor. So, in Bacon's famous hypothetical the instinct for self-preservation was thought to excuse a person, struggling to survive following a shipwreck, forcing another from the surviving plank. Later, self-defence was understood as capable of negating the basic core of wrongdoing—unjustified aggression— which crimes of violence express. Even intentional homicide may be justifiable if the circumstances dictate. Necessity, whose justificatory credentials emphasise the desirability of advancing collective interests rather than the acceptability of vindicating individual autonomy, underwent no such formal recognition, least of all in cases of murder. In *Dudley and Stephens,* where shipwrecked sailors killed and ate a cabin boy after several days without food, the Court of Queens Bench said

---

[45] 109 Minn, 456, 124 N.W. 221 (1910).

[46] G Fletcher, *Rethinking Criminal Law*, 761.

[47] See generally G Fletcher, *ibid*, 856–60; S Uniacke, *Permissible Killing*, 34 *et seq*.

quite reasonably that there was no principle of law which entitled a person to take the life of an innocent to save his own life.[48] This left unaddressed the possibility, envisaged in Bacon's hypothetical, that such action might nevertheless be excused. It also ignored the broader self-evident truth that acting as the letter of the law requires may under appropriate conditions oppose the very values which the law sustains. One way of understanding the drive towards defences such as necessity is to see it as adding flesh to the moral principles underlying offences. Sometimes the reasons in favour of committing a prima facie act of wrongdoing are so compelling that the only thing certain is that some doctrinal method should and will be found to ensure just treatment.[49]

Hitherto case law has resisted a rational exposition of the principles by which necessity may justify our actions. Outside the field of medicine, necessity has been recognised only in its excuse form of duress of circumstances. Peter Glazebrook has demonstrated how necessity operating as a justification has, however, long existed in an inchoate form.[50] The cases of *Steane* and *Adams* are well known illustrations of how, in cases of morally justified action, the courts have traditionally sought to marry moral and legal principles in an uneasy accommodation.[51] In each of the above cases the courts conceived of the respective defendant doctors as lacking the basic criminal intention necessary to sustain criminal liability. At any level other than analytical precision this makes undeniable sense. It is a moral untruth to say, for example, that a doctor exercising himself to relieve pain may intend to kill his patient.[52] As explained earlier, however, doctrinal hygiene discourages defining intention in this motive-sensitive fashion. It requires justifying defences which are superimposed onto the basic conditions of liability. In this way the criminal law's purposes can be rationally discharged ensuring that it is the law's own values rather than the values of individual subjects which dictate the content of our legal obligations.[53]

[48] (1884) 14 QBD 273.

[49] See generally P Glazebrook 'The Necessity Plea in English Criminal Law' [1972] *CLJ* 87.

[50] *Ibid*; also 'Structuring the Criminal Code' in AP Simester and ATH Smith (eds), *Harm and Culpability* (Clarendon Press, Oxford, 1996), 196.

[51] For further discussion see ch 6.

[52] AR White, *Misleading Cases* (Clarendon, Oxford, 1991), 57–8; W Wilson and KJM Smith, 'Necessity and the Doctors Dilemma' [1995] *Med L International*; AJ Ashworth, 'Good Intentions' in AP Simester and ATH Smith (eds), *Harm and Culpability*, 173.

[53] J Horder, 'The Irrelevance of Motive in Criminal Law' in J Horder (ed), *Oxford Essays in Jurisprudence* (OUP, Oxford, 2000), 174.

Setting the Limits

The major practical concern posed by self-defence and necessity is par-celling up their respective spheres of operation so as to ensure that whatever it is which justifies us in taking action against the interests of others is properly catered for by defence doctrine. Consider, for exam-ple, a routine 'doctor's dilemma'.

Case 1

A is a doctor in a hospital which has only one life support machine, at presently benefiting patient X. He transfers the machine from patient X, who is failing, life support notwithstanding, to patient Y whose con-dition is such that life support will probably enable him to make a full recovery.

Transferring scarce medical facilities is obviously a 'good thing' and, where appropriately motivated, should not incur criminal liability whatever the consequence for the patient at the wrong end of the trans-fer. But how do we account for this? It is obviously not a case of self defence or defence of others. X is not unjustly attacking or threatening Y. Is it then a case of necessity? If it is, justifying the transfer seems to require resort to consequentialist arguments.[54] But the moral justifica-tion needs more than a satisfactory outcome of the felicific calculus. Somehow our moral intuition that scarce medical resources should be allocated to those most likely to profit needs to be voiced in such a way as to ensure that respect for the sanctity of life is the winner rather than the loser in any doctrinal response. We need to be assured, in other words, that the reasons for transferring the life support machine from one patient to another does honour to the reasons why such machines are there in the first place—as human kind's compassionate attempt to minimise the suffering of its members.

Setting limits is of concern because of the different basis upon which the two defences are ordered. Necessity demands that we act for the best—assessed from the collective point of view and justifies our action when we do. Self-defence, however, permits us to put our own interests

---

[54] See Fletcher, *Rethinking Criminal Law*, 144 'When probability factors are included in assessing the competing interests it is clear the defendant engages in conduct with a higher expected loss (near certain death) that expected gain (a probability of death).'

first—to kill, if need be, to protect ourselves from unjustified attack. Cases showing features of both necessity and self defence pose problems, therefore, as it will profit a person, or somebody acting on his behalf, who does nothing more than that which is immediately necessary to save the former from harm, to be able to present the case as one of self defence.

The problems posed by conduct at the interface of self-defence and necessity were encountered in graphic form in the well publicised case of Mary and Jodie, the conjoined twins.[55] An operation was needed to save the life of Jodie whose heart was being put under unsustainable strain by the fact that her sister Mary's own blood supply depended upon it, her own heart being inoperative. The issue raised was whether an operation to separate the two could be lawful when the inevitable side effect of maximising the chance of survival of the stronger of the two was the death of the weaker. At first blush the operation was unlawful, constituting murder since, although designed to benefit Jodie, it was certain to kill Mary and there was no compensatory facet of the operation which might, from Mary's self-interested point of view, make that worthwhile and therefore a clearly justified clinical intervention. Nevertheless the moral intuition of many favoured the operation.

A straightforward utilitarian calculation was the most usual justification encountered. It is better for Mary to die now than for them both to die later. But this ignores a basic truth about the way necessity is organised at least in domestic doctrine. It is not the case that one patient can be killed in order to save another. A doctor cannot say remove the heart, liver and kidneys of a living patient, although four might live at the expense of only one. The basic justification for medical intervention appears then paradoxically for traditional theory to be anti-utilitarian. It is autonomy led. Autonomy places a limit on what doctors can do and constitutes the basic framework for justifying what they do. Doctors act lawfully in advancing a patient's clinical interests with the patient's consent and may, so long as the boundaries of social acceptability are not breached, equally be acting lawfully in compromising those interests with the patient's consent . The corollary is that doctors cannot act for their patient's benefit in the absence of consent—a doctor is not justified in performing a life-saving amputation on a patient's gangrenous leg if this is contrary to the known wishes of the patient. *A fortiori* he cannot

---

[55] [2000] 4 All ER 961.

also harm their patient in the interests of another patient unless he consents. He cannot even cause minor harm for major benefit, say by performing a coerced blood transfusion.[56]

The Limits of Self-Defence

An obvious escape route from this theoretical *cul de sac* is to reconstitute the doctor's dilemma as one of self-defence rather than necessity. This creates a basis for action which does not require Mary's interests to be treated with concern and respect equal to that of Jodie.

This option was rejected in *Re A*. Only Ward LJ was able to analyse the case as one of 'quasi' self-defence since Mary was threatening the life of Jodie. It is clear, however, that the case of Jodie and Mary has little to do with the internal moral agenda of self-defence. While representing a fatal threat to Jodie, Mary did not actually constitute or pose that threat.[57] The threat she represented was ordained by nature rather than anything by way of dangerous conduct attributable to Mary. She had not say managed to hook herself up to Jodie as a means of parasitising on her or had decided to take poison thus threatening the life of both. The implications are that the operation cannot be justified because it is in Jodie's self-interest. It can only be justified on the basis of a moral imperative to advance the cause of life in general.

This analysis may be thought over elaborate given that, as Brooke LJ in pointed out in his judgment,[58] self-defence suggests action taken to resist a culpable act of aggression, which was clearly not present in *Re A*. This is not uncontroversially the case, however. There is widespread agreement that the right to take defensive action is a right to take action against wrongful aggression, whether or not it is also culpable. This would permit defensive action taken against some aggressors lacking responsibility such as infants and the insane.[59] What is less clear is

---

[56] Subject only to the possibility, discussed earlier, that considerations of utility may justify confounding interests where they are both hierarchically inferior and of a different nature to those to be advanced (eg committing theft/criminal damage justified as a life-saving measure). For discussion see W Wilson, *Criminal Law: Doctrine and Theory* (Longmans, London, 1998), 216–7, 280–5.

[57] At 1016. For discussion of self-defence as limited to cases of 'unjust threats' see J Horder, *Oxford Essays in Jurisprudence*, 153–5.

[58] At 1067.

[59] See for example G Fletcher, *Rethinking Criminal Law*, 869–70; S Kadish, 'Respect for Life and Regard for Rights in the Criminal Law' in *Blame and Punishment* (Macmillan, New York, 1987) S Uniacke, *Permissible Killing*, 177–89; J Horder, *Oxford Essays in Jurisprudence*, 144–6.

whether the right to defend oneself is a right arising by virtue of the defence of necessity or that of self-defence. This is of key doctrinal concern not least because, as explained above, the matter of proportionality of response stands to be assessed more favourably to the defender under self-defence than under necessity. Assuming the vindication of autonomy is the defence rationale a person faced with an uplifted knife which he believes is probably bound for his abdomen must surely be permitted to 'get in first' with his own knife in a 'defensive' thrust to the heart.[60] If, by reason of the attacker's lack of culpability, the defender is forced to leave the protective doctrinal shield of self-defence for that of necessity he must then rely on the social desirability of his defensive action which inevitably will lend more prominence to the interests of the attacker and the severity of the threat the latter represented.

What is also unclear is whether, assuming self-defence is the appropriate defence in all cases of wrongful aggression, it may not extend still further to permit defensive action against all unjust threats. A quite plausible case can be made that self-defence is not limited to cases of wrongful and culpable aggression but vindicates a more general permission to take action for purposes of self-preservation.[61] This view would instantiate a higher level of coherence between the norms governing offences and defences. The overall structure tells us that to the extent that violence unjustifiably attacks personal autonomy it is unlawful. To the extent that it secures (self-defence) or vindicates (consent) personal autonomy it is within limits lawful. This leads quite naturally to the conclusion that the moral acceptability of using force in self-defence does not vary with the normative status of the aggressor. Shifting the focus from the attitude of the attacker to the predicament of the defender reflects common sense understandings operative in social life generally which are embedded in its linguistic forms. We make no analytical distinction between fending off a dangerous cricket delivery, fending off an (over) friendly dog, and fending off/defending ourselves against a sociopath's hostile attack. Each action is defensive in character as is indicated in the action verb used to describe it—'fending off'.

Where everyday usage parts company with its juridical counterpart is that the former treats the question as to whether action is defensive as a

---

[60] See R Christopher, 'Self Defense and Objectivity '[1998] *Buffalo Crim LR* 537 generally.
[61] See G Fletcher, above n 59. S Kadish, above n 59, 119–122; S Uniacke, *Permissible Killing*, ch 5.

purely empirical matter. For example, a batsman is acting defensively for the purpose of the laws of cricket wherever action is taken for the purpose of avoiding harm.[62] He may be acting defensively, therefore, although there is absolutely no objective reason for her doing so. She may experience a sudden apprehension that the next ball will be a bouncer and so duck without first checking to see if her apprehension were justified. In the juridical setting, by contrast, whether a person is acting defensively is a matter of normative evaluation. It must be an acceptable response. This reflects the fact that the actor is claiming that something he is doing which is not usually permitted (using force against another human being) is in fact permitted. Jeremy Horder, in adopting Suzanne Uniacke's analysis of self-defence,[63] thus characterises defensive action as action which is necessary and proportionate to ward off an 'unjust threat' and a threat is unjust where it is 'posed for no objective justificatory moral reason'. So, A can avail himself of the defence wherever the threat posed is undeserved, whether or not it takes the form of unlawful aggression. But he cannot avail himself of self-defence if the threat is deserved, say if he is acting to resist a lawful arrest by B or where B is using force to counter the unjustified threat that A himself was posing to C as where A was trying to kill C. In such cases B is not permitted to use force since the force opposed is itself permitted. The point of limiting defensive action to cases of warding off 'unjust' threats is to sustain the normative credentials of self-defence which is to permit direct action to be taken against the interests of another only to sustain the point of coercive law itself, namely to facilitate the mutual existence and co-operation of autonomous individuals. In the core case of self-defence, namely culpable aggression, the aggressor, by virtue of his attack on the autonomy of the defender, attacks also society's core value. By so doing he is readily analysable as having forfeited his right to be treated with concern and respect equal to that of the defender since society values defensive before aggressive conduct when the two collide. This is not to say, for example, that in a toss up between the defender's and the aggressor's life the latter forfeits his right to life. This stays intact. What he forfeits, and must forfeit if individuals are to be proof against aggression, is his right to life overriding the corresponding right of the defender.[64]

---

[62]   That she is acting defensively may have certain important consequences for the batter such as the right to score a run if the ball hits the body rather than the bat.

[63]   S Uniacke, *Permissible Killing*, ch 5.

[64]   G Fletcher, *Rethinking Criminal Law*, 857–8; See also Judith Jarvis Thomson, 'Self-Defense' (1991) 20 *Phil & Pub Aff* 283.

Approaching self defence from the normative position of the person seeking to justify his use of force (is he defending himself against an unjust/undeserved threat?) rather than that of the person against whom force is directed (is he unjustifiably attacking?) means that conduct may be defensive even where there is no semblance of wrongdoing let alone culpability on the part of the other. So if A pushes B against C, C is acting in self-defence by fending off B although B does no wrong. *Vis a vis* C, B represents an unjust threat, that is one which is undeserved and unwarranted, although B does no wrong. If the same events occur on the ski slopes and in the split second available to him C can do no more than stick out his pointed ski poles on which B becomes impaled the same analysis follows.[65] If his action is necessary and proportionate to ward off a threat posed to C by B, as it may well be if C was standing near a precipice , it is justified.

A serious objection can be posted to this 'unjust threat' rationale of self-defence, namely that it lacks a compelling account of why the permissible **level of response** should be tailored to the moral agenda of self-defence rather than necessity. The former, it will be remembered allows a defender to use more force than that to which he is subject. In the case of non-culpable aggressors such as the insane there is a ready explanation, namely that what justifies the forfeiture of the innocent aggressor's right to be treated with equal concern and respect is that he is, irrespective of any culpability on his part, committing a wrong against the defender. This justifies the cancellation of the defender's usual obligation not to secure his interests through the use of violence, and justifies a level of response other than a lesser of two evils basis, as a vindication of his own status as a protected person. The criminal law offers us protection against wrongdoing rather than against harm. When it is harm alone we are faced with, it is reasonable to suppose that we must look to matters other than our own self-interest in determining the appropriate level of response since there is no objectively validated basis for supposing that more concern is owing the autonomy and welfare of C than of B. We can accept that C's conduct is excusable by virtue of the fact that it is certainly necessary from his point of view, is designed for purely defensive purposes and that C cannot be expected to prefer his own sacrifice to that of B. But why should we go that extra step involved in holding that it is justified and permitted?

---

[65] This hypothetical is a reworking of one considered by R Nozick in *Anarchy State and Utopia* (1974), 34–5, considered by both Uniacke and Horder.

A related difficulty with this account concerns a paradox which presents itself in the case of those who, though innocent of any wrongdoing, are the objects of defensive action. If an unjust threat is one which is posed for no 'objective justificatory moral reason' and if, as so defined, unjust threats may be opposed by force the paradox concerns action taken under conditions of necessity. As explained earlier, under such conditions a person may with justification act in such a way as to present an objective threat of harm to an innocent person—say by seeking to destroy the latter's property for the purpose of creating a firebreak—and yet under such circumstances the innocent person would nevertheless also be permitted to resist the threat. If this is correct we need to qualify the notion that a person may not use force in self defence where the threat is posed for an 'objective justificatory moral reason'. The kind of just threat which one is not permitted to resist is one which is just in the sense that it is itself permitted by virtue of the conduct of he who would seek to use defensive force. Troublingly, however, even as so described, a just threat might well from the point of view of the person subjected to it be one against which he is rightly permitted to defend himself. Suppose, for example, B witnesses C extending his ski-poles towards him in his 'defensive' posture such that C no longer constitutes 'the soft cushion' he was counting on to interrupt his progress and is now a mortal threat. Would B not be permitted to get his 'defence in first' by impaling C on his own slightly longer pointed ski-poles, as a means of warding him off? It may be argued that C, being the first threatened, has the prior claim. But this rather specious means of evaluating the moral credentials of their respective actions presents a formidable analytical difficulty, namely that it is in fact C, rather than B, who first 'presents arms' and therefore from an objective point of view can appropriately be designated as the prior threat.[66] Although this is a theoretical problem dogging many accounts of self-defence,[67] it is particularly pertinent in an account which seeks to justify self-defence as a basis for defensive action taken not merely against wrongdoers but anyone who poses an undeserved threat to the defender.

Although there are very good reasons then for permitting defensive action against some who are innocent of both blame and wrongdoing, the implications of so doing should not be underestimated. Self defence

[66] See generally R Christopher, 'Self Defense and Objectivity '[1998] *Buffalo Crim LR* 537, 551–574.

[67] See Thomson, above n 64, 283–304; cf R Christopher; J Waldron, idem.

and necessity necessarily boast different notions of proportionality of response, and action permitted under self defence ostensibly cannot be resisted which would seem to create doctrinal dissonance, if not paradox, in the type of case described above where both parties can legitimately view each other as posing a threat necessitating defensive action.

The Limits of Necessity

If *Re A* is not a case of self-defence we are left with the problem posed earlier concerning the limits of necessity. It was suggested that those limits included the prioritisation of rights over utility, which explains both why a refusal of consent in medical cases overrides clinical need and why coerced organ transplants or blood transfusions are unlawful. If rights limit as well as drive the defence in this way, how is it possible to justify the victimisation of an innocent person for the benefit of another? Quite clearly this is not a case where the justification offered is that it serves the patient's best interests. It cannot be in Mary's best interests that her life is sacrificed for the benefit of Jodie.

In *Re A* Ward LJ adopted a solution implicit in the judgment of McNaghten J in *Bourne* where the doctor was, in effect, facing what might loosely be termed a double no-win emergency. The moral no-win was that, on the facts found, some 'body' was likely to die, the mother or the foetus. Whatever the doctor chose to do this was the prospect. The legal no-win was that if he chose to perform the abortion the law supposes he was guilty of the statutory offence. If he chose not to and the mother (and foetus) died he was guilty of manslaughter.[68] No rational system of law can incorporate rules which deprive a citizen of the ability to act lawfully whatever he/she chooses to do.[69] The juridical options in such a case would be either to cancel the doctor's duties altogether so that he is liable for the death of neither if he chooses to do nothing. Or more plausibly, given that the purpose of these rules is to affirm the value of life, it is to privilege the higher interest. Rights, freedoms and responsibilities are not hermetically sealed but interrelate and inform each other which is why crimes of recklessness are constituted

---

[68] *Bourne* [1939] 1 KB 687, at 693–4.

[69] For an extended analysis of the legality of 'impossible demands', see Lon Fuller, *The Morality of Law* (Yale University Press, New Haven, 1969).

only upon it being established that the accused had no good reason for taking the risk. Necessity fulfils a comparable role by offering a necessary legal escape route for those challenged by a conflict of duties. The 'necessity' then is not so much the moral imperative to infringe the primary rule as the legal imperative to afford the actor on the horns of a dilemma a legal escape route. In such circumstances the defendant's position must be supposed to transcend the normal scheme of the criminal law requiring him to choose to perform the duty which vindicates the higher interest. The choice facing the doctor is very different from the choice facing the victim of duress or duress of circumstances, taking it outside the realm of excuses. The latter is a coerced choice. The former, by contrast, can be analysed as a legal requirement.[70]

Although there are obvious reasons why a defence of necessity is required in legal no-win emergencies, there is, however, no obvious reason to limit the justification to such cases.[71] Consider the following variation of the well known hypothetical known as the trolley problem.[72]

Case 2

An aircraft is out of control and about to crash into a densely populated part of a city resulting in a huge loss of life. The pilot is dead in his seat. Adam, the air steward, in the time available, has only one option which is to press a special button in the cockpit which will eject him from the aircraft to safety and, after a twenty second time delay, explode the plane, killing the passengers but with a correspondingly reduced death toll.

The key point here is that whatever the law may say Adam may not do, it cannot help him to decide what it is which he may not do. It is something which can only be decided there and then on the basis of the information before him. How does one best honour innocent lives in a situation where, whatever one does, lives must be lost.[73] In this moral no-win one-off emergency, where the outcome is bound to be bad, it

---

[70] For discussion HLA Hart, *Concept of Law* (Clarendon Press, Oxford, 1961), ch 2.

[71] A Brudner, 'A Theory of Necessity' [1987] 7 *OJLS* 339; S Gardner, 'Necessity's Newest Inventions' [1991] 11 *OJLS* 125, 131–3.

[72] See JJ Thomson, 'Killing, Letting Die and the Trolley Problem' (1975–6) 59 *The Monist* 204.

[73] See Horder, 'The Irrelevance of Motive' in *Oxford Essays in Jurisprudence*, (2000) 157.

seems plausible that Adam, irrespective of any legal duty he may owe and irrespective of his understandable desire to save himself, is under a legally supported moral obligation to intervene to ensure the least worst outcome.

The second equally well-known case supporting the intuition that an actor may sometimes be justified in victimising an innocent arises out of the Herald of Free Enterprise Ferry disaster.[74] As the ferry was sinking fast a passenger, traumatised by the awful emergency, 'froze' on the staircase to safety, unable to move forward or back. Those behind him could only escape to safety if they dislodged him from the step and threw him into the water rising to engulf them. This is clearly not a straightforward case of self-defence since the frozen passenger does not constitute the threat, which is an external one, namely death by drowning. Rather, he sustains the conditions, without exacerbating them,[75] by which the threat may be actualised. While one can appreciate the analytical force in this analysis—would we wish to call it a case of self-defence if the passenger was not 'frozen' but unconscious or bound to a wheel chair?—it is a position which perhaps unduly emphasises matters which, from both frozen and blocked passengers' point of view at least, are of little moral consequence. It is a case whose moral force seems to derive from our intuition that people cannot be expected to sacrifice themselves for the good of others who present a threat to them. And make no mistake this is what the frozen passenger does, no less than the out of control skier against whom there are strong grounds, as has been suggested, for defensive action to be permitted.

Treating it as a case of necessity, by contrast, leaves this personal appeal untapped. Horder has proposed an analytical model by which conditions of necessity are evaluated on a casuistic basis designed to identify which facts happen, in a given case, to carry moral salience and which therefore might be expected to make a difference to our assessment of the reasonableness of the course of action adopted or proposed. He identifies three such features capable of generating a conclusion that action can and should be taken against the frozen passenger, although he poses no independent threat to the other passengers which would entitle them to take defensive action. The first, already discussed, is that the situation involves a one-off emergency

---

[74] See JC Smith, *Justification and Excuse in the Criminal Law* (Sweet & Maxwell, London, 1989), 73–8.
[75] Say by rocking the staircase, further imperilling the other's safety.

which calls, from the imperilled passenger's point of view, for immediate action. The one-off nature of the emergency deprives the latter of any plausible guidance in the form of norms of behaviour as to what should be done It is something which can only be decided there and then on the basis of the information before them. As such it has no implications for future cases and does not render the passenger a legislator in his own cause.[76]

The second feature is that it is easier to justify action directed against an innocent person, say the frozen passenger, if that person is subject to the conditions of his own threat. In such cases, his interest—which is the only countervailing consideration to the undeniable advantages which would attend his being dislodged—can no better be safeguarded by leaving him there than dislodging him. This is a strong ground for overriding his right not to suffer interference. The position would be otherwise if the person was not subject to the conditions of his own threat. For example, say the stricken ship had lodged on the bottom of a shallow harbour and the frozen passenger was, on his position on the staircase, able to access a pocket of air and thus breathe the very oxygen of which the others below were about to be deprived. There would be a clear moral value in leaving the frozen passenger undisturbed, namely to honour his innocent life. Not doing so would necessitate reliance upon consequentialist reasoning, prioritising collective interests before individual rights which, as explained earlier, runs counter to the principles by which the criminal law is organised.[77]

The third salient feature which might justify taking action not categorisable as defensive against V is perhaps the most telling. This is that V is 'standing in the way' of innocent persons whose only means of escape is to 'remove that person by a method which involves or entails killing them'.[78] Of what moral significance is it that the victim is 'standing in the way' of an actor's escape route? Horder's answer is that it enables the case to be distinguished from the taking of direct victimising action against someone as a means of securing one's own survival as occurred in *Dudley and Stephens*, where the cabin boy was used as

---

[76] 'The Irrelevance of Motive ' and see J Griffin, *Value Judgement* (OUP, Oxford, 1996), 98 *et seq*.

[77] Significantly, if the passenger were blocking the way out of self interest—say to conserve a scarce resource for himself, this would, on Horder's view, apparently change the passenger's normative position for the worse. He would now be part of the threat to which the others were subjected which would entitle them to use defensive force.

[78] J Horder, 'The Irrelevance of Motive', at 159.

a resource rather than simply removed from a position of threat. Beyond this he is careful not to say that this fact justifies the action taken only that it is clearly a less contentious basis for justifying direct action than using another as a 'resource'. Removing people who block an escape route does not involve exploiting another for one's own purposes. It is not undertaken with the intention of harming the other. And the bad consequence is an undesired and unavoidable side effect of an otherwise justified act of self/life preservation. There can be little argument that this is of huge moral significance. It is something which is done, and one presumes quite lawfully, on a routine basis when individuals crossing dangerous roads need to push slow-moving individuals in front of them to avoid encroaching cars.

JUSTIFYING SELF-PRESERVATION: NECESSITY AND DURESS

This casuistic method of uncovering the justificatory credentials of a given course of action has clear advantages over the attempt to produce an abstract organisational principle such as the lesser of evils approach of the Model Penal Code. The latter's enduring weakness, and probably the reason why it has rarely if ever been invoked successfully,[79] is that it is rarely able to identify what it is in any given case which allows us to say that the action proposed is the lesser of two evils and why ultimately this should matter.[80] In *Re A* the Court of Appeal showed themselves fully alert to this and embraced a comparably casuistic approach offering no general principle capable of providing guidance for future cases.[81] Here another salient feature was exposed, however, embracing an important normative dimension of the case of the frozen passenger. This is that the action by which the actor seeks to protect himself from harm is the self-same action which opposes itself to that of the other. If an innocent person can be victimised in an emergency simply because 'he stands in the way' this may well be because it is a case of putative necessity requiring action taken to be for 'the best'. But there may be another reason why this may be justified, namely that it is a simple instantiation of a broader principle, namely that people are not legally

---

[79] S Kadish, 'Fifty Years of Development in the Criminal Law' (1999) 87 *Cal LR*.

[80] For a general exploration of the strengths of casuistical reasoning in cases of moral dilemma arising under the common law see A Jonsen and S Toulmin, *The Abuse of Casuistry* (University of California Press, London, 1989) ch 16.

[81] See Ward LJ at 1018.

required to make unjustified sacrifices for the good of others. This in turn suggests that we are nearer the terrain of duress or self-defence than necessity.

The morally significant feature of the medical intervention was therefore that Mary's death was incidental to an act of healing, rather than the means by which such healing was to be achieved. Mary was not being used as a resource to advance Jodie's interests. This is an application of the so-called doctrine of double effect, another instantiation of the casuist's art which significantly was most famously exploited by Aquinas to solve the (then) problem of intentional killings in self-defence.[82] In its modern forms the doctrine holds that a (bad) outcome cannot be justified as a means to another (good) outcome. But it can be justified as an unpurposed side effect of action taken for a good outcome as long as there is no reasonable alternative to the action taken and the good outcome is in appropriate proportion to the bad.[83]

Analysed in this way the justifying reason proposed is nearer the moral terrain of self-defence rather than duress. Of the three judges deciding the case of Mary and Jodie only Robert Walker LJ considered this analysis as potentially determinative of the legality of the operation.[84] But it is noteworthy that the spokesperson for the surgeons involved in the separation insisted that the latter had done everything they could to prevent Mary dying when the nature of the conjunction (one heart for two blood supplies) meant that once the major arteries were severed nothing could be done to prevent it. Implicit in their own sense of justification, in other words, is that Mary's death was a tragic side effect of, rather than a necessary means to, securing the survival of Jodie.

Most other cases of protective/self-protective action falling outside the contours of self-defence or necessity involve personal moral justifications sufficient to raise an excuse but not a justification.[85] The excuse is duress of circumstances which kicks in to excuse those who would have to suffer an unreasonable personal sacrifice (death or serious injury) if they were to act in conformity to the law. So Bacon's mariner on the plank

---

[82] For discussion see A Jonsen and S Toulmin, above n 80, ch 11.

[83] See generally J Finnis, 'Intention and Side Effects' in RG Frey and CW Morris (eds), *Liability and Responsibility* (St Pauls, Minn, 1991), 32; S Uniacke, *Permissible Killing*, ch 4.

[84] 1068.

[85] In *Perka et al v The Queen* MacDonald J presented such cases as ones of personal necessity or duress of circumstances: 'Generally speaking the defence of necessity covers all cases where non-compliance with the law is excused by an emergency or justified by the pursuit of some greater good.' (1984) 13 DLR.

case is not a case of justificatory necessity. That this is so can easily be demonstrated by the fact that it would make no moral sense for a third party to assist the drowning mariner by dislodging the occupant of the plank on his behalf. What would render it imperative to do so?[86]

There are, however, other cases of self-preservation not involving the victimisation of others and falling outside the traditional boundaries of self-defence which are capable of recognition as involving permissive justifications in such circumstances.[87] An example is the case of the motorist who speeds to avoid a tailgating lorry, met in the previous chapter. The practical significance of channelling cases of personal necessity into duress of circumstances concern the latter's inability to marshal an irresistible case for excusing or justifying murder.[88] Particular problems arise where the actor is faced with a kill or be killed choice, as in the following example.

Case 3

Adam is driving his car on a narrow mountain road and encounters a party of hikers who cannot be avoided unless he makes the ultimate self sacrifice and plunges off the cliff.

If Adam eschews the sacrifice and plunges through the middle of the hikers our moral intuition reacts to this as a case of justified rather than simply (if at all) excused action.[89] But what is the justification? Again, Adam is not acting in self defence, even in Horder's unnaturally expansive version, and necessity faces the objection that Adam's action is not morally imperative, it cannot ordinarily justify the death of an innocent person and is limited in any event to lesser of two evils choices. The hikers might appear to be people who 'stand in the way', which, were Adam's action to be genuinely the lesser of two evils, might keep open this option. Looked at more closely, however, even this argument appears suspect since presumably to rely on this feature an actor must be subject to an encroaching danger (an unjust threat) for the purpose

---

[86] Horder, 'The Irrelevance of Motive', at 160.
[87] See S Uniacke, *Permissible Killing*, 143–55.
[88] RF Schopp, *Justification Defences and Just Convictions* (OUP, Oxford, 1998), ch 5.
[89] Uniacke doubts this at p 148. She suggests a justificatory form of duress in such cases 'Killing under Duress' (1989) *J of Applied Phil* 53.

of avoiding which he must remove the victim from the sole available escape route. This does not happen with our driver upon encountering the hikers. He is not, unlike the frozen passenger or slow moving pedestrian, seeking an escape route from a danger bearing down on him, which route the latter are blocking. The only danger in this scenario is in fact one which he himself poses. The issue is, therefore, whether he is required to do something about it, say to sacrifice himself for the good of others.

Judges, speaking of duress, have flirted with the idea that we may owe a duty of self-sacrifice for the good of others.[90] But this is an idea which appears closely connected to the fact that, in most cases of this nature, the defendant's choice is to (purposely) kill or be killed. Absent this stark predicament there are doctrinally supported grounds for allowing strangers to put their own interests before the interests of others wherever this does not necessitate them taking direct exploitative action against the latter.[91] This is most evident in the doctrinal underpinnings of omissions liability which provides no general duty of rescue. Other cases can be produced which sustain a comparable claim of justification.[92]

Case 4

A is crossing a busy road, the central reservation of which is packed solid with people waiting to cross to the other side. A car bears down on him at great speed just as he is about to reach the reservation. In the split second available A realises that unless he thrusts himself onto the reservation he will be killed. He realises also that if he does so it will unavoidably result in others being pushed off the reservation into the line of traffic with inevitable loss of life. This is what he does. He jumps onto the reservation sending X and Y sprawling forward. In the resulting disorder C, D and E are displaced onto the roadway and killed by encroaching cars.

On the face of it this may appear to be another reworking of Bacon's mariner on the plank case which, given there is no objective moral reason in favour of A's action, would provide an excuse at best based upon

---

[90] See for example Lord Hailsham in *Howe* [1987] 1 AC 417.

[91] DW Elliot, 'Necessity, Duress and Self-Defence' [1989] *Crim LR* 611.

[92] See S Uniacke, 'Killing under Duress', above n 90 at 55.

personal necessity/duress of circumstances. And yet it appears central to the inherent wrongfulness of the mariner's (M1) action that he directs his action against the other mariner (M2) who posed no threat to M1 and so had a right not to be subjugated to the latter's will. This does not commit us to conclude that M1 would not be permitted to do something else to preserve his life with an equally inevitable concomitant that M2 would be pitched into the water and drown. If M1 in the struggle for survival had hauled himself up onto an unstable plank occupied by M2 in seas so rough as to render it inevitable that M2 would both be pitched off and be unable to recover his situation, it is plausible that his conduct is justified and not merely excused. This is because, as has been explained, action is easier to justify where its object is unobjectionable and the harm wrought is incidental to rather than constitutive of the act concerned. It is for this reason that where the basis of a person's moral responsibility is located in what he foresees, the corresponding fault element is constructed as recklessness rather than intention. It is not that we foresee the harm issuing from our actions which renders us blameworthy. It is that the reason we have for acting is not good enough to offset the harm which is threatened.

Adam's, A's and M1's actions straddle the defences of duress of circumstances, necessity and self-defence. They are not cases where a person is compelled to kill another as a means of saving himself. It is not a case where he has acted for the best. It is not a case of action directed against someone who poses an undeserved threat.[93] It is a case where a person has preserved his life by an act which. while entirely apt for that purpose, has as its unavoidable side effect the death of another. One and the same intentional action, avoiding a car/escaping the sea produces good consequence (preservation of life) and bad side effect (death of others). If there are cogent grounds for holding that intended consequences extend to side effects as well as aims and objects, this does not necessarily commit us to hold that double effects are of no significance in the establishment of defences. If A cannot rely on his socially acceptable objective by reason of the undesirable and undesired side effect, it commits us in effect to hold that a person has a duty of self-sacrifice in the interests of others who may benefit from such sacrifice. That this seems problematic at best suggests that the grounds of justified action extend beyond the boundaries of duress, necessity and self-defence as traditionally understood.

[93] Cf S Uniacke, *Permissible Killing*, 30 *et seq.*

11

Excusing Wrongdoing: Capacity and Virtue

INTRODUCTION

In an earlier chapter it was discussed how, rather than engage in general moral evaluation of the defendant's conduct for the purpose of assessing the defendant's fitness for condemnation and punishment, the criminal justice system makes its decision via an analytical prism, which fractures the fault element in criminal liability into more basic elements. This prismatic approach aims to effect a separation of the attitude of mind brought to the action performed by the actor from the reasons which prompted that attitude of mind. The point of compartmentalising the fault element in this way is to exercise control over the reasons which do or do not affect criminal liability and to minimise the scope for ambiguity and dissent governing what is and what is not censurable behaviour. The resulting gap which opens up between excuses and justifications operative at the moral level and those operative at the legal level is thought by some to create an inbuilt tension within doctrine to defy its own organisational structure.

Without wishing to fan the flames of an already well-rehearsed debate still further, this latter criticism, if undeniably cogent, does not in my view represent a fatal attack upon the moral authority of the state to subject individuals to coercion. This moral authority accrues through the efforts made to strike a balance between justice to the individual and society's collective needs, such that the content of the rules can be experienced as fair from the (reasonable) subject's point of view although adverse to him. The central values celebrated by criminal doctrine will usually, one way or another, be realised in doctrine. The perennial problem concerns the failure to dovetail offence and defence elements satisfactorily so as to ensure the **systematic** exculpation of blameless citizens. As has been suggested this does not commit us to concede, however, that these values cannot systematically be realised

326 Central Issues in Criminal Theory

by the form of criminal law; only that in the rush to deliver substantive justice the essential form of law can be distorted.

Other examples of this tendency in English case law are not hard to come by. A topical concern is the manner in which defence elements can become skewed so as to afford an excuse where an individual's personal context or psychological make-up renders rule-governed behaviour more than usually difficult. In diminished responsibility, where responsibility for a killing is substantially impaired by mental abnormality, the defence has been successful in cases where the aetiology of the defective choice is not obviously attributable to mental abnormality as opposed to the kind of events which make normal minds take extreme, unbridled measures. So the defence has been allowed in cases where a killing has been prompted by the emotional and psychological disturbances caused by a severely handicapped child to a loving parent,[1] by paranoid jealousy and fear of burglary,[2] or by persistent physical violence over a long period of time.[3] These are cases where the defendant, as in provocation and duress, seems to be raising questions about whether it was fair to demand conformity with the rule rather than a status-based incapacity to conform.

Such doctrinal ambiguity and inconsistency points to an underlying lack of clarity as to the moral basis to excuses and the way this finds expression in criminal doctrine. In the following sections I shall make some preliminary observations concerning how excuses are constituted at the moral level. Thereafter I shall examine the way in which excuses operative at the moral level are filtered through into criminal doctrine. I shall suggest that if a person's action is morally defensible this is a strong but not conclusive reason for holding it also to be legally defensible. If a person's action is morally indefensible this is a strong but not conclusive reason for holding it to be legally indefensible. Finally I shall examine the leading contemporary theories of excuses with a view to considering whether a unified theory of excuses is either possible or desirable.

---

[1] *Price, The Times* 22 December 1965, cited in G Williams, *Textbook of Criminal Law* (Stevens, London, 1983), 692–3.
[2] *Eeles* (1972) *The Times*, 22 November, *ibid*.
[3] *Ahluwalia* [1992] 4 All ER 889.

THRESHOLDS OF RESPONSIBILITY

Sometimes ordinary people do things they should not. They may be drunk; they may be tired; they may be angry; they may be emotional; they may be confused; they may be fearful; they may have lost their job; their partner may have left them. Under what circumstances do we hold them not to be morally responsible for what they do? Consider the case of *Acott* who killed his mother, apparently in the course of a frenzied attack following an argument. The two had had a stormy relationship.[4] Mother may have had a tendency to belittle her son. It was possible that this had provoked him to lose his self-control. However, no evidence of any specific act of provocation was adduced. The House of Lords agreed with the Court of Appeal that the mere fact that A had lost his self-control was insufficient to enable him to rely upon the partial excuse of provocation. To have an excuse required there to be evidence that something had happened to provoke him, not merely that he was provoked. Lord Steyn put it this way:

> A loss of self control caused by fear, panic, sheer bad temper or circumstances (eg a slow-down of traffic due to snow) would not be enough. There must be some evidence tending to show that the killing might have been an uncontrolled reaction to provoking conduct rather than an act of revenge.[5]

It may have been better if Lord Steyn had not qualified his statement by reference to 'an act of revenge' since there was no evidence of this either and it is not solely to prevent the exculpation of revenge killers that the provocative prompt is required.[6] But taken as whole the statement is a fairly representative statement of the way excuses are constituted at the moral level and how they reach a threshold capable of incorporation into the criminal law. The key feature to be noted in the decision is an acknowledgement that the standards of behaviour binding upon one as a member of a society do not vary with an actor's personal characteristics or the context within which he acts. Losing one's self control in the course of an argument or other stressful conditions, however unpleasant, is not excusable. In a loose way a person who attacks another in the throes of a bout of, say, 'road rage' may be said to have an 'excuse', but it is such a weak excuse that it counts for little.

---

[4] [1997] 1 All ER 706.
[5] At 712–3.
[6] See generally J Horder, *Provocation and Responsibility* (OUP, Oxford, 1992), ch 9.

It tells the moral audience that the actor is not a lost cause, that he is not normally like this, that his normal compliant attitude was subverted, that he was acting out his stress rather than innate aggression.[7] The 'excuse' does not excuse—indeed loss of self-control is likely to be a matter of great regret to the actor for which he feels blameworthy. However, it may render the actor's behaviour understandable, may elicit compassion and empathy and ultimately, therefore, help the actor to be reconciled with his critics.

Provocation exemplifies something common to most claims of excuse (and justification), namely that the accused's was a (partially) normal reaction to an abnormal event—here a kind of psychic attack. Why is it not enough simply that the actor lost his self-control? The moral basis to restricting excuses in this way is to keep faith with the idea that we are responsible both for who we are and the choices we make.[8] We are supposed to make the best of things. General morality does not allow us to excuse our behaviour on the basis that we were dealt a bad hand—that we were born aggressive, hot-headed, poor, or cowardly. True we are not morally blameworthy for conditions not of our making which render us unduly susceptible to coercion, temptation or violence. It was not Acott's fault if he was born with a difficult mother. But in life, as in cards, being dealt a bad hand requires us only to develop and exploit our skills and virtues rather than capitulate to circumstances or resort to cheating.[9] Being who we are and the context we are in may dispose us to the kind of behaviour we engage in but this enables us only to explain our behaviour, not excuse it. So the pressures of poverty help to explain why the poor are more prone to steal than others just as the pressures of finding a parking space during the school run explain why frazzled parents double park or drive erratically. In neither case, however, do we expect the moral audience or indeed the offenders themselves to consider this to be much of an excuse for their wrongdoing. But where crisis strikes—a lost and starving individual takes food from an unoccupied dwelling, a parent parks illegally in the urgency of delivering a sick infant to hospital; where we are the victim

---

[7] S Morse, 'Diminished Capacity' in Shute *et al*, *Action and Value in Criminal Law* (Clarendon Press, Oxford 1993), 239.

[8] S Kadish, 'Excusing Crime' (1987) 75 *Calif LR* 257; J Dressler, 'Reflections on Excusing Wrongdoers: Moral Theory, New Excuses and the Model Penal Code' (1988) 19 *Rut LJ* 671 at 675.

[9] An ethical viewpoint dating back to Aristotle. See, for example Aristotle *Ethics*, Book 3 (Penguin, Harmondsworth, 1953) chs 5 and 6.

of events rather than our own psychology, history or context, general morality bids us excuse rather than criticise.

It is only in response to such opportunistic crises that it is plausible to claim that our actions are not authentically ours and, therefore, not ones for which as decent self-respecting human beings we should own up and take responsibility. It is perhaps for this reason that tragedy in literature and drama—from the Greeks, through Shakespeare to Racine, Flaubert, Dostoyevsky and Ibsen proves so psychologically troubling. At the root of it is the moral ambivalence we feel when strong, apparently steadfast human beings are undone and brought to account by their own history, context and personality. We are moved by the tragedy of Orestes fleeing the implacable vengeance of the furies for having, at his sister's instigation, avenged his father murdered by his mother. We are moved by the tragedy of Othello who murdered his beloved wife, deceived into believing her unfaithful. We are moved by the tragedy of King Lear whose egotism and susceptibility to flattery causes him to lose forever his beloved daughter, forgo his lands, power and ultimately his sanity. But it is not a deep sense of moral injustice which moves us. We do not claim that Orestes lacks moral responsibility for the murder of Clytemnestra, Othello for murdering Desdemona, Lear for his part in the ultimate death of Cordelia, though our sympathy and empathy in each case is more overwhelming than for those whose actions we would excuse or justify. We conclude in each case that, while the price paid was rather steep and in each case the actor was impelled along the route they took, they had only themselves to blame for the events which overcame them. They had no excuse for what they did and, indeed, they offered none. You cannot excuse the inexcusable. That's the tragedy.

EMBODYING CRIMINAL DEFENCES

And so it is with the criminal law. Core criminal defences reflect underlying moral precepts and they share a basic organisational formula, namely that the actor was reacting to, or subjugated by, a one-off external crisis or prompt. It may take the form of an unjustified threat of harm (self-defence, duress, necessity),[10] an act of considerable provocation, or a rationality-subverting shock to the psyche (automatism). This pattern derives from our natural moral inclinations. We differentiate

---

[10] See J Griffin, *Value Judgment* (OUP, Oxford, 1996), 98 *et seq.*

the things which happen to us by virtue of who we are and the things which happen to us opportunistically, where we are singled out by an unruly fate to be the person to face a crisis. We should hesitate, then, before drawing unduly radical conclusions about the seemingly narrow range of excuses incorporated into criminal doctrine, why it excuses insanity but not psychopathy, why self-defence, duress and provocation may exculpate, but not road-rage, jealousy, or pre-menstrual tension. Rather than acting to effect a politically motivated closure upon the possible range of criminal excuses, as some would have it, the basic defence formula operates largely as a reflection of limits placed upon excuses and justifications at the level of general morality. It is not simply a device designed to exert maximum control over those whose behaviour we have most cause to fear, although incidentally it may have this effect. It feeds off deeply rooted moral assessments of what it is to be responsible human subject. Crisis upsets the natural order of things. It deprives rules of behaviour of their moral relevance. It deprives individuals of their susceptibility to control by rules. Far from being an unholy moral compromise with the demands of penal efficacy the formula sets the moral limits within which a workable system of norm enforcement can be achieved.

This basic formula also sets necessary political limits to the range of defences. When citizens face moral dilemmas outside the special circumstances envisioned by the defences of duress, necessity and self-defence they are likely to be in a position of 'partial moral ignorance' which requires them to defer to the collective effort at addressing the problem that is embodied in a legal prohibition.[11] It is the fact that one's moral dilemma or something like it has been deliberated upon in advance at a collective level which creates and sustains a duty of compliance. In one-off emergency situations this reasoning will often not apply and the actor will be uniquely placed to grasp exactly what needs to be done. There are no slippery slopes, moral, political or evidential, when the law exculpates those who act in a one-off emergency to prevent harm where there is no recourse to official protection and/or guidance. Affording a defence in such circumstances means the law's co-ordinating function is not imperilled.

For obvious reasons such an account does not explain the construction of criminal defences such as provocation or automatism. Requiring

---

[11] For elaboration see J Horder, 'The Irrelevance of Motive in Criminal Law' in J Horder (ed), *Oxford Essays in Jurisprudence* (Clarendon Press, Oxford, 2000), 174, 181–4.

an external crisis in cases where the defendant has temporarily lost the capacity or will to conform ensures that criminal defences are not available to those who are undone by their own weak character. It ensures that those with constitutional weaknesses which render them susceptible to rule breaking are brought within the coercive powers of the state, whether punitive or otherwise. The centrality of the extraneous crisis or one-off emergency allows us an insight into those defences which are constituted in its absence. What distinguishes automatism from say status defences such as insanity and diminished responsibility is that the latter are, by their very nature, more deeply rooted in the actor's personal circumstances. So a person obtains a true excuse if he commits a crime while under the grip of concussion following a blow on the head but a capacity-based exemption (or worse) if that blow on the head causes a long-term personality change disposing to violence. There are obvious reasons of penal policy attached to this structuring process.[12] Primarily there is the need to ensure that those who display a disposition to break rules are subject to appropriate control and this is no less urgent a priority for the fact that such disposition does not reflect badly upon the actor. There is the practical need to devise rules, evidential or substantive, which can be trusted to identify those lacking this capacity or realistic choice to obey the law.[13] Finally, there is the need to avoid a proliferation of defences capable of offering immunity to dangerous people and encouraging the invention of divisive social categories.[14]

Occasionally cases crop up which afford us some insight into possible tensions between legal and moral excuses. A topical example is that of involuntary intoxication. This is recognised in the United States[15] but not in England,[16] where the moral excuse (this act was morally involuntary/did not reflect my authentic character) does not

[12] See for example *Bratty v AG for Northern Ireland* [1963] AC 386 and discussion in KJM Smith and W Wilson, 'Impaired Voluntariness and Criminal Responsibility' [1993] *OJLS*, 69, at 79.

[13] See N Lacey, 'Partial Defences to Homicide' in A Ashworth and B Mitchell (eds), *Rethinking English Homicide Law* (OUP, Oxford, 2000), 107 at 121 *et seq*; F Kaganas, 'Domestic Homicide, Gender and the Expert' in A Bainham, S Day Sclater and M Richards (eds), *Body Lore and Law* (Hart Publishing, Oxford, 2001).

[14] G Fletcher, *Rethinking Criminal Law* (Little Brown and Company, Boston, Toronto, 1978), at 846.

[15] LaFave and Scott (West, St Pauls, 1972) cite *Prather v Commonwealth* 215 Ky 714, 287 S.W. 559 (1926) as authority at 347–8.

[16] By the Model Penal Code involuntary intoxication is a defence 'if by reason of such intoxication the actor at the time of his conduct lacks substantial capacity either to appreciate its criminality [wrongfulness] or to conform his conduct to the requirements of law.' Section 2.08(4).

translate into the corresponding legal excuse.[17] On the face of it involuntary intoxication is then illustrative of a lack of even-handedness in defence doctrine. The involuntarily intoxicated offender is being treated less favourably than the subject of coercion, who is also prompted to do wrong by external events outside his control, and there is no principled reason for it—only a desire to ensure the non-proliferation of difficult to disprove 'soft' defences. As will be suggested later, there may be good reasons of principle for treating coercion and involuntary intoxication differently. Even were we to concede this point, however, this would not necessarily commit us to condemning the differential treatment as a failure of justice. Justice is not an absolute but a standard—something to be striven for. In addition to individual fair treatment, due process, social defence, efficiency and speed are all laudable objectives of a criminal justice system. Only if the successful pursuit of these objectives unfairly compromise individual rights to fair treatment is the justice of the system as a whole imperilled. Rules which generate personal injustice can be morally justified, therefore, on an all-things-considered basis. The pursuit of moral perfection can be inimical to the very values the system is designed to uphold.[18]

If there is then a natural inclination for excuses and justifications to kick in where behaviour can be regarded as a normal reaction to an abnormal one-off event it remains to be discussed how this filters through into the theories offered of criminal defences. There are two leading theories.[19] The capacity approach is rooted in the idea that moral responsibility follows from an actor freely choosing to commit a criminal wrong. Excuses operate to negate the free choice to do wrong which punishment seeks to counter. The character approach holds, by contrast, that it is an actor's bad character against which punishment is directed. Where rule infringement occurs in circumstances which block the usual inference that a person who infringes a rule is of bad

---

[17] For discussion see W Wilson, 'Involuntary Intoxication: Excusing the Inexcusable' [1995] 1 *Res Publica* 25; GR Sullivan, 'Making Exuses' in AP Simester and ATH Smith (eds), *Harm and Culpability* (Clarendon Press, Oxford, 1996), 131.

[18] For further discussion see J Feinberg, 'Justice, Fairness and Rationality' (1972) 81 *Yale LJ* 1004, 1005; J Dressler, 'Exegesis of the Law of Duress: Justifying the Excuse and Searching for its Proper Limits' (1989) 62 *S Cal L Rev* 1331; S Kadish, 'Moral Excess' (2000) 32 *McGeorge Law Review* 1 at 15.

[19] For general discussion see G Fletcher, *Rethinking Criminal Law*, ch 10; M Bayles, 'Character, Purpose and Criminal Responsibility' (1982) 1 *Law and Philosophy* 5; RA Duff, 'Choice, Character and Criminal Liability' (1993) 12 *Law and Philosophy* 345.

character punishment and condemnation is unjust and excuses (and justifications) interpose themselves to ensure justice is done.

THE CAPACITY APPROACH

The basis of the orthodox approach to excuses is a denial of a voluntary act of rule-defiance. It is this latter feature, uniquely, which justifies state coercion being used to underwrite what is as explained above a central feature of everyday life, namely the assertion of values through the process of expressing moral criticism for people who act in an antisocial fashion. On this approach it is not enough that people act in an antisocial fashion, it must be appropriate to blame them and, moreover, it must be fair to **punish** them. Acting unreasonably or immorally while a precondition of moral criticism is neither a necessary nor a sufficient condition of state punishment. Since punishment attends a rule violation the liberal state's authority to punish is conditional upon the presence of all the necessary conditions for a human subject to obey that rule. Non-conformity to the law must, before all else, express an attitude towards the rule itself rather than the values underpinning it. That attitude at root is 'I shall not conduct myself in this way, although the rule bids me do so.' In so acting the actor expresses his own autonomy, choosing both to violate the rule and the punishment price tag attached thereto.[20]

If we examine the structure of criminal liability there are obvious features which support this choice-based view of criminal responsibility. The most obvious is that the fault element for crimes which have the censuring of moral wrongdoing as their rationale tend to be cognition-based. So crimes of violence, typically, are established only upon proof of an intention of causing injury to the victim or subjective recklessness. The (non-definitional) excuses also appear to kick in where the relevant behaviour was involuntary under some description or other. This absence of choice is most marked in cases where the defendant's conduct does not issue from a decision on his part to act in the relevant fashion, that is where his conduct is **literally** involuntary as where a driver ignores a traffic signal in the throes of heart attack. It is less marked in other excuses where the essence of the defendant's claim

---

[20] RP Wolff, 'The Conflict between Authority and Autonomy' in J Raz (ed), *Authority* (Duckworth, London, 1990) 20–31.

to avoid punishment is not that he made no choice but that it was not freely taken.[21] Thus, the rationale for the defence of duress is that although the defendant chose to commit crime rather than suffer injury, it would not be reasonable or fair (as he is only human) to expect him to choose otherwise. On this analysis all claims to avoid censure and punishment lie on a voluntariness spectrum stretching from, at the one extreme, 'actions' which are not, in any sense relevant for culpability, attributable to the actor as a reasoning goal-centred human being and, at the other extreme, actions which are so freely chosen that we could offer no better explanation for the action than that the actor 'wanted to'. As one continues along this continuum the actor's claim to avoid punishment, namely 'I could not help doing what I did' becomes ever less compelling until it meets with the response. 'You could and you should.'

The idea that it is personal choice which stands at the heart of the state's authority to punish is opposed by other features within the make-up of criminal liability. Most damning it might appear is that not all crimes are crimes of subjective *mens rea*. Indeed the vast majority of criminal offences bear strict liability, where it is not incumbent upon the prosecution to prove any criminal fault let alone a conscious flouting of the relevant rule. But the existence of crimes of strict liability is, in theory, quite consistent with a choice-based system of criminal punishment. It can be explained, as suggested earlier, on the ground that their overriding nature is regulatory and that the penalties which attach are preventive rather than retributive in function. As such the criminal law can be seen to exhibit two separate paradigms of responsibility which operate to separate law's censuring and preventive functions where individual rights and utility conflict.[22] It is only where punishment is an expression of moral criticism involving stigmatic penalties that fairness in punishment requires conscious rule flouting.

A more serious problem is posed by negligence liability which, since it predicates censure and punishment upon proof of moral fault but requires no conscious wrongdoing, seems to contradict the idea that choosing to flout rules is a precondition of state punishment. So, liability for manslaughter can be incurred without proof that the accused adverted to the risk of death or indeed any injury if the accused's conduct

---

[21] S Kadish, 'Excusing Crime' (1987) 75 *Calif LR* 257; KJM Smith and W Wilson, 'Impaired Voluntariness and Criminal Responsibility' [1993] *OJLS*, 69.

[22] A Brudner, 'Agency and Welfare in the Penal Law' in Shute *et al* (eds), *Action and Value in Criminal Law* (Clarendon Press, Oxford, 1993), 21, and see ch 1.

nevertheless provoked mortal danger. The existence of such crimes is supported by a generally held intuition that the kind of moral fault which is properly punishable is not limited to cases of conscious wrong-doing.[23] Sometimes our indignation is aroused precisely because a person was not conscious of the risks attending his conduct. Where the circumstances surrounding our conduct provoke the objective risk of death or serious harm we feel that a failure to be conscientious in the weighing and taking of risks may be equally if not more blameworthy than in the case of someone who takes the risk consciously. Who is more blameworthy, the anaesthetist who does not notice the patient under-going surgery has become starved of oxygen in the excitement of filling in his crossword puzzle or the over-optimistic driver who takes a conscious gamble when overtaking on a blind corner?

In the most influential modern version, HLA Hart attempts to reconcile choice theory with liability for negligence and to provide the essential ground rules for determining justice in punishment. He does so by reformulating the question 'Did the actor choose to flout this rule?' as '(Did the actor have the) normal capacities, physical and mental, for doing what the law requires and abstaining from what it forbids, and a fair opportunity to exercise those capacities?' If these capacities and opportunities are absent, as in cases of coercion, mistake, insanity etc it is morally wrong to punish.[24] But if they are present, Hart insists that it is no injustice to punish someone for not acting in conformity with them. Negligence liability is justified on this basis. Punishing negligence is not unfair by reason that negligent actors do not have harm 'in mind'. Rather it is fair by reason that they 'ought' to have had such considerations in mind as a reason for not acting as they did. In his view justice in punishment requires, however, the actor to have the reasonable person's normal capacities for foresight and carefulness. Capacity, therefore, replaces choice as the basis of responsibility.[25]

The basic scheme offered by Hart separates excuses into two categories—those which involve a denial of the physical or mental attributes which are a precondition of successful and consistent rule-following and

---

[23] K Huigens, 'Virtue and Criminal Negligence' (1998) *Buffalo Criminal Law Review* 431, at 434–9; and see generally; Horder, 'Gross Negligence and Criminal Culpability' (1997) 47 *U Toronto LJ* 495.

[24] Hart, *Punishment and Responsibility* (Clarendon Press, Oxford, 1968), 155.

[25] *Caldwell*, the leading case on criminal damage, represents a clear expression of a system of blame based upon capacity theory. See S Field and M Lynn (1992) 12 *LS* 74 at p 87.

those which involve a denial that the normal conditions under which people with those attributes are expected to conform their behaviour to law subsisted. Thus insanity and involuntary behaviour involve a denial of the capacity to conform one's behaviour to the law. In other words, the actor's conduct was not the expression of a deliberated choice on his part. Duress, by contrast, involves the claim that the actor's choice was made more difficult by the abnormal conditions which subsisted at the time of acting and that because of this it would not be fair to attribute that choice to him. The first difficulty occasioned by this rationale of excuses is that of delimiting a cogent notion of voluntariness so that all people who claim that they 'could not help doing what they did'—are treated even-handedly. We have seen already how some theorists consider that this is a knock-down criticism against the present structure of criminal defences Consider some of the problems which result from this capacity approach to excuses.

Free Will

Implicit in whatever justification of punishment we are minded to adopt is the fact not only that some social harm is attributable to the defendant's act but also that he bears personal responsibility for its occurrence. At the root of this equation and also the theories of punishment lies an assumption about the nature of human beings and the part they play in the world of events—that they have free will and that social harms can be morally attributed to the choices which people make. If we examine this assumption of free will closely it discloses a degree of fragility. There is no doubt that we experience life as structured by our choices; so much so that words such as *anomie* and alienation have been coined to describe the absence of such psychological experience. But, as Buzz Light Year discovered, experiencing ourselves as the master of the universe (or of our own destiny) is not the same as being such master.[26] Except perhaps at the level of quantum physics everything which happens in the material world is thought to have a cause and those causes have causes and so on *ad infinitum*. Chaos theory asks us to consider whether today's storm force wind may not have been caused by last month's butterfly flapping its wings in some

---

[26] In the film *Toy Story* Buzz, a toy astronaut, thought he was the real thing. His friend Woody, a toy cowboy, could not convince him otherwise.

distant tropical rainforest. The causality assumption is built into the very structure of our minds. We find the idea of the virgin birth so sublimely implausible that we perversely take comfort in the fact that Mary was first visited by an angel with a message the better to prepare us for the ultimate subversion of the laws of biology. Why, then, do we presume that our action-choices are not subject to these same rules and insist that our actions, absent any intervening determinant such as duress or insanity, are the products of our own free choice? When, say, we eat a cream bun how can this be explained in terms which are qualitatively different from a dog that does the same thing? In both cases the action of eating a cream bun seems to be determined by something. It may be a predilection for cream buns. It may be hunger. We may be hungry because, lacking money, we cannot afford enough food. We may be hungry because we have an unusually large appetite. Environment, genes, biochemistry or hormones may themselves cause any of these determinants of our hunger or desire. All that differentiates us from the dog, it seems, is that our decision to eat a cream bun is executed via a reasoning mind which in the moment of decision contemplates or is capable of contemplating its opposite. 'Shall I have a cream bun? I am hungry, I think I shall' or, 'Shall I have a cream bun? No not today. That would be piggy.' Consider a more extreme example. Two people arrive simultaneously at a waterhole in the desert. One has not drunk for two days. The other has not drunk for two minutes. They both drink water. If it is implausible to understand the former action simply as an exercise of free will then it is no less implausible so to understand the latter. We just need to look a little harder for the cause.

Capacity theory and indeed criminal theory generally takes note of the plausibility of determinism but, by and large, is not daunted by it.[27] Given that state coercion is almost universally recognised as, at worst, a necessary evil and, at best, a force for human well-being and flourishing, theories which seek to evaluate the operation of criminal defences are entitled to concentrate upon identifying the conditions under which rule infringement **should not** suffer punishment. After all few would advocate a system where (grave) censure and punishment could be meted out irrespective of the conditions under which the infringement took place. It is difficult to counter the intuition that some

---

[27] Hart, *Punishment and Responsibility*, 48; M Moore, *Placing Blame* (OUP, Oxford, 1997), 504.

of us are more responsible for our (harmful) deeds than others and that both the occasion and quantum of punishment should reflect such degrees of responsibility. It is towards identifying what underpins this intuition which criminal theory is generally engaged and with which Hart's capacity theory, specifically, is grappling. Under what circumstances or conditions is whatever free choice we may exercise in relation to our deeds compromised so that attributing responsibility/full responsibility is inappropriate?[28] Hart's general conclusion, as we have seen, is that both moral and criminal responsibility is fairly attributable to a given actor where he has the physical and mental capacity to conform his behaviour to law and where he has a fair opportunity of choosing to act otherwise than he did.

Drawing the Line

An unresolved doubt exposed by this rationale concerns the point at which a person's capacity or opportunity to conform is sufficiently compromised to render censure and punishment inappropriate. Outside paradigm cases such as involuntary behaviour, when inappropriate bodily movements owe nothing to an actor's deliberative processes, and duress, when action is compelled, when is responsibility lacking? This is significant both in connection with evaluating the doctrinal elements of offences and defences and also setting limits upon the potential scope of excuses. If the capacity theory of criminal responsibility is to be at all plausible it must somehow separate those determinants of our choices which are fairly treated as part of the actor's authentic choice-making resources and so reflect badly upon him from those which are not and so do not reflect badly upon him. What yardstick does it possess for assessing whether the defendant, in any sense relevant for the attribution of criminal responsibility, had a fair opportunity to avoid acting as he did? The criminal law's yardstick is its perennial paragon, namely the reasonable man. The fairness or otherwise of the actor's opportunities turn on whether the reasonable man, whoever he or she is would have done so. It is the use of this overworked creature which poses the greatest problem for the credibility of capacity theory. Does the drug addict born into penury and brutalisation genuinely have a fair opportunity of avoiding infringing the law?

[28] A Norrie, *Punishment, Responsibility and Justice* (Clarendon Press, Oxford, 2000), ch 1.

Does the cowardly person subject to weak coercion, the hot-tempered person subject to weak provocation, or the paedophile subject to temptation genuinely have a fair opportunity of conforming? Central to capacity theory it seems is an idealised notion of human beings. They are people who are morally resistant to environmental, genetic and biochemical determinations of their character and choices. Whatever their race, class, gender, upbringing, personal psychology or intellect, their range of choices are not significantly affected. Rule-breakers are punished without regard to their real capacities and opportunities to conform save in the case of certain penologically non problematic exculpatory claims such as duress and self defence which no criminal justice system could sensibly do without and which hardly, therefore, need accounting for. Those critics which complain of the lack of even-handedness in the excuses recognised in domestic law gain support from capacity theory's inability to theorise cogently exactly what it is which negates the fairness of the actor's opportunity to conform.

Most plausibly this is, as indicated earlier, that fair opportunity-based excuses tend to arise from some opportunistic external crisis, leaving the few recognised capacity-based excuses more deeply rooted in the actor's personal circumstances. Although the state no doubt profits by drawing the line in this way this is a matter of general morality rather than self-serving penological convenience. Capacity theory is able to explain and justify this form of closure on the basis that the choices made by the actor in non-excuse situations are authentically the actor's own choices. Censure and punishment address the person as he is rather than the person he might have been but for his own personal history. By addressing the person as he is he is treated with respect. Even the poor, the hot-headed and the intemperate have the power of choice—the power to do what they know to be the right thing—even if those choices are weighted against 'doing the right thing'. By filtering defences in this way, we do justice to the true nature of the choice made. Consistent with this analysis the general form of excuses distinguishes those who failed to resist an impulse **upon which they desired to act** and those whose condition or circumstances **causes them to fail** to resist an impulse **upon which they desired not to act**.[29] So conditions and contexts such as pre-menstrual tension,[30] battered women's syndrome, poverty, alcoholism, intellectual inadequacy and

[29] D Meyerson, 'Fundamental Contradictions in Critical Legal Studies' (1991) 11 *OJLS* 439.
[30] Compare 'brain-washing'.

psychopathy do not fall squarely within the template of any recognised defence although it is well known that sufferers are less able, compared with non-sufferers, to conform their behaviour to the law.[31] An actor is offered no excuse for failing to resist the temptation of a briefcase full of money and this is so even where she is poor and unable to feed and clothe her children. Having reason to be tempted is not the same as having reason to act upon temptation. On the other hand, an excuse is available in both cases where a person is coerced into behaving in such a manner? What does it tell us about a person who acts against his own inclinations other than that his choice is not authentically his?

Related to this drawing the line problem posed by capacity theory is that of determining whether the actor was in fact deprived of the relevant capacity/fair opportunity. There is a big gap opened up between the presentation of evidence that the accused was subject to coercion, provocation, intoxication, concussion or mental abnormality and concluding that this event or condition, in fact, deprived the actor of the capacity or fair opportunity of conforming his behaviour to law. For example, in relation to diminished responsibility how is it possible to determine whether a given mental abnormality is operative and/or such as to diminish substantially an actor's responsibility for a killing? How much weight do we accord the opinion of experts when, as so often they do, they fail to reach agreement in criminal trials and everyone, experts included, is in the dark about the connection, moral and psychological, between mental abnormality and rule-breaking[32]? Is being a psychopath a reason to (partially) excuse or to pile on the blame? The problems opened up can also be seen in relation to provocation. For every person who is taunted, nagged or bullied by another and reacts by killing there are thousands of people who do not. Upon what basis, then, can we say that the accused was deprived of a realistic choice? Would we rather not explain the disposition to excuse on the basis that even people of good character 'lose it' sometimes.

The capacity model raises other important questions. On the one hand it presupposes that justice in punishment requires the actor to have the reasonable person's normal capacities for foresight and carefulness. This poses a serious problem for the normative status of all

---

[31] Provocation and diminished responsibility which fall outside this model can be explained as deriving from their special status as partial defences to murder. N Lacey above n. 13, *Murder* 115.

[32] F Kaganas, 'Domestic Homicide, Gender and the Expert' in A Bainham, S Day Sclater and M Richards (eds), *Body Lore and Laws*.

exculpatory claims.[33] If the claim 'I am not like ordinary people' excuses one from liability for crimes of negligence why should it not also form the basis of all other exculpatory claims—I am more cowardly, hot-tempered, and so on, than normal people? Individualising the conditions of liability in this way is fairly exceptional in criminal doctrine and where it happens receives little by way of support from the commentators. More usually it is the fact of acting unreasonably rather than having the capacity to act reasonably and failing which attracts condemnation[34] and those who lack moral restraint or fortitude are under most people's perception of moral fault damned from their own mouths.[35]

On the other hand it does not fully explain why it is justified to punish those who cause harm inadvertently but negligently. Hart argues that those who fail to exercise their own capacities for conscientiousness and care are properly censurable and punishable. But what are they properly censurable and punishable for? Consider a person who kills in the course of driving dangerously. Granted that a person must bear responsibility for the way he behaves, if dangerous driving results in death or injury does it necessarily follow that it is appropriate to hold the driver responsible for that consequence? When a person intends a consequence it is easy to attribute responsibility for that consequence to the defendant's action. When a person's action is goal-directed it would not do to claim that the consequence aimed at 'was nothing to do with the way I chose to behave'. Indeed, it has everything to do with it. The outcome is in every sense of the word 'his choice'. But where, as in cases of causing death on the road, a consequence is not aimed at, factors other than the actor's lack of care bear on the outcome, perhaps the weather, the conduct of the victim and other drivers, the responsiveness of the driver's and or victim's car. Assigning responsibility for outcomes on the basis of a person's capacity to prevent their occurrence starts very much to look like liability for being in the wrong place at the wrong time in the wrong context.

---

[33] Kopsch (1927) 19 Cr App R 50 CCA.

[34] Hence also the standard of fortitude required in duress of 'a sober person of reasonable firmness'. See RA Duff, 'Choice, Character and Criminal Liability' (1993) *Law and Philosophy* 345, 346.

[35] See for example, S Kadish, 'Excusing Crime' (1987) 75 *Calif LR* 257; J Gardner, 'The Gist of Excuses' (1998) *Buffalo Criminal Law Review* 587.

THE CHARACTER APPROACH

We have seen that the capacity approach has difficulty creating objective, even-handed distinctions between freely and unfreely chosen wrongdoing. The capacity view pretends that our opportunities to avoid wrongdoing are basically similar when they clearly are not. A currently influential challenge to capacity theory, which can be traced back to Aristotle, attempts to provide a model of responsibility which is not dependent upon an assessment of the actor's capacities or opportunities to avoid doing wrong. Rather it turns its attention to the richer conception of responsibility to be derived from an evaluation of character. That this should be so is deceptively simple to understand since it seems, unlike capacity theory, to follow our standard moral intuitions. At its simplest, we reserve moral condemnation (and punishment) for bad people. And our deeds, consciously chosen or otherwise, do not provide direct unmediated access to our characters.[36] The moral claim to avoid punishment, reflected throughout the range of criminal defences, is, on this view, 'Do not blame me. My act does not reflect the kind of bad character which fits me for censure and punishment,' rather than 'Do not blame me I could not have helped acting as I did.' To make the leap between deed and character it is necessary to examine an actor's reasons for having acted as he did and the overall context within which he acted.

Apart from the light it sheds on the moral filtering mechanism for criminal defences, character theory affords also an uncomplicated explanation for the persistence of negligence based liability and related doctrinal features such as the non-exculpatory effect of voluntary intoxication and unreasonable mistakes. It is that behaviour which can only be accounted for by confessing to character traits falling short of what is reasonably to be expected is not excusable. This accounts also for the tendency for doctrine to punish those who may be unable to resist doing what is wrong and to eschew consideration of whether the defendant had the normal capacities to act as he did.[37] The point of state punishment is to control those who manifest an antisocial disposition and, by denouncing wrongdoing, communicate appropriate standards of behaviour.[38] As an obvious illustration, recent doctrinal

[36] J Gardner, *ibid*, 593.
[37] N Lacey, in *Rethinking English Homicide Law* at 119
[38] N Lacey, *State Punishment* (Routledge, London, 1988), 65–8, 71–3.

development in the field of criminal damage points up the appropriateness of punishing those who act without 'evil in mind'. Limiting liability by requiring proof of a given mental attitude accompanying antisocial acts such as vandalism ignores the symbiotic relation existing between individual virtue and collective wellbeing. Vandals exhibit a dangerous and frightening character defect. This generates its own imperative to replace capacity with (good) character as the basis of responsibility.[39] Responsibility derives from the prosecution of the kind of life career which makes for poor judgment, deliberation, and ultimately morally unstructured choices. People who allow themselves to deviate from the path of virtue must take responsibility for the consequences of getting lost.[40]

Still to be discussed is how character works as a benchmark of liability. There are two main accounts. The first is that responsibility is avoided where the accused's deed is not representative of the accused's own (good) character. Defences, on this view operate where the defendant's wrongdoing is 'out of character'. The second is that responsibility is avoided where the defendant's reasons for doing wrong manifests a character consistent with what can be expected of responsible citizens placed in the context in which the defendant found himself.

Acting out of character

The standard version of character theory discussed here is initially plausible both in its ability to record what it is about certain occasions of wrongdoing which renders censure inappropriate and as a means of explaining existing doctrine. When say a person robs a bank under duress or kills under provocation we excuse/partially excuse his conduct because we understand that persons of good character can, in extreme conditions, act in defiance of their own standards, that is in defiance of their own good character. A couple of illustrations may be in order. It may not be commonplace; it may not always be meant; but it is not unheard of for loving partners to declare in the presence of others that

---

[39] RA Duff, 'Choice, Character and Criminal Liability' (1993) *Law and Philosophy* 345, 363.

[40] Aristotle, *Ethics* (Penguin, Harmondsworth, 1953), 90–1. For discussion see K Huigens, 'Virtue and Criminal Negligence' in (1998) *Buffalo Criminal Law Review* 431, at 434–9; cf L Zaibert, 'Intentionality, Voluntariness and Culpability' idem, 459 generally.

they would kill the other and/or the lover if it were found that they were cheating. Neither is it unheard of for there to be a rumble of approval from the audience when such fierce emotions are articulated. Such approval, expressed in terms such as 'I'd do it myself', indicates that where the things we do reflect our essential humanity rather than some defect of humanity they are thought to be excusable. Righteous indignation expresses rather than opposes our humanity. Equally strongly we condemn those whose violent outbursts, whether prompted or otherwise, express a violent disposition. We excuse the cheated spouse because they are not violent people. We denounce the jealous bully because they are. Yet more frequently we hear loving parents confess to ungovernable anger when dealing with inconsolable infants during sleepless nights. Here again 'I could have killed him/her' is met with 'I've been there'. National helplines are run not only for the child victims of parental abuse but also for those parents whose good will and humanity is tested by the stresses of child rearing. Here of course we are not talking about righteous indignation but another emotion which is a constituent element of the human condition, namely anger. And once again we distinguish between those whose anger expresses an individualised inability to deal with their situation and those whose anger expresses humanity's own inability. The not always coherent practices of blaming visible in tabloid newspapers express this difference in the black and white polarities of defendant mothers lacking emotional support and living in cramped conditions, treated as victims of circumstance, and defendant fathers/stepfathers treated as drunken, brutish bullies. Although the capacities to resist doing harm may be identical in any given case, moral intuition discerns a difference between the one-off (re) action of the oppressed carer and the more or less equally determined (re) action of the psychologically, and hence morally, fragile non-carer. Criminal doctrine seems to reflect this moral basis to provocation by denying a defence to those whose behaviour was dispositional and thus was not out of character. By contrast it is thought by some to be unfair 'to hold people responsible for actions which are out of character, but . . . fair to hold them so for actions in which their settled dispositions are centrally expressed.'[40a]

If we examine the out of character premise more closely, however, it begins to look less plausible. What is it, after all, to act out of character? It cannot surely mean simply acting inconsistently with the (good) standards of character we are wont to expect of the actor. If so a person could escape liability for theft or murder far too easily.

[40a] N Lacey *State Punishment* (1988), 68

Case 1

John, a person of previously good character, finds that his bank has, by mistake, credited his account with a huge sum of money. Although he knows he is not entitled to the money he withdraws it and spends the lot.

Case 2

John, a person of previously good character, having been left by Janet, his wife, and children, kills her and the children, preferring a dead family to an estranged one.

In both cases John's action appears out of character. He has never killed before and he has never stolen before. He acts as he does because of a never-to-be-repeated accident of fate which operates to subdue his usual rule-following disposition. When he looks back on what he did perhaps he cannot believe he did it, as it seems so alien to his character. Despite all these considerations few people are likely to conclude that John's conduct is even partially excusable. Indeed his action is inexcusable, previous good character notwithstanding. He had every opportunity to avoid acting as he did. In both cases he allowed his feelings, greed, possessiveness, to get the better of him and we feel that he is responsible because he should not have done.[41]

It is of course possible to justify a finding of responsibility within the parameters of this version of character theory by allowing people's actions to constitute them in their character.[42] As Duff puts it 'we are our characters, and are for that reason responsible for the actions which flow from them.' People who steal from or attack others display, by this very act, something about themselves which is authentically theirs.[43] In the above examples John shows himself to be the kind of person who is prone to flout rules even if the conditions had not previously arisen in which this disposition had manifested itself. Everyone has his or her price and John's is a little higher than your typical villain. To be a thief the reward must be large and the appropriation easy. To be a killer the cause must be existential. But previous good character

---

[41] Moreover, it would be morally nonsensical to treat John's responsibility as being any different if, in either case, what he had was in line with past behaviour.

[42] Fletcher, *Rethinking Criminal Law*, 801.

[43] RA Duff, 'Choice, Character and Criminal Liability' (1993) 12 *Law and Philosophy* 345.

seems to become then something of a red herring since any freely chosen action is liable to subvert it.[44] This version of character theory
offers little more guidance than capacity theory as to when moral
responsibility may be absent notwithstanding intentional wrongdoing.
Both are underpinned by a conception of virtue. The only relevance to
the ascription of liability that something is out of character is to under-
line the difficulty the virtuous actor may have had in acting otherwise.
No doubt for reasons such as these an out of character basis to the construction of criminal responsibility has not found favour in doctrine. It
is no answer to manslaughter that a doctor's disastrous blunder was
quite out of keeping with his usual admirable standards of competence.
It is no answer to murder that the accused would never hurt a fly save
the one person in the world, her spouse, whose very existence she experienced as an intolerable affront. These facts may mitigate the actor's
wrong but they do not excuse it.[45]

Occasionally, however, cases crop up where a person of apparently
good character has chosen to do something which is out of character
but in circumstances which block the usual inference that she is in fact
a person of bad character. A famous example is that of Patti Hearst, a
wealthy American heiress, who was kidnapped by a revolutionary
group, known as the Symbionese Liberation Army. After a long period
of indoctrination and abuse she adopted the values and beliefs of her
captors and engaged, apparently voluntarily, in various revolutionary
activities including bank robbery. Just as it would seem unfair to hold
her responsible for the change in character effected by this experience
so also it might be thought that punishment for these activities would
not be deserved.[46]

A rather different case was *Kingston* where the defendant committed a serious sexual assault on a young boy having had his drink spiked
by villains who had set him up for this purpose. Involuntary intoxication may negate *mens rea* or subvert a defendant's ability to engage in
practical reasoning. In such cases it clearly may ground a defence of
automatism along with concussion, post-traumatic stress syndrome
and hypoglycaemia.[47] Here, however, involuntary intoxication acted

---

[44] M Moore, *Placing Blame* (1997) 241 *et seq*. For an extended critique of this weakness within character theory see A Norrie (2000) 127–30.

[45] J Gardner, *The Gist of Excuses* (1998) n 7 citing J Murphy and Jean Hampton,
Forgiveness and Mercy (1988).

[46] For discussion see GR Sullivan, 'Making Excuses' in AP Simester and ATH Smith
(eds), *Harm and Culpability* (Clarendon Press, Oxford, 1996) 131.

[47] See M Moore, *Placing Blame*, 502.

merely as a disinhibitor. Is it an excuse that the accused's criminal intention was caused by the intoxication and would not have been formed otherwise? The Court of Appeal, allowing Kingston's appeal, had accepted his defence which amounted, in effect, to a claim that his conduct was out of character since the operative cause of his wrongdoing was not his own inclinations but the wrongful act of another.[48] Lord Taylor CJ drew a plausible comparison between involuntary intoxication and duress, namely that in both cases it may prompt an actor to form a (criminal) intention which would not otherwise be present. The comparison echoes the features described earlier in relation to the basic excuse template. Spiking a person's drink is a one-off external behavioural determinant having a normative significance akin to a crisis or emergency. What could be more abnormal than having one's drink spiked? What can be more normal than to lose one's normative 'radar' in response? Nobody can follow rules when they are drunk. Intoxication disables people from doing things they otherwise are able to do and causes people do things they would not otherwise do.

The House of Lords rejected such a basis for the defence. In their view, responsibility for the outcome would follow from the fact of forming an intention to commit the offence and **not from** the fact that this intention expressed a disposition to flout the relevant rule. On the face of it the reasoning is quite cogent. Kingston's 'excuse' seems to reduce to a form of moral buck-passing. I am not responsible because this other person is more responsible. What system of morality excuses on the basis that a person was induced, by the stratagem of others or otherwise, to act out of character? Do we excuse Othello for being Iago's dupe? Not likely. As explained earlier, it is not true that our actions are not properly deemed authentically ours simply because they are heavily determined by events outside our control. Authenticity of action is largely a matter of relating action to appetite. If action follows appetite it may be authentic even if the appetite itself is determined. By committing the offence Kingston was essentially owning up to a morally discreditable character trait.[49] It might be objected that this is more assertion than argument—a partial moral truth self-consciously designed to restrict the development of out of character excuses. But a moment's reflection suggests that this conception of authenticity is of

---

[48] W Wilson, 'Involuntary Intoxication: Excusing the Inexcusable' [1995] 1 *Res Publica* 25; GR Sullivan, 'Making Excuses' in AP Simester and ATH Smith (eds), *Harm and Culpability* 131.

[49] M Moore, *Placing Blame*, at 241.

more general application in criminal doctrine. In rape, for example, it may not simply be the rapist who is unable to disown his behaviour when prompted by intoxication. The consent of the victim may likewise not be vitiated simply because a mood change has been effected by the involuntary consumption of alcohol, even, it has been said, where the mood change is procured by the accused.[50]

On the other hand his was a character trait whose suppression is arguably a signal of virtue in itself. If Kingston had been a celibate priest with no experience of sex or alcohol moral condemnation let alone punishment would surely have been too much to stomach. All the criminal law can expect of us surely is that we keep our obnoxious desires under control and avoid the conditions under which such control may be subverted? But since Kingston was also in no way to blame for falling into his disinhibited state we cannot fairly attribute the actions prompted by this state to him either since these did not reflect the commitment, indicative in the pursuit of the life plan hitherto prosecuted, to the values his appetites opposed. To punish him would be unjust because the object of our punishment would be somebody quite different, namely the person he temporarily became for reasons outside his control. Of course there would be significant practical and evidential problems with recognising such a defence. Not only the obvious ones. Was this person intoxicated? Was this person involuntarily intoxicated? But more subtle ones. Do we acquit because he was intoxicated or because it made a difference to his behaviour? If the latter, upon what evidential basis do we decide whether the involuntary intoxication was operative in releasing his inhibitions? Do we take into account past behaviour? Such problems are not irremediable, however. For example, such a defence could operate with a reversed burden of proof and restricted in its operation to persons of previously good character;[51] similar to defences such as section 27 (3) Theft Act 1968 in relation to handling and section 6(3) Sexual Offences Act 1956 in relation to unlawful sexual intercourse with a minor.

Rejecting this approach Lord Mustill nevertheless allowed that an excuse might be available where a fundamental but temporary character change had been effected, rather than, as here, temporary disinhibition.[52]

---

[50] *Lang* (1975) 62 Cr. App R 50. G Williams, *Textbook of Criminal Law* (Stevens, London, 1983), 569.

[51] An argument proposed by Sullivan, above n. 7, 143–4.

[52] Cf Fletcher who insists that bad character is of the essence of the retributive theory of punishment. He distinguishes between those acts which are a mark of character, even

'The drug is not alleged to have created the desire to which the respondent gave way, but rather to have enabled it to be released.' Significantly such a distinction is capable of informing a limited out of character defence. One's settled dispositions, on this view, are those which would be acted upon in the absence of self-control. As such they form part—a hidden part—of an actor's character. They do so although they are never in fact acted upon. So on this argument a person would not have a defence if, like Kingston, he had been tempted by say the stratagem of others to steal a briefcase containing a sum of money too large to activate his usual sense of honesty. But a defence may be available if the defendant had had his drink spiked which led him to form an intention, preposterous for a person of his character and values, to steal a policeman's helmet. It would also seem to exculpate Patti Hearst, at least for the period during which her normal character was being subverted, since she can hardly be held responsible for doing things which owe no part to the normal process by which we constitute ourselves as human beings and moral agents.[53] Such an analysis goes some way to explaining the decision in *T*, encountered in chapter 4. The defendant was able to raise a defence to a charge of malicious wounding upon adducing evidence that she was suffering post-traumatic stress syndrome consequent upon having been raped a few days previously. There was no suggestion that she lacked *mens rea* or that her behaviour was compelled in any way. On the face of it, therefore, she escaped liability because her act was out of character. The case can be reconciled with *Kingston*, however, if we distinguish between events which release hidden character/personality traits (*Kingston*) and events which create alien character traits (*T*).[54]

The fact that an act is out of character may be the most plausible basis for certain existing defences, in particular provocation, but possibly also duress. The out-of-character account is here the most plausible because it seems unrealistic to suppose that there is any meaningful empirical grounding for the claim that the accused 'lost his self control'. What is it which is lost when one loses 'self-control'? Is it the

---

if that character has been foisted on the defendant against his will say by penury or brutalisation, and those which represent a temporary derangement of character (802).

[53] Whether or not she initially chose to become the character she adopted, it is appropriate to hold her morally responsible if the character traits, at the time she engaged in the relevant conduct, were constituent elements in her then personality and identity. Sullivan, n 51 above, 137. For further argument see Moore, *Placing Blame*, 560–80.

[54] In fact, it appears that the basis of her excuse was a temporary impairment of practical reasoning. It was the fact that she was confused and did not know what she was doing which excused rather than that her act was out of character, whether or not it was.

capacity to behave otherwise or more simply the obedient disposition? In everyday speech we talk of a person 'losing it'. Perhaps this phrase brings us close to what the defence of provocation is all about, namely a person who loses touch with himself so that he no longer acts as he is wont to do in accordance with the reasons which normally inform his actions. How else can we account for the fact that the defendant obtains a (partial) excuse although there is clearly nothing other than (justified) anger upon which to base it?

An out-of-character basis to excuses is less easily extended to cover other contexts where the actor 'loses it' as where he is involuntarily intoxicated. This is not an excuse like duress or provocation is an excuse where the actor is, in effect, saying 'anybody might have done this given the context'. 'Anybody' would not commit a serious sexual assault simply because they are intoxicated. It is not something virtuous people are motivated to do, even if intoxicated. The problem posed by such a basis to defences is the unlimited and unfocused range of villainy the defence could exculpate. With most currently recognised excuses operating to confess and avoid liability, such as duress, self-defence and provocation there is an objective referent which make the excuse fit for a workable system of norm enforcement. This is a requirement of a direct relationship between the crime committed and the external prompt. The actor kills because he is provoked. He robs a bank because he is forced to. He hits an aggressor to prevent the aggressor hitting him. This direct relationship makes it easy for us to determine whether it is fair to excuse and also, it must be acknowledged, to assess the evidence; it is easier to put ourselves in the defendant's shoes, experience what he experienced and thus evaluate his behaviour.

By contrast, involuntary intoxication creates no unmediated and proportionate link to a given crime. Who knows what evil dispositions the actor might act out having been slipped his Mickey Finn. We are left with few anxieties when we excuse say defendants who kill, in hot blood, a person who has just abused them whereas we will always be left in doubt whether Kingston's conduct was, in any sense relevant for the ascription of moral responsibility, attributable to the drug and whether, ultimately, it matters. Restrictions in the range of criminal defences are not necessarily a sign of a systemic failure to deliver criminal justice. There may be good reasons as well as bad reasons for allowing personal injustices to occur.[55] There are obvious reasons in

[55] For further discussion see W Wilson, 'Involuntary Intoxication: Excusing the Inexcusable' [1995] *Res Publica* 25, 34–6.

the case of an appetite-orientated behaviour such as sexual activity to conclude that disinhibition rather than subversion of the preconditions (rationality) for successfully rule-following is inexcusable whatever the circumstances. It may well be then that a defence of involuntary intoxication is best conceived as a capacity-based excuse in which the claim to avoid punishment is that the actor suffered a temporary failure of rationality. Such claims have already been accepted in contexts, such as T, which give the appearance that the actor's excuse was that he was acting out of character. In this case, however, the court's conclusion was that T, unlike Kingston, was deprived of the mind's normal ability to reason practically about what is or is not acceptable and/or a good thing to do. In this sense, at least, the consequence was to make her temporarily lose touch with who she actually was.

It is not necessarily unjust then to hold an actor responsible for wrongdoing simply because it does not reflect the character manifested in his usual behaviour but it may be unjust if it issued from a temporary derangement of character brought about for reasons beyond the actor's control. What about the corollary? Is it a fair basis for holding an actor responsible for his wrongdoing that it did 'express his settled dispositions'? This presents another problem. Excuses are needed for the things we do wrong rather than the people we are. We punish paedophiles, psychopaths and inveterate thieves not because they are bad people but because they have done bad things. Under appropriate conditions the things we do wrong, if done for a good reason, say under conditions of duress, do not lead to just censure and this is so whether we are of good or bad character. This is so also with justifications. We make no plausible moral distinction, for example, between the habitually violent person who, in a fit of uncharacteristic altruism, uses (reasonable) force to protect an innocent third party against unlawful attack and similar force used by an habitually pacific person for the same purpose.[56] If the basis of responsibility were otherwise there would be no reason, other than for reasons of evidence or possibly maintaining the moral hygiene of law enforcement, to await a criminal deed before we instituted punishment.[57] We could punish the paedophile for being a

---

[56] G Fletcher, *Rethinking Criminal Law*, 801; GR Sullivan, 'Making Excuses' in AP Simester and ATH Smith (eds), *Harm and Culpability*, 131, at 135–40.

[57] G Fletcher, *ibid*, 800–01, holds that it is enough that an actor commits one wrongful act to entitle the inference of bad character. This may be artificial but if we do not limit the inquiry in this way we subject the defendant to the prospect of an intrusive investigation into the state of his character. Cf RA Duff, 'Choice, Character and Criminal Liability' (1993) 12 *Law and Philosophy* 373, for a contrary view.

paedophile, the psychopath for being a psychopath. This we do not think morally justifiable, although in extreme cases we may be prepared to advocate some form of preventive detention.[58] We hold to a deed-centred view of moral responsibility because of a general understanding that characters, more so than actions, are so much a hostage to different determinants, including heredity, psychology and social and economic background.[59] It is what people do rather than what they are disposed to do which renders them a proper subject of condemnation and punishment. If we are not justified in holding people morally responsible for their characters we may, given our assumption of free will, be justified in censuring and punishing them for constituting and displaying their characters in their deeds.

Another Look at Character: Deploying Reasons

The above discussion makes the case that, provocation apart, an out of character rationale to excuses offers few insights unavailable to capacity theory to explain our disposition to hold responsible people of apparently good character who 'fall from grace' and excuse people of bad character where they had good reasons for acting as they did. John Gardner has recently sought to refine the manner in which character is thought relevant to criminal responsibility.[60] While character is still the touchstone of desert in punishment that desert is not linked to the question of whether or not a particular act is out of character for the defendant. Rather desert is linked to an evaluation of the actor's conduct as manifested in his deeds. The process of assigning criminal responsibility taps directly into the manner in which individuals morally evaluate the behaviour of others, that is by dint of the reasons for which people act. Praise for good deeds follows closely an actor's reasons for acting whereas censure for wrongdoing does not. We do not make the same distinction between an actor who harms another for harming's sake, say he burns down a rival's shop to steal a competitive advantage, and

---

[58] A suggestion of Lord Woolf, *The Times* 15 December 2001; *cf* P Robinson, 'Punishing Dangerousness' (2001) 114 *Harv LR* 1429.

[59] Cf M Moore, *Placing Blame*, 571. The idea probably accounts for the astonishing decision in *Gilks* [1972] 3 All ER 280 in which the court held that a person might be excused for a crime of dishonesty if, due to his social background, he believed, against normal social standards, his action not to be dishonest.

[60] J Gardner, 'The Gist of Excuses' (1998) *Buffalo Criminal Law Review* 575.

an actor whose actions harm others as avoidable side effects of morally neutral actions, say he fails to extinguish a cigarette before dropping it on a neighbour's rug. Both actions manifest a character lacking virtue.

Excusing or justifying action by the giving of reasons is a way of indicating commitment to the values expressed in the standard allegedly infringed. At the very least this may be successful in deflecting anger and hostility, if not necessarily the moral criticism which censure expresses. Where one is successful with the reasons offered one presents oneself as a person who can be trusted to do the right thing. In so doing one shows oneself fit for the role that one is discharging, whether friend, colleague, neighbour, fellow road user, spouse, police officer, politician and so on. People are subject to moral criticism when their deeds show them in a poor light in their different roles. The 'gist of excuses' is not then that an act is out of character nor that the actor lacked the capacity to have acted otherwise. Lack of capacity is no excuse at all if that incapacity signals a character flaw. And acting in defiance of one's settled dispositions is no reason to excuse either since, as shown in Cases 1 and 2, there is no gap between one's global character and the character one displays at any given time.[61] Rather it is that the conduct of the actor does not depart significantly from the standards to be expected of good citizens in the role inhabited by the actor. The important conclusion to be drawn from this is that excuses, like justifications, derive their moral force from the objective reasonableness of the defendant's action rather than its aberrational nature.[62] So, with duress it is not because the defendant is acting is out of character that we excuse him; it is because the circumstances surrounding his action prevents us from taking inferences about his general character. In Gardner's view his claim to be excused is a normative judgment 'I was not a coward' rather than an empirical one 'I am not normally one'.[63]

The reasons approach to character-based responsibility accounts for the doctrinal requirement that the defendant meets objective standards for crimes of negligence and acts reasonably when raising defences such as duress, provocation, and self-defence. The standards required to **exculpate** are societal standards of good citizenship and to **inculpate** deviations from such standards. These do not vary with a person's

---

[61] J Gardner, *ibid*, 576–8.

[62] In this, Gardner largely adopts a view previously espoused by S Kadish in 'Excusing Crime' (1987) 75 *Calif LR* 257

[63] Gardner, above n 61 at 577.

capacities or virtue. So it is no answer to a charge of driving without due care and attention that one was on one's first lesson and did one's best if that best fell short of the standards of ordinary, prudent motorists. Again, it is no excuse for an inexperienced soldier panicked into using more force than is reasonable that he showed as much level-headedness as he was capable of showing in the circumstances. In each case the excuse is tailored not to the individual capacities of the defendant but to expectations driven by the role he was performing.[64] The capacity approach, by contrast, finds the reasonableness ingredient less easy to account for since our capacities and opportunities inevitably vary with our own personal circumstances and history. It is unable to provide a principled explanation for the persistence of doctrinal features in offence and defence doctrine which prevent exculpatory claims being tailored according to the individual capacities of the defendant. Reasonableness requirements become therefore a way of cutting defences down to size for purpose of penal efficacy rather than inherent in the defence itself.

Left unaccounted for by this explanation are defences such as insanity, diminished responsibility and infancy where it is no part of the claim to be exempt from punishment that the actor conformed to societal expectations. On this approach such defences do not operate to excuse a person. Infants and the insane need no excuse for what they do. Rather personal incapacity to conform to generalised prohibitions exempts subjects from the kind of moral condemnation which excuses serve to counter.[65] The gist of excuses proceeds from the contrary assumption, namely that the accused is a normal member of society and, by virtue of that membership, deserves to be treated with respect, that is, as answerable for any act which falls short of the standards to which we expect normal people to conform. Like justifications, therefore, and unlike exemptions,' excuses are available only to those whose actions have intelligible rational explanations, ie whose actions properly reflected reasons for action that they took themselves to have.'[66] They are reasons sufficient to block the inference of bad character that rule infringements excite without being reasons sufficient in themselves

---

[64] Gardner, above n 61 at 587. Valid excuses must conform to this requirement of not falling short of the role standards applicable.

[65] *Ibid*, 589. 'Excuses rely on reason not the absence of it. People who cannot meet this condition are not responsible for their actions and need no justification or excuse'.

[66] J Gardner, 'Justifications and Reasons' in AP Simester and ATH Smith (eds), *Harm and Culpability*, 103, 121–2.

to defeat the reason to obey the rule. So, as explained earlier, a person has an excuse if, mistakenly though with good reason, he believes himself the subject of an imminent attack and uses force for the reason of deflecting the supposed attack. His reason for acting as he did was a good reason but it left his conduct unjustified since there was no actual (guiding) reason for it.[67]

An important by-product of this latter taxonomy of defences is that it offers a more reliable blueprint for the development of criminal defences than is offered by capacity theory, which depends upon the structure of existing defences to ensure that defence developments do not subvert the point and efficacy of the normative system. This is because the reasons which people offer for rule infringement are more easily systematisable and validated as reasons which ordinary responsible people would or may respond to. Any anxieties that opening up the range of defences in this way would destabilise the imperative quality of legal norms can be allayed by the development of partial defences/offences of lesser gravity along the lines of provocation in homicide. It is easy to see, for example, how the law of criminal homicide could generate a number of defences and partial defences grounded in socially validated judgments of character formed on the basis of the defendant's reasons for acting. These may include guiding reasons such as self-preservation or altruism or emotions, such as fear, anger, compassion or righteous indignation. Examples of defences fit for immediate inclusion into criminal doctrine on this basis include mercy killing, duress and disproportionate force in self-defence. In each of these cases there is a well understood reluctance to judge the actor as responsible/fully responsible when the reasons for disobedience do not show the actor in a bad/unduly bad light.[68] More broadly the jury are well positioned to evaluate any reasons offered by the defendant for his conduct as they do already in theft when assessing dishonesty. A reasons based approach affords the possibility that juries be given a central role in fitting an actor to a graduated list of crimes more precisely than a voluntariness/capacity based approach. Possible problems are that it may prove impractical as a guide to behaviour and would, in any event, be heavily dependent upon decontextualised moral judgments and attendant discrepancies in jury decisions.

---

[67] *Ibid*, 107–114.

[68] N Lacey, 'Partial Defences to Homicide' in A Ashworth and B Mitchell (eds), *Rethinking English Homicide Law*, 107 at 117–21.

Separating excuses from exemptions also lends a plausible coherence to defence doctrine. It creates a structure of liability which is responsive to the two morally uncontroversial reasons why censure and punishment for rule infringement may be unwarranted, namely that the actor had good reason for the infringement or that he lacked the reason necessary to conform. Separating defences in this way has an undeniable advantage lacking in capacity theory, namely that it maximises the possibility that criminal defences stay true to their moral counterparts. Either the defendant has an excuse or he lacks personal capacity. He cannot have it both ways and excuse himself on ground of personal fallibilities falling short of incapacity.[69] Availing oneself of duress asserts that one acted for reasons 'intelligible to the moral audience. A denial of responsibility rules all of this out and that is, accordingly, the line of defence which counts as an admission of defeat for any self respecting person.'[70] Capacity theory, by contrast, has no clear mechanism, as explained earlier, for excluding morally discreditable failures of voluntariness.

A UNITY TO EXCUSES?

While it must be admitted that in the general social context the disposition to blame and censure is heavily dependent upon the extent to which as individuals we conform to the expectations generated by our various roles we must, however, beware of extrapolating from this that the content of criminal excuses is similarly dependent. Left rather under-theorised by this account are defences such as duress and provocation where, since there is no guiding reason/moral justification for the defendant acting as he did, there is no good reason either. Good people do not kill in response to provocation, although admittedly they do kill if they mistakenly believe they are about to be attacked.[71] They do not feel justified in robbing banks in response to coercion, although admittedly a (good) counter assistant may well hand over to the robber the contents of her till at his insistence.[72] This suggests that an alternative rationale for these defences may be appropriate.

---

[69] The only concession to individual weakness that Gardner would make is perhaps in developing exemptions eg defences of impaired capacity extending beyond the remit of murder.

[70] J Gardner, 'The Gist of Excuses' (1998) *Buffalo Criminal Law Review*, 590.

[71] Gardner conflates such excuses.

[72] See discussion in ch 7.

What seems lacking in this account is a failure to accommodate one constant theme in the literature and cases governing excuses, namely the idea that state coercion is not a fair response to ordinary human frailty. Emergencies of any kind are apt to expose our weaknesses. We may be lucky and sail though life without having such weaknesses exposed. But if we are not; if we are the unlucky ones who are threatened with violence, who are subjected to provocation, who are placed in apparent danger, only chance controls whether we have been dealt the cards which enable us to conform our behaviour to the standards we expect our fellow citizens to reach. The point about criminal excuses is not, surely, that they are necessarily occasions when the actor acquits himself reasonably or in the cases of partial excuses part reasonably in the role he was placed although this is a judgment we may nevertheless be prepared to accede to. It is that as human beings our capacity and willingness to follow rules is not absolute and the authority of the state will suffer if it is not sensitive to that fact. Joshua Dressler makes this point particularly well:

> We (must avoid) . . . overzealous or even self-righteous use of the criminal law. The criminal law is not intended to correlate perfectly with our personal moral values . . . Thus although in the general run of cases we should expect excuse law to conform roughly with our feelings about blame and guilt, a perfect relationship should not be expected. In some cases, it is proper for the law to excuse me, although I do not excuse myself. We should set the criminal law standards of conduct somewhat *below* the level to which we tend to hold ourselves in our private lives.[73]

Doctrinal appearances may deceive, therefore. Excuses, like justifications, seem to be rooted in socially validated standards of good citizenship. These and deep-seated personal incapacity no doubt account for a large proportion of exculpatory claims. However, we need a richer conception of criminal excuses than this. Excuses are also needed where the defendant's character and/or ability to make the right choices has been subverted by some external trauma or crisis which renders the defendant unable to reason practically through to action or otherwise decide upon the morally appropriate response to a given prompt. Cases of involuntary intoxication and temporary insanity following trauma, concussion or hypnotism are obvious examples of

---

[73] J Dressler, 'Exegesis of the Law of Duress: Justifying the Excuse and Searching for its Proper Limits (1989) 62 *S Cal L Rev* 1331. For a similar view see S Kadish 'Moral Excess' [2001] 32 *McGeorge Law Review* 1 at 15.

these.[74] But ordinary people wishing to rely on cognate defences such as duress and provocation may also be deprived temporarily of their usual character or ability to engage in practical reasoning. They may be so scared, so enraged and so on that the fact that behaving in a particular way is unlawful and wrong does not register as a reason to behave accordingly.

Most people recognise that the most balanced among us can 'lose it' on occasions. If the fact of 'losing it' expresses a general human failing rather than a failing specific to this actor it seems proper that this should count as a criminal excuse, if it is not entirely successful in deflecting the moral condemnation that such excuses normally embody. Accommodating human weaknesses by fashioning extensions to the range of exemptions does not seem to meet the case of ordinary decent people acting inappropriately in the face of one-off crises or emergencies. If we examine duress it is clear that under threat of death a person may act reasonably in acceding to another's demand that he commit a criminal wrong, say he hands over the money in his till to an armed bank robber. And yet equally we can conceive of duress cases where the defendant's claim to avoid punishment is not that he acted reasonably in his own eyes. On the contrary his will may be so overborne by fear that reason played no part in what he was doing. In such cases his claim to avoid punishment and censure is not grounded in the reasonableness of what he did but in the unfairness of expecting people to behave properly when their rule-following disposition has been subverted for reasons outside their control.[75]

Again if we examine provocation, it is hard to see that our propensity to excuse derives from the fact that the response, as Gardner puts it, 'exhibits as much self restraint as we have a right to demand of someone in her situation.'[76] This is clearly not the case. Rather, the propensity acknowledges that even good, well balanced people may sometimes act in defiance of their own character standards. This is not to argue that an excuse is potentially available wherever a person acts out of character or loses the capacity to conform his behaviour to the

---

[74] As Lacey puts it: 'The seriously involuntarily intoxicated defendant is simply not engaged in the usual process of practical reasoning, and it seems obtuse to insist on judging her as if she is or consigning her to the category of exemptions.' See N Lacey, 'Partial Defences to Homicide' in A Ashworth and B Mitchell (eds), *Rethinking English Homicide Law*, 107 at 121.

[75] For discussion see RA Duff, 'Rule Violations and Wrongdoings: What does the Criminal Law Say to Citizens?' (2002), 47.

[76] Gardner, above n 70 at 579.

law. The excuse must be grounded in social morality and it must be consistent with an effective system for the enforcement of criminal norms. It is for both these reasons that there is a requirement for most excuses that the defendant could not reasonably be expected to act otherwise. It is not solely to limit the range of defences to cases where the defendant is acting for reasons sufficient in either his own eyes or the eyes of others to justify acting in this way. Rather, more loosely, it is to ensure that the defendant temporary aberration of character or loss of capacity to obey is socially validated. Ordinary people sometimes 'lose it'. We may not approve but if it signals a characteristic which is to do with being a human being rather than being a bad person it is right to take this into account.

Recent doctrinal developments in the area of duress and provocation support this conclusion. There is an increasing tendency, lamented by most, to excuse those who failed to live up to objective standards of self control and courage.[77] For, example, in *Emery* the defendant had been convicted of cruelty for having failed to protect her child from violence by her partner, having suffered from prolonged physical abuse, herself, at his hands. The Court of Appeal held that it would be right for the jury to be allowed to consider whether there were special reasons why she may have excusably acted with less fortitude than ordinary people. Clause 25(1) of the Draft Criminal Code adopts a comparable method of 'personalising' the excuse requiring the jury to consider whether 'the threat is one which in all the circumstances (including any of [the defendants] personal characteristics that affect its gravity) he cannot reasonably be expected to resist.' It should be noted that this test centres the excuse in what we can reasonably expect of the defendant not what we expect of the reasonable man. The argument currently being advanced is that this is quite fair since it is the defendant who is asking to be excused.[78] This is treated as self evident in the neighbouring field of self defence where the test of proportionate reaction is sensitive to without being dictated by the predicament faced by the defender.[79] The overzealousness referred to by Dressler counsels against requiring citizens routinely to match up to the standards which jurors might reasonably set for themselves.

---

[77] See for example J Horder, 'Diminished Responsibility and Provocaction (1999) *Kings College Law Review*; J Gardner and T Macklem, 'Compassion without Respect? Nine Fallacies in R v Smith' [2001] *Crim LR* 623.

[78] See also *Bowen* [1996] 4 All ER 837; *Martin* [2000] *Crim LR* 615.

[79] *Palmer v R* [1971] 1 All ER 1077.

Similar decisions have been reached in the field of provocation but with less reason. Cowardice is not a character trait which is constitutive of certain forms of wrongdoing. Having low standards of self-control is. It is the reason for most crimes of violence. Nevertheless in *Morgan Smith* the House of Lords held that it was not fatal to the defence of provocation that the defendant's loss of self-control may have been attributable to some constitutional weakness in the defendant. In attempting to convey to the jury the standard of self-control expected of the defendant, the judge should not use the reasonable man as a comparator. The jury should be told that the same standards of self-control are expected of everyone regardless of their psychological make-up. But occasionally they should also be told that this is a principle and not a rigid rule which may sometimes be trumped by a yet more important principle, which is to do justice in the particular case. Lord Hoffman concluded 'the jury may think that there was some characteristic of the accused, whether temporary or permanent, which affected the degree of control which society could reasonably have expected of **him** and which it would be unjust not to take into account. If the jury take this view, they are at liberty to give effect to it.'

The strength of a theory is to be found in its explanatory potential and in its capacity to predict. Capacity theory, by and large, explains very well the normative basis of criminal liability and the full scope of the defences on offer. What it fails to do is to account for the paucity of these defences. Character theory attends to many of these weaknesses but in its attempt to render moral virtue the basis of responsibility ignores some basic ethical limits placed upon the state's authority to punish. One of these, exemplified in *Emery*, is that if it is more than we can reasonably expect that a person conforms her conduct to the standards required then it is wrong to punish unless the actor's failure discloses the very vices—cruelty, dishonesty, lack of concern for others, and so on which criminal norms serve to underwrite. *Emery* disclosed no such vice. Her vice was that she lacked fortitude. Since she was not responsible for this it cannot be right to punish her for it. As we are wont to say 'There but for the grace of God.' Or as Victor Tadros, more analytically, puts it, 'Imposing criminal liability expresses not just that an individual has been at fault, it expresses the indignation of the state, as a representative of society, towards the individual in question. But such indignation is only appropriate when the individual has failed to show adequate consideration to the interests of others.[80] He does not so fail where, whatever the incentives to have acted otherwise, say there was a policeman at his shoulder, he would have been unable to have acted differently. We cannot truly say the same of *Morgan Smith*. The vice he disclosed, the vice of unjustified anger and aggression, is exactly the kind of vice towards which criminal norms are directed. That he lacked the capacity or inclination to control his hostile urges may be a reason to exempt him from liability partially or fully on the grounds of personal incapacity or weakness but it can be no reason to excuse.

---

[80] 'The Characters of Excuse' (2001) *Oxford Journal of Legal Studies* 517.

Bibliography

Alexander, L, 'Affirmative Duties and Limits of Self-Sacrifice' (1996) 15 *Law and Philosophy* 65

——, 'Criminal Liability for Omissions' University of San Diego School of Law, Working Paper 22, 2000–01

——, 'Harm, Offence, and Morality' (1994) 7 *Canadian Journal of Law and Jurisprudence* 199

——, 'Insufficient Concern: A Unified Conception of Criminal Culpability' (2000) 88 *Cal LR* 955

Alldridge, P, 'The Doctrine of Innocent Agency' (1990) 2 *Crim LR* LF 45

Allen, FR, *The Decline of the Rehabilitative Ideal: Penal Policy and Social Purpose* (Yale University Press, New Haven, 1981)

Andenaes, J, 'The General Preventive Effects of Punishment' (1966) 114 *U Pa LR* 949

Aristotle, *Ethics*, Book 3 (Penguin, Harmondsworth, 1953)

Ashworth, AJ, 'Belief, Intent and Criminal Liability' in J Eekelaar and J Bell (eds), *Oxford Essays in Jurisprudence*, third series, (Clarendon Press, Oxford, 1989)

——, 'Criminal Attempts and the Role of Resulting Harm under the Code and under the Common Law' (1988) 19 *Rutgers LJ* 725

——, 'Criminal Liability in a Medical Context: The Treatment of Good Intentions' in AP Simester and ATH Smith (eds), *Harm and Culpability* (Clarendon Press, Oxford, 1996)

——, 'Testing Fidelity to Legal Values' (2000) 63 *MLR* at 320

——, 'Good Intentions' in AP Simester and ATH Smith (eds), *Harm and Culpability* (Clarendon Press, Oxford, 1996)

——, 'Is the Criminal Law a Lost Cause?' (2000) 116 *LQR* 225

——, *Principles of Criminal Law* (OUP, Oxford, 1999)

——, 'Self Defence and the Right to Life' [1975] *Camb LJ* 272

——, 'Sharpening the Subjective Element in Criminal Liability' in RA Duff and N Simmonds (eds), *Philosophy and the Criminal Law* (Wiesbaden, 1984)

——, 'Taking the Consequences' in S Shute, J Gardner and J Horder (eds), *Action and Value in the Criminal Law* (Clarendon Press, Oxford, 1993)

Ashworth, AJ, 'The European Convention and the Criminal Law' in *The Human Rights Act and the Criminal Justice and Regulatory Process,* Cambridge Centre for Public Law (Hart, Oxford, 1999)

——, 'The Scope of Criminal Liability for Omissions' (1989) 105 *LQR* 424

Ashworth and Steiner, 'Criminal Omissions and Public Duties: The French Experience' [1990] *LS* 153

Ashworth and von Hirsch *Principled Sentencing* 2nd edn (Hart, Oxford, 1997)

Atiyah, P, *Promises, Morals and Law* (Clarendon Press, Oxford, 1981)

Austin, JL, 'A Plea for Excuses' (1956-7) *Proceedings of the Aristotelian Society* 57

Austin, J, *Lectures on Jurisprudence* (John Murray, London, 1869)

Bayles, M, 'Character, Purpose and Criminal Responsibility' (1982) 12 *Law and Philosophy* 5

Beale, J, 'The Proximate Cause of an Act' (1920) 33 *Harv LR* 633

Benn, SI,' 'Interests' in Politics' (1960) *Proceedings of the Aristotelian Society* 60

Bennett, J, *The Act Itself* (OUP, Oxford, 1995)

Beyleveld, D, 'Deterrence Research as a Basis for Deterrence Policies' (1979) 18 *Howard Journal of Criminal Justice* 135

Bhaskar, R, *Dialectics: The Pulse of Freeedom* (Verso, London, 1993)

Braithwaite, J and Pettit, P, *Not Just Deserts* (OUP, Oxford, 1990)

Brody, SR, *The Effectiveness of Sentencing: a Review of the Literature* (Home Office Research Study No 35, 1976)

Brudner, A, 'Agency and Welfare in the Penal Law' in S Shute, J Gardner and J Horder (eds), *Action and Value in Criminal Law* (Clarendon Press, Oxford, 1993)

——, 'A Theory of Necessity' [1987] 7 *OJLS* 339

Campbell, K, 'Offences and Defences' in I Dennis (ed), *Criminal Law and Criminal Justice* (Sweet & Maxwell, London, 1987)

Carson, WG, White Collar Crime and the Institutionalisation of Ambiguity, in M Fitzgerald *et al Crime and Society* (Routledge, London,1990)

Christopher, R, 'Self Defense and Objectivity' [1998] *Buffalo Crim LR* 537

——, 'Unknowing Justification and the Logical Necessity of the *Dadson* Principle in Self- Defence' (1995) 15 *OJLS* 229

Cicca, S, 'Sterilising the Intellectually Disabled: The Approach of the High Court of Australia in *Department of Health v JWB and SMB*' (1993) *Med LR* 186

Clarkson, C, 'Context and Culpability in Involuntary Manslaughter' in AJ Ashworth and B Mitchell (eds), *Rethinking English Homicide Law* (Clarendon Press, Oxford, 2000)

Collingwood, RG, 'On the So-Called Idea of Causation' (1938) *Proceedings of the Aristotelian Society*

Crocker, L 'Harm and Culpability: Which Should be the Organising Principle of the Criminal Law? A Retributive Theory of Criminal Causation' (1994) 1 *Contemp Leg Issues* 65

Cullen, FT and Gilbert, KE, *Reaffirming Rehabilitation* (Cincinnatti, 1982)

Dan-Cohen, M, 'Decision Rules and Conduct Rules: On Acoustic Separation in Criminal Law' (1984) 97 *Harv LR* 625

Davies, M, 'Why Attempts Deserve Less Punishment Than Complete Crimes' (1986) 5 *Law and Philosophy* 1

Dennis, I, 'The Critical Condition of Criminal Law' [1997] *Current Legal Problems* 213

——, 'The Elements of Attempt' [1980] *Crim LR* 758

——, 'The Mental Element for Accessories' in PF Smith (ed), Criminal Law: *Essays in Honour of JC Smith* (Butterworths, London, 1987)

Dickens, Charles, *Pickwick Papers* (Random House, New York, 1943)

Dressler, J, 'Does One Mens Rea Fit All? Thoughts on Alexander's Unified Conception of Criminal Culpability' (2000) 88 *Cal LR* 955

——, 'Exegesis of the Law of Duress: Justifying the Excuse and Searching for its Proper Limits' (1989) 62 *Cal L Rev* 1331

——, 'Reassessing the Theoretical Underpinnings of Accomplice Liability: New Solutions to an Old problem' (1985) 37 *Hastings LJ* 111

——, 'Reflections on Excusing Wrongdoers: Moral Theory, New Excuses and the Moral Penal Code' (1988) 19 *Rut LJ* 671

——, *Understanding Criminal Law* (Matthew Bender, New York, 1988)

Duff, RA, 'Acting, Trying and Criminal Liability' in S Shute, J Gardner and J Horder (eds), *Action and Value in Criminal Law* (Clarendon Press, Oxford, 1994)

——, 'Choice, Character and Criminal Liability' (1993) 12 *Law and Philosophy* 345

——, *Criminal Attempts* (OUP, Oxford, 1996)

——, *Intention Agency and Criminal Liability: Philosophy of Action and the Criminal Law* (Basil Blackwell, Oxford, 1990)

——, 'Intentions Legal and Philosophical' (1989) 9 *OJLS* 76

Duff, RA, 'Rule Violations and Wrongdoings: What does the Criminal Law Say to Citizens?' (1999)

——, *Trials and Punishment*, (CUP, Cambridge)

——, in RA Duff (ed.), *Philosophy and the Criminal Law* (CUP, Cambridge,1998)

——, 'Rule Violations and Wrongdoings;' in S Shute and A Simester (eds) Criminal Law Theory: Doctrines of the General Part (OUP, Oxford, 1999)

——, and von Hirsch, A, 'Responsibility, Retribution and the Voluntary' [1997] *Camb LJ* 103

Durkheim, E, *The Division of Labour in Society* (Macmillan, London, 1984)

Dworkin, R, *Life's Dominion* (Fontana, London, 1993)

——, 'Obligations of Community' in J Raz (ed), *Authority* (Duckworth, London, , 1990)

——, *Taking Rights Seriously* (Duckworth, London, 1977)

Elliot, DW, 'Necessity, Duress and Self Defence' [1989] *Crim LR* 611

Engels, F, *The Origins of the Family, Private Property and the State* (Lawrence and Wishart, London, 1972)

Evans, EP, *The Criminal Prosecution and Capital Punishment of Animals* (Faber and Faber, London, 1987)

Feinberg, J, *Harm to Others* (Clarendon Press, Oxford, 1984)

——, *Harm to Self* (Clarendon Press, Oxford, 1986) chs 18–19

——, 'Justice, Fairness and Rationality' (1972) 81 *Yale LJ* 1004

Field, S and Lynn, M, 'The Capacity for Recklessness' (1992) 12 *LS* 74

Finnis, J, 'Authority' in Raz (ed.), *Authority* (Duckworth, London, 1990)

——, 'Intention and Side Effects' in RG Frey and CW Morris (eds), *Liability and Responsibility* (St Pauls, Minn, 1991)

Fletcher, G, *Basic Concepts of Criminal Law* (OUP, Oxford, 1998)

——, 'Fall and Rise of Criminal Theory' [1998] *Buffalo Criminal Law Review* 275

——, 'On the Moral Irrelevance of Bodily Movements' (1994) 142 *U Pa LR* 1443

——, *Rethinking Criminal Law* (Little Brown and Company, Boston, Toronto, 1978)

——, 'The Right Deed for the Wrong Reason: A Reply to Mr Robinson' (1975) 23 *UCLA LR* 293

Foucault, M, *Discipline and Punish: The Birth of the Prison* (Penguin, Harmondsworth, 1976)

Fuller, L, *The Morality of Law* (Yale University Press, New Haven, 1969)

Fumerton, R and Kress, K, 'Causation and the Law: Pre-Emption, Lawful Sufficiency and Causal Sufficiency' (2001) 64 *Law and Contemporary Problems* 83

Gardner, J, 'Justifications and Reasons' in AP Simester and ATH Smith (eds.), *Harm and Culpability* (Clarendon Press, Oxford, 1996)

——, 'On the General Part of the Criminal Law' in RA Duff (ed), *Philosophy and the Criminal Law* (CUP, Cambridge, 1998)

——, 'Rationality and the Rule of law in Offences Against the Person' [1994] *Camb LJ* 502

——, 'The Gist of Excuses' (1998) *Buffalo Criminal Law Review* 575

Gardner, J and Jung, H, 'Making Sense of Mens Rea: Antony Duff's Account' (1991) 11 *OJLS* 559

Gardner, J and Macklem, T, 'Compassion without Respect? Nine Fallacies in *R v Smith*' [2001] *Crim LR* 623

Gardner, S, 'Necessity's Newest Inventions' [1991] 11 *OJLS* 125

Glazebrook, PR, 'Should We Have a Law of Attempted Crime?' [1969] 85 *LQR* 28

——, 'The Necessity Plea in English Criminal Law' [1972] *CLJ* 87

——, 'Situational Liability' in PR Glazebrook (ed.), *Reshaping the Criminal Law* (Stevens, London, 1978), 108

——, 'Structuring the Criminal Code: Functional Approaches to Complicity, Incomplete Offences and General Defences' in AP Simester and ATH Smith (eds), *Harm and Culpability* (Clarendon Press, Oxford, 1996)

Goff, R, 'The Mental Element in the Crime of Murder' (1988) 104 *LQR* 30

Greaves, CF, The Criminal Law Consolidation and Amendment Acts of the 24 & 25 Vict. (2nd edn., London, 1862)

Griffin, J, *Value Judgement* (OUP, Oxford, 1996)

Gross, H, *A Theory of Criminal Justice* (OUP, New York, 1979)

——, *A Theory of Punishment* (OUP, Oxford, 1979)

Hall, J, *General Principles of Criminal Law* (Bobbs Merrill, Indianapolis, 1960)

Hart, HLA, *Punishment and Responsibility: Essays in the Philosophy of Law* (Clarendon Press, Oxford, 1968)

——, *The Concept of Law* (Clarendon Press, Oxford, 1961)

Hart, HLA, and Honore, HM, *Causation in the Law* (Clarendon Press, Oxford, 1982)

Hassett, P, 'Absolutism in Causation' (1987) 38 *Syracuse L Rev* 683

Holmes, OW, *Lectures on the Common Law* (Boston, 1881)

Honderich, T, *Punishment: The Supposed Justifications* (Penguin, Harmondsworth, 1984)

Honore, A, 'Are Omissions Less Culpable?' in P Cane and J Stapleton (eds), *Essays for Patrick Atiyah* (Clarendon Press, Oxford, 1991)

Horder, J, 'Crimes of Ulterior Intent' in A Simester and ATH Smith (ed), *Harm and Culpability* (Clarendon Press, Oxford, 1996)

——, 'Gross Negligence and Criminal Culpability' (1997) 47 *U Toronto LJ* 495

——, 'Intention in the Criminal Law: A Rejoinder' [1995] *MLR* 678

——, 'Occupying the Moral High Ground/ The Law Commission on Duress' [1994] *Crim LR* 334

——, 'On the Irrelevance of Motive in Criminal Law' in J Horder (ed), *Oxford Essays in Jurisprudence* (Clarendon Press, Oxford, 2000)

——, 'Provocation and Diminished Responsibility' (1999) *Kings College Law Review*

——, Provocation and Responsibility (OUP, Oxford, 1992)

——, 'Rethinking Non-Fatal Offences Against the Person' [1994] *OJLS* 335

——, 'Self Defence, Necessity and Duress' [1998] *Can J of Law and Juris* 143

——, 'Varieties of Intention, Criminal Attempts and Endangerment' (1994) 14 *LS* 335

Hornsby, J, 'On What's Intentionally Done' in S Shute *et al* (eds), *Action and Value in the Criminal Law* (Clarendon Press, Oxford, 1994)

Hughes, G, 'Criminal Omissions' (1958) 67 *Yale LJ* 590

Huigens, K, 'Virtue and Criminal Negligence' (1998) *Buffalo Criminal Law Review* 431

Hume, D, *An Enquiry Concerning Human Understanding*, (Open Court, Illinois,1907)

Jarvis Thomson, J, 'Self Defence' (1991) 20 *Phil & Pub Aff* 283

Jonsen, A and Toulmin, S, *The Abuse of Casuistry* (University of California Press, London,1988)

Kadish, S, 'Complicity, Blame and Cause: A Study in the Interpretation of Doctrine' (1985) 73 *Calif LR* 323

——, 'Excusing Crime' (1987) 75 *Calif LR* 257

——, 'Fifty Years of Development in the Criminal Law' (1999) 87 *Cal LR*

——, 'Moral Excess' (2000) 32 *McGeorge Law Review* 1

——, 'Respect for Life and Regard for Rights in the Criminal Law' in *Blame and Punishment* (Macmillan, New York, 1987)

Kaganas, F, 'Domestic Homicide, Gender and the Expert' in A Bainham, S Day Sclater and M Richards (eds), *Body Lore and Laws* (Hart Publishing, Oxford, 2001)

Kahan, D, 'Punishment Incommensurability' (1998) 1 *Buffalo Criminal Law Review* 691

Kant, I, *Prolegomena to any Future Metaphysics* (Bobbs Merrill, Indianapolis, 1950)

——, *The Metaphysical Element of Justice* (Bobbs Merrill, Indianapolis, 1965)

Katz, L, *Bad Acts and Guilty Minds* (University of Chicago Press, Chicago, 1987)

——, 'Why the Successful Assassin is More Wicked than the Unsuccessful One' (2000) 88 *Calif LR* 791

Kelman, M 'Interpretive Construction in the Substantive Criminal Law' (1981) 33 *Stanford LR* 591

Kennedy, I *Treat Me Right* (OUP, Oxford, 1988)

Kenny, A 'Intention and Purpose in Law' in RS Summers (ed), *Essays in Legal Philosophy* (Blackwell, Oxford, 1968)

Lacey, N 'A Clear Concept of Intention: Elusive or Illusory?' (1993) 56 *MLR* 621

——, 'Contingency and Criminalisation' in I Loveland (ed) *The Frontiers of Criminality*, (London, Sweet & Maxwell, 1995)

——, 'Contingency, Coherence and Conceptualism: Reflections on the Encounter between 'Critique' and the Philosophy of the Criminal Law' in RA Duff (ed) *Philosophy and the Criminal Law* (CUP, Cambridge, 1998)

——, 'In Search of the Responsible Subject' [2001] *MLR* 320

——, 'Partial Defences to Homicide' in A Ashworth and B Mitchell (eds), *Rethinking English Homicide Law* (Clarendon Press, Oxford, 2000)

——, *State Punishment* (Routledge, London, 1988)

LaFave, W, and Scott, A, *Criminal Law* (West, Minnesota, 1978)

Lanham, D, 'Accomplices and Withdrawal' (1981) 97 *LQR* 575

——, 'Larsonneur Revisited' [1976] *Crim LR* 276

——, 'Primary and Derivative Liability' [2000] *Crim LR* 707

Law Com Report No 131, *Assisting and Encouraging Crime* (1993)

Law Com Report No 218, *Legislating the Criminal Code: Offences Against the Person Act 1861* (1998)

Law Com Report No 237, *Legislating the Criminal Code: Involuntary Manslaughter* (1996)

Leavens, A, 'A Causation Approach to Criminal Omissions' (1988) 76 *Cal LR* 547

Lucas, JR, *On Justice* (Clarendon Press, Oxford, 1980)

Lord Macauley, *Introductory Report upon the Indian Penal Code* (Longmans Green & Co, 1898)

MacIntyre, A, *After Virtue* (Duckworth, London, 1981)

——, 'A Mistake About Causality in the Social Sciences' in P Lazlett and D Runciman (eds), *Philosophy, Politics and Society* (OUP, Oxford, 1956)

Mackie, JL, 'The Grounds of Responsibility' in PMS Hacker and J Raz (eds), *Law, Morality and Society* (Clarendon Press, Oxford, 1977)

Mahoney, M, 'Legal Images of Battered Women: Redefining the Issue of Separation' (1993) 90 *Mich L Rev* 1

Marshall, SE and Duff, RA, 'Criminalisation and Sharing Wrongs' [1998] *Can J of Law and Jurisprudence* 7

McColgan, A, 'In Defence of Battered Women who Kill' (1993) 13 *OJLS* 508

——, *Women Under the Law, The False Promise of Human Rights* (Pearson, Harlow, 2000)

Mclaughlin, 'Proximate Cause' (1921) 39 *Harv LR* 149

Meyerson, D, 'Fundamental Contradictions in Critical Legal Studies' (1991) 11 *OJLS* 439

Mill, JS, *A System of Logic* (Longmans, London, 1843)

——, 'On Liberty' in J Gray (ed) *On Liberty and Other Essays*, (OUP, Oxford, 1991)

Moore, GE, *Ethics* (Thornton Butterworth, 1912)

Moore, M, *Act and Crime: The Philosophy of Action and its Implications for Criminal Law* (Clarendon Press, Oxford, 1993)

——, 'Causation and the Excuses' (1985) 73 *Calif LR* 1091

——, *Placing Blame* (Clarendon Press, Oxford, 1997)

——, 'The Metaphysics of Causal Intervention' (2000) 88 *Calif LR* 827

Morse, S, 'Diminished Capacity' in Shute et al (eds), *Action and Value in Criminal Law* (Clarendon Press, Oxford, 1993)

——, 'The Moral Metaphysics of Causation and Results' (2000) 88 *Calif LR* 879

Murphy, JG, 'Marxism and Retribution' in Duff and Garland (eds) *A Reader on Punishment* (OUP, Oxford, 1994)

Murphy, J and Hampton, J, *Forgiveness and Mercy* (1988)

Norrie, A, 'A Critique of Criminal Causation' (1991) 54 *MLR* 685

——, *Crime Reason and History* (Weidenfeld and Nicolson, London, 1993)

——, *Law Ideology and Punishment* (Kluwer, London, 1991)

——, 'Oblique Intention and Legal Politics' [1989] *Crim LR* 793

——, *Punishment Responsibility and Justice* (Clarendon Press, Oxford, 2000)

——' 'Simulcra of Morality'? Beyond the Ideal/ Actual Antinomies of Criminal Justice' in RA Duff (ed), *Philosophy and the Criminal Law* (CUP, Cambridge, 1998)

——, 'After Woollin' [1999] *Crim LR* 532

Nozick, R, *Anarchy State and Utopia* (Clarendon Press, Oxford, 1974)

Packer, HL, *The Limits of the Criminal Sanction* (OUP, Oxford, 1968), 296

Patient, I, 'Some Remarks about the Element of Voluntariness in Offences of Absolute Liability' [1968] *Crim LR* 23

Paton, HJ, *The Moral Law: Kant's Groundwork of the Metaphysic of Morals* (Hutchinson, London, 1948)

Perkins, R, 'Criminal Attempt and Related Problems' (1955) 2 *UCLA L Rev* 319

——, and R Boyce, *Criminal Law* (Foundation Press, New York, 1982)

Popper, K, *Conjectures and Refutations* (Routledge, London, 1959)

Porter, R, *The Greatest Benefit to Mankind: A Medical History of Humanity from Antiquity to the Present* (Harper Collins, London, 1997)

Quinton, A, 'On Punishment' in P Lazlett and D Runciman (eds), *Philosophy, Politics and Society* (Clarendon Press Oxford, 1956), 83

Raz, J, *The Authority of Law* (OUP, Oxford, 1979)

——, *The Morality of Freedom* (Clarendon Press, Oxford, 1986)

Ripley, C, 'A Theory of Volition' 11 *Am Phil Q* 141

Robinson, PH, 'A Theory of Justification: Societal Harm as a Prerequisite to Criminal Liability' (1975) 23 *UCLA LR* 266

——, 'Causing the Conditions of One's Own Defence' (1985) 71 *Virg LR* 1

——, *Criminal Law Defences* (West, St Paul, 1984)

——, 'Criminal Law Defences: A Systematic Analysis' (1982) *Col L Rev* 199

——, 'Punishing Dangerousness' (2001) 114 *Harv LR* 1429

——, 'Rules of Conduct and Principles of Adjudication' (1990) 57 *Univ of Chicago LR* 729

Robinson, PH, 'Should the Criminal Law Abandon the Actus Reus–Mens Rea Distinction?' in S Shute, J Gardner, J Horder (eds), *Action and Value in Criminal Law* (Clarendon Press, Oxford, 1993)

——, *Structure and Function of Criminal Law* (OUP, Oxford, 1997)

Ryle, G, *The Concept of Mind* (Hutchinson's University Library, 1949)

Salmond, J, *Jurisprudence* (Stevens, London, 1947)

Sartre, JP, *Existentialism and Humanism* (Methuen, London, 1970)

Saunders, K, 'Voluntary Acts and the Criminal Law: Justifying Culpability Based on the Existence of Volition' (1988) 49 *U Pitt L Rev* 443

Sayre, J, 'Criminal Attempts' 41 (1928) Harv *LR* 821

——, 'The Present Significance of *Mens Rea* in the Criminal Law' (1934) *Harvard Legal Essays* 399

Schopp, RF, *Automatism, Insanity, and the Psychology of Criminal Responsibility* (Clarendon Press, Oxford, 1991)

——, *Justification Defences and Just Convictions* (Cambridge University Press, Cambridge, 1998)

Shapira, R, 'Willed Bodily Movement' (1998) *Buffalo Criminal Law Review* 349

Simester, AP, 'Can Negligence be Culpable?' in J Horder (ed), *Oxford Essays in Jurisprudence* (Clarendon Press, Oxford, 2000)

——, 'On the So-called Requirement for Voluntary Action' [1998] *Buffalo Criminal Law Review* 403

——, 'Why Distinguish Intention from Foresight?' in AP Simester and ATH Smith (eds), *Harm and Culpability* (Clarendon Press, Oxford, 1996)

Singer, P, *Rethinking Life and Death* (OUP, Oxford, 1995)

Smart, A, 'Criminal Responsibility for Failing to do the Impossible' (1987) 103 *LQR* 532

Smith, JC, 'Criminal Liability of Accessories: Law and Law Reform (1997) 113 *LQR* 453

——, *Justification and Excuse in the Criminal Law* (Sweet & Maxwell, London, 1989)

——, [1986] *Crim LR* 539

Smith, JC and Hogan, B, *Criminal Law* (Butterworths, London, 2002). (1999 also cited)

Smith, KJM, 'Duress and Steadfastness' (1999) *Crim LR* 363

——, *Lawyers, Legislators and Theorists* (Clarendon Press, Oxford, 1998)

——, 'Proximity in Attempt: Lord Lane's Midway Course' [1991] *Crim LR* 576

——, (*A Modern Treatise on the Law of Criminal Complicity* (Clarendon Press, Oxford, 1991)

——, 'The Law Commission Paper on Complicity: (1) A Blueprint for Rationalism' [1994] *Crim LR* 239

——, 'Withdrawal in Complicity' [2001] *Crim LR* 779

Smith, KJM and Wilson, W, 'Impaired Voluntariness and Criminal Responsibility' [1993] *OJLS* 79

—— and —— 'Necessity and the Doctors Dilemma' [1995] *Med L International* 315

Stapleton, J, 'Damage as the Gist of Negligence' (1988) 104 *LQR* 213

Stein, A, 'Criminal Defences and the Burden of Proof' (1990) *Coexistence* 26:70

Stephen, JF, *A Digest of the Criminal Law of England* (London, 1877)

Strahorn, D, 'The Effect of Impossibility on Criminal Attempts' (1930) 78 *UPA L Rev* 962

Strawson, PF, *Freedom and Resentment* (Methuen, London, 1974)

Stuart, D, 'The *Actus Reus* in Attempts' [1970] *Crim LR* 505

Sullivan, GR, 'Intent Purpose and Complicity' [1988] *Crim LR* 641

——, 'Making Excuses' in AP Simester and ATH Smith (eds), *Harm and Culpability* (Clarendon Press, Oxford, 1996)

Tadros, V, 'The Character of Excuse' (2001) *OJLS* 517

Taylor, RD, 'Complicity and Excuses' [1983] *Crim LR* 656

Thompson, EP, *Whigs and Hunters: The Origins of the Black Acts* (Allen Lane, London, 1975)

Thompson, J, 'A Defence of Abortion' (1971) 1 *Phil. and Pub. Aff* 47

Thompson, JJ, 'Killing, Letting Die and the Trolley Problem' (1975–6) 59 *The Monist* 204

Toulmin, SE and Flew, AN, 'The Logical Status of Psycho-analysis' in *Analysis*, December 1948

Tur, R, 'Objectivism and Subjectivism' in Shute *et al*, *Action and Value in Criminal Law* (Clarendon Press, Oxford, 1994)

Turner JCW, (ed), *Kenny's Outlines of the Criminal Law* (Cambridge University Press, Cambridge, 1962)

Uniacke, S, 'Killing under Duress' (1989) *J of Applied Phil* 53

——, *Permissible Killing: The Self-Defence Justification of Homicide* (Cambridge University Press, Cambridge, 1994)

von Hirsch A, *Censure and Sanctions* (Clarendon Press, Oxford, 1993) von Hirsch A, *Doing Justice—The Choice of Punishments* (Report of the Committee for the Study of Incarceration) (NewYork, 1976)

——, 'Extending the Harm Principle: Remote Harms and Fair Imputation' in A Simester and ATH Smith (eds), *Harm and Culpability* (Clarendon Press, Oxford, 1996), 259

—— and Jareborg N, 'Gauging Criminal Harms: a Living Standard Analysis' (1991) 11 *OJLS* 1

Waldron, J, 'Self Defense, Agent-Neutral and Agent-Relative Accounts' (2000) 88 *Cal LR* 711

Walker N, 'Punishing, Denouncing, or Reducing Crime' in P Glazebrook (eds) *Reshaping the Criminal Law* (Stevens, London, 1978)

——, 'Modern Retributivism' in H Gross and R Harrison (eds), *Jurisprudence: Cambridge Essays* (Clarendon Press, Oxford, 1990)

Wasik, M, 'Abandoning Criminal Attempt' [1980] *Crim LR* 785

——, 'Form and Function in the law of Involuntary Manslaughter' [1994] *Crim LR* 883

Weigend, T, 'Why Lady Eldon Should be Acquitted: The Social Harm in Attempting the Impossible' (1978) 27 *DePaul L Rev* 231

White, AR, *Misleading Cases* (Clarendon Press, Oxford, 1990)

Williams, B, 'Moral Responsibility and Political Freedom' [1997] *Camb LJ* 96

Williams, G, 'Complicity, Purpose and the Draft Code' [1990] *Crim LR* 4

——, 'Oblique Intention' [1987] *Camb LJ* 417

——, 'Offences and Defences' (1982) 2 *LS* 233

——, 'Rationality in Murder: A Reply' (1991) 11 *LS* 204

——, *Textbook of Criminal Law* (Stevens, London, 1983)

——, *The Mental Element in Crime* (OUP, Oxford, 1968)

——, 'What Should the Code do About Omissions?' (1987) *LS* 92

——, 'Wrong Turnings on the Law of Attempt?' [1991] *Crim LR* 416

Wilson, M and Daly, M, 'Till Death Do Us Part' in J Radford and DEH Russell (eds), *Femicide. The Politics of Woman Killing* (Open University Press, Buckingham, 1992)

Wilson, W, 'A Plea for Rationality in the Law of Murder' [1990] *LS* 307

——, *Criminal Law: Doctrine and Theory* (Longmans, Harlow, 1998)

——, 'Doctrinal Rationality after Woollin' [1999] *MLR* 447

——, 'Involuntary Intoxication: Excusing the Inexcusable' (1995) 1 *Res Publica* 25

——, 'Murder and the Structure of Homicide' in A Ashworth and B Mitchell (eds) *Rethinking English Homicide Law* (Clarendon, Oxford, 2000

——, 'Consenting to Personal Injury: How Far Can You Go?' (1995) 1 *Contemporary Issues in Law* 45

——, 'Impaired Voluntariness and Criminal Responsibility' [1993] *OJLS* 79, with KJM Smith

Winch, P, *Ethics and Action*(Routledge and Kegan Paul, London, 1971),

Wittgenstein, L, *Philosophical Investigations* (Basic Blackwell, Oxford, 1953)

Wolff, RP, 'The Conflict between Authority and Autonomy' in J Raz (ed), *Authority* (Duckworth, London, 1990)

Wootton, B, *Crime and the Criminal Law* (Sweet & Maxwell, London, 1981)

Wright, R, 'Causation in Tort Law' (1985) 73 *Cal LR* 1735

Yeo, S, 'Blameable Causation' (2000) 24 *Crim LJ* 144

Zaibert, L, 'Intentionality, Voluntariness and Culpability' (1998) *Buffalo Criminal Law Review*? 459

Index

accessorial liability 198–9,
  see also complicity
act:
  actions and 79–81
  as condition of liability 78–86
  omissions and 84–9
  requirement 78–80
actions:
  absence *see* omissions
  acts and 79–81
  inapt, as subject matter of criminal
    attempts 254–6
  volition and 105–10
actus reus:
  mens rea and 263–8
  offences and defences 268–9, 271–4
affirmative duties 92–5, 126
agency 27, 32, 115, 118
attempts 225–57
  adjudicative framework 242–3
  dangerousness and 229–30, 255
  impossible 252–7
  inapt actions 254–6
  incomplete 235–43, 249
  intention and 226–9, 232–5
  kinds of 231–2
  last-act test 237–8
  luck and 228, 249–52
  limiting principle 228
  mental element 232–5
  objectivist accounts 235–42, 254–6
  prevention of harm and 228
  proximity test 239–43
  punishment 249–52
  resulting harm and 249–52
  Rubicon test 240–41, 244–5
  subjectivist accounts 236–7, 254
  temporal proximity 242
  ulterior intent crimes and 10, 226–8,
    232, 248–9
  voluntary abandonment 243–9
attribution, and wrongdoing 278–82
authorship:
  control and 118–21

involuntariness and 116–18
automatism 107, 119–21, 331
autonomy:
  communitarian goals and 41–2
  criminal omissions and 39–40, 91–5
  freedom restrictions and 19–20, 26,
    31–2, 37–8
  morality and 38–43
  omissions and 91–5
  personal capacities for 40–41

behaviour 82
blameless instrumentality *see* innocent
  agency
'but for' connection 173–4, 177–8, 191–3

capacity:
  character theory and 360–61
  excuses and 333–6, 338–41
  free will and 336–8, 339–41
  negligence and 335
  theory 335–6, 355–6, 360
  thresholds 338–41
causation 163–5
  abnormal coincidences 176–81
  accountability 163
  assigning responsibility 170–86
  blameability 162
  'but for' connection 173–4, 177–8,
    191–3
  complicity and 200–204, 218–23
  as criminal liability requirement 166–7
  'dangerous forces which come to rest'
    182–3
  Draft Criminal Code 177–8
  explanatory and normative accounts
    163–9
  free will and 337
  novus actus interveniens 173–86
  omissions and 89–91, 186–93
  potency approach 182–3
  reactive conduct 182
  socio-political basis 184–5
  tort and 167–8

causation (*cont.*):
    trial procedures and 171–2
    unforeseen consequences and 175–6
    voluntariness and 181–2
character
    capacity and 354–6, 360–61
    excuses and 342–56
    acting 'out of character' 343–52
    reasons and 352–6
choice theory 333–6
coercive rules 18–20, 41–2
communitarianism 40–1
complicity 195–6
    agency and 198–9
    authorisation 205–6
    causal basis 200–04, 218–23
    derivative liability 207–12, 221–3
    dual standards in attribution 12–13,
        219–20
    forfeiture theory and 199–200
    innocent agency 208–12
    joint enterprise 204–8
    'perpetrators and participators' 196–8,
        219–23
    'principals and facilitators' 219–23
    responsibility relationships 220
complicity, withdrawal from:
    attempt contrasted 212–3
    effective withdrawal 216–17
    motivation and 217–18
    public policy and 214, 217
    theoretical rationale 215–16
consequentialism 51–3
constitution of wrongdoing 259–63,
    see also offences and defences
    mens rea / actus reus and 263–8
    paradigmatic wrongs 259–60, 262
control, authorship and 118–21
criminal assault 226
criminal attempts *see* attempts
citizen's codes 280–82, 289–92
criminal omissions, and autonomy
    39–40
criminal prohibitions 99–102
    motives and 131–2
criminalisation:
    ethical constraints 18–20
    harm principle 20–26, 31, 33–37, 42
    immorality and 34–8
    offensive conduct 33–4
    propriety of 17
    remote harms and 29–31
    wrongdoing and 18–20

culpability:
    intention and 133–5, 139–42, 155–6,
        282–7, 306–7
    wrongdoing and 265–8

deeds 80–81
deeds and reasons 319–43, 363–4
defences, *see also* offences, and defences
    character and 342–56
    duress 289–92, 303–6
    justifications and excuses and 279–80,
        282–9, 325–6
    self-defence and 303–6
    separating justifications and excuses
        and 282–9, 325–6
derivative liability 207–12,
    see also complicity
determinism 337–8
dominion 52
duress:
    excuses and 359
    justification and 293–303
    nature and scope of the defence
        289–92
    proportionality and 302
    self-defence and 303–6
    self-preservation and 319–23

endangerment 172–3
excuses 282–9, 325–6, 356–61
    capacity and 333–6
    character and 342–56
    criminal law and 329–33
    exemptions and 288–9
    provocation and 328–9, 330, 359–60
    social morality and 359
    thresholds of responsibility 327–9
exemptions 288–9

forfeiture theory 199–200
free will 103, 336–8

general part:
    destabilising doctrines of the 143–5
    special part and 3–7, 11, 102, 123–7,
        232–5
grading offences 24–5, 138–42

harm 19–25
    remote 22–3, 29–31
    wrongdoing and harm principle 19–25,
        31, 33–37, 43
hierarchy of offences 138–42

independence *see* autonomy
innocent agency 208–212, 221
intention:
    criminal liability and 135–6
    culpability gap 155–9, 306–8
    definition 154
    foresight and 144–8, 150–1, 153–6,
      158–9, 319–23
    grading of offences and 138–42
    imputing 136–8
    Law Commission and 149–56
    motive and 129–35, 156–8, 319–23,
      rational fault system and 156–9
    wrongdoing and 142–8
involuntariness, *see also* voluntariness
    actions 110–113
    authorship and 116–18
    literal and metaphorical 114–15
    omissions and 121–3
involuntary intoxication 331–2, 350–51

justifications, *see also under* defences
    common framework 293–303
    excuses distinguished 282–9
    immediacy requirement 295–9
    necessity 294–5
    proportionality and 299–303
    reasons and 273–8, 285–6, 352–5

'kill or be killed' choices 321–3

last-act test 237–8
legal moralism 35–7
libertarianism 36
luck 170–2, 228, 249–52, 341,357

manslaughter, murder and 145–8
mens rea 130
    actus reus and 263–8
    offences and defences 268–9, 271–2
    rule of conduct and 266
minimalism 31–2, 35, 41–2, 236–7, 250
moral responsibility *see* responsibility
moral wrongdoing 32–8
morality:
    autonomy and 38–43
    legal moralism 35–7
    rule-infringement and moral wrongdo-
      ing 57–8
    social context 56–7
motive:
    criminal liability and 129–35
    suppression and social control 133–5

ulterior intent and 10, 142–4, 226–8,
    232, 248–9
    withdrawal from complicity and
      217–18
murder:
    complicity 195–6
    manslaughter and 145–8

necessity:
    duress and 303–6
    as justification 294–5
    self-defence and 306–10, 315–19
    self-preservation and 319–23
negligence 126
    capacity and 335

obligatory behaviour 37
offences:
    definition *see* constitution of wrongdoing
    grading 24–5, 138–42
offences, and defences 268–78
    actus reus/*mens rea* and 268–9, 271–2
    cogency of distinction 268–278
    consent and 275–8
    justificatory defences 273–6
omissions 82–4
    autonomy and 91–5
    as causes 186–93
    constructing duties 97–99, 186–90
    criminalisation and 91–2, 95–9
    forbearance 85–6
    harm and 186–93
    impossibility defence 123–5, 127
    interventions and 189–90
    involuntary 121–3, 127
    liability and 97–8
    negative acts 84–6
    responsibility and 84–91, 125–7
    tort and 99
    utilitarianism and 91–2
'out of character' actions 343–52
outcomes 100–101

packaging liability *see* constitution of
    wrongdoing
paradigmatic wrongs 259–60, 262
'perpetrators and participators' 196–8,
    219–23
premeditation 149–50
'principals and facilitators' 219–23
prior fault 117–18
prohibitions *see* criminal prohibitions
proportionality, justification and 299–303

provocation, excuses and 328–9
punishment:
  of attempts 249–52
  censure and 61–2
  as communication 63–5
  conceptual and functional elision
    66–71
  consequentialism 51–3, 67–8
  definition 43–5
  desert theory 54–61
  dominion 52
  efficacy 53
  exceptional cases 70–71
  justification 45–7
  protectionist approach 53–4
  cardinal and ordinal proportionality 65
  public censure and 61–2
  reductionism 43, 49–52
  rehabilitative ideal 49–50
  restorative 71–6
  retributivism 43, 54–61, 67–8, 250–51
  rule-infringment, and morality 57–8
  social control and 47–8
  state role's justification 58–60
  unfair advantage theory 60–61
  utilitarianism and 49–52
  vengeance 71–6
  victim's viewpont 75–6

rational fault system 156–9
reasons:
  action and outcome 100–2
recklessness 126, 154
regulatory offences 27–9
rehabilitative ideal 49–50
remote harms 22–3
  criminalisation 29–31
responsibility:
  causation 170–73
  complicity and 220
  excuses and 327–9
  omissions and 84–91, 125–7
  voluntariness and
  Rubicon test 240–41

secondary parties, liability *see* complicity
self-defence:
  duress and 303–6
  necessity and 310–15
  self preservation and 319–23

unjust threats and 311–15
self-preservation 319–23
set-back of interest 21–2, 24
social control, and suppression of
  motives 133–5
socio-political basis for harm 184–5
state coercion 26–32
  as punishment 46–7, 58–60
  societal and ethical constraints 18–20
strict liability offences 118
  paradigms of responsibility 71–6

thresholds of harm 23–5
tort:
  causation and 167–8
  omissions and 99

ulterior intent:
  crimes of 10, 142–4, 226–8, 232, 248–9
unfair advantage theory 60–61
utilitarianism 49–52
  omissions and 91–2
  proportionality and 299–300

vengeance 71–6
volition 105–110
voluntariness:
  capacity to act otherwise 113
  definition 105–113
  excuses and 105, 123–7
  harm and 181–2
  involuntary actions and 110–13
  as legal defence 113–16
  omissions and 121–7
  requirement 103–5
  variable standards 123–5
  volition and 105–10
  wrongdoing and 77–8

Waltham Black Acts 226–7
wrongdoing:
  act requirement 78
  attribution and 278–82
  criminalisation 18–20
  culpability and 265–8
  differentiating wrongs 141
  intention and 142–8
  offence-specific definitions 156–9
  as voluntary action 77–8
wrongs, paradigmatic 259–60, 262